SEP 0 3

DATE DUE

FEB 27 '04		
GAYLORD		PRINTED IN U.S.A.

BY G   AN

Other Play Collections from Applause

19th Century American Plays

Amazon All-Stars: 13 Lesbian Plays

Before Brecht

Best American Short Play Series

Black Heroes

Chekhov: The Major Plays

Classical Comedy: Greek & Roman

Classical Tragedy: Greek & Roman

Elizabethan Drama

A Flea in her Rear and other Vintage French Farces

Life is a Dream and other Spanish Classics

Medieval & Tudor Drama

Misanthrope & other French Classics

National Black Drama Anthology

Plays by American Women 1900-1930

Plays by American Women 1930-1960

Seeds of Modern Drama

Servant of 2 Masters & other Italian Classics

Women Heroes

Women on the Verge

Womenswork

THREE COMEDIES

BY GEORGE S. KAUFMAN

&

EDNA FERBER

The Royal Family

Dinner at Eight

Stage Door

An Applause Original

THREE COMEDIES
BY GEORGE S. KAUFMAN & EDNA FERBER

Copyright © 1999 Applause Books

ISBN 1-55783-334-6 (trade paperback)

Information about performance rights is found before each play.

Library of Congress Cataloging-In-Publication Data

Library of Congress Catalog Card Number: 99-64645

British Library Catalogue in Publication Data
A catalogue record for this book is available from the British Library

APPLAUSE BOOKS

211 West 71st Street
New York, NY 10023
Phone (212) 496-7511
Fax: (212) 721-2856

 PRINTED IN CANADA

Contents

THE ROYAL FAMILY

GEORGE S. KAUFMAN
AND EDNA FERBER

*The following is a copy of the program of the first performance of
the revival of "THE ROYAL FAMILY" as presented at the Helen
Hayes Theatre, New York, N.Y., on December 30th, 1975:*

Barry Brown, Burry Fredrik, Fritz Holt, Sally Sears present
THE ROYAL FAMILY
a Comedy by George S. Kaufman and Edna Ferber
Directed by Ellis Rabb

THE CAST (In order of appearance)

DELLA	Rosetta Le Noire
JO	John Remme
HALLBOY	James C. Burge
McDERMOTT	Sherman Lloyd
HERBERT DEAN	Joseph Maher
KITTY DEAN	Mary Louse Wilson
GWEN	Mary Layne
PERRY STEWART	Forrest Buckman
FANNY CAVENDISH	Eva Le Gallienne
OSCAR WOLFE	Sam Levene
JULIE CAVENDISH	Rosemary Harris
ANTHONY CAVENDISH	George Grizzard
CHAUFFEUR	Miller Lide
GILBERT MARSHALL	Donald Barton
ANOTHER HALLBOY	Mark Fleischman
GUNGA	James C. Burge
MISS PEAKE	Eleanor Phelps

THE ROYAL FAMILY

SCENE: The scene is the duplex apartment of the Cavendish family, in the East Fifties, New York. The room is spacious, high-ceilinged, has a balcony. Rear center of balcony is an alcove, from which two doors, right and left, lead into bedrooms. A door at left of balcony that leads to additional rooms. A staircase leads to the balcony from about left center. Leading off the main room there are three doors. One is the outer door, set at a right angle. Under the stairs, right, is the door leading into the rear of the apartment. Down left is a double door leading into the library. A large window down right.

The room has about it nothing of the commonplace. At a glance one sees that it is lived in by an unusual family. It is rich, careless, crowded, comfortable. Almost cluttering it are deep cushioned chairs, little corner clusters of couch, table, lamp; photographs in silver frames are all about; magazines, cushions. A profusion of flowers. Tapestries and rich shawls hang over the balcony railing. A grand piano is partly under the balcony, slightly to the left. A colorful brocade is thrown over this, and a lamp stands on it, together with photographs, etc. All sorts of periods and styles have gone into the making of the room. Prominently placed is a portrait in oils of the late Aubrey Cavendish in his most celebrated role, all bristling mustachios, high stick, romantic cape, glittering orders, gold braid, silk and boots and swagger. A shadow light is over this picture.

Down stage at the extreme right there is a table. In front of window is a bench at the upper end of the bench and facing the audience is a large over-stuffed chair. Directly back of this chair against the back flat is a secretary and chair. A grand piano is directly center with the keyboard right There is a piano bench. In front of piano is a large sofa. Left of the sofa a small table. Next an armchair. Above the doors left is a commode, a chair and a coffee table. Below the doors is a small table and a chair. There is a French telephone, stands on the piano. Another (the house telephone) is under the stairs. The time is about one o'clock of a November afternoon. The Cavendish is a family of actors, are only now stirring for the day.

AT RISE: At the rise of the curtain the stage is briefly empty. Immediately DELLA, *the maid, comes from one of the bedrooms off the balcony, a breakfast tray in her hands. She looks a capable person, in the thirties, and intelligent enough to cope the often surprising situation that arise in the Cavendish household.*

She has some difficulty in manipulating both the tray and the door. Finally manages to close the door with her foot. Then she rests the tray on the balcony rail for a moment of readjustment before starting the length of the balcony to descending the stairs. As she starts down the stairs the telephone rings. JO, *the houseman, enters down right, also carrying a laden tray. He is wearing a white housecoat. He is a man of about forty-eight or fifty.*

DELLA, *downward bound, naturally is the one to answer it. She hastens on down, looks about and puts her tray on a "coffee" table left of stairs.*

(HOUSE TELEPHONE)

DELLA: Hello! *(The house phone off stage, right, rings.* JO *is at top of the stairs, and looks about in indecision, then puts the tray on the top step and comes hurriedly down and off right under stairs to the house phone. In the meantime* DELLA *is speaking on the outside phone.)* Yes . . . No, she's not up yet . . . I say she's not up yet. Well, I don't know. About an hour, maybe.

*(*JO *is now at the house phone, off. His conversation can be heard running through the rest of* DELLA's *talk.)*

JO: Hello . . . You can sign for them . . . All right, send him up and I'll sign for them. *(He hangs up.)*

DELLA: Who is it, please? . . . Mr. Who? . . . Oh, Mr. Wolfe ! Yes, Mr. Wolfe? *(A more personal tone)* Yes, Mr. Wolfe? You know how it is here when the phone starts . . . Yes, certainly, Mr. Wolfe, I will. All right.

*(*JO, *having finished his telephone conversation, has crossed rapidly and is well up the stairs.)*

DELLA: Who was on the house phone?

JO: Nothing. Only some flowers.

DELLA: *(A glance around the flower-laden room)* Just what we need.

(TELEPHONE)

(Reaches for tray. Again the telephone)

DELLA: Hello!

(BUZZER)

(The sound of the back door buzzer.)

DELLA: The back door, Jo! (JO *disappears into* JULIE'S *room.)* Hello!
. . . Yes . . . Who is it, please? . . . Oh . . . Yes, she's up, but she
can't come to the phone . . . Yes, I'll take . . . Dinner at Mrs.
Sherwin's——(JO *appears from* JULIE'S *room.)*

(BUZZER)

DELLA: Will you wait a minute, please? Jo, that was the back door.
Katie'll never answer.

JO: *(Annoyed)* All right. *(Exits right— under stairs.)*

DELLA: *(Again at phone)* Now what was that again? . . . Dinner at
Mrs. Sherwin's, four thirty-six Park Avenue, November 26th,.
at seven . . . Seven! I'll tell her, but Miss Cavendish has got to
be in the theatre before eight she always eats dinner six-thirty.
. . Yes, I will. *(Hangs up.)*

(JO enters from under stairs. In his arms stacked high and tied to-
gether are pasteboard boxes, very large ones at the bottom, and
smaller ones at the top. These reach almost to JO'S *chin.)*

JO: Where do you want these?

DELLA: Who they for? Miss Julie? Take 'em up to her room. *(Jo*
goes toward stairs. A HALLBOY *enters behind him, bundle laden. He*
pauses just a moment, peers around his stack of boxes to get his bear-
ings.) Right on up.

HALLBOY: There's more. *(Follows* JO *up.)*

(DELLA exits right. MCDERMOTT, the trainer, enters on balcony
from JULIE'S *room, whistling. A dapper, slim, quick ferret with a*
left cauliflower ear and an amazing co-ordination of muscle. He

reeks of the ring. He is wearing a white flannel sleeveless under-shirt, trousers, a belt. Has on one boxing mitt, carries the other.)

McDERMOTT: *(Speaking as he enters)* All right, Miss Julie, I'll see if I can—(McDERMOTT, *on balcony, steps aside for Jo, who is at the top of the stairs. Surveys the laden two.)* Somebody moving in?

Jo: One side! Heads up!

McDERMOTT: G'wan! *(DELLA enters from under stairs carrying additional boxes.)* Je's!

(DOOR BELL.)

(Jo exits JULIE's room. HALLBOY still ascending stairs. The door-bell rings. DELLA has an instant of indecision. Puts down her boxes. Starts for door. Telephone rings. DELLA goes toward it. Changes her mind, continues to door. Telephone continues. McDERMOTT comes down. Jo reappears on balcony. Comes down.)

(TELEPHONE.)

DELLA: Jo, answer the telephone. *(Exits in hallway.)*

Jo: Let it ring!

McDERMOTT: *(To DELLA)* Seen Miss Julie's mitts?

DELLA: In the library.

McDERMOTT: Where?

(VOICE OFF.)

MESSENGER: *(Voice off. Very loud)* Telegram for Cavendish.

Jo: *(Picking up DELLA'S pile of boxes)* Only ring again if I do answer it. *(Starts for stairs.)*

McDERMOTT: Where'd you say? *(DELLA down from door, with telegram in hand.)*

DELLA: In the library. Jo, you got a pencil?

(McDERMOTT exits into library, left.)

Jo: *(Over the top of his boxes)* Have I got a pencil!

(HALLBOY out of JULIE's room. Down stairs.)

DELLA: Well, I can't answer—Oh, for heaven's sake!

(HALLBOY *exits.*)

(*Stop* PHONE.)

DELLA: (*In phone*) Hello! Miss Julie Cavendish? . . . Well, she can't just now.

McDERMOTT: (*Enters front library, whistling*) I found 'em!

DELLA: Oh, I should think in about an hour.

McDERMOTT: I bet Jo was using them.

(JO *enters from* JULIE'S *room. Starts down. He carries a pair of women's shoes.*)

(*BUZZER.*)

DELLA: All right. I'll tell her. (*Hangs up. The back door buzzer sounds.*) What's that?

JO: I guess it's those flowers.

DELLA: I'll go. Here, you take this up to her. (*Hands him telegram.*) Give me those. (*Takes shoes. Buzzer sounds again.*)

(*BUZZER.*)

(McDERMOTT *has taken off his gloves, put on the other pair. Tucks original gloves under his arm.*)

DELLA: Oh, all right, all right! (*Exits right.*)

JO: (*Gets card tray from hallway, places telegram on it— then comes to piano*) How's the battler, huh? Pretty good?

McDERMOTT: Say, I'm always in good condition. A little boxing wouldn't hurt you none. You got flat feet carryin' trays.

JO: (*Lays tray on piano—picks up cigarette box*) Any fellow goes around boxing women for a living I guess I could take 'em on.

McDERMOTT: Yeah! I've took on some of the best in the world in my time.

JO: (*Crosses left with cigarette box*) I know your record. You was known as Canvasback McDermott. You're right in your class now, all right. Running a gymnasium racket, hiring out as a punching bag for workmen to keep their figures. *(Has come left to commode and filled the cigarette box)*

MCDERMOTT: All right, and let me tall you something. I got some clients could make jelly out of you, and what do you know about that!

JO: Yeah!

MCDERMOTT: Yeah. *(Points to stairs)* She give me a poke yesterday would have held you for the count.

JO: I'd like to see her try it. *(Crosses back to piano puts down cigarette box picks up tray and telegram)*

MCDERMOTT: I trained a lot of stage people, but I never seen anybody pick it up quicker than Miss Cavendish.

(DOOR BELL)

JO: I bet the old lady herself could take you on. Now, I been here upwards of ten years, and—*(The outer door bell rings. Jo starts toward it, still talking)* and nothing they could do—*(Remembers telegram. Gives it to* MCDERMOTT*)* Here. Take that, will you? You're going up to Miss Julie's room. *(*MCDERMOTT *is on his way up the stairs.)* Say, do you think you could get me into the Garden Friday night? I've never seen this Delaney.

MCDERMOTT: Sure. Just mention my name.

(Takes the last few steps in a great leap. Exits. JO *opens outer door. The well-rounded tones of* HERBERT DEAN *are heard in greeting.)*

DEAN: Ah, good morning, Jo, my boy! Good morning!

JO: Good morning, Mr. Dean.

*(*DEAN *strides to the room.* JO *shuts outer door and follows.* DEAN *is about fifty-seven, very dressy, an excellent actor, beginning to show his age. The flower of the Lambs Club. Necktie, shirt and handkerchief always blend. Massage has been his most active form of exercise. His appearance inevitably brings to mind the adjective "well-preserved." Clothes a shade too well tailored. His topcoat is one of those which define the waistline. His walking stick is London.)*

Under his arm is a play manuscript. His entrance is a characteristic one, done in state. That springy walk)

DEAN: Well, well, well! Where's the family! Where's everybody!

(Drops script on sofa—gives JO *hat and stick)*

JO: They're not down, Mr. Dean. It's hardly half past one yet.

DEAN: *(Removes coat)* I was up a full hour ago. Setting up exercises! Cold bath!

JO: *(Taking coat)* Yessir! You always took care yourself. That's how you kept your figger.

DEAN: *(Goes up right, looks in mirror)* Yes. Well, look here. They're all awake, aren't they? Miss Julie's awake? *(Takes out cigarette-case finds it empty— fills it from box on piano)*

JO: *(Takes hat and coat in hall)* Oh, yes. Her and the trainer been exercising half an hour and more. She ought to be down any minute now.

DEAN: I see. I see. I want very much to talk to her before we're interrupted. *(Picks up his script.)* How about my sister? *(Goes left.)* She up? *(A glance to balcony bedroom door)*

JO: *(Enters)* She's been stirring quite a while. Doesn't sleep so well lately. Mrs. Cavendish doesn't. Wide awake at nine thirty every morning. Wide awake at nine thirty every morning.

DEAN: *(DEAN has noticed the breakfast tray and drifts toward it, talking as he walks, but intent on the tray.)* Well, of course she's getting along in years.

(DOOR BELL. Two Long Peals.)

(DOOR BELL rings. He feels the coffee pot to learn if it's hot. Dreamily picks up a breakfast roll. Butters it)

DEAN: Trouble is, she won't give in. Pretends she's well—

(Two long and determined peals of the door bell. An apprehensive look in Dean's face. Munching the roll, crosses down left. JO opens outer door to admit KITTY LEMOYNE DEAN.)

JO: Good morning, Mrs. Dean! And how are you this morning?

KITTY: *(Off stage)* Is Mr. Dean here?

JO: Yes, he just got here! *(Off stage. KITTY enters. About forty-eight but doesn't believe it. An actress for many years, never more than mediocre. She is obviously in a temper. She remains right. Stands regarding him with a baleful eye. They glare at each other. DEAN turns away with a snort. JO comes down, is in a genial mood and essays a pleasantry.)* That's funny. You getting here just a minute after Mr. Dean. He must got here a minute ago himself. *(He looks expectantly from one to the other, for appreciation of this coincidence. Something in their faces tells him that things are not so jolly.)* Well, I'll tell Miss Julie you're both down here. *(He retreats, somewhat gingerly going to stairs. DELLA enters from under stairs breezily. She is carrying box of flowers tied with ribbon.)*

DELLA: Good morning, Mrs. Dean! Mr. Dean! You two are out bright and early!

JO: Psst! *(A bit of warning pantomime from JO to DELLA. DELLA gives to JO an uncomprehending look.)*

DELLA: H'm? *(KITTY barely glances at DELLA. A movement of the lips that is a frigid imitation of a smiling assent)* Well, I'll tell Miss Julie you're here. *(DELLA exits upstairs. JO picks up tray that DELLA brought down earlier. Starts toward door, right.)*

DEAN: Yeh! Here, here! *(Snatches another roll from tray.)*

JO: Why, you're hungry, sir. Won't you let me bring you a bite of breakfast!

DEAN: No, no, no, no! . . . *(JO starts right)* I'll tell you what. You might bring me a cup of coffee.

JO: *(Stops center)* Yessir! I'll have it made fresh for you.

DEAN: Thanks, Jo I wasn't permitted to finish my breakfast this morning, what with one thing and another. *(With a meaning glare at KITTY.)*

JO: Yes, sir! *(A backward look around the edge of the upraised tray that inquires as to KITTY's possible need of refreshment.)*

(READY PHONE)

JO: Perhaps—you—would like—(KITTY'S *stony look defeats him.* JO *exits under stairs.* KITTY *and* DEAN *are alone.* DEAN *takes a vicious and defensive bite of roll.*)

KITTY: And further more up by sneaking off to this family of yours—

DEAN: Sneaking, my good woman! I believe I am privileged to walk out of my own home and call on my niece and my sister without asking your formal permission. If you think, I'm going to stand by and see another woman play that part— (*Simultaneous*)

KITTY: You're mighty mistaken. That part was made for me! I'd be marvelous in it! And if you imagine for one minute, Herbert Dean——

DEAN: For heaven's sake, Kitty. I've been waiting ten years to get a play like this—but I tell you it isn't for you! It's—

(*Both stop at the sound of a door opening on the balcony. They glance up.* DELLA *appears.* DEAN *throws the manuscript back on the table with a slam and turns left.* DELLA *comes down. She has just exited right and* KITTY *has taken breath for a renewal of attack it when the the phone rings.* DELLA *returns.* KITTY *sits on sofa.*)

(*As* DELLA *comes Down Stairs,* PHONE)

DELLA: (*At phone*) Hello! Yes. Mr. Anthony Cavendish? Oh, no, Mr. Anthony Cavendish is not here . . . Yes, he lives here when he's home, but he's in Hollywood . . . I don't believe he's expected. (*To* DEAN) Is Mr. Tony expected?

DEAN: I don't know.

DELLA: No, he isn't expected . . . Who is it, please? . . . The Graphic?

DEAN: (*A warning whisper*) You don't know anything.

DELLA: (*In phone*) I don't know anything.

(*Hangs up*)

DEAN: What did they want?

DELLA: Said Mr. Tony. I told them he was in Hollywood.

DEAN: The Graphic. What's that young devil up to now? *(Sits in chair left of center)*

KITTY: A Cavendish can do no wrong.

DEAN: I told Miss Julie you wanted to see her in a hurry. (DELLA *exits right)*

KITTY: In a hurry, h'm? Before I could get here!

DEAN: Now, Kitty, let's not go all over this again. Look at me! I'm all unstrung. I've had no sleep.

KITTY: You had as much sleep as I had.

DEAN:Whose fault was it! Let me tell you, madam, one more night like that and I move to the Lambs' Club.

KITTY: Move! Where do you think you live now!

DEAN: *(Rises picks up script)* I won't have any more talk about it.

KITTY: No, I'm not allowed to say a word. But you sent a script over for Julie to read last night—Julie and that sister of yours.

DEAN: And why shouldn't they read it! I have never done a play without consulting Fanny and Julie.

KITTY: Maybe that's why you never have a hit.

DEAN: I'll have one this time! I can see myself in every line of it, every gesture! Take the Nero scene! *(A pose)* And as Abraham Lincoln. But you, my dear Kitty—you are no longer—uh—h'm! You see, your technique is more—uh—mellow.

KITTY: Are you by any chance telling me I'm too old!

DEAN: Oh, my dear Kitty!

KITTY: Then I suppose I'm not good enough actress! I was good enough to support Mansfield, though, wasn't I!

DEAN: Plenty!

KITTY: I'm as good an actress as your precious Julie. And I'm better than that sister of yours ever was.

DEAN: My dear Kitty, please do not embarrass me by comparing yourself with Julie Cavendish, or with my sister, the greatest Lady Macbeth of her day.

KITTY: Cavendish! Cavendish! I'd had the royal family Cavendished up to me for twelve years. God, but I'm sick of them!

DEAN: You are sick of the Cavendishes! You are—— And who are you, I'd like to know,-to be sick of the Cavendishes! What were you when I married you!

KITTY: I was understudying Mannering in "The Garden of Allah."

DEAN: You were an off-stage noise!

(JO *enters with* DEAN'S *tray. Slight pause on threshold to make certain battle is not too thick)*

JO: Here you are, Mr. Dean. Nice hot pot of coffee pick you up right away. *(Puts tray on table, left of stairs)*

DEAN: Thanks, Jo, thanks. Coffee! That's fine!

JO: Hot buttered toast. *(Lifts a napkin.* KITTY *sits on sofa.)*

KITTY: Oh, Jo! (JO *pauses)* I feel a little faint. *(An eye on the tray.* DEAN *looks hopeful.)* Perhaps if I forced myself to swallow a mouthful of coffee—

JO: Right away, Mrs. Dean. And a little toast?

KITTY: The tiniest sliver . . . Or perhaps I ought to try to eat an egg.

JO: I'd try, yes, ma'am. Soft boiled?

KITTY: I think, shirred. With just a thin curl of bacon.

JO: Thin curl of bacon. Yes'm. *(Turns to go.)*

DEAN: I. . .uh h'm—I might have an egg, Jo, while you're about it.

(Slam DOOR)

JO: Yes, sir. Same as Mrs. Dean's? *(The sound of the outer door closing.)*

DEAN: Why—ah—

(GWEN enters from outer door. She is in riding clothes; a slim lovely young thing of nineteen. She is, perhaps, less a CAVENDISH *than*

any of the others of the family. PERRY STEWART *enters behind her and lingers a moment uncertainly in the doorway.* PERRY STEWART *a personable young fellow of about twenty-eight. Piping Rocking, Long Island bonds. He is wearing an overcoat. His driving gloves are rather indicative of the Minerva at the curb.)*

GWEN: M-m-m, Jo, I've got to have some lunch. *(*JO *exits.* DEAN *and* KITTY *say "Hello" to* GWEN. *To the* DEANS*)* Hello . . . What some lunch, Perry?

DEAN: Lunch?

PERRY: Not a chance! If I'm going to dress and get back here I've got to blow.

GWEN: This is Perry Stewart. Oh, I guess you've met. My Uncle— and Aunt Kitty. *(*PERRY *steps forward and shakes hands with* KITTY.*)*

KITTY: Been riding?

GWEN: Mm. It was marvelous. Jo, what've you got to eat? . . .

PERRY: Look here, don't you waste a lot of time on lunch. *(Looks at wrist watch.)* I'll be back here at half past two, and you're going to be ready.

GWEN: Very well, m'lord.

PERRY: No fooling, Gwen. It's an hour's drive, and a guest of honor has to be on time.

GWEN: That sounds scary.

PERRY: Well, you know—one thing mother's fussy about is people being on time.

GWEN: I'll be sitting on the curb.

PERRY: She thinks actresses are temperamental, or something. So let's show her. *(To* DEAN *and* KITTY*)* Goodbye.

(They say goodbye. PERRY *goes out.)*

GWEN: Goodbye, Perry! *(*GWEN *follows him in hallway.)*

*(*DEAN *and* KITTY *also say "Goodbye.")*

JO: *(Enters to* DEAN*)* Did you say the same as Mrs. Dean's, sir? The eggs?

DEAN: Oh. Yes. A little bacon—chicken livers—anything.

JO: Yes, sir. *(Starts to exit.)*

GWEN: *(Enters from hallway)* What you got for me, Jo? Cold meat, or a chop— I don't care so long as it's food.

JO: Yes, Miss Gwen. *(*JO *exits right.)*

GWEN: Gosh, I'm hungry! I was up at half past seven. *(Removes hat)*

DEAN: Half past what!

KITTY: I think he's awfully good looking, Gwen. *(Coming down)* I'll tell him.

KITTY: What's the function this afternoon? It sounds formal.

GWEN: Oh, no. Perry's mother is giving a tea for me, that's all. *(Is going up the stairs)*

DEAN: Uh—Gwen. You might remind your mother that I am waiting. And also your grandmother.

GWEN: Sure.

KITTY: Incidentally, so am I

DEAN: No more morning rides after this week, eh, Gwen, my child? Rehearsals. Rehearsals.

GWEN: I'm afraid so.

DEAN: You ought to be very proud, my dear. At your age, to be appearing with your mother. Quite an event! Quite an event in the theatre! *(Toast and napkin in hand, he gives the effect of a speech as his mood gains in warmth and splendor)* Yes, sir! About to enter into your great inheritance? To come before the public as the descendant of a distinguished family! It is not a trust to be taken lightly, my dear. Remember that not only will all of us be watching you, but your gifted ancestors as well. *(A heavy "Ahem" here)*

*(*GWEN *has lingered politely near the top of the stairs.* FANNY CAVENDISH'S *door opens and she enters quickly from the balcony. She speaks simultaneously with the opening of the door.)*

FANNY: I think that speech needs cutting, Bertie.

(FANNY CAVENDISH *is seventy-two. Managerial, pungent rather magnificent. Given to domineering and to reminiscence. Her clothes are rich, but careless and somewhat out-dated.*)

GWEN: How are you, baby? Feeling all right?

FANNY: Splendid . . . Have a nice ride?

GWEN: Glorious! The sun over the frost—

FANNY: Spare me. (GWEN *exits door right on balcony.* FANNY *starts down stairs.*) Yes, Bertie, they'd be up the aisles and out before you'd really got your teeth in it. (*Is descending stairs*) Isn't that hat a little ingenue, Kitty? (DEAN *goes to meet* FANNY, *foot of stairs.*)

DEAN: How are you this morning, Fanny? What did the new doctor say? Anything?

FANNY: What do they know? Parcel of fools! . . . (*As* DEAN *tries to assist her. Descends the last step*) Well, what brings you two love birds around at the break of day?

KITTY: Your devoted brother is calling one of his family conclaves.

DEAN: I'm here to see Julie, that's all.

FANNY: (*Crossing to her chair*) Family conclave, eh? Sounds very repulsive.

DEAN: (*Following and trying to assist her*) Allow me.

FANNY: It's all right. Don't fuss, Bertie. I'm not helpless. (*Sits*) Julia not down yet, eh?

DEAN: She is not. I've been waiting half an hour. (*Crosses left*)

FANNY: That prize fighter's here, I guess. When I was Julie's age I didn't have to have prize fighters to keep my figger. You could span my waist with your two hands.

KITTY: I like a nice womanly figure myself.

FANNY: You ought to be very happy.

DEAN: Well, Fanny, you certainly don't seem an invalid. You're looking splendid. (*Crosses to his tray.*)

FANNY: Invalid? Well as I ever was. I am going into rehearsal as soon as Wolfe can pick a cast.

DEAN: Now, now, Fanny. You've had a long siege of it. After a year's illness—*(Picks up his cup of coffee)*

KITTY: Nearer two, isn't it?

FANNY: And what if it is! Two years out of a lifetime! I played fifty-three years without missing a performance, except when Tony was born.

KITTY: And surely when Julie was born!

FANNY: No, sir. She knew her business better than that. Julie was born during Holy Week.

DEAN: But look here, now, Fanny. What are you going to do? You haven't a new play, have you?

(Sits left center, sips coffee)

FANNY: Who said anything about a new play! I'm reviving "Mrs. Castlemain."

DEAN: But that's rather old-fashioned, Fanny. New York won't come to see that, even with you in it.

FANNY: New York! You talk like a Follies girl! I'm going to take it on the road.

DEAN: The road? You're mad.

FANNY: I know your views, Bertie.

DEAN: I don't belittle the road. It's quite all right in its way. But my public is in New York.

KITTY: Or was, when last heard from.

FANNY: Well, I'm not like you, Bertie. I've been a trouper all my life, and I'm going to keep on trouping. I'd rather pack 'em into a tent in Texas than play highbrow matinees at the Teacup Theatre in New York.

DEAN: But you've been ill, Fanny. You can't stand what you used to. Those dreadful small town hotels! Sleeping in Pullmans . . .

FANNY: I did it when there weren't any Pullmans! When many a time I had to sit up all night —yes, with Julie asleep on one side, and Tony generally yelling his head off on the other.

DEAN: But that belongs to the past, Fanny. You're too important a figure today.

FANNY: *(In spite of her infirmity rises to her feet)* I was Fanny Cavendish then, just as I am now. When the bills said Aubrey and Fanny Cavendish people knew what they were going to see. You had to know how to act—*(A slow turn toward* KITTY*)* when you went on the stage in those days.

KITTY: You had your method. We of the younger school have ours.

FANNY: Ah, youth, youth!

DEAN: *(Rise. In the manner of a formal announcement)* If you do go back this season, Fanny, that's going to mean the whole family on the boards. *(Returns his cup to tray)*

FANNY: The whole family?

(DOOR BELL)

DEAN: Except Tony, of course. You can't call pictures acting . . . But with you in "Castlemaine," Julie and Gwen in their play, and— *(A triumphant reach for the manuscript on the table. The doorbell rings)*—for your humble servant as the star of—

FANNY: *(In a surprising shout—picks up daily paper from piano)* Della! Della! *(Turns to* DEAN *again)* What's that about your being the bright particular star?

DEAN: I sent the manuscript of my next play over to Julie last night.

FANNY: I know it. *(*KITTY *rises,* DELLA *enters right. Goes to outer door)*

DEAN: Have you read it?

FANNY: Only the first four scenes. *(*JO *enters with* KITTY'S *tray.)*

DEAN: Well?

FANNY: I was afraid to read the second act for fear you played two parts at once. *(Sits in her chair right)*

DELLA: *(At door)* Good morning, Mr. Wolfe.

WOLFE: *(Off)* Morning, my girl. Good morning.

JO: *(Speaks through others)* Here you are, Mrs. Dean. All nice and hot. *(Places tray at window right.)*

KITTY: Oh—food!

(The thought palpably repels her, though she begins to eat. Jo places tray on tray bench up right and brings it in front of armchair near window. OSCAR WOLFE enters, followed by DELLA, who waits. WOLFE is a figure of authority; dark, stocky, slightly gray, dressed with a picturesque richness. A rakish black velour hat. Altogether the entrepeneur)

WOLFE: Well, well. Good morning, folks! Hello, Bert! *(Gives his coat, hat and stick to DELLA.)*

DEAN: Ah, Oscar! Just the man I want to see.

WOLFE: *(Shakes a chiding finger)* Calories, Kitty! Calories!

KITTY: *(Her mouth full)* I didn't have a bite of breakfast!

WOLFE: Fanny, my girl, how are you! *(Takes her hand, pats it warmly)*

FANNY: What brings you around this hour?

WOLFE: What draws me here always but the one great passion of my life! You, my dear Fanny!

FANNY: Now now—what are you here for?

WOLFE: The heartlessness of this coquette! The best years of my life I've given her.

DEAN: Ah—Oscar—just—

WOLFE: *(Not heeding DEAN. To FANNY)* Where's your gifted daughter?

FANNY: I thought so . . . Della, tell Miss Julie.
(GWEN appears from center door, balcony. DELLA exits under stairs.)

GWEN: My lunch ready? I'm dying. *(Wears silk riding shirt, breeches, mules and gay bathrobe)*

JO: I'll bring it right in. *(Exits right.)*

WOLFE: Hello, there, young lady! How's the child actress! *(Meets* GWEN *at foot of stairs)*

GWEN: Well, if it isn't Oscar himself! Here at the first pale crack of dawn!

WOLFE:. Crack of dawn, huh? Say, you good-for nothing actors can sleep till noon. You know your poor old manager's done a day's work for you already. That's quite a costume! What are you supposed to represent?

GWEN: *(*JO *enters with* GWEN'*s tray. He takes it left below door)* I'm the Spirit of Quick Lunch . . . Bring it over here, Jo. Don't you want something, Mr. Wolfe? H'm? Haunch of venison or a couple of bear steaks?

FANNY: Jo, Time for my eggnog, isn't it?

JO: Yes, Mrs. Cavendish. They're beating it up.

WOLFE: *(A slow inclusive look around that takes in the three trays)* Don't you ever get mixed up, Jo, about who wants breakfast and who wants lunch?

JO: Yes, sir, certainly do, Mr. Wolfe. Still, you get used to it. *(*JO *transfers one dish to* DEAN'*s tray.)*

WOLFE: Say, do you realize that there actually are families in this town that sit down in a dining-room all at the same time and eat a meal! Together!

FANNY: Quaint!

GWEN: I think it would be nice.

JO: Sure you wouldn't care for anything, Mr. Wolfe? Glad to get it for you.

WOLFE: No, not me, thanks, Jo. Lunch is a meal I never eat. *(*JO *exits at right.)*

FANNY: No. Just a little thick soup, and a mixed grill and coffee and French pastry at the Astor.

WOLFE: You're your old self this morning, Fanny.

(Crossing to FANNY*)*

FANNY: My old self, Wolfe, and ready to go back to work. (*A quick movement from* DEAN. *He wants to speak of himself.*)

WOLFE: Now, now, Fanny! Not so fast!

FANNY: Don't you now-now-Fanny me! I know whether I'm well or not. You haven't time for anything nowadays but Julie and Gwen productions.

DEAN: (*Manuscript in hand, taps* WOLFE *on the shoulder*) Oscar, I tried to reach you all day yesterday—

WOLFE: Yesterday? A crazy day. This is the last theatre I'll ever build. Contractors—(*crosses center*)—plasterers, license commissioners! Where the devil is Julie? She can't stay in bed all day. (JO *enters with eggnog, places it on* FANNY'S *table—then exits.* WOLFE, *at foot of stairs*) Julie!

FANNY: Julie! (*A shout that tops* WOLFE'S)

JULIE: (*A voice from behind the bedroom door, balcony*) I'm busy.

FANNY: Wolfe is here!

JULIE: Give him my love!

WOLFE: I'm in a hurry!

(*Nothing from the uppers regions. A moment's expectant pause.* WOLFE *turns away with an impatient shrug.*)

DEAN: Well, Oscar—I have finally found the play!

WOLFE: All right, all right. Later on. You're a fine actor, Bert, but remember that last opus you handed me. Well, well! (*Cross to* FANNY) What you got there, Fanny? Something good?

FANNY: Eggnog. I'm being built up.

WOLFE: Got a little schnapps in it, huh?

FANNY: Milk and eggs.

WOLFE: Say, to do you good it's got to have something in it. Let me send you a few bottles sherry to-morrow. I got some fine Amontillado over at the office.

FANNY: That'll help.

DEAN: Now, Wolfe. (*Slips the manuscript under* WOLFE'S *arm*) There's the script.

(DELLA, *who has gone up on balcony by back stairs, now enters from* JULIE'S *room, a great pile of garments in her arms, so stacked that she scarcely can see over them. Down the stairs, exits right*)

WOLFE: All right. (*Up toward the piano. Tosses manuscript on piano*) I'll keep it in mind. (*Strikes note or two, idly*)

DEAN: What a play! Richness, characterization, verisimilitude!

WOLFE: M-m-m-m! I read it anyhow. (*A bar or two of music*) That other piano as bad as this?

DEAN: I'll drop in on you first thing in the morning. Hear what you think. (*He goes back to his tray, right.*)

(WOLFE, *becoming more interested in the music, runs another bar or two. Then he sits and concentrates a bit more on a few notes, preparatory to playing the thing he has in mind.*)

FANNY: What's the name of it again, Bertie? This masterpiece.

DEAN: "The Conqueror." (*Another brief run on the piano from* WOLFE)

FANNY: Are you going to do it soon?

DEAN: Oh, around the holidays, if that suits Oscar?

(*A glance toward* WOLFE. WOLFE *is now playing, lightly a melodious, slightly sentimental air that continues for a few bars without interruption.*)

GWEN: (*Goes to piano, gets cigarette, goes back to her tray. During a moment's lull in the music*) What's that?

WOLFE: I don't know.

(*For a moment they give an ear to the music.* JO *comes down to* FANNY *with a plate of rolls.* FANNY *refuses it. While the music is still playing,* JO *crosses to* KITTY, *offers her the rolls. They have all resumed eating. Their attention is fixed on the food before them. A brief lull. The music softly continues. The tinkle of silverware and the clatter of china is distinctly heard. The door of* JULIE'S *bedroom opens slowly.* JULIE *appears, balcony.* JULIE CAVENDISH *is thirty-nine, beautiful, slim, mature. She is wearing a smart, rather tailored afternoon gown. Is evidently dressed for the day. She comes out slowly, curious to know who is playing. She crosses the width of the balcony, stands at the railing, looking.down. Her first glance is toward the piano. She sees* WOLFE *there. Her gaze encompasses the rest of the room. Four of its occupants are busily eating. One at a time, she takes them in.)*

JULIE: Have you a table for one, Jo, not too near the music? (WOLFE *stops playing. Turns quickly to took up at* JULIE. DEAN *also looks up at her; and* KITTY.)

WOLFE: How do you ever make it on matinee days, Julie?

JULIE: *(Starts toward stairway)* By being the star, Oscar. They wait for me. *(She is leaning over the stairway rail, one hand posed just a little too carefully on the bannister.)*

FANNY: A very good entrance, Julie.

JULIE: Dear little mother! Wouldn't you like to go up and come down again? *(Comes on down.* GWEN *rises from her table, a bit of food in her hand, munching as she goes. She meets* JULIE *at the foot of the stairway)* Have a nice ride, Gwen? *(A glance at her)* Don't you look terrible!

(DELLA enters, right, carrying a gay orange and purple figured box.)

GWEN: I know it, mother. I'm going right up and change.

JULIE: No, wait a minute. *(Flicks open the telegram in her hand and holds it out)* For lo, I bring tidings! Guess what!

FANNY: Tidings?

GWEN: Well?

DEAN: What?

DELLA: *(Indicates hat box)* A center O.D. package, Miss Julie. Thirty-nine dollars.

JULIE: What?

DELLA: Thirty-nine dollars. A package.

JULIE: Thirty-nine dol—What did I buy for this—Such a strange sum. Who has thirty-nine dollars? *(Surveys the group rapidly)* Oscar! Let me have it, will you? That makes—how much do I owe you now?

WOLFE: Enough. *(MCDERMOTT appears from center door, balcony. He wears a coat, small black derby; little black bag in his hand. Starts down.)*

GWEN: Mother, I can't wait. You haven't any news, anyhow.

JULIE: Oh, but I have, Gwen, so come right back here. *(Glimpses McDermott coming swiftly down the stairs)* I'll want you tomorrow, you know, Mac.

MCDERMOTT: *(Shifts his hat slightly by way of deference)* Yes, Miss Cavendish, we'll have a real workout to-morrow. Same time? *(Crossing right)*

JULIE: No, come at eleven—No—Bendel! Ten? . . . Oh, my God, no! . . . Twelve . . . one . . . one, Mac.

FANNY: Matinee tomorrow.

JULIE: Oh, good Lord, I can't make it tomorrow at all, Mac . . . Monday.

WOLFE: Watch out there! You got rehearsals starting Monday.

JULIE: Wait a minute, Mac. So I have. Let me think . . . could you give me Sunday?

MCDERMOTT: I don't generally work Sundays as a rule. But, seeing it's you. One o'clock.

JULIE: One's fine. You're a dear.

MCDERMOTT: So long. *(MCDERMOTT starts to go.)*

JULIE: Good Lord! Mac! I can't Sunday! Make it to-morrow at twelve! I'll get it in some way.

MCDERMOTT: Yes, ma'am. *(Exit.)*

(DELLA exits with package. JO on and off with GWEN's tray. JULIE picks up her photographs from secretary— looks them over.)

JULIE: Special fitting on Sunday, and it may take hours. Oscar, her second-act dress is going to be lovely. And, of course, the sable wrap will make it perfect.

WOLFE: Sable wrap?

JULIE: Why, of course. For the opera scene. She has to have a sable wrap.

FANNY: Wouldn't surprise me if the whole cast wore 'em. My day it was Fanny Cavendish's costumes by Fanny Cavendish. With one little dress and a guipure lace flounce I could be anything from Camille to Two Orphans.

JULIE: I've seen that one little dress in the storehouse. The investment for whalebone and buckram alone would have kept me in sables a lifetime.

(Goes left center)

GWEN: Mother, are you going to read that telegram or aren't you?

WOLFE: First. let me tell you what I came about. Then I get right out. *(A sigh of impatience from GWEN)*

JULIE: No, no! You've got to hear this. We need you.

GWEN: Well, then, come on with it!

FANNY: Yes, Julie, I think you've built up a good suspense.

JULIE: *(Surveys her position)* Am I centre? . . . It's dear little brother Tony again.

FANNY: Tony!

DEAN: I knew it.

WOLFE: What's he done now, that bum?

KITTY: Plenty, is my guess.

JULIE: Well, his telegram is rather sketchy, but as nearly as I can make out, I gather that he's killed somebody.

FANNY: Anyone we know?

JULIE: *(Reads)* "Pay no attention to possible accounts of Deming incident injuries not fatal takes more than a lousy movie director I arrive New York Saturday California police have no authority outside state on no condition talk to reporter Zeta Kaydak on this train but no trouble so far as am locked in drawing room love to all of you he was dirty hound anyhow, Tony." Good old Tony.

KITTY: What did I tall you! *(Rises)*

JULIE: It lacks a certain clarity, doesn't it?

FANNY: California police!

DEAN: What's this, what's this! *(There now ensues a babel of sounds— exclamations, conjectures, questions spoken together.)*

FANNY: What's it mean?

KITTY: You know Tony!

GWEN: What's it all about?

DEAN: Who's this Zeta Kaydak?

WOLFE: *(Comes over to JULIE)* Now, now— now! Just a minute. Let's get at this. This may not be so funny. *(Takes telegram)*

FANNY: Do you think it's serious?

JULIE: Of course not, Mother. It never is.

WOLFE: *(Re-reading fragments of the telegram to himself, but aloud)* Possible accounts of Deming incident—

GWEN: Deming is his director.

WOLFE: Arrive New York Saturday.

DELLA: That's tomorrow.

WOLFE: . . . Zeta Kaydak on this train . . .

KITTY: She's that Polish hussy.

(JO enters, gets eggnog glass and KITTY's tray—exits.)

WOLFE: A fine business.

FANNY: What's she on the train for?

WOLFE: On no condition talk to reporters . . .

JULIE: Reporters? Have there been any reporters?

DEAN: Before you were down. The Graphic.

JULIE: The Graphic. Whatever we've done, we've always kept out of the tabloids. *(Sits on sofa.)*

WOLFE: Yes, and who's kept you out, I'd like to know? Wolfe!

JULIE: Here's another chance for you. What are we going to do?

WOLFE: Now, wait a minute. Let's look this over. Maybe it's not as bad as it seems.

FANNY: No.

GWEN: Of course not, Grandma. Such a fuss because Tony's punched some director. I'm sure to be late. *(On her way up the stairs. GWEN exits center door, balcony.)*

WOLFE: *(Still concentrating on the telegram)* Now, the way I figure it, it was like this. The fella says something Tony doesn't like. Tony knocks him down, of course. And to keep from having to answer a lot of questions about it, he gets on this train.

JULIE: With the picture half finished, naturally.

WOLFE: Omaha he sent this from. Omaha last night. That means he got to Chicago this morning. Naturally he got on the Century. To-morrow morning you'll be just one happy family.

JULIE: Now we've got to keep the newspapers off him. They've been laying for him ever since that Mauretania thing.

KITTY: I must say I don't blame them.

DEAN: Yes, he never should have thrown that reporter overboard.

WOLFE: A big mistake.

JULIE: They're sure to know he's on the Century. They'll swarm on him at the station. He'll start to smash cameras. *(A gesture that says "Whoop!")*

FANNY: That poor boy

WOLFE: *(Snaps his fingers)* I tell you how I fix it. He don't come into Grand Central. He gets off at 125th Street.

JULIE: It doesn't stop there.

WOLFE: Tomorrow it will—for one second. *(Points wisely to himself)* I get him off the train, I bring him here before the newspapers know it, he stays quiet a couple of weeks. If they find it out, he's having a nervous collapse—and nobody can see him.

JULIE: *(Rise)* Oh, Oscar! That'll be wonderful! There you are, Mrs. C. Everything grand.

FANNY: Everything grand! Who's this Zany woman? What's she doing on the train?

JULIE: Well—uh—Oscar, tell mother the facts of life. *(Crosses to stairs.)*

WOLFE: *(Pats FANNY'S shoulder)* Satisfied, Fanny? Huh? Your boy ain't in danger? *(KITTY crosses and sits on bench right.)*

FANNY: You're the manager.

WOLFE: Good! Now! If nobody else has got anything to do, that you would like to have me wait until you do it—Julie, you don't want to take a massage first, or something? . . . No? . . . Well, then, do you mind if I waste just a minute of your time on my business?

DEAN: *(Rises)* That's what I say! After all, we—

WOLFE: No, no, no, no! This is Julie. Julie, my girl, it is now— *(His watch)* My God! Five minutes after two! I want you down town in my office—you and Gwen—three o'clock, sharp.

JULIE: Down town! What for? *(Protesting.)*

WOLFE: Now, don't start to holler before I tell you. I'm not so stuck on it, either, but we've all got to do it.

JULIE: Do what?

WOLFE: Who do you think came in on the Mauretania last night? Out of a blue sky—St. John Throckmorton.

JULIE: Oh! Is that all? *(Turns upstage—picks up magazine from commode left— then sits)*

KITTY: Who's he?

WOLFE: Who's he? Only the fellow that wrote Julie's new play, that's all.

DEAN: Oh, the author!

JULIE: Send him back.

WOLFE: Now, now, hold on a minute. We got to be nice to this fellow. He's given you a beautiful play here, and the point is he's going to write more of them. Now, you do that for me, huh, Julie? Be there with Gwen at three?

FANNY: The less you have to do with authors the better.

WOLFE: *(To* FANNY*)* That's right! Make it harder! *(To* JULIE*)* We call it settled, huh? You'll be there? Remember this fella's come all the way over from England.

JULIE: But an English author! If he landed last night, won't he be lecturing this afternoon? *(They all laugh)*

WOLFE: If you comedians will keep still a minute, I'll tell you what it is. This Throckmorton is a new playwright, and English to boot, and nothing will satisfy him he wants to read his play to the entire company. *(A shout of derision from them all)* Now hold on a minute. This is a serious fellow—monocle, spats, gardenia—everything. With him this is part of being a playwright, reading the play aloud. The chances are he saw one of those photographs in the Green Room of His Majesty's Theatre, the whole company grouped around,—Sir Beerbohm Tree in the middle—and What's-his-name reading "The Gay Lord Quex" to 'em. You should try to talk him out of it. I spent the morning.

JULIE: I never heard anything so idiotic in my life! *(Rises)* It's fantastic! But if you're really serious, and you want me to do this, I'll sit through it—only it can't be this afternoon.

WOLFE: It's got to be this afternoon.

JULIE: Oh, no! *(Comes down)* Then the whole thing's off. It would take hours. I have an appointment.

WOLFE: Julie, how often do I ask a favor? Now, this fella has got another play that I'm crazy to get hold of. If we're all just a little bit nice to him—jolly him along—tell him how good he is. What do you say?

FANNY: To hell with him!

JULIE: But Oscar, why in the name of heaven does it have to be just this afternoon! Can't it be some other time?

WOLFE: Say, what's going on this afternoon? You going to be married?

JULIE: *(A startled look)* I can't, that's all, Oscar. I can't! It's got to be some other time.

WOLFE: To-morrow you got a matinee. Monday you begin rehearsals.

JULIE: Well—Sunday.

WOLFE: Sunday he's out at Otto Kahn's. I tell you there is no other time for it. If you knew what you mean to him! He's all impressed about having you and Gwen in his first play. He knows all about you. Everything you've been in—all of you.

DEAN: Really!

KITTY: You don't say!

WOLFE: So you wouldn't even do this for your old manager, huh? You got some little appointment-tea, or to buy a hat—and compared to that Oscar don't matter.

JULIE: Oh, now, Oscar.

WOLFE: Well—never mind. The next time you ask me to do something for you—*(Turns right)* I do it anyhow.

FANNY: I don't believe in humoring playwrights, but if it's such a favor to Oscar, that's different . . . *(Then turns directly to* JULIE*)* What're you doing that's so important this afternoon?

JULIE: Well, I—

KITTY: I'd do it, busy as I am. *(Cross to piano)*

FANNY: Pay no attention to her, Oscar—I'll see that she's there.

JULIE: Mother, you don't understand.

FANNY: Oscar's done a lot of things for you.

JULIE: You win, Oscar. At three o'clock—Enter Julie Cavendish, laughing.

WOLFE: That's my girl! *(Starts briskly toward hallway)* Now don't forget. Three o'clock at my office.

DEAN: Oscar, you're not going? *(Crossing—grabs up play and stands right)*

(JO enters, crosses left, gets DEAN's tray. WOLFE enters from hallway, putting on hat and coat. Takes out his watch again, his coat half on)

WOLFE: It's now two-twenty. You and Gwen leave here quarter to three, sharp. *(Comes down again, stands near Julie)* All right? I can depend on it?

JULIE: I'll be there. *(Stands near stairs.)*

WOLFE: That's the way to talk. Good-bye, everybody! *(Starts upstage toward outer door.)*

DEAN: *(Eager for a few last words to WOLFE about his play)* Heh! Oscar!

WOLFE: *(A little bewildered, glancing at the manuscript)* What's this?

DEAN: *(Highly offended)* Well, on my word! This is the play that—

WOLFE: Oh, yes, yes, yes, yes——*(Into the alcove up. DEAN follows him rapidly. KITTY has been easing over toward WOLFE at the first sign of his departure. She now comes swiftly to the alcove, bent on pressing her own claim.)*

DEAN: Now, as I told you, there's a scene or two where I could use a better entrance.

WOLFE: Sure, sure! I read it to-night. Give you a ring in the morning. Excuse me if I run. *(To elevator)* Down! *(Exits)*

(DOOR slam)

(Exits. The slam of the door. JO exits with DEAN's tray.)

DEAN: *(Talking through WOLFE'S speech, continuing from his own last speech)* But that's a simple matter. The main thing is to get an absolutely——Kitty, for God's sake! *(DEAN enters and goes left.)*

KITTY: *(Starts speaking cue—when DEAN says "A scene or two")* You are going to remember about me, aren't you? I've played nearly all those parts and there isn't one—*(At the slam of the door both* DEAN *and* KITTY *break off.* DEAN, *at the slam of the door at* WOLFE'S *exit, strides on and across to left, hands in pockets, very disgruntled.* KITTY *follows him, bristling.)* I'm on to you all right. You're afraid I'll give too good a performance. You won't surround yourself with anything but second-rate people—you don't want anybody that's really good. Let me tell you I don't purpose to be held down artistically just because I'm married to Herbert Dean. I'm important, too, don't forget. Ask any producer in New York.

DEAN: *(Cuts in about at "You're afraid I'll too good a performance")* Good God, Kitty, I've been a star for years! It's simply that you're not suited to this play, that's all. It's entirely the wrong kind of part for you. I should think you'd want to help instead of hindering. You know very well you drive me crazy by your infernal——

JULIE: *(Cutting in on the double conversation. Cue—*KITTY—*"That's really good")* Oh, stop it, you two, will you! Stop it or get out of here! Go on in there and argue. I've been a star, you've been a star I can't stand it, I tell you. Get out! Get out! Get out! *(Takes an arm of each and, while they are still arguing, propels them rapidly into the library, left. Slams the door on them. Turns swiftly her back to the door, slumps a little against it, exhausted. A deep breath. Leans against door. The telephone rings on stage.* JULIE'*s sigh breaks off in the middle)* Oh! *(A mock nod of deference in the direction of the phone)*
*(*TELEPHONE *Business)*

FANNY: Let it ring.

JULIE: Oh, you never can tell. *(Picks up the receiver)* Yes . . . this is Julie Cavendish . . .Yes, this is Miss Cavendish speaking Yes? . . .Yes . . . *(To* FANNY, *picks up cigarette—looks for match)* You were right . . .Well, I'll tell you, it's very difficult for me to take part in any benefit performances just at present . . . December third . . . Well, you see, I'll be playing and rehearsing at the same time. I'm afraid . . . Yes, I'm sure it's a very good cause . . . The Newark Newsboys . . .The little . . . Oh, yes . . . Well, I will if I possibly can. *(One of those mirthless laughs in response to a bit of fulsome praise. Goes left—sits—gets match)* That's very kind of you. I'm so glad you enjoyed it . . . No, I won't forget . . . Century Theatre, December third. *(Hangs up. To* FANNY) Mother, will you remind me? Bronchitis on December third.

FANNY: I shall do no such thing! If you promised to play that benefit you'll play it—bronchitis or double pneumonia.

JULIE: The honor of the family! *(Sits on sofa)*

FANNY: Now, Julie Cavendish, what's all this mooning about? What was this big renunciation scene? "I can't this afternoon. I can't . . ." *(A gesture)*

JULIE: Gilbert's back.

FANNY: Gilbert?

JULIE: Gil Marshall. He's in New York. I had a note from him; and some flowers.

FANNY: So that's it. *(Rises left)*

JULIE: You see, it would have been nice to have had the afternoon clear.

FANNY: Was he going to come here?

JULIE: He's calling up at four to find out. Della will have to explain to him, that's all. A play reading! I'd better not tell him that.

FANNY: So! *(Sits on sofa)* He's come back to New York to spend his millions, h'm? What's that they call him? South American Diamond King?

JULIE: Emerald, mother. Much nicer.

FANNY: Emeralds or diamonds. When I think that if it hadn't been for me you'd have gone off to South America—given up your career everything.

JULIE: I wonder what he's like now. He may have grown very charming. South America, and millions, and perhaps a little gray here. *(Touches her temple)* Sounds rather romantic.

FANNY: No more romantic now than he was nineteen years ago! Ah! What a siege that was!

JULIE: And what a demon you were!

FANNY: I had to be. You thought because he looked serious and didn't say much that he was doing a lot of deep thinking. I knew it was because he couldn't think of anything to say.

JULIE: You certainly acted like a mother in a melodrama.

FANNY: I told him, I said, "Here's a girl that's going to have fame and fortune the world spread before her. Do you think that you can make up to her for all the things you'd rob her of!"

JULIE: Yes, yes, I know, mother. He went away, and we both lived happy ever after.

FANNY: How I ever got you where you are today is more than I know. You were always at the point of running off with some young squirt.

JULIE: But I never did. So it couldn't have been so serious.

FANNY: Serious enough for them! That young Earl of Pembroke who went off to Africa, and that Boston fellow that shot himself—

JULIE: He was cleaning his gun.

FANNY: They were always cleaning their guns. And when you finally married Rex Talbot!

JULIE: Mother, out of the whole crowd of them, why did I marry Rex?

FANNY: He was the weakest, I guess.

JULIE: I always said I wouldn't marry an actor. And Rex wasn't even a good actor. What was there about him, mother?

FANNY: Rex Talbot was a brilliant young loafer! And he had the most beautiful manners. He was the kind of man who could kiss your hand without looking silly.

JULIE: I guess that was what he was always doing when I needed him. That's one thing you will admit about Gil, Mother. He would have been dependable.

FANNY: When you're eighteen you don't marry a man because he's dependable.

JULIE: But when you're a little older, you begin to think that maybe—

FANNY: What's that?

JULIE: Don't be alarmed. But I am curious to see him again. I had it all staged so beautifully, too. I was going to wear my rose beige, and a hat with a brim, and be dignified and wistful, yet girlish withal.

FANNY: You can put on that act for him just as well after the show tonight. It's been nineteen years. What's a couple of hours more!

JULIE: No. Midnight isn't as kind to me as it used to be. I'm just vain enough to want to look my best.

FANNY: You are, eh?

JULIE: I want to look fresh and young and radiant.

FANNY: Is that all?

(GWEN *enters from the center door on the balcony. She is smartly dressed in an afternoon frock, and on her arm she carries her coat. Her hat is in her hand. She is singing blithely and carelessly the newest jazz song hit. She comes quickly down the stairs.*)

GWEN: *(At the foot of the stairs)* Has anybody seen my tan bag? *(Throws coat and hat on nearby chair)*

JULIE: *(Remembering the engagement with* WOLFE*)* Gwen, you're not going out?

GWEN: *(Crosses left, looking about, then goes on swiftly down left to the library door)*I left it down here somewhere last night when— *(Opens the library door.* DEAN'*s voice and* KITTY'*s are heard in conflict.* DEAN'S *rising clearly above* KITTY'S*)*

DEAN: *(Offstage)*—over my dead body—

KITTY: *(Offstage)*—a woman like Fanny Ward—*(*GWEN *bangs the door shut with bewildered and startled expression.)*

FANNY: *(Half to herself)* Shouts and murmurs off.

GWEN: But I think it's in there.

JULIE: Gwen was it this afternoon that you were going out to Westchester with Perry?

GWEN: Of course. He'll be along any minute.

(Coming left center)

JULIE: Gwen, you've just got to leave word for him, that's all. You can't go.

GWEN: Why not? What's the matter?

JULIE: We've got to go right down to Oscar's office. I promised.

GWEN: But, mother—

JULIE: I know. I just forgot you were going with Perry. It's all a reading of the play by Throckmorton. He got in last night. He's set on it. Wolfe made an awful fuss about it—a favor to him—we —

GWEN: Mother, that's absurd. You know I've had this date with Perry for a week. I've never met his mother. She's giving this tea just for me. It's the first time she's asked me. She's having all these people in. How can I—— *(Fanny rises, goes to her chair right.)*

JULIE:. You can do it as well as I can, Gwen. I'm only doing it. for Oscar.

GWEN: But it can be some other time.

JULIE: No it can't. I've been all over it, and there isn't any other time. It's got to be this afternoon.

GWEN: *(Stamping childishly away frown them)* Oh, for the Lord's sake!

FANNY: He picked a good day for it, this Mr. Thingambob.

GWEN: Why do I have to be there! I've read his old play!

JULIE: So have I, for that matter.

GWEN: *(On the verge of tears)* Why didn't you tell me sooner? You knew I had this date—

JULIE: I'm sorry, Gwen, but I gave up something just as important—and more so. If you think it's going to be any fun for me to sit there and hear a play read——

GWEN: *(Starts speaking cue "And more so")*—I wouldn't care if it wasn't Perry's mother, but she'll probably never ask me again. And I couldn't go if she did ask me. I'll be rehearsing all the time, and then, I'll be acting, and it'll just go on like that forever. First thing you know I'll be an old woman—*(Two long rings at the doorbell, followed by a terrible hammering at the outer door. The clamor is enough to stop them, mid-speech.)*

(DOOR BELL)
(Pounding)

JULIE: *(Started)* What's that! . . . Jo! . . . Della! *(Goes up to alcove.)*

GWEN: What is it! *(Runs up to alcove.)*

(FANNY pounds rapidly on the floor with her stick. JO appears swiftly, right, followed by DELLA. Both go to alcove, JO on a half run, DELLA walking very quickly. At the same time the unusual doors of the library are thrown open as DEAN and KITTY emerge, brought out by the unusual noise.)

DEAN: What's the matter? What' s going on?

KITTY: My, what a racket!

(With the others they go up toward outer door. They are huddled in a group as JO opens the door. From offstage you hear their voices in surprise and alarm. FANNY alone is on stage.)

JULIE: *(Off)* Tony!

GWEN: *(Off)* Tony!

GWEN: *(Off)* Tony!

FANNY: *(In a tone of unbelief)* Tony?

DEAN: *(Over his shoulder, to FANNY)* It's Anthony! *(At this point the group at the door break into a confused chorus of surprise, unbelief, amazement, interrogation, "But how did you get here!" "You were in Chicago this morning!" "We just got your telegram!" "What does this mean!" "I don't understand how you ——" "Well, this is a surprise,*

*Mr. Tony!" (*JO*) "Well, of all people!" (*DELLA*)* TONY'S *"Sh-shs-shs-sh!" attempting to silence them, sounds through this babel)*

(TONY *enters, dramatically, elaborately, stealthily, his look. and gesture cautioning silence. He is wearing an all-enveloping fur coat, the collar of which is turned up so that his face is concealed. The brim of his soft felt hat is pulled over his eyes. He comes down swiftly, almost in the manner of one who is backing away frown something he fears. His face is turned away so that he is looking over his shoulder. His left coat sleeve, scarcely seen by the audience, hangs empty.)*

TONY: Sh-shs-sh! Sh-sh, I tell you!

FANNY: Tony! It's really you!!

(JULIE, GWEN, DEAN, KITTY *have followed a few feet behind him, bewilderment in their faces. They are still exclaiming.* JO, *laden with luggage, follows. A hallboy and chauffeur, also carrying* TONY'S *belongings.* JO, *laden with baggage, enters last.* DELLA *enters, stands upstage. Distributed among servants are a violin case, half a dozen bags and suitcases, very smart and glittering; an overcoat, a rug, golf sticks, hatbox, tennis racquet. The barrage of questioning opens up again with* JULIE, DEAN, *and* KITTY *in the lead, overlapping each other's speech.* GWEN, *after the first flurry of the entrance, remembers her own problems. And while she is interested in* TONY'S *explanation etc., she is plainly disturbed about* PERRY STEWART.)

JULIE: But Tony, how did you get here? It isn't possible!

DEAN: My dear boy, this is rather bewildering!

KITTY: Well, you're a great one! Of all the surprises!

FANNY: If this is one of your jokes, Tony Cavendish——

TONY: Sh-sh! Be quiet, will you, everybody! Shut up! (*Complete quiet then, for a brief moment*) Somebody go out there—(*Points to the entrance, right*) and lock the back door! (*JO exits.*) Gwen! (*Indicating library*) Take a look out of that window! See if there's a man out there in a long overcoat! (*JO enters.* GWEN *vanishes a second only through library doorway. Appears again immediately*) Take everything up to my room, Jo!

JO: This way, boys. (*JO starts quickly up the stairs, laden with luggage, a glance over his shoulder to indicate that the hallboy and the chauffeur are to follow him with their share of the burden. They follow.*)

TONY: Julie, have you got some change? I want a lot of change. (*Turns toward his mother. Tilts up chin gaily. Kisses her*) How's America's sweetheart? Aren't you glad to see your baby boy?

JULIE: Tony, will you explain this trick entrance? How did you get here?

TONY: I'll tell you in a minute. First I want some money. (*Glances up toward chauffeur, hallboy, JO, on stairway. To CHAUFFEUR*) Let me see. You get twenty dollars. (*Aside to others*) He brought me in from Mineola . . . You get ten—— (*To the HALLBOY*) And ten apiece for those fellows downstairs. How many are there?

HALLBOY: Three, sir. Two, and the doorman.

TONY: All right. You take forty, and you get twenty . . . and now remember, you fellows, if any of those reporters ask you, you didn't see me, I never came in here. You don't know anything about me. Do you get that?

HALLBOY: Yes, sir.

CHAUFFEUR: I get you.

TONY: Julie, let them have the money, will you?

JULIE: Jo, you attend to it. My bag's on my dresser.

JO: I'll see to it.

> (*At the end of his own last line* TONY *has started to throw off his fur coat, shrugging his left shoulder free and revealing his left arm in a silk sling. A little shriek from* FANNY)

FANNY: Tony! Your arm!

JULIE: You're hurt!

DEAN: Is it a serious injury?

KITTY: (*At sight of the arm*) Oh!

GWEN: (*Half aloud*) Oh, Tony!

TONY: It doesn't amount to anything. I hit him too hard, that's all. (FANNY *makes a pitying sound between tongue and teeth.*)

JULIE: How did it start in the first place?

DEAN: Let's hear about it.

(DELLA *enters right and starts toward stairway.*)

TONY: Della, I'm starved. I haven't had a bite for twelve hours. Bring me everything you've got. (DELLA *turns and exits right.*) First I've got to have a hot bath. Come on upstairs, everybody, while I take a bath.

(*With* KITTY *and* DEAN *in the lead,* KITTY *having one foot on the stairway, they all go up toward the stairs.* FANNY *goes to* DELLA— *instructs her regarding* TONY'S *food.*)

JULIE: Tony, will you listen to me! How did you get here today? You were in Omaha yesterday!

TONY: I flew, of course. Came by aeroplane from Chicago.

DEAN: Aeroplane!

KITTY: Flew!

JULIE: Tony Cavendish!

TONY: I couldn't come on a train. They're watching the trains. I've got to lay low in this apartment till I sail. (JO *is seen to cross to* JULIE'S *room and returns counting money.*)

FANNY: Sail?

JULIE: Sail where?

TONY: Europe, of course. To-morrow on the Aquitania . . .God, I hate pictures . . . I've got to have a bath. If you want to hear the rest of it, come on up!

(TONY *starts again for the stairway, and* KITTY *and* DEAN *mount quickly ahead of him.* KITTY *in the lead.* JULIE *follows just behind.* GWEN *remains on stage. As they ascend the stairs,* TONY, JULIE, DEAN *and* KITTY *are talking constantly and simultaneously.*)

DEAN: What happened out there, Tony? How did you get into this fight?

TONY: Oh, this alleged director—he had it coming to him ever since we started to shoot. He put his girl into the picture and when she got stuck on me he got sore. The blow off came when we were out on location. Doing a desert scene and Deming picked out the worst camel in the pack, and said to me: "You ride that one." I took one look at it and said: "The hell I will!" He said: "Who's directing the picture?" "You're directing the picture, but you're not directing me. I'm through with it, and you can take this to remember me by." *(Exits in* FANNY'S *room.* FANNY *starts towards stairs, when* TONY *says, "Like hell I will," nods approvingly.)*

JULIE: *(Cue when* DEAN *says "fellow in his place")* Unless you've killed him, Tony, I don't see why they're making all this fuss. And as for your going to Europe, I think it's the most ridiculous thing I've ever heard of. And you walked out in the middle of the picture, of course. They'll probably sue you for a million dollars, and you'll never get another picture job. *(Over balcony railing at* GWEN, *just exiting)* Get your things on, Gwen—I'll be right down.

KITTY: *(Cue when* JULIE *says "Making all this fuss")* I've always heard things about those directors, though I must say I met David Wark Griffith and you couldn't ask for a more perfect gentleman. He said to me, "Miss Le Moyne," he said, "if you ever want to go into pictures, come right to me."

DEAN: *(Cue when* TONY *says, "Remember me by")* Perfectly right to put the fellow in his place. Catch me letting any whipper-snapper tell me what to do. I'd show him!

*(*TONY *exits ahead of the rest.* DEAN *and* KITTY *follow, then* JULIE. FANNY *is last.)*

FANNY: Who's this train woman? This Zickery Zackery. *(Exits)*

*(*GWEN'S *mood throughout this scene has been one of thoughtful depression. After the general exit she stands upstage for a moment. She drifts down toward the sofa where her hat and coat have been thrown, and sits. Without glancing at it, she picks up her hat. The hallboy and the chauffeur appear on the balcony and descend the stairs quickly. The* HALLBOY *leads. He is counting a little sheaf of*

crisp bills. The CHAUFFEUR *is just putting his bills into his pocket. They exit under stairs.* GWEN *merely glances at them, resumes her position. With a little spasmodic gesture that is almost despairing she crumples her hat in her hand, beating one hand softly with the crushed felt hat. A deep sigh. She sits staring ahead of her.* JO *follows the chauffeur onto balcony, descends the stairs. The doorbell rings. The sound electrifies* GWEN *into sudden action.)*

*(*DOOR BELL, PERRY*)*

GWEN: I'll go, Jo. *(Exits outer door)*

*(*JO *picks up* TONY'S *fur coat and hat. Exits under stairs)*

PERRY: *(Off. With exaggerated elegance)* Why! Fancy meeting you here!

GWEN: *(Off)* Oh, shut up, Perry!

*(*DOOR *Slam)*

(The sound of the door closing. GWEN *comes down immediately, followed by* PERRY. *He is speaking the next line as he comes)*

PERRY: Come on, get your bonnet on. I'd like to stop at the Riding Club and look at that horse, wouldn't you? It'll only take a minute.

GWEN: Oh, Perry!

PERRY: What's the matter?

GWEN: I can't go.

PERRY: What do you mean—you can't go!

GWEN: They're going to read the play down at Wolfe's office.

PERRY: What?

GWEN: The author's going to read the play. And of course they had to pick this afternoon.

PERRY: What are you talking about?

GWEN: I can't go with you, Perry. I've got to go to Wolfe's office to hear the play read. There's no way out of it. I've got to do it. Isn't that damn!

PERRY: You're joking.

GWEN: But Perry. I'm not! I know it sounds silly——

PERRY: Silly! It's cuckoo! I never heard anything so ridiculous in my life. You can't mean you're breaking this date just to go and hear somebody read a play . . . What play?

GWEN: The play! The play that goes into rehearsal on Monday. That Mother and I are doing.

PERRY: Why, good God, you've read it a thousand times. You read it to me!

GWEN: But this is different. The author's going to read it.

PERRY: Well, let him—the silly ass! What do you care!

GWEN: (A long breath) Now, Perry, please try to understand this. It's part of my job, and it's important.

PERRY: Important to hear some idiot read a play that you've read again and again!

GWEN: But it's more than that it's a ceremony! (Sits on bench.)

PERRY: Gwen, you know as well as I do that we planned this thing a week ago. Mother's no Victorian, but, listen, you can't do a thing like this. She wouldn't understand

GWEN: Perry! I want horribly to go! I made an awful fuss. But what could I do?

PERRY: (Crosses right center) You know, Gwen, this isn't the first time you've done this to me.

GWEN: Perry, please don't be unreasonable.

PERRY: I don't think I was unreasonable about New Haven, when we were all set to go to the game ——

GWEN: But I explained. (Rise) I told you. You said you understood. Wolfe suddenly phoned—I had to go down to see the chap he'd got as juvenile. If it was somebody I couldn't stand——And Wednesday I had to be photographed with Mother.

PERRY: Yes, I know. I know.

GWEN: Don't look so stern. You know this is all just because of the new play.

PERRY: Yeh, But there'll always be a new play. *(Looks directly at her)* Won't there?

GWEN: I realize it's inconvenient sometimes. It is for me, too.

PERRY: But what are we going to do about it, Gwen?

GWEN: If I can't go——I can't. *(Turns away right)*

PERRY: *(Follows her over)* I'm not talking about that. I mean us! Look here, Gwen. You're no blue-eyed babe. I haven't dropped down on one knee and said will-you-be-mine, but you know I'm absolutely crazy about you. Don't you?

GWEN: Uh-hm.

PERRY: But what are we heading for? That's what I'd like to know. How's it all going to work out?

GWEN: Why——I don't know. What is there to work out?

PERRY: After all, you marry the person that you'd rather be with than anyone else in the world. But where'll you be half the time? Rehearsing, or something. *(Turns right center)*

GWEN: Now, don't be fantastic! Rehearsals last three weeks.

PERRY: All right. And then what! You're at the theatre every night. Your work will just begin when mine is all over. You'll have dinner at six. I'll probably not even be home. By midnight you're all keyed up and ready to start out, but I've got to be at work in the morning.

GWEN: But those things adjust themselves. Lots of other people have got around it. *(Sits on bench.)*

PERRY: I'd do anything in the world for you, Gwen. I'd die for you! But I can't be one of those husbands. Hanging around dressing rooms! Sidestepping scenery. Calling up the costumer. What am I going to do every night. See the show?

GWEN: But you wouldn't want me to be one of those wives, would you! Bridge and household and babies!

PERRY: Well, why not! What's the matter with that!

GWEN: *(Rise)* Because I can't do that sort of thing any more than you can do the other. I'm an actress, Perry. An actress!

PERRY: Oh, what does that mean! Suppose you turn out to be as good as your mother or better! What is there to it when it's all over? Get your name up in electric lights, and a fuse blows out and where are you!

GWEN: I won't let you belittle my work. It's just as important as yours. I suppose the world would go to pieces if you didn't sell a hundred shares of Consolidated Whatnot for ten cents more than somebody paid for it!

PERRY: You can't compare business with acting. *(Goes right center)*

GWEN: Is that so? I can give you the names of actors and actresses of three hundred years ago—dozens of them! Name me two Seventeenth Century stock brokers.

PERRY: All right, I'll give up my work. That'll be dandy! And trail along behind you carrying your Pekinese, huh?. . . Not me!

GWEN: It's not a Pekinese! Oh, Perry, what are we talking like this for! It's horrible. *(Goes to him)* Forgive me! How could I talk like that to you!

PERRY: It's my fault. I didn't know what I was saying.

GWEN: Perry — dear! *(He takes her in his arms.)*

PERRY: Oh, what does anything matter!

GWEN: Weren't we a couple of idiots! We've never quarreled before.

PERRY: And we won't again. There isn't anything that matters to me except you. Business and acting. We must have been crazy!

GWEN: And you're all that matters to me.

PERRY: Gwen darling! *(They kiss again)* You're wonderful. Now, come on, honey. It's late. *(Gets hat)*

GWEN: What?

PERRY: Why, you are coming with me, aren't you?

GWEN: Oh, Perry!

PERRY: Huh?

GWEN: You haven't heard a word I've said. *(Crosses and sits in chair right)*

PERRY: I heard everything you said. You heard what I said, too, didn't you!

GWEN: Oh, Perry, we're not going to go all over this again, are we!

PERRY: No. We're not going all over it again. Not at all. We're not going over any of it again. It just comes down to one thing, that's all. *(Up stage slowly)*

GWEN: It's like a bad dream! I can't go, Perry! Haven't I explained to you that I can't.

PERRY: Oh! . . . Yes . . . Well, I've got to get started, of course, if I'm going to get there. Good-bye. *(He has been making a confused withdrawal. Hurt, angry. You hear the door bang.)*

(DOOR Slam)

(GWEN sits, her head up, defiantly. Then, as the realization of what has happened creeps upon her, she becomes less confident. Even terrified. JULIE appears on balcony from FANNY's room. She is in hat and coat. She is first heard talking over her shoulder to DEAN and KITTY, who are unseen in the hallway off balcony.)

JULIE: If he'd only try persuasion now and then instead of knocking people down right away . . .*(Glances at her wrist watch.)* Good Lord! *(Coming down stairs, calls over the railing)* Are you ready, Gwen?

DEAN: *(Entering)* Well, I'll be on my way, too.

KITTY: Where are you going?

JULIE: *(Descending the stairs. Sees that GWEN is not dressed for the street)* Good heavens, Gwen! Get your things on! What have you been doing? I must say you weren't much interested in Tony. *(Exit into library)*

(FANNY enters on balcony from center door. She is talking in a rather high-pitched voice to an unseen TONY in the room she has just left.)

FANNY: Stay on the stage where you belong, you wouldn't get mixed up with all that riff-raff! *(A mumble to herself as she stumps along the balcony and toward the stairs)*

JULIE: *(From the library)* Is the car downstairs?

DEAN: (Has gone up to alcove. Starts to plunge into his coat) Drop me at the Lambs', Julie?

KITTY: *(Goes right)* You're late, aren't you? Lackaye'll be worried. *(Into her coat)*

(TONY enters from center door balcony, carrying a snow-shoe, singing a snatch of an aria. He is wearing a gay silk bathrobe, monogrammed, embroidered, tasseled. He advances with a romantic swing to the balcony rail. Reaching it, he strikes a magnificent pose aided by a high topnote. FANNY picks up the melody and carries it a phrase further.)

JULIE: *(Re-enters from library, pulling on her gloves)* Lord, we're terribly late!

TONY: *(Shouts toward door right)* Jo, where the hell's my lunch!

JULIE: *(Making a last dash)* Gwen, will you get your things on? . . 'Bye, mother! . . . *(Kisses FANNY)* Where do you want to go, Bert? . . . *(Cross right)* See you later, Tony! . . . Gwen, what the devil's the matter with you! Why don't you come?

GWEN: I'm not coming.
(JULIE, during this speech, has crossed almost to the alcove. DEAN is above her in the alcove doorway. KITTY has put on her coat and has crossed toward the piano. FANNY has dropped down left. TONY is sitting on balcony rail fixing the snow-shoe, surveying the departure of the others.)

JULIE: *(Turns quickly, comes down a step or two)* Now, Gwen, don't start all that again. It's so silly.

GWEN: *(Rise)* I'm not going, do you understand! I'm not ever going. I'm not going, to act in it at all.

JULIE: *(Impatiently)* Oh, for heaven's sake!

FANNY: Don't be sulky.

DEAN: My dear Gwen!

KITTY: What's the matter with her?

JULIE: Will you put on your hat and coat? *(Turns again as if to go.)*

GWEN: Listen to me! *(A note in her voice makes them realize that here is something serious.)* I don't just mean I'm not going to be in this play. I'm not going to be in any play.

DEAN: What!

JULIE: My offspring has gone mad.

GWEN: I mean it. I'm through with the stage. I'm never going to act again.

JULIE: What are you talking about!

KITTY: She does mean it!

DEAN and FANNY: Not act again! Why—why—brrrrr—why—The child's sick!

TONY: Don't go into pictures.

GWEN: Please! I've made up my mind, and all of you put together can't stop me. I'm through with the stage and I'll tell you why, if you want to know. I'm not going to have it mess up my whole life! *(An hysterical jumble of attempted explanation.)*

KITTY: What are you talking about?

JULIE: What do you mean, your whole life?

DEAN: What—what is this—

GWEN: *(Her talk is pierced from time to time by exclamations from the others of the family)* . . . Do you know what he did! He walked right out of the room . . . If you think I'm going to give him up for a miserable little stage career just because we've always done it . . . we'd never see each other . . . he's get up in the morning and I wouldn't go to work till night . . . Look at this afternoon with his mother waiting out there. . . it'll be like that for years and years . . . You're not going to ruin my life. *(Tumbled explanation)*

JULIE: What do you mean, ruin your life?

DEAN: What kind of talk is this?

KITTY: Ain't you ashamed of yourself——

GWEN: I'm going to marry Perry Stewart and be a regular person. And nothing you can say is going to stop me!

JULIE: *(Comes toward her)* I never heard such silly rot in all my life.

(From DEAN, FANNY, TONY, KITTY, *such lines as: "Why, it's preposterous! Quit and get married!")* *(*TONY. *"Who's Perry Stewart?")* *(*FANNY. *"Never thought I'd live to see this day.")*

JULIE: I don't know what you're talking about.

GWEN: Well, I know what I'm talking about. I'm sick of all this. I'm sick of being a Cavendish! I want to be a human being *(From the others a shocked murmur)*

FANNY: What's that!

DEAN: But you are a Cavendish!

JULIE: Of course you are.

GWEN: But I don't want to be! *(Crosses to sofa and sits.)*

JULIE: You've got to be. What do you think we've worked for all these years!

FANNY: You can't do this to us!

JULIE: My God! What anyone else would give for your chances!

DEAN: Yes!

FANNY: It's absurd!

JULIE: You can be the greatest of us all. Aubrey and Fanny Cavendish have just been stepping stones for you—

FANNY: What's that? What's that!

JULIE: Oh, Mother, please!

FANNY: I'll be a stepping stone for nobody! And as for Aubrey Cavendish, there's nobody since his day that can touch him. *(Cross to stairs)*

(NOTE: The following speeches overlap. Individual speeches carry no weight—it is the ensemble that counts. However, we do hear

KITTY *and* JULIE *say,* "*Well, if you want my opinion——*" "*Well, we don't want your opinion.*")

DEAN: One minute, please! *(Crosses to* FANNY*)* I believe my Macbeth ——

GWEN: Listen to them! That's what I mean!

DEAN: Still takes rank as the finest interpretation of its day and age.

FANNY: You miserable upstart! Do you expect me to stand here and allow you to mention yourself and Aubrey Cavendish in one and the same breath? Aubrey Cavendish was an artist. He wouldn't have had you for his dresser. The greatest actors of his generation have sat at the feet of Aubrey Cavendish.

Henry Irving, Beerbohm Tree, Richard Mansfield! And you have the presumption to fancy that your absurd struttings are comparable in any way with the histrionism of Aubrey Cavendish, the greatest actor that the English speaking stage has ever seen! And you stand there and tell me——

DEAN: *(Cue—"You miserable upstart"—)* Role for role, my dear Fanny, I'm a much better actor than Aubrey Cavendish ever dreamed of being. You must remember that his was the day of provinces, and while I have no doubt that he was a great favorite in the hamlets, it is quite another thing to win critical acclaim in London and New York. And you may recall that on three successive nights I played Othello, Iago and Petruchio. And that never under the historic roof of Wallack's Theatre have there been such three ovations, and a year later, at the Old Vic, I——

JULIE: *(Cue——"Ever dreamed of being——")* *(Crossing to them)* For heaven's sake, you two! Telling how good you are I'm pretty good myself, but you don't hear me talking about it!

KITTY: Well if you want my opinion——

JULIE: Well, we don't want your opinion! This is purely a family matter, and it seems to me that you'll save yourself a good deal of trouble if you'll just keep out of it. *(To* DEAN*)* Oh, who cares which of you was the best actor! And, while we're about it, Herbert Dean, will you tell that wife of yours to stop talking.

This is no concern of hers. Why doesn't she keep out of it? And why shouldn't Gwen be a greater actress than any of us! At least she's got intelligence on her side, and that's more than I can say for any of the rest of you. *(To* KITTY*)* Oh, all right! You're Bernhardt! You're Modjeska! You're Duse!

KITTY: *(Cue ——"Don't want your opinion——")* No, I suppose not. Just because I am not one of your precious Cavendishes, I have no right to speak. But I want to tell you that Kitty LeMoyne can hold her head up with the best of them when it comes to acting. I may not have reached my present position by stepping on the heads of other people—I've won out by talent and hard work. It isn't always the people who have their names in electric lights that are the best actors. I may not be a tradition in the theatre, but just the same—

(NOTE: When DEAN *says "in London and New York"* DELLA *enters from under stairs with* TONY's *tray.)*

TONY: *(On seeing the tray)* Lunch!

CURTAIN.

TONY: *(Dashes down stairs)* Right over there, Della——*(As the curtain descends)*

(Tableaux)

*(The curtain goes—the argument is still raging——*TONY *is over right with his tray of food—*GWEN *still seated on the sofa. The telephone bell is ringing and* DELLA *answers the phone for the second.*

CURTAIN

ACT II

SCENE: The scene is the same as in Act I.

The time is about six o' clock on the following afternoon, Saturday The table at the end of the sofa left is moved up by the piano. The armchair at the foot of stair is struck. A small bench now stands at the left of the sofa. A table above the door left contains considerable mail matter, a small vase to break stands on the table. There are fresh flowers in bowls and vases. Two of the lamps are lighted. The room is not yet fully lighted for the evening, however. The double doors leading into the library, left, are closed. The lamp on the commode is lighted.

AT RISE: At the rise of the curtain there is heard the clash of fencing foils, the thud of feet, and male voices calling an occasional fencing term, sometimes in earnest, sometimes mockingly. "Have at thee, varlet!" in TONY'S *voice.*

The library doors open. FANNY *enters. As she opens the doors she calls. She walks with her cane.*

(READY Lights Up.)

FANNY: Jo! *(She glances toward the balcony, from which comes the sounds of combat.)* Jo! *(Goes toward center, turns up lamp on piano. Shivers a little, draws about her a little shawl that hangs at her shoulders.* DELLA *enters right.)* Della, the fire's nearly out in the library.

DELLA: *(Over her shoulder)* Jo! Bring some wood—*(Turns on lamp on secretary. A muffled answer from* JO, *off)*

FANNY: I must have dozed off. *(Another little shiver)* What time is it, anyway?

DELLA: *(Tidying the rooms, picking up the papers, plumping cushions)* It's near six, I guess. Miss Julie's late. Said she was coming right home after the matinee. Course Saturday lots of young girls in the house, crowding back stage, taking her time up.

FANNY: More likely it's that passport of Tony's that's keeping her. Europe! Got to sail for Europe! Huh!

DELLA: One of those reporters tried to get up in the service elevator a little while ago, but they got him. *(Puts golf stick under arm)*

FANNY: That crowd still standing around down there? In the wet snow? *(Crosses to window)*

DELLA: There certainly is a mob of 'em. Jo says there's a bigger crowd than the time Mr. Tony got his first divorce.

(Clash! Clash! From the balcony the sounds of combat up there swell into an uproar as the battle grows hot. "Aha!" from TONY. Shouted speech or two, unintelligible but loud, from the panting combatants)

DELLA: I wish Mr. Tony'd stop that fencing. Poor Miss Gwen feeling the way she does.

FANNY: Tony! Hush that racket! . . . He's carved his way through every room in the house this afternoon. I had to lock the door of my bathroom.

(JO enters from right. He carries an armful of fireplace wood)

JO: Gee! Ought to see the crowd down there now! And they just rolled up one of those trucks with a lot of lights on it. *(Crossing left)*

DELLA: Good grief! What for?

JO: Going to take movies, I guess. Catch everybody, going in and out.

FANNY: They'll take no movies of me.

JO: And there's a fellow down there selling hot dogs and doing quite a business . . .You want your tea, Mrs. Cavendish? *(Exits into library)*

FANNY: Too near dinner time.

(The clash of foils comes up again. MCDERMOTT and TONY, fencing, enter center of balcony, the former backing away from TONY'S attack.)

DELLA: *(Going up stairs)* I brought a cup of tea up to Miss Gwen but she wouldn't take it again.

FANNY: Still in her room, is she?

DELLA: Hardly eaten a mouthful in twenty-four hours.

(The combat leads across the balcony and down the stairs, TONY maintaining the advantage, and keeping up at the sametime a running comment, couched in a mixture of medieval and movie subtitle style. JO enters, watches the sword play.)

TONY: Ha! He gives ground! Black Jennifer knows now the dark fate that soon is to o'ertake him. *(DELLA goes up stairs and breaks through the two swordsmen. She exits in JULIE'S room.)* Came the dawn, and yet they battled grimly upon the ancient parapet.

(JO enters and watches the sword play.)

McDERMOTT: Je's! Go easy, there!

TONY: *(On stairs)* Ha! He begs for quarter! Too late! Expect no mercy from Anthony the Elegant.

FANNY: "Ah the immortal passedo! the punto reverso! the hai!"

TONY: Ha, ha, varlet! Thou didst not know, what time thou didst hash a flagon of Burgundy from this hand, thou hadst run smack up against the niftiest little swordsman in all of Gascony.

McDERMOTT: Hah!

TONY: And now, thou cur, prepare to meet thy end!

Prince, call upon the Lord!

I skirmish . . . feint a bit.

I lunge . . . I keep my word.

At the last line, I hit.

(He disarms McDERMOTT.)

JO: Hot dog!

TONY: Come, a kiss, my pretty wench! *(FANNY falls into TONY's mood. Takes a few mincing steps to the victor's arms.)* For have I not won thee fairly! *(Turns his sword.)* Here, you are, Mac. I'll be up in a couple of minutes.

JO: I told you he was good. *(Exits into library.)*

McDERMOTT: *(Starts up stairs)* Yah! Gee!

(McDERMOTT exit on balcony.)

FANNY: You should have seen your father hold off eight of them——What a swordsman——what an actor——Aubrey and Fanny Cavendish in "A Gentleman of France." *(She works her way toward the stairs, her cane in one hand. She accompanies her next few lines with graphic illustration, in which the cane becomes the weapon.)* He'd send one head first right down the stairway, throw another one over the banister, quick as a wink he'd whirl and get one creeping up behind him—thrust — pierce — parry — exit — that scene alone took a full bottle of liniment every week. *(Sits on stairs)*

TONY: *(Pats the withered cheek)* Those were the days, Fanny. *(Sits beside her)*

FANNY: *(Sighs)* Those were the days.

(As FANNY, nodding her head in reminiscent confirmation, turns away, TONY rolls down the sleeve of his shirt. A realization of the hour disturbs him.)

TONY: Say, where the devil is Julie? What time is it, anyhow? It's late!

FANNY: Maybe the weather's delaying her. She rings down quarter to five.

TONY: Well, my God, is she getting my passport or isn't she? I've got to get out of here! I can't sail without a passport! She ought to know that!

FANNY: Now, now! Wolfe is helping her. You'll get it all right.

TONY: But when? The boat sails at midnight! I've got to get aboard early if I'm going to dodge that mob down there! *(A vague gesture toward the downstairs region)* I ought to crack a couple of them in the jaw—that's what I ought to do!

FANNY: You've done enough jaw cracking. How are you ever going to get past them anyhow, even if Julie does get you a passport?

TONY: Oh, the hell with them! *(Rises, goes right)* I've got to get on that boat to-night! God! If Julie hasn't got that passport!

FANNY: *(With something of* TONY'S *fire)* Suppose she hasn't? Who says you've got to get on the boat? What for?

TONY: A million reasons! I feel like it! I want to get so far from Hollywood and sunshine—I never want to hear camera again! Or stage, either, for that matter! You can have it! I'm through! *(Comes center)*

FANNY: Through! You've been saying that ever since "Fauntleroy."

TONY: I mean it this time! That's why I'm going abroad! *(Sits on bench left of center)* Give me two years in Munich with my violin under Ascher, and I'll show you what the stage means to me! I can be a great musician! Or I may go away into India with Krishnamurti and study Hindu philosophy! It's the only real thing in the world! You wear just one garment—a long white robe—and you eat just one food! Rice!

FANNY: That'll be restful!

TONY: *(Rises, goes left)* The stage! I'd rather spend ten minutes in the Cathedral at Chartres——I don't give a damn if I nev—— *(In the course of making a sweeping gesture he encounters the huge pile of letters on the table.)* What the hell is all this stuff? They've been here all day! What are they?

FANNY: *(Shouting at him)* They're for you! We've told you a dozen times! It's your mail we've been saving!

TONY: Well, why didn't you say so?
(He looks at it a moment— then he dumps them all into the wastebasket, goes right)

FANNY: *(Advancing on him)* Don't think you're fooling me about why you're going to Europe. Cathedrals, and violins, and rice! It's this Dago woman you're running away from. Else why was she on the train with you? *(She is center)*

TONY: Oh, I'm not afraid of her. I gave her the slip at Chicago.

FANNY: Just the same, that's why you're going to Europe! Don't lie to me, Tony Cavendish!

TONY: (*Reluctantly giving ground*) Well, suppose I am! (*Flares up again*) Only I'm not afraid of her!

FANNY: Then what is it?

TONY: (*Paces a bit first*) It's that God damned process server she's got after me!

FANNY: That God damned process server?

TONY: (*It is being torn out of him*) The breach of promise suit.

FANNY: Breach of promise?

TONY: (*Scornfully*) Two hundred thousand dollars! She wants two hun—(*On fire again*) That's why I've got to stay cooped up here! You don't think I'm afraid of reporters, do you? But if they ever clap that paper on me I can't sail!

FANNY: Why wasn't I told of this? I suppose I was too young to know?

TONY: Fanny, darling——

FANNY: Keep away from me! Two hundred thousand for breach of promise. Assault and battery on this director probably another hundred thousand. And breaking your contract with the picture company——I guess half a million will cover it. (*Goes left.*)

TONY: It's worth it, I tell you! God, that sunshine! (*Throws himself on sofa*)

FANNY: (*Back of sofa, fiercely*) What did you ever promise this movie actress that's worth two hundred thousand dollars?

TONY: Oh, she claims to have some letters——I didn't want her in the first place! She was Deming's girl! That's why he got sore! (*Lies on sofa*)

FANNY: Who is she, anyhow? Where'd she come from?

TONY: Zeta Zaydak! She's a Pole.

FANNY: Look out for Poles!

(PHONE)

(The phone bell rings. TONY *takes the receiver off the hook and listens for a second. Then he quietly puts the receiver down on the table; edges away.)*

FANNY: A woman's voice?

TONY: No, but I'm not taking chances.

(As he hangs up, Ring)

(He goes back to the phone, a little furtiveness in his manner; takes up the receiver and listens again. Apparently he is satisfied that the caller is gone; he hangs up the receiver. Instantly the bell starts to ring again; TONY *quickly takes the receiver off again. Puts it once more on the piano; slides away quickly from the instrument. The sound of the outer door opening)*

(DOOR Slam, JULIE)

TONY: Who's that? *(The slam of the door.)*

*(*JULIE *enters. She has come in from the matinee. She is wearing smart winter street clothes—a luxurious fur coat and a costume to match. There is a bristling sort of vigor in the way she stations herself in the doorway.)*

JULIE: *(Talks as she enters)* Damn your dear public, Tony!

TONY: Did you get it?

JULIE: The entire population of New York is standing on the doorstep, howling for a glimpse of America's foremost screen lover. In the meantime they take what fortune sends, and it just happened to be me.

FANNY: Your coat's ripped.

TONY: Julie! The passport! Have you got my passport?

JULIE: *(Calls)* What a dandy day this has been! *(Sits on sofa.* DELLA *appears on balcony. Exits into* JULIE'S *room)* . . . I had to get out at the corner—you don't dare drive up. And my dear Mrs. Cavendish, have you ever played to an audience made up entirely of sea lions! *(She is energetically tearing off hat, coat, kicks off her shoes.* DELLA, *meantime, comes down with mules. During* JULIE'S *speech she kneels and assists her with slippers, etc.)* They came in wet to the knees and never did dry off. They spent the first act taking galoshes off and the last act putting them on. You know— *(Stoops to pull imaginary zippers)* . . . I looked out once during the last act and couldn't see a face. And cough! I think they had a cheer leader. Lincoln couldn't have held them with the Gettysburg address. How's Gwen, mother? Is she better?

TONY: Now, look here, Julie!

JULIE: Shut up, Tony! . . . Has she eaten anything? What's she doing?

FANNY: No. Wouldn't take her tea.

JULIE: I'll go up.

DELLA: Dinner at the usual time, Miss Julie?

JULIE: No, hold it awhile, Della.

DELLA: *(Edging toward door right, as she talks, delivering the day's messages in a sort of monotone)* Mr. Cartwright phoned, and Mrs. Blair's dinner's postponed till a week from Sunday, and—

JULIE: Not now, Della, please.

DELLA: And the La Boheme Shop says your dress is all ready *(DELLA exits, right.)*

TONY: Dress be damned! My boat sails at midnight. What have you done about my passport!

JULIE: Tony, my love, Wolfe is bringing it.

TONY: He is? Why didn't you say so? Thank God! *(Sits chair right)*

JULIE: He's been pulling all sorts of wires. He's been in and out of my dressing room all afternoon. Everybody's been in and out of my dressing room all afternoon. Compared to my dressing room, Grand Central Terminal was a rustic retreat. And all on account of you, my baby. Reporters, and process servers, and sob sisters . . . I'm going up to Gwen.

FANNY: *(Detains her)* Gwen's all right. You lie down and take it easy —with another show to play.

TONY: Listen, Julie, how soon'll he get here?

JULIE: *(Lies on sofa)* Oh, I don't know. Right away. And he's bringing the money for you too. They kept your reservation, and I've paid for it. You neglected to tell me that you were roughing it across in the royal suite.

TONY: I can't travel like a stowaway.

JULIE: Hire a battleship for all I care! But remember I'm a working girl. What do you do with all your money, anyway? You go out to Hollywood with a billion dollar contract and you buy a pink plaster palace for one hundred and fifty thousand, an Isotta Fraschini for twenty thousand and an Hispano Suiza for twenty-five, a camp in the Sierras for another fifty—good God, you were sunk a quarter of a million before they ever turned a crank on you! . . . And as soon as they start to take a picture you knock out the director and quit.

TONY: It'll all blow over in a month. That's why I want to get away.

JULIE: But why does it have to be Europe! What are you going to do when you get there!

FANNY: He's going to eat rice and play the violin.

TONY: I'm going to bathe in the pure beauty of Athens! I want to lose myself in the Black Forests of Bavaria! *(Cross to window.)*

FANNY: Mm! Switched your bookings.

TONY: I don't know where I'm going. Any place where it rains all the time.

(DOOR Bell)

JULIE: All right. Go to Pago-Pago. But attend to your own passport. I got my art to look after. *(Door bell rings.* TONY *dashes for stairs, turns.)*

JULIE: Keep calm. They can't get up here.

TONY: Think we'd better open it?

JULIE: You'll have to go out to catch the boat, won't you? They can't back the Aquitania up to the door.

TONY: I'll get out, all right, when the time comes. *(*JO *enters right.*

Starts toward outer door) Wait, Jo! . . . *(To* JULIE*)* Maybe it's Wolfe, huh?

JULIE: Shoot from the hip, Jo.

JO: *(Genially)* Reminds me of the time the Grand Jury was after you. Remember that sheriff? *(In the alcove* JULIE *sits up.)* When you took his gun away!

DEAN: What! What!

TONY: Keep a foot against the door!

JO: Who's out there?

DEAN: *(A tufted voice off)* This is Herbert Dean!

JO: *(Opening door)* Oh, come right in, Mr. Dean.

*(*HERBERT DEAN *enters with* JO *following him on. His entrance is marked by relieved sighs from* JULIE, FANNY *and* TONY.*)*

DEAN: They ought to be arrested, those fellows. *(Flicking from his garments the contaminating touch of those who had waylaid him on the sidewalk. This finished he starts to remove his coat.* JO *takes it with hat and stick.)* Pushing me all around.

TONY: You didn't tell them I was here?

DEAN: Of course not. But I hope, Anthony, that your next director will prove more congenial to you.

TONY: There isn't going to be any next director, old socks . . . Come on, Jo . . . I've got to pack and get out of here. *(Leaps up the stairs, followed by* JO*)* Tell you what I want you to do. Want you to sneak out and get me three taxis exactly alike—and have them lined up in front of the door . . . *(Exits center door balcony, with* JO*)*

DEAN: What the devil's he up to!

JULIE: Mother'll tell you. I'm going up to see Gwen.

DEAN: Wait—wait!

FANNY: I'm going in by the fire, Bertie, if you want to talk to me. *(Goes left)*

DEAN: No—Julie—I want to talk to you. I've had a devil of a day.

In the first place, where's Oscar? I gave him my play to read last night and I haven't been able to find him since. (JULIE *rises, goes to stairs.*)

FANNY: Isn't that funny! (FANNY *exits library.*)

JULIE: He's coming here, Bert. Nail him. (JULIE *starts upstairs.*)

DEAN: Fine! Ah— just one thing more! (*Detaining her*) And this is what I really came about. (*Goes to her*)

JULIE: Oh, Bert, not now, please.

DEAN: Now, hold on, Julie. I've got to talk to you. It's vital.

JULIE: Bert, can't it be some other time? I've simply got to see Gwen.

DEAN: No, no. I never needed you worse than I do now. I wouldn't tell this to anyone else, but I know you'll understand. Give me just a minute. Please!

JULIE: Why—what is it? What's the matter?

DEAN: You see, it's this way. These last five or six years I haven't— things haven't exactly—damn it all, it's youth! Youth! They write all the plays for young whipper-snappers! You've got to be built like a—uh—greyhound. Now mind you, I'm just as youthful as anybody. I keep in good condition. Try to. But it's impossible to get a good massage nowadays.

JULIE: Your figure's grand, darling.

DEAN: Not bad. But you see—I can't go around—sit in offices they've got to come to me! I sit and wait for letters, rush to the telephone—think each time—first thing you know it's months and months—What am I to do! (*Sits on sofa*)

JULIE: Oh, you're just a little down. Something may come along any minute. (*Down to* DEAN, *arm on his shoulder*)

DEAN: That's just it! I've got it! This play! It's a Godsend! Just what I need! It'll put me on my feet again. I can easily get in condition for it. Diet! Exercise!

JULIE: Yes, I know. I read it. It struck me then, that if instead of trying—if you'd be willing to play one of those attractive—uh—slightly greyed parts—

DEAN: Oh, I can't get around that. Pink lights—and I don't look over thirty-five. But here is the real difficulty. It's the girl. She's got to be young—beautiful! A vision! I can't have—*(Very confidentially)*—To tell you the truth, Kitty will ruin it. She'll ruin me! She'll kill the first real chance I've had in years.

JULIE: But you know I can't do anything with her.

DEAN: But you can! That's just it. For God's sake, Julie, say you'll do it.

JULIE: Do what!

DEAN: Give her that part in your play—you know—the colonel's wife. She'd be very good in that—

JULIE: But, Bert, I've got a good woman——*(Going to stairs)*

DEAN: *(Follows her, stands left of the stairs)* Yes, yes—I know. But you could let that woman out. The point is, you're big enough, Julie. It wouldn't hurt your play. You're so admired, and popular—nothing can stop you. Now, I've never asked a favor before —little things, maybe—but we've always stood by each other— the family. Let me go and tell Kitty you suggested it.

JULIE: But I had Kitty once before, and——

DEAN: I know. But this will be different. She'll be very good in that part . . . It means I am sure to have a hit. I could pay back everything I owe you — you, and different people ——

JULIE: Oh, that's all right. Don't think of that now.

DEAN: *(Pats her hand, gratefully)* You're a brick, Julie . . . You've been very kind—I hadn't meant to come to you again—but I wonder—I was going to ask if you could spare another five hundred—just a few weeks——

(DOOR BELL, *Three Rings*)

(*Outer door bell rings sharply, three times.*)

JULIE: That's Oscar.

DEAN: Oh! Splendid! Now, what do you say, Julie? Will you do that for me? Will you? (DELLA *enters starts for door.*)

JULIE: *(Weakly)* Bert, I'll try to dig it up. I don't know——Della, that's Mr. Wolfe. Tell him I'll be right down. I've got Gwen up here.

DELLA: *(Pausing on her way to the door)* How about dinner, Miss Julie?

JULIE: Oh, I can't right now, Della.

DELLA: It's getting late.

JULIE: I don't know what to say about Kitty, Bert. (DELLA *exits to outer door.*) You've given me an awful problem. Fortunately I've got so many that one more doesn't matter.

DEAN: Then you will do it, huh? Good!

JULIE: Good! Hell, it's perfect. (*Exits center door balcony*)

WOLFE: *(As DELLA opens the door for him)* Say, what a mob scene you got down there!

DELLA: It certainly is terrible, all right.

WOLFE: *(Entering on this speech)* And what's more, it's bad publicity.

(*Sees* DEAN, *breaks off. From his look in* DEAN'S *direction he is plainly far from delighted.* DELLA *follows. Waits to receive* WOLFE'S *coat*)

DEAN: Ah, Oscar, my boy!

WOLFE: Oh, hello.

DEAN: This is fortunate!

DELLA: Miss Julie'll be right down. Shall I take your coat?

WOLFE: No, thanks. I don't stay.

(FANNY *appears in doorway, left. She is carrying a manuscript of a play.*)

FANNY: Hello, Wolfe! I thought it was your voice. (DELLA *goes out right.*)

WOLFE: *(Up)* Your gifted daughter, Mrs. Cavendish, certainly gave a fine ham performance this afternoon.

FANNY: Did you get his passport?

WOLFE: Well, I want to talk to Julie about it. Where is she?

FANNY: She's up with Gwen.

WOLFE: Yah? How is Gwen? Come to her senses yet?

FANNY: Stubborn as ever. *(Comes down. Sits on sofa)*

WOLFE: She'll come around.

DEAN: Now, Oscar, I've got a dinner engagement. *(Going to* OSCAR. *His watch)* Tell me how the play impressed you. Wonderful, isn't it? Tremendous!

WOLFE: *(Hesitatingly)* M-m-m, yes—but——

DEAN: I knew you d be crazy about it! *(Goes to hallway)* Now, I'll start lining up a cast and come in to see you to-morrow. About what time, say?

WOLFE: I don't know——Oh—uh—any time.

DEAN: *(A dignified scamper up to the alcove, throws his coat over his arm, claps on his hat, takes his stick)* That's fine! Fine! We can start rehearsals in about ten days, eh? *(Picks up hat and coat)*

WOLFE: *(Strolls uneasily up toward alcove)* Now, not so fast, Dean. Pretty heavy show you got there. Take a pile of money to put that on.

DEAN: *(In protest)* Oh, no, no, no, no.

WOLFE: No, no, no——Yes, yes, yes. Fourteen scenes. Grand Central Terminal, Garden of Eden—

DEAN: Just a few drapes. *(Exits hallway)*

OSCAR: Court of King Solomon. Battle of Waterloo

(The door is heard to slam. WOLFE *comes down, puffing at his cheeks in rather stunned perplexity. His eye roves to* FANNY, *a grim figure in her chair. The two are in accord.)*

FANNY: I think Bertie has retired and doesn't know it.

WOLFE: I wish they were all like you, Fanny. *(Comes over to pat her shoulder)* What d'you think? Going to be able to troupe again after the Holidays?

FANNY: Tried to tell you yesterday, but you were so busy with your English playwrights.

WOLFE: Say, if I had to pick one actress out of the whole caboodle of 'em, you know who it'd be. Come on, tell me. Think you can start out again? Sure enough?

FANNY: You can dust off the "Castlemaine" scenery, and I'd just as soon you'd route me to the Coast.

WOLFE: At a girl! *(Crosses to the left)* You're worth a dozen of these New-York-run actresses. No foolishness about you. No private cars and maids in the contract, and telegrams from the company manager you won't go on because the theatre's cold. No, sir! You're the girl that does twenty-eight hundred in Boise City, Idaho, and catches the six-fourteen next morning for Pocatello.

FANNY: I did twenty-nine hundred in Boise City.

WOLFE: Chairs in the aisles, h'm? I tell you, if Bert—*(A gesture toward the departed figure)*—had taken his hits out on the road he wouldn't be in this jam to-day. But by nature Bertie is a Lambs' Club actor, and look what happens! In a couple more years he'll own six toupees, and be playing Baron Stein in an all-star revival of Diplomacy.

FANNY: *(Getting to her feet to take the oath)* May God strike me dead if I ever appear in an all-star revival!

(She sits again. Then JULIE enters on balcony from center door. Starts downstairs)

JULIE: Well, she's promised to dress and come out of that room, anyhow. That's more than she's done all Day.

WOLFE: Say, what kind of a show are you going to give tonight, with all this hullabaloo!

JULIE: Once Tony goes, things will be a little better. It's so restful to think that at midnight he'll be rounding Sandy Hook.

WOLFE: M-m, that's what I came to talk about.

JULIE: *(Alarmed)* What!

WOLFE: It don't go so quick. These fellows——

JULIE: You don't mean you can't get it! Oh!

WOLFE: Well, now, hold on. I don't say I can't yet exactly. There seems to be some sort of monkey business going on. Maybe they got wind of something and don't want him to get away.

JULIE: Oscar, another twenty-four hours with this caged lunatic and you can order straight-jackets for two. He's impossible to live with—and those terrible people on the street!

WOLFE: Now, now, now! Did Oscar ever fail you? We'll all get it right—I hope. Anyhow, here's his money. That's that much. *(Cross right center)*

FANNY: How much?

JULIE: What's the difference, Mother? He has to have it. *(Tosses money on the piano)* Oscar, I owe you a ghastly lot of money, don't I? How much?

WOLFE: The money you're welcome to, Julie. But it oughtn't to be that you got to come to me like this. You make as much money as any woman in the business. What the devil do you do with all your money, anyhow!

JULIE: Why—I don't know. What do you mean—do with it?

FANNY: What does anybody do with it?

WOLFE: Well, just for argument's sake, let me ask you once! Forty-one weeks. You've made sixty thousand since you opened in this play, and that says nothing about all the other ones. In the past twenty years, I bet you, you made a million dollars. Now how much of it have you actually got?

JULIE: Let's see—where's my bag? I've got over three dollars in that, and Della owes me seventy-five cents——*(JO enters on balcony; starts to descend stairs.)* Oh, I don't know, Oscar. It just goes. *(To JO, who is crossing to the door at right)* Jo, tell Della caviar for Miss Gwen's dinner.

JO: Yes, Miss Julie

JULIE: *(To* WOLFE *and* FANNY*)* Perhaps that'll tempt her.

WOLFE: Well. *(Quick little gesture and a squeeze of* FANNY'S *hand.)* I stayed longer than I meant to. *(Starts up to alcove.)* I let you know the minute I see this fellow, huh?

JULIE: *(Following him up a step or two)* Oscar, you're an angel! Would it interest you to know that you are adored by the most beautiful actress on the American stage?

WOLFE: *(Airily)* Nope.

JULIE: My Galahad!

FANNY: Goodbye, Wolfe. *(*WOLFE *goes hallway. The slam of the door.* (DOOR *Slam.)*

JULIE: Gwen . . . Oh, I hope he gets that passport! I don't dare tell Tony there's any doubt of it—let's just hope he gets it—— Gwen! *(A second's vain pause for an answer.)* She promised she'd come down.

FANNY: I thought she'd get tired of moping in her room like Elsie Dinsmore.

JULIE: Gwen, dear! *(Goes to stairs.)*

GWEN: *(Heard upstairs)* Yes, mother.

JULIE: Aren't you coming down, dear? I wish you would.

GWEN: *(Off)* Yes, mother.

FANNY: Who is this What's-his-name of hers, anyway? Doesn't seem to me like anything but an average young man.

JULIE: They're all average young men.

FANNY: Speaking of average, how's Mr. Gilbert Marshall? Have you seen him yet?

JULIE: No. I suppose when he telephoned yesterday, and they told him I was out, he just thought I didn't want to see him. Perhaps it's just as well. It's a long time ago, and he's probably bald, and fat, and talks about conferences.

*(*GWEN *appears on the balcony. She is in one of those chiffon neg-*

ligees; there is something of the Ophelia about her appearance. She has been cooped up with her resolution for twenty four hours, and it's beginning to wear her down.)

GWEN: *(Advancing to the rail)* Nobody else there, is there?

(GWEN comes slowly, pensively, down the stairs.)

JULIE: Only your aged relatives.

FANNY: Speak for yourself.

(GWEN has come down.)

JULIE: *(FANNY is seated on sofa right JULIE is to sit on bench left of sofa. GWEN is between them on sofa)* Do you want to sit here, dear? Or shall we go in by the fire?

GWEN: *(Sits)* Oh, this is all right. *(Glances up with a rather wan smile)* I don't mean to act like a prima donna. I just feel like hell, that's all.

JULIE: *(Standing over her)* I know you do, dear. I hate to see you unhappy like this. *(Leans over, kisses the top of her head lightly)* But you have so little sense.

GWEN: *(Her lip quivering. Very low)* He didn't even telephone. He might at least have telephoned.

FANNY: How do you know he didn't? Tony had the receiver off most of the day.

JULIE: *(Puts receiver back on hook)* Yes.

GWEN: *(Eagerly)* Do you think so! He might have, mightn't he? Oh! *(A little whimper of dismay. She even weeps, weakly.)*

JULIE: *(Pats her shoulder tenderly)* Now, Gwen.

GWEN: Oh, Mother, I love him so!

JULIE: There's nothing to cry about. *(A hand on her shoulder, patting her into calm)* There! *(A moment's pause while GWEN grows quieter)*

FANNY: You can love him and marry him, too, can't you?

JULIE: Of course you can marry him, Gwen, and live happy ever after.

FANNY: Only why you think you have to quit the stage to do it is more than I can figure out.

JULIE: It's hard for us to realize that you wouldn't want to keep on, Gwen.

FANNY: Your mother and I both got married. But we didn't drop more important things to do it.

GWEN: There isn't anything more important.

FANNY: Fiddlesticks! Marriage isn't a career. It's an incident! Aubrey Cavendish and I were married in the Church of St. Mary Redcliffe, in Bristol, England, just before the matinee. The wedding super was served on the stage of the Theatre Royale between the matinee and the night performance — we played "She Stoops to Conquer" in the afternoon, and "A Scrap of Paper" was the night bill. They sent the supper in from the George and Lion next door, and very nice it was, too, but I remember they'd gone and put nutmeg in the gooseberry tarts, and Aubrey never could abide nutmeg. It must have been that that upset him, for he gave the only bad performance that night that I ever saw him give.

GWEN: I know, Grandma. But that's got nothing to do with me. You married an actor, and—(*Turning to her mother, swiftly*)—so did you. You lived the same sort of lives.

JULIE: Oh, I knew some rather nice men who weren't actors—didn't I, Fanny? (*A gesture from* FANNY *of utter dismissal of this subject as being too vast and agonizing to go into*) There were lots of times when I thought that being a wife and mother was all that mattered in the world. And then each time I'd learn all over again that that wasn't enough for me.

FANNY: I should say not.

JULIE: Earthquakes, and cyclones, and fire and flood, and somehow you still give the show. I know it says in the contract that you stop for "acts of God," but I can't remember that I ever did. (*Rise*)

FANNY: Nor I. Nor your grandfather. Nobody ever knew what a sick man Aubrey Cavendish was those last months. But he played a full season of thirty-five weeks. Dropped dead on the stage of Macauley's in Louisville two minutes after the curtain fell on Saturday night, the week we closed. Not only that, but he waited to take four calls.

GWEN: I know, I know. (*Rises—goes right*) But—I'm not like that, that's all. (*Sits near window*)

JULIE: (*Rises, crosses to* GWEN) You think you're not, but you are! Marry him if you love him, Gwen, but don't give up everything to do it! The day might come when you'd hate him for it.

GWEN: Hate Perry! (*A little bitter, scornful laugh.*) You just don't know what you're talking about.

JULIE: Gwen, do you think it's going to be any fun for me to have them see you step out—acting with me in my play, and, for all I know, walking away with it! You'll be so fresh, and such a surprise! And it'll be your night. I'll be very proud and happy, of course. (*A very little pause, and then, almost as though to convince herself*) . . . of course. They'll say, "That's her daughter." But ten years from now it'll be, "That's her mother."

GWEN: I'll never be half the actress you are.

JULIE: Gwen, if I could only make you realize that the thrill you get out of doing your work is bigger than any other single thing in the world! (*A little gesture of protest from* GWEN) Oh, I know! There's love. But you can be the most fortunate person in the world, Gwen. You can have both. But for God's sake don't make the mistake of giving up one for the other.

FANNY: No, child!

GWEN: Work! Acting isn't anything. What's acting compared to—

FANNY: It's everything. It's work and play and meat and drink. They'll tell you it isn't——your fancy friends——but it's a lie! And they know it's a lie! They'd give their ears to be in your place. Don't make any mistake about that.

JULIE: There'll be plenty of things that you'll have to give up — gay things and amusing things—I've missed dinners (DELLA *appears in doorway right, evidently meaning to get* JULIE'S *attention*)—and parties and rides and walks and —

FANNY: What is it, Della?

DELLA: How about dinner?

FANNY: Don't bother us! (DELLA *exits, slowly and unobtrusively, puzzled. Stealing* JULIE'S *thunder*) Yes, you've got to leave, and go down to a stuffy dressing room and smear paint on your face and go out on the stage and speak a lot of fool lines, and you love it! You love it! You couldn't live without it! Do you suppose I could have stood these two years, hobbling around with this thing—(*Brandishing her cane*)—if I hadn't known I was going back to it!

JULIE: Long as I've been on the stage there isn't a night when I stand in the wings waiting for my cue that I don't get that sick feeling at the pit of my stomach. And my hands are cold and my cheeks are hot, and you'd think I'd never been on the stage before.

FANNY: Yes, yes! That's it! Every night when I'm sitting here alone I'm really down there at the theatre. Seven-thirty, and they're going in the stage door. Good evening to the doorman. Taking, down their keys and looking in the mail rack. Eight o'clock! The stage hands are setting up. (*Raps with her cane.*) Half hour, Miss Cavendish! Grease paint, rouge, mascara. Fifteen minutes, Miss Cavendish! My costume . . . More rouge . . . Where's the rabbit's foot! . . . Overture! . . . Good evening, everybody . . . How's the house tonight? . . . The curtain's up! . . . Props! . . . Cue . . . Enter. (*Rise*) That's all that's kept me alive these two years. If you weren't down there for me, I wouldn't want to live. . . I couldn't live. You . . . down there . . . for me . . . going on . . .going on . . .going on . . .

(*The excitement and the strain are too much for her. Suddenly she goes limp, topples, crumples.* JULIE *and* GWEN, *standing near her, catch her as she is about to fall, and place her in the chair from which she has risen. She is briefly unconscious.*)

JULIE: Mother! Mother, what's the matter!

GWEN: Grandma! Grandma!

JULIE: Jo! Tony! Della! Quick!

GWEN: *(At* FANNY'S *side, frantic and remorseful)* It's all right, grandma. I'll do it. I will. I will! Grandma! I'll do it.

*(*JO *and* DELLA *enter.* JO *picks up* FANNY *places her on sofa.)*

JULIE: Some water—whisky—quick!

*(*MCDERMOTT *appears on balcony, followed by* TONY, *in answer to* JULIE'S *calls.* JO *dashes off after a flask.* MCDERMOTT *comes down to assist* JO.)*

TONY: What's the matter? What is it?

JULIE: She fainted! We were talking!

TONY: Do something! For God's sake, do some-thing! What are you all standing around for! Where is everybody? *(On stairs)*

GWEN: It's all my fault! Grandma! Grandma!

*(*JO *enters swiftly, with flask. Ad libs. Exclamations, suggestions, broken speeches from group. "She's coming around." "She's better." "There, mother." "It's me, mother. It's Julie." "Telephone the doctor." "You're all. right." "You're all right, mother." "You're all right now." "There, take that, mother. Just a sip. You'll be fine in a minute. There. She's taking it. Moisten her forehead with it," etc.)*

TONY: Mother! Mother! It's me . . . Tony. *(The confused murmur of talk slowly dies.)*

GWEN: I'm going to do it, Grandma. I didn't mean it. I will! Of course I will!

JULIE: Did you hear? It's all right! Everything's going to be all right

TONY: She's better now! Aren't you, mother?

FANNY: *(Struggles rather feebly to rise; to assert her independence. Her voice is little more than a whisper.)* I'm all right. There's nothing the matter. But I think I'll go up and lie down. *(They gather round to assist her.)*

JULIE: Jo, get a hot water bag. Della, run ahead and turn the bed down.

TONY: Let me alone. I've got her.

(JO *and* DELLA *run up the stairs ahead of the others.* DELLA *exits into* FANNY'S *room, the first door on the balcony.* JO *exits into* JULIE'S *room.*)

McDERMOTT: That's the stuff. Just lean on me, You're doing swell.

TONY: Here we go! Now!

JULIE: Careful, Tony. Slow. (*They move cautiously up the stairway.*) She oughtn't to be walking up stairs.

TONY: She won't let me carry her.

FANNY: (*They are half-way up the stairs*) Wait a minute . . . Wait . .

JULIE: What is it! Mother, do you feel faint again?

FANNY: I just want to rest a minute . . . Just a minute . . . (*A long sigh.* McDERMOTT *is on her left.* TONY, *as she pauses and turns, a step below her, on her right.* JULIE *is a step behind her.* GWEN, *her back to the audience, is about at the foot of the stairs.*) No use . . . No use fooling myself. . . I'm through . . . I'll never go back again. It's finished.

McDERMOTT: Look out there! (TONY *catches her up in his arms and starts up with* FANNY.) You better get a doctor.

(JO *comes hurrying out of the center door carrying a hot water bag, goes swiftly into* FANNY'S *room left.*)

JULIE: How white she is. (*They stream into the bedroom.* JULIE *is heard giving orders to* DELLA. GWEN, *during the latter part of this scene, has taken a few slow steps up the stairs, so that she is by now about half-way up. The movement of the door's closing finds her quite still on the stairs. She brings her hands together in a little gesture of desperation. You hear the impact of her closed fist against her palm. Stumbles on up, heavily. Exits, center. Off*) Spirits of ammonia. Bring the whole thing. (JO *exits hurriedly into* JULIE'S *room.*)

(NOTE: *The following conversation is heard in* FANNY'S *room, and continues until* JULIE *enters and talks to* GIL *left.*)

JULIE: Look out! That's hot! Put it at her feet.

FANNY: I hate hot water bags——

TONY: Here. This'll pick you up.

JULIE: Give it to me. Let me do it. Just a sip, darling.

MCDERMOTT: Why'n't you open a window?

JULIE: No. Her hands feel so cold.

FANNY: Stop this clatter or I'll get right up.

JULIE: Just you dare, Fanny Cavendish!

TONY: That stuff's no good. Swig of whisky's the thing.

FANNY: I won't drink it.

GWEN: Oh, what a bad girl you are!

JULIE: Darling, are you all right now.

(As DELLA *comes down stairs. Door bell.*)

(DELLA *follows* JO *into* FANNY'S *room, goes downstairs.* JO *enters from* JULIE'S *room, carrying a heavy medicine case.*)

DELLA: (*Calls up to* JO) I'll go. (JO *goes on into* FANNY'S *room.* DELLA *goes to outer door.*)

GILBERT MARSHALL: (*Off*) Miss Cavendish in? Miss Julie Cavendish?

DELLA: Yes, sir.

GILBERT: Will you tell her—Mr. Gilbert Marshall?

(DELLA *reappears from alcove a little ahead of* GILBERT.)

DELLA: Yes, sir, if you'll just . . . I'll ask her if she can see you. (*Exits under stairs*)

(GILBERT MARSHALL *enters at* DELLA'S *exit. He is forty-seven, quiet, dominant, successful. He gives the effect of power and control. Hair slightly graying. Very well dressed. He is in topcoat now as he stands surveying the charming empty room. His hat and stick in his hand. As* JO *opens the door to* FANNY'S *room, there comes from it a chorus of high-pitched voices.* MARSHALL *has come down so that he is now somewhat right of center. At the sound of what evidently is a scene upstairs he turns and surveys the balcony. There is something of recognition in his glance and manner as he hears this. After a moment* MCDERMOTT *rushes hurriedly out of center door, balcony. He goes to* TONY'S *room.* JO *comes out. He comes down the stairs.* MCDERMOTT *enters carrying bottle of alcohol. He goes to* FANNY'S *room.* JO *glances inquiringly at* GILBERT MARSHAL.)

GILBERT: Is there something the matter? Is Miss Cavendish?

JO: It's Mrs. Cavendish, sir.

GILBERT: Oh, I'm sorry. (DELLA *enters from servants' quarters carrying a glass. She exits upstairs in* FANNY'S *room. The sound of voices is heard again.*) Maybe I'd better not wait.

JO: Oh, she's all right now. Just a kind of fainting spell.

GILBERT: I won't intrude now. Just say I'll telephone.

JO: I'm sure Miss Julie'll be right down.

GILBERT: (*Doubtfully*) Well—

JO: Just be seated, sir. (JO *exits under stairs.*)

(GIL *stands a moment, uncertainly. The door of* FANNY'S *room opens from the inside. No one is to be seen in the doorway, but* FANNY'S *voice is heard, high-pitched and querulous.*)

FANNY: (*From off*) Fiddlesticks . . . go to bed in the middle of the day!

(GIL *picks up gloves from table where he has laid them, puts on hat, starts toward outer door.* JULIE *comes out of* FANNY'S *room quickly. A small towel is pinned across the front of her gown. Her hair is somewhat dishevelled. One sleeve is rolled up. She sees* GIL, *about to depart.*)

JULIE: (*Down the stairs swiftly*) Gil! Gil! Don't go!

GILBERT: Julie! (*Comes quickly to foot of stairs*) Can I help? What's wrong?

JULIE: It's nothing. I'm—it's just—(*Begins to cry—helplessly. Clings to him, a refuge*)

GILBERT: I'm so sorry. Is she very ill? I shouldn't have come, should I?

JULIE: I'm so ashamed. I don't know why I——She's all right now. She's perfectly all right. It's been such a hellish day. Everything in the world that could happen——Gil, you're still sane, aren't you?—and solid, and reliable, and sure!

GILBERT: I hope so.

JULIE: How nice! . . . *(Suddenly aware of her appearance. Glances down at towel)* And I was going to be so ravishing on our first meeting. I had it all planned. *(Unpins towel. Throws it aside)* Let me make another entrance, will you? I'll say, "It's really you, Gil! After all these years!" And you'll say ——

GILBERT: *(One stride, takes her hand)* I'll say——

(DELLA enters on balcony from FANNY'S room. The sound of the door interrupts GILBERT MARSHAL. Both glance up quickly.)

JULIE: Do you want me, Della?

DELLA: *(Comes swiftly down the stairs)* No, she's fine, Miss Julie. Mr. Tony's telling her stories about Hollywood to quiet her. *(Exits under stairs)*

GILBERT: Julie, I know I'm in the way I——*(Goes right)*

JULIE: Ch, please stay, Gil. This is the first peaceful moment I've had to-day.

GILBERT: No wonder, with that mob downstairs.

(DELLA enters.)

JULIE: You've seen the papers, of course.

DELLA: Pardon me, Miss Julie, but it's twenty minutes after seven. I thought perhaps——*(An apprehensive glance at GILBERT. Dinner is on DELLA'S mind.)*

JULIE: It's all right, Della. Never mind. I'll let you know.

DELLA: Yes, ma'am. *(Goes under stairs. A moment's silence as the two are alone. They look at each other. Then they speak together.)*

GILBERT and JULIE: You haven't changed a bit. *(A light laugh as they realize the absurdity of this)*

GILBERT: Do you know, Julie, I haven't gone to see you once in all these years?

JULIE: I think I'd have felt it if you'd been out front. And you never were? *(Sits on sofa)*

GILBERT: No. I've only been in New York a few times since then. South America's a long way off. But I kept track of you. I took the New York Times and——the Theatre Magazine, is it?

JULIE: You haven't been exactly hidden from the public gaze, Gil. What was it you found down there? Radium—lying around in chunks?

GILBERT: Oh, no, not radium. Platinum. *(Sits on sofa.)*

JULIE: Anyhow, you've got millions and millions.

GILBERT: I've done—pretty well. But say! You're certainly top of the heap in your line.

JULIE: Oh, the Zenith!

GILBERT: And you have a daughter, haven't you? Seventeen.

JULIE: That was last year's paper. Gwen's eighteen.

GILBERT: I want so much to see her.

(PHONE)

JULIE: We're going to be in a play together for the first time. Think of it!

GILBERT: That ought to be exciting.

(PHONE)

JULIE: It's been exciting enough. Gwen got a sudden horrible idea that——*(The telephone rings. JULIE glances quickly toward door right, as though expecting DELLA to answer. Goes to telephone. GILBERT rises, goes right.)* Hello! *(GILBERT removes overcoat—places it right)* Yes . . . Oh, Oscar! . . . Oh, dear! . . . Yes, I'm sure you did, but., . . .Oh, Oscar! *(TONY enters balcony from FANNY'S room, carefully closing door behind him, his attention all on the tele-*

phone below.) Well, of course, if you can't, there's no use . . . There's nothing to be . . . Yes, I know it is. I'm leaving right away . . . Don't worry. I'll give a swell performance. *(Hangs up)*

TONY: Was that Wolfe? *(Comes down stairs)*

JULIE: Oh, Tony! . . . How's mother? All right?

TONY: Asleep . . . Who was that on the phone? Wolfe, wasn't it?

JULIE: Now, Tony, I don't want you to hit the ceiling——

TONY: *(With a snarl)* He hasn't got it!

JULIE: It's not so vital. You haven't done anything so terrible——

TONY: You don't know what you're talking about! You'll find out if it's vital! Why, my God! If this woman——

JULIE: Oh, don't be childish, Tony! What can she do to you? You talk like somebody in a melodrama! Now calm down and shut up. Gil, this is my brother Tony.

TONY: What can she do to me? I'll tell you what she can do to me! She can——

JULIE: Tony, will you be quiet? This is Mr. Gilbert Marshall. Gil, my brother Tony.

TONY: *(Through his teeth)* Charmed! . . . *(Turns again to* JULIE*)* What the hell kind of a jam do you think I'm in, anyway? *(During the following speech he is down the stairs, up and down the room furiously, up the stairs again, and into center door balcony.)* What do you think I blew all the way from California for! The ride! I've got to get out of here, I tell you! Zaydak's in town by this time. Do you know what what that means! You don't know that Polecat! Why I've seen her pick up——(Snatches a fragile glass ashtray off the table, which he uses to accent his gestures as he goes on, forgetting meanwhile that he has it.)* She's a killer! She'll do anything! She'd just as soon shoot as look at you. She's a Pole. She's cuckoo about me, and she knows I'm through with her. Now if you don't want to do anything to help me, why, all right. *(Turns, starts upstairs)* You're a Hell of a sister—I'm only your brother and why should you bother about me! But I'm telling you now, if they get me I'll be all over the front page, and so will you, and so will Gwen, and the whole damned family! Now if that's what you want, believe me, you're going to get it! *(On the balcony, discovers ornament still in his hand. A smothered exclamation of disgust at finding it. Smashes it to the floor)* . . . Pleased to have met you, Mr. Gilson. *(Exits balcony—left)*

(A moment's pregnant pause. GILBERT *stands looking up after the departed whirlwind. His gaze comes back to* JULIE.)

GILBERT: Is he always like that?

JULIE: Oh, no. That's the brighter side.

GILBERT: But what is it he wants? What didn't you do for him?

JULIE: He wants to sail to-night on the Aquitania, and we can't get a passport.

GILBERT: A passport? And he's putting you through all this for a— Well, no wonder you're upset.

JULIE: This! What you've seen is practically the rest hour. We've had Gwen deciding to leave the stage forever——

GILBERT: What!

JULIE: —Mother having a little collapse. Uncle Herbert—you remember Uncle Herbert, don't you? Well, we won't go into that.

GILBERT: Look here, Julie. When does Tony want to sail? *(Cross to phone)*

JULIE: Midnight. The Aquitania. *(*GIL *goes directly to the telephone, takes up the receiver.)* Why? Gil, do you mean you know someone that can——

GILBERT: Bowling Green ten-five-one-six. . . How soon can he get down there? Tony, I mean.

JULIE: Why—right away, I guess, if he can slip by the reception committee.

GILBERT: Tell him to get ready—no, wait a minute—Hello! John? . . . Let me talk to Moran . . .

JULIE: Gil, do you mean you can get it? Oh, if you only could!

GILBERT: Don't you know there isn't anything in the world that I wouldn't . . . Hello! . . . Why, if I thought you needed me, Julie, I'd go to the ends of the . . . Hello! Moran? This is Marshall . . . Now get this . . . I want an emergency passport Aquitania to-night . . . That's right . . . I want you to meet me on the Cunard dock in half an hour? *(To* Julie*)* Can he make it in half an hour?

Julie: *(Eagerly)* Yes, yes!

Gilbert: *(In phone)* Now, no slip-up on this.

Julie: *(Sotto voce)* Twenty minutes.

Gilbert: *(In there)* I'll give you the details when I see you . . . Right. *(Hangs up)*

Julie: Oh, Gil!

Gilbert: I'll meet Tony and smuggle him on board. Moran will do the rest.

Julie: *(Goes to stairway; even mounts a step or two)* Tony! Tony! *(Turns to* Gilbert*)* It's wonderful of you, Gil. Why, you're one of these strong, silent men, aren't you! *(*Tony *enters from door left, balcony.)* Tony, we've got it. Hurry up! Get ready!

Tony: What! You mean the passport!

Julie: Yes! Yes! Gil got it for you. He's going to meet you there and fix——

Tony: *(Racing down the stairs)* Whee! *(A leap)* That's the stuff! *(Bounds over to* Julie*)* You're a swell sister!—Jo! Jo!

Julie: Now, Tony, you understand, you're to go right down there. Gil will meet you on the dock. He'll have the passport.

*(*Jo's *head is seen in doorway, right.)*

Jo: Yes, sir.

Tony: Jo, I'm going to leave in five minutes. You got everything ready?

Jo: Yes, sir. It will be.

Tony: All right. Go to it. *(Leaps for the stairs as* Jo *exits)* Sis, you're a grand kid! I knew I could count on you. Old reliable. *(To* Gilbert, *who has crossed left)* Much obliged, old fellow! *(To*

JULIE, *in the same breath)* Who is he, anyway? *(Exits, on balcony left)*

JULIE: *(Groping uncertainly for a chair. Rather mockingly utters the trite phrase of the theatre to cover her own shaken condition)* Won't you—sit down? *(Sits on sofa)*

GILBERT: Why do you stand for all this?

JULIE: Oh, Tony doesn't mean anything. He's always like that.

GILBERT: What do you mean? That you have this kind of thing all the time, and that you go ahead and put up with it?

JULIE: Oh, sometimes families are . . . It just happens to-day that blood is thicker than usual.

GILBERT: But these other things that you were talking about. You oughtn't to allow them to do that! You're a successful actress. Head of your profession! You ought to be the one they're running around for. And look! Everybody dumping their troubles on you.

JULIE: Oh, it isn't always like this.

GILBERT: *(Sits on small bench left of sofa)* You know, Julie, the reason I went away was so that you could go ahead and be an actress. All that stuff about Cavendish, and the stage being your real life, and the only way you could be happy. Well, you've got everything you went after. And how about it? Are you happy?

JULIE: Happy! I don't know.

GILBERT: Of course you're not, Julie. I've stayed away all these years because I thought at least you were living the life you wanted most. And then I come back and find this. You ought to have everything in the world. You ought to have everything done for you — done for you by some one who loves you . . .

JULIE: Oh, don't, Gil—don't say things that will make us both—

GILBERT: Don't you know what you ought to be doing instead of this? The way you ought to be living! Why, you ought to be in a country house somewhere, with a garden around it, and trees. Julie, if you could see the place I've got in England. An old stone house, and a rose garden that's famous. It's a beautiful place, Julie, and there it stands, empty.

JULIE: Oh, Gil!

GILBERT: Or we can go any place else you want—Cairo, St. Moritz—anywhere you say. Don't you know that's the way you ought to be living! Don't you?

JULIE: *(Rises)* I don't know! I don't know!

GILBERT: Julie! *(Takes her in his arms)* What fools we've been! What fools!

JULIE: Gil—wait! Let me think a minute. Let me get my breath.

GILBERT: You've had too long to think. It's settled.

JULIE: *(As she gently frees herself)* No—please! I-I'm not quite sure what's happened. I can't think very clearly——

GILBERT: I'll tell you what's happened. Something that should have happened twenty years ago. That's what's happened.

JULIE: Well, perhaps if—maybe—Gil, you'd better go now. I think you'd better go. It's late.

GILBERT: All right . . . Must I?

JULIE: Please.

GILBERT: I—I can't take you to the theatre?

JULIE: No——*(Crosses left)* please. I must get Tony away on that boat—I couldn't give a performance if—just a minute alone—

GILBERT: It'll only be for a few hours—this time.

JULIE: You'll call for me at the theatre?

GILBERT: At eleven? Is that all right? *(Gets hat and coat)*

JULIE: At eleven.

GILBERT: I'll be waiting.

JULIE: That'll be wonderful.
GILBERT: Good-bye.

(*BUZZER*)

JULIE: *(Gayly)* Good-bye.

(GILBERT goes. JULIE stands a moment. A step toward him as he departs. The buzzer off stage, right, sounds. TONY leaps out on balcony, clad in his B.V.D.'s and a bathrobe of silk worn open and billowing away behind him.)

TONY: *(Very loud)* Jo! Jo! Where's that bastard!

JULIE: Tony, be quiet! You'll wake mother!

TONY: Well, God damn it, I've got to get out! Jo!

(DELLA enters, right, carrying a covered cup of hot soup on a small tray.)

JULIE: Tony, will you shut up!

DELLA: Miss Julie, you'll have to be going. You've just got to have something hot in your stomach. Now, you drink this soup.

TONY: *(Simultaneous with DELLA'S speech above. Starting down the stairs, his robe ballooning behind him)* Della, where the hell is Jo? *(JO enters, right, followed by HALLBOY in uniform.)* Jo, where the hell have you been? Come on! Bring that boy and come up here. I've got to get out!

JO: *(Crossing to a little flat-footed dog-trot)* Yes, sir. On the job. Got it all fixed. *(JO and HALLBOY go upstairs and exit in TONY'S room.)*

JULIE: *(Speaking on DELLA'S "You drink this soup")* What time is it? . . . Good heavens! . . . I can't stop to eat, Della . . . No, I can't! . . . Get my things. I've got to run. . . Look after mother, won't you? . . . Bring her some hot soup . . . Tony, what's all this hullabaloo! Oh, if you were only out of this! What I wouldn't give for a little peace and quiet!

TONY: *(Toward stairs. Talks through last part of JULIE'S speech)* I'm not making any racket! You're making all the racket. Nobody'll be gladder than I am—— *(FANNY enters.)*

DELLA: *(Has placed tray on piano. Gets JULIE'S hat and coat. From the time of JULIE'S refusal to take the soup she speaks on JULIE'S "only out of this.")* You know very well you can't give a performance on an empty stomach. Go fainting in the wings, and then what! You wouldn't even have to sit down to it. You could swallow this cup of good hot broth.

(As the three voices climax, speaking together, FANNY *appears on balcony from her room. She wears a rich and handsome dark silk dressing gown, voluminous and enveloping.)*

FANNY: Hush that clatter! Person can't get a wink!

JULIE: *(Goes toward her)* Mother! What are you doing up?

TONY: *(Is about to exit as he turns and sees* FANNY——*goes to her)* Hi there, Fanny! All right again! *(Pats her shoulder)*

DELLA: Why, Mrs. Cavendish!

JULIE: Go back into your room this minute, Fanny Cavendish! Go back to bed!

*(*FANNY *starts down, assisted a step or two by* TONY, *who leaves her to* JULIE, *who has come up part way to meet her mother.* DELLA, *hat and coat in hand, remains right)*

FANNY: What's going on here! What's the excitement!

TONY: There you are! You're the comeback kid!

JULIE: Mother, I wish you hadn't done this. I've got to go to the theatre . . . Gwen!

FANNY: I know. I know. Run along.

JULIE: I will not run along until you go back to bed. I want you to go back to bed.

FANNY: But I want to see Tony go! I can't stay in bed with Tony going!

JULIE: Tony, for heaven's sake, hurry up! How soon will you be ready?

TONY: All set! I'll be gone in thirty seconds. . . All board for Europe! *(As* TONY *turns on balcony,* GWEN *comes out center door, balcony. She is still white and shaken. To* GWEN*)* Hello, there! *(*TONY *exits, center door.)*

GWEN: Mother, did you call me?

JULIE: Oh—yes, Gwen. I want you to look after mother. *(*GWEN *starts down stairs.* JULIE *is descending with* FANNY.*)* I'm terribly late. Mother, lean on me. Gwen, taker her other arm.

FANNY: I don't need any arm.

JULIE: Yes, but you do, though. You oughtn't to be up at all. Now Gwen's going to look after you—and Della, if you need me you're to telephone the box-office, you understand, and ask for Mr. Friedman—you know. I'll come right home after the performance——No! Yes, I will! There! *(She has settled* FANNY *in her chair.)* Now Della'll bring in your dinner, and Gwen'll get you anything you want, and oh, Gwen, you've been crying.

GWEN: No, I haven't.

DELLA: *(Still with* JULIE'S *hat and coat)* Miss Julie, it's quarter to eight. You know what the traffic is.

JULIE: *(Has gone over to the piano on which soup stands. Starts to drink a mouthful of it during this speech)* Oh, I've got to go through that crowd downstairs again! . . . Whew! This is hot! . . . And how Tony's ever going to manage it . . . *(Calls)* Tony . . . are you ready?

TONY: *(Voice from balcony, off)* Right!

JULIE: I've got to know he's on that boat or I won't be able to play . . . Mother, I want you to promise me to go back to bed the minute Tony's gone. Have your dinner in bed.

FANNY: Don't fuss about me.

JULIE: But don't wait up for me, will you? Della, I can't take this. I'm not hungry. I haven't got the time for it anyhow . . . *(Calls)* Tony! Are you coming? . . . *(To* DELLA*)* Hat! *(With a quick movement she seizes the hat from* DELLA'S *hand and pulls it down on her head.)*

TONY: *(Heard off)* All right! Go!

(Out of the balcony entrance and down the steps sweeps the cavalcade. It consists of JO *and* MAC, *laden with all the luggage that* TONY *arrived with on the preceding day. Then comes the* HALLBOY, *disguised in* TONY'S *hat and coat—the upturned fur collar, the pulled-down slouch hat, just as* TONY *entered in the first act. His face is concealed almost entirely by the coat collar and the hat.* JULIE *and* GWEN *follow the group up into the alcove, shouting their good-byes and last-minute instructions.* FANNY *rises and*

stands about the center, her arms out, as though expecting TONY *to come to her before he goes out.)*

JULIE: The end of a perfect day. Thank God. Tony, don't charter a tug and come back—that's all I ask. Now, Jo, stay with him no matter what happens. *(*JO, MAC *and* HALLBOY *exit in hallway.* JULIE, GWEN *and* DELLA *follow off.)* How he's going to do it I don't know. I ought to go down with him.

GWEN: No, don't, mother!

FANNY: Good-bye, Tony! Good-bye, my boy!

JULIE: Take care of your sinus. Keep out of Russia. Why do you have golf clubs? *(From this point the voices of* FANNY, JULIE *and* GWEN *are heard simultaneously offstage.)* Don't start anything rough with anyone downstairs, for Heaven's sake! Jo, make him behave himself. Mac, I'm trusting you, too. They're sure to know him in those clothes. Why do you have to go to Europe! Well, anyhow, good-bye! Good-bye!

GWEN: Tony, take care of yourself. Send us a radio. Be sure! Be sure! I think it's absurd to take all that stuff. He could buy it all over there. Good-bye! Good-bye!

DELLA: *(Off)* Good-bye, Mr. Tony——good-bye.

FANNY: *(Standing at hall door)* Tony! Tony! Aren't you going to say good-bye!

(The three figures have swept down the stairs, been joined by DELLA, *have moved quickly across the room, and are now in the alcove on their way out.* JULIE, FANNY, *and* GWEN *stand aghast as they realize that* TONY *is not stopping to say good-bye.)*

JULIE: *(Off)* Tony, aren't you saying good-bye to us? He isn't saying good-bye.

GWEN: *(Off)* Tony! Wait a minute! Say good-bye to us all. Why isn't he stopping! He's going! He's gone!

FANNY: Don't let him go! He's never gone like that! Come back and say good-bye! He didn't even talk to me! He didn't even look at me! Tony! . . . Tony! . . . Tony! *(Growing weaker.* GWEN *goes to her.)*

JULIE: *(Rushing back to her)* Now, mother! He's all right! You wouldn't want him to stop! He'll send you a radio. Now don't! You'll only make yourself sick!

GWEN: Never mind, grandma—it'll be all right. I think it's a rotten shame.

JULIE: *(Darting toward the alcove, then realizing that her mother needs more)* Tony! Tony!. . . No, I guess I'd better not! *(Runs back to her mother)* Mother, you're all right, aren't you? Don't worry. I've got to go to the theatre! *(Through the outer door* KITTY *and* DEAN *enter* KITTY *leading.)*

KITTY: *(Off)* Why, the door's open.

DEAN: *(As he and* KITTY *enter)* What was that? Tony?

GWEN: Are you all right, Grandma?

JULIE: I wish I didn't have to go, Gwen. Do you think she's all right?

DEAN: What's the matter? Fanny sick?

KITTY: Listen, Julie Cavendish! I've got something to say to you.

JULIE: What?

*(*TONY*, in hallboy's uniform, darts out onto the balcony . . . He does not pause, but skims the balcony and down the stairs.)*

TONY: Hello, folks! Farewell appearance!

JULIE: *(In a sort of squeak that dies in her throat)* Oh! . . . Oh! . . . Oh, for. . .

FANNY: Tony!

GWEN: Oh!

DEAN: What is this?

KITTY: What's he doing?

TONY: *(Glances down at himself complacently)* How do you like it? Good on me? Isn't it?

JULIE: Tony! What are you going to do?

TONY: Going to the boat, of course.

FANNY: Like that!

TONY: Sure! They'll make a dash for their taxi—the crowd will all swarm after them—give 'em a nice run up Fifth Avenue. Then I go down, get into my cab, ten minutes I'm on the dock, voila!

DEAN: What's it all about?

FANNY: Tony, my boy!

TONY: (*A swift leap across the room*) Good-bye, everybody! (*Takes* FANNY'S *head in his two hands. Kisses her*) Good-bye, mother! (*A pose*) The open sea, the salt spray! The arctic wind! . . . I'm on my way! Remember it's the Guaranty Trust——(*Exit* TONY, *outer door.* GWEN *sits on bench right*)

FANNY: (*Rather feebly*) Tony! Tony! (*Sits on bench left of sofa*)

DEAN: Why! What! . . . What!

JULIE: (*Who is standing near the sofa, sinks into it*) Ooooooh!

KITTY: (*Comes to* JULIE; *stands over her*) And now I want to ask you a question.

DEAN: Kitty!

KITTY: (*Sharply*) Did you offer me that part of your own accord, or did Bert put you up to it?

DEAN: Oh!

JULIE: (*From the position into which she slumped in the chair,* JULIE *begins to uncoil. Her eye is baleful. She rises slowly. Her whole attitude is so sinister and desperate that* KITTY *shrinks back a little.*) No. No, it isn't possible! You! You come to me with your miserable little . . . Your part! Bert's. . . (*A little high hysterical laugh*) After all that I've . . . it's too . . . I can't . . .

GWEN: Mother! Don't! (PERRY *enters*) Perry!

PERRY: What's the matter? What's going on?

JULIE: Well—what else? What else? Come on! What else? Perry! for God's sake take her out of this! Take her away before it's too late. Take her where she'll never hear stage again! Take her away!

FANNY: Julie! Julie!

GWEN: No! I'm not going to marry him! (*A Warning.*)

JULIE: (*Pushes her hair back from her forehead with her open palm—a gesture of desperation*) Not going to marry him! Not going—— (*A finger pointing to the spot where* JULIE, GWEN *and* FANNY *have talked earlier*)

GWEN: I'm not going to marry him and spoil his life!

PERRY: Gwen!

GWEN: No, no!

JULIE: Oh, no, you won't! If you think I'm going to let you throw away your whole life! . . . And for what? . . . This! So that nineteen years from now you can be standing here as I am, a mad woman in a family of maniacs! Money for this one, jobs for that one, rehearsals and readings and tickets for God knows where. I'm damned if you're going to! You're going to marry——Perry Stewart.

GWEN: No, no!

JULIE: Oh, yes, you are! You're going to do what I didn't do. They told me I had to be a Cavendish. (*A movement from her mother*) Oh, yes, you did! (*Wheeling to Gwen again*) Well, you're not going to be one. You're going to marry him now-to-night—to-morrow. And I'm goring to be there with you, and stand up beside you, and cry for happiness, and wish to God it was me! (*Her voice suddenly low, thoughtful*) And why not? I'm not dead yet. I've got some of my life left. And I'm going to live it to suit me! You've all had your turn. Who's crazy now! I can walk out and nobody can stop me.

FANNY: What nonsense!

DEAN: You're mad!

JULIE: You don't believe it, him? I'll show you. I'm going to marry Gil Marshall and go to Egypt and Venice and Constantinople—and what do you know about that? As far as the stage is concerned—I'm through with it, Cavendish! To hell with Cavendish! I'm never going to act again. I'm never going to set foot on another stage as long as I live. I'm never going inside a theatre! I'm ne——

JO: *(Aghast at finding Julie still at home, has heard her voice, high-pitched. In a voice of alarm)* Miss Julie! It's eight o'clock!

JULIE: *(Grabs her coat from* JO. *Rushes in a panic toward the outer door)* Oh, my God!

CURTAIN

ACT III

The scene is the same. The time, a year later. November. As al-
ways, flowers are everywhere. The small table upstage, left of the
stairs, is decked with a rich lace tea cloth. The table and armchair
have been restored to their former position—left of the sofa. The
door at right is open; so are the doors to the library. At the rise
DELLA enters from right. She is carrying a silver tea service—
gleaming with cups and silver pitchers. She puts it down on the lace
covered table; starts to arrange the cups. JULIE strolls casually out
onto the balcony, from her room. She wears a costume slip of gold or
silver, with only straps over the shoulder. Obviously a tea coat is
presently to be slipped over this. She is polishing her nails with a
buffer. She throws a careless glance toward FANNY'S room; her gaze
takes in the room below.

JULIE: Oh, Della.

DELLA: Yes, Miss Julie.

JULIE: Let's have tea in the library. I think it'd be cozier.

DELLA: All fight. *(Starts to pile up the cups again.)*

FANNY: *(Her voice through the open door of her room)* What's that
smells so good?

JULIE: *(Sniffs)* Gingerbread, I guess, for tea. *(Jo enters at right, car-*
rying a little stack of plates.)

DELLA: Library, Jo.

JO: *(Crossing to tea tray)* Oh . . . How many there going to be?

DELLA: Half a dozen, she said. Better count on twelve.

(JULIE on balcony, putting some last touches to the adjustment of her
costume)

JULIE: Jo, did you start a fire in the library?

JO: Yes, Miss Julie. Nice bright one. *(Exits into library)*

DELLA: I told him to build one soon's I heard Miss Gwen was
bringing the baby over.

JULIE: *(Coming down stairs)* Coming down, mother?

FANNY: *(From her room)* Minute.

JULIE: *(Descending)* Got on your plum silk?

FANNY: Yes, sir!

DELLA: *(Indicating a vase of roses)* I brought Mr. Marshall's roses out into this room. I thought you'd want 'em where he'd be sure to see them.

JULIE: Thanks, Della.

DELLA: Wonder what Mr. Marshall will say to Miss Gwen's baby. He knows about him, doesn't he?

JULIE: I wrote him, Della—let's hope he approves. *(Sits on sofa. Gathers up a few letters from the table. JO enters and crosses.)* You might shake up a few cocktails, Jo. Somebody'll want them.

JO: Right. *(Exits right)*

DELLA: He'd better approve. *(Crosses right)* I never saw a grander baby in all my life. Two months old, and you'd think he was twice that.

JULIE: *(Absorbed in a letter. Absently)* You must tell that to Miss Gwen.

DELLA: I bet he don't see babies like that down in South America. Anyhow, they're black, ain't they?

JULIE: M-m well, maybe cafe au lait.

DELLA: *(A moment's hesitation. Then, with determination to know)* Miss Julie, are you going to live down there in South America when you marry Mr. Marshall?

JULIE: *(Looks up)* Mr. Marshall doesn't live there, Della.

DELLA: Well, he's been there twice this year and this last time about six months. That's living there, ain't it?

JULIE: Oh, he won't be there much, next year. *(Again turns her attention to her mail.)*

DELLA: You see, I'm only asking you on account-Excuse me, Miss Julie, but I don't know if you're going to give up the apartment or what. You see, with Miss Gwen with her own place now, and you going to get married and go traveling——

JULIE: Well, I wouldn't worry about that, Della. We may not give up the apartment after all.

DELLA: But who's going to live in it? With Mrs. Cavendish going touring on the road——

JULIE: I don't know about that, Della. The doctor doesn't think she ought to go on the road.

DELLA: But she was only telling me five minutes ago——

JULIE: Yes—yes, I know. But mother is not going to be able to travel again, Della.

DELLA: What? (JULIE *turns and looks at* DELLA) Oh, my God! (FANNY *is heard coming.*)

JULIE: Be quiet!

(FANNY *enters from her room onto balcony. She wears the plum silk gown, very proud. Her cane has been discarded. Her step is quick and firm. She descends the stairs.*)

FANNY: "And purple her habiliments and scarlet was her soul. Romeo, wherefore art thou, Romeo?" Well, where's your young man? You'd think he'd come bounding right up from the dock after being away so long. (DELLA *exits, right.*)

JULIE: He'll be along presently. He phoned from the hotel.

FANNY: Well, if he said he'd come, he'll come. He's what they call steady-going. Regular habits. Look at those two dozen American beauties—(*A gesture in their direction*) that have been arriving every morning, like the milk.

JULIE: I think it was very sweet of him to leave an order like that.

FANNY: If there's one way to take the romance out of roses, it's knowing that you're going to get them every day.

JULIE: But the very qualities he's got are the ones I need. I've had enough of temperamental people.

FANNY: I'll bet he's worked out your honeymoon in algebra. Arrive Constantinople January twelfth. Arrive Cairo February twenty-fourth. He'll tell you that the next Sahara sunset is at 6:49 and it had better be. And while you're sitting on the hill at Fiesole he'll know to the minute when you'll be in Copenhagen.

JULIE: Even that'll be restful. After twenty years of practically checking my own trunk.

FANNY: If you wanted to marry him why didn't you do it a year ago? Why didn't you marry him then?

JULIE: You know why I didn't. There was Wolfe with a new theatre all built—a new production on his hands—and then Gwen dropping out of it. I had to agree to play the New York run. How'd I know it was going to be a whole year!

FANNY: Where're you going on your wedding trip? Made up your mind yet?

JULIE: Why, I don't know. It'll depend on what Gil says, a good deal. I'm not keen about these faraway aces.

FANNY: Since when! Why, it's been Baghdad and Venice and the Vale of Kashmir every day of the past year!

JULIE: Well, I love the sound of the names, but they are awfully far away.

FANNY: If you're going to marry him at all, you might as well see the world. You'll need it.

JULIE: I just thought I'd like to be around in case you needed me—you or Gwen.

FANNY: What for? Gwen certainly doesn't need you. Settled and through with the stage.

JULIE: Yes . . . still . . .

FANNY: And as for me, while you're drifting down the Nile I'll be playing Ogden, Utah, and doing pretty well. I sold out there in 1924.

JULIE: Now look here, mother. I've been thinking it over—your going on this tour—and I'd ever so much rather you wouldn't go.

FANNY: What!

JULIE: You haven't been well. I wouldn't have any peace if I had to think of you galloping around those terrible towns—Tulsa, Albuquerque, Oklahoma City. I know. I couldn't stand a tour like that.

FANNY: I'm tougher than you are. When I quit it'll be for the same reason that Aubrey did. And no other.

JULIE: Well, I don't think you ought to go. Besides, there's Gwen. She's awfully young . . . I'd feel so much better if you were here to look after her.

FANNY: What's the matter with her husband?

JULIE: Besides, there's this place——Della was just asking if you were going to give it up——And then there's Bert

(DOOR BELL)

FANNY: And Kitty. *(Outer door bell rings.)*

JULIE: You see, if you stay here, all comfortable, it'll mean I'll have some place to come back to when I'm in New York.

FANNY: Oh! So as to make you comfortable I'm to give up my whole career.

JULIE: No, no. It isn't me. It's you. You must admit it's a hard trip, and——(JO *enters right, goes toward outer door.)*

FANNY: *(Rising slowly)* This'll be your Emerald King.

JULIE: I suppose so.

DEAN: *(His voice heard off as* JO *opens the door.)* Good afternoon.

JO: Afternoon, Mr. Dean.

FANNY: It's Bert.

JULIE: Oh, mother!

(BERT and KITTY enter from the alcove, followed by JO. During the next few speeches JO takes their coats and DEAN'S hat; hangs them in alcove closet. KITTY is dressed with some expensiveness—perhaps a fur coat. DEAN, who has been quite gray and nearly bald in the preceding acts, displays, when he removes his hat, a fine and unexpected crop of coal black hair.)

KITTY: Isn't it a marvelous day?

DEAN: Ah! Here we are!

FANNY: Hello, there, Bertie. Kitty.

JULIE: *(Weakly)* Why, hello.

DEAN: Just thought we'd drop in and see how you all were.

KITTY: Mm, what a smart tea coat, Julie!

JULIE: Do you like it?

KITTY: Oh, yes. I think the color's a little trying.

DEAN: Thanks, Jo, *(As he helps him with his coat. He is up near alcove)* Marshall's boat get in? I see he's due.

JULIE: Yes, it did. He'll be here very soon.

KITTY: Oh, won't that be nice? We'll be here to greet him. *(Sits on sofa)*

JULIE: Tha-t's—lovely.

DEAN: *(Crossing left)* Queer fellow, Marshall. Always talking about the Panama Canal . . .Well, Fanny, still determined to go out into the hinterland?

FANNY: Why not?

DEAN: No reason. Just be careful, that's all. You're not as young as you were, you know.

FANNY: Who is?

KITTY: Won't be many more chances for family gatherings, will there, Mother Cavendish? *(DELLA enters and exits library with tray with cake, etc. A bitter look of resentment from FANNY)* You won't be keeping this great big place when the family breaks up. *(DELLA enters with tray containing cake—pitcher of hot water for tea. She crosses left.)*

FANNY: I was not aware that the Cavendish family is breaking up. *(Rises. JO enters from hallway and exits under stairs.)*

KITTY: Well, after all, with you on the road, and Julie God. knows where, and Gwen married—I don't see that you'll have any use for it. You can't count on Tony. It looks as if he's going to stay in Europe forever.

DEAN: *(Intercepting* DELLA *as she passes him with her laden tray, gathers up a rich and crumbly piece of cake, which he negotiates with some difficulty through the following lines)* Just what are your plans, Fanny? *(Pauses, cake in hand, ready for a bite)* How about all this stuff? *(A huge bite)* What are you going to do with everything? *(A gesture that indicates the room about him, but which does not disturb the precarious business in hand)*

*(*DELLA *exits, library)*

FANNY: *(Crosses up)* It'll all go to the storehouse, I suppose. And Aubrey there along with it. . . But we're held together by something more than tables and chairs. *(Comes down)*

KITTY: It occurred to me this morning—remember I was saying to you, Bert—that aside from Fanny on the road, it will be Bert and I who'll be carrying on the family tradition.

FANNY: Thanks for including me, anyhow.

KITTY: Has Bert told you what we're planning to do?

FANNY: Why, no.

JULIE: No.

DEAN: *(All eyes on him)* Well, I was keeping it as a sort of surprise.

JULIE: Why, Bert, what is it?

FANNY: What are you going to do?

BERT: Why, it seems that the vaudeville people are very anxious to elevate the tone of their entertainments.

FANNY: Vaudeville?

DEAN: Why not? Why not? They don't want good plays any more. They proved that in the way they received "The Conqueror." Finest play of my career, and what happened?

FANNY: It closed. *(Sits)*

DEAN: Now, here comes this opportunity to reach a wide public, to create an audience for the finer things.

KITTY: We're getting eighteen hundred dollars a week, together.

DEAN: Ah—yes, and twenty weeks right in New York, and around it. They've got up a very neat little act for us. Amusing. Human. Now, here's the plot.

JULIE: Oh, yes, tell us.

FANNY: I'm all a-twitter.

DEAN: I'm a sort of a bachelor chap——thirty-five or thereabouts—very rich, and have had an unhappy love affair that I tell the butler about.

KITTY: Ever since then you've been a woman hater.

DEAN: Yes, yes.

KITTY: Yes, yes.

DEAN: Then comes this letter from Australia. It seems that an old college friend has died out there, and it was his last wish that I should take care of his little girl——be her guardian.

JULIE: The letter is delayed in transit, so that it happens to arrive just before the little girl herself.

DEAN: You've read it.

JULIE: Oh, no. No.

DEAN: All events, presently there's a lot of noise outside——automobile horn, so on—the door's opened, and instead of the little child they were expecting, there stands an exquisite young girl of eighteen.

FANNY: Kitty. (FANNY, *without a word, rises and starts for the library.*)

(DOOR BELL)

DEAN: Hold on, Fanny—I'm not through.

FANNY: (*Going left*) Oh, yes, you are. Besides, that's probably Marshall. Why don't you two come in here with me for a while?

(DELLA *enters from library. Goes toward front door*)

DELLA: Tea's all ready, Mrs. Cavendish. (*Crosses and exits under stairs.* JO *enters and goes to door.*)

FANNY: Come on. Have some tea. *(A step or two toward library door. A feeling of general movement of the group, left)*

KITTY: I come in with my little dog Rags, that my father gave me— *(As she talks she is walking toward left in what evidently is meant to be the way in which* BERT'S *ward will walk)*—and I'm sort of a pathetic figure

FANNY: You don't say!

WOLFE: *(Heard as* JO *opens the door)* Well, Jo! The whole family, here?

DEAN: *(At the sound of his voice)* Ah!

KITTY: Well!

JULIE: Ah, Oscar.

WOLFE: *(Entering. To* JULIE*)* Don't Oscar me, you renegade! *(Gives* JO *hat and coat, who takes them in hallway)* Hello, folks! Fanny, my girl! *(Turns again to* JULIE*)* A lot you care about Oscar. All you're thinking about is this Whozis. The boat gets in today, huh? It couldn't sink or anything?

JULIE: Your own fault, Oscar. Why didn't you marry me?

WOLFE: *(Cross on speech)* Say, it's bad enough to manage you. . . Well, Fanny, how are you? Good as ever?

FANNY: Certainly am. Come on—I want my tea.

WOLFE: Don't you go back on me like these other loafers. With Julie a millionaire's bride, and Gwen a society matron, all I need is you should marry John D. Rockefeller and my season is over.

FANNY: About time you had to concentrate on me. I want a brand new play for next season, and none of your cold storage tidbits.

WOLFE: *(To* JULIE*)* You hear that? There's a trouper for you!

JULIE: Anyhow, Oscar, I was a good fellow when I had it.

DEAN: And I'll comeback to you, old fellow. This little flyer in vaudeville.

WOLFE: Mm . . . Oh, Fanny! I knew there was something. Can you open a week earlier, do you think? Toledo on the 14th—all right with you?

FANNY: *(Doubtfully)* Full week in Toledo?

WOLFE: Well, maybe we should split it with Columbus, huh? Toledo ain't so good this year.

FANNY: *(With asperity)* I can play the full week.

(Turns to exit)

KITTY: *(Following her as all drift toward library doors)* Now I want to tell you about my part. Did we tell you it's called "The Bachelor's Baby?" Well, of course, my part is really just as important as Bert's——(FANNY, KITTY *and* BERT *exit into library.* WOLFE *is about to follow.)*

JULIE: Oscar, Oscar!

WOLFE: Huh?

JULIE: Wait a minute. *(*JULIE *quietly closes the library doors.)*

WOLFE: What's going on?

JULIE: I've got to talk to you. *(She stands listening a brief moment to make sure that the others cannot hear.)*

WOLFE: What's the matter?

JULIE: It's about Fanny.

WOLFE: Yeh? What's up?

JULIE: *(Pause)* Oscar, she can't go on this tour.

WOLFE: Why not?

JULIE: I don't know how you're going to do it, but some way or other you've got to keep her from going. Without her knowing it.

WOLFE: *(His keen gaze on her)* What are you trying to tell me, Julie?

JULIE: I went to see Randall yesterday.

WOLFE: Yes?

JULIE: She's through, Oscar.

WOLFE: *(Dully)* What!

JULIE: She can't go on this tour. She can't do anything.

WOLFE: What do you mean?

JULIE: She's got to have absolute quiet and rest. The least strain of exertion, and she's likely to go—like that.

WOLFE: . . . Fanny?

JULIE: (Crosses right) She never can play again—anywhere. She may never even leave this house.

WOLFE: Let me—let me realize this. Fanny Cavendish—in there— it's all over? (JULIE nods.) I don't know why I'm so—after all, she's been sick now a long time; she ain't young any more—but she never seemed sick—always going on again—busy with plans—sweeping us all along—it don't seem possible that——

(JULIE'S warning hand halts WOLFE'S speech. FANNY appears in library doorway.)

FANNY: Della! Della! No more mind than a rabbit.

WOLFE: (Elaborately casual) So I says to him, that's one way of look-ing at it. Everybody's got his own ideas——

JULIE: I think you're quite right, Oscar. I thought of that myself.

FANNY: Don't you two ever talk anything but business! . . . Della! (DELLA appears, right.)

DELLA: Yes, Mrs. Cavendish.

FANNY: Where's that gingerbread?

DELLA: We tried to cut it and it crumbled.

FANNY: Bring it in anyhow. (DELLA goes.) Don't you two want your tea?

JULIE: Right away, mother.

FANNY: Kitty's reached the love interest. (Draws her skirts and very coquettishly exits the library)

JULIE: (Talking for FANNY'S benefit as she goes quietly up to close library door) Of course, Oscar, in one way I agree with you, but on the other hand, I don't think it wise—— (Closes door. Turns to Oscar) What are we going to tell her, Oscar? How are we going to manage it?

WOLFE: I tell you how I fix it. First I tell her on account of booking troubles we can't open just yet—make it March, say, instead
of January. Then when March comes along, it's late in the season, the road ain't so good any more—maybe we ought to wait
till next year. And I guarantee you, the way I do it, she won't
suspect a thing.

JULIE: Oscar, what a grand person you are.

WOLFE: I wish I could really do something. Thirty-five years we
been together. They don't make them like her anymore . . . I
wish you could have seen her the first time I did, Julie. Her
face. Young, and gay, and beautiful—but so much more than
beautiful. And how she treated me that first meeting. Me—a
beginner, a nobody. I went into there, I tried not to show how
I was shaking. I came out, I could have been Sir Charles
Wyndham.

JULIE: Oscar, if I could only tell you what you've meant to all of us!
But you wouldn't listen.

WOLFE: And—you, Julie?

JULIE: What?

WOLFE: What about your plans, with this news? Still Egypt and
India?

JULIE: Oh, no. But—what am I going to do, Oscar? Gil's got his
heart set on the ends of the earth—he hates New York; I don't
dare go far away.

WOLFE: Well, say. You tell him how things stand, what the situation is. After all, he can't be quite a—I mean, in the face of
something like this, surely now——

JULIE: Oscar, why don't you like Gil? I wish you did.

WOLFE: Marshall? I like him all right. He ain't just my kind, but
maybe I ain't his, either.

JULIE: Oscar, do you think if I asked him he'd be willing to take a
house here in town for a while? Then I could look after her—
be here if—anything happened.

WOLFE: How could he say no—a time like this?

JULIE: I'd feel so relieved.

WOLFE: Only what would you do with yourself all the time? New York—you've seen New York. Running a house—what's that for you? What are you going to do?

JULIE: Why, I don't know. It's all so sudden—I hadn't thought about it yet.

WOLFE: Well, then, say! You're living in New York anyhow; you haven't got anything to do; what's the difference if——

JULIE: No, no! I'm through with it, Oscar. Through with it forever.

WOLFE: So. You—Gwen—Fanny—that ends it, huh? And for you there's no excuse.

JULIE: I'm going to be married, Oscar. That's a pretty good excuse.

WOLFE: Tell me, what do you talk about when you're alone with this fellow? The theatre he says he don't care about. Imagine!

JULIE: There are other things in the world beside the theatre.

WOLFE: Sure! But not for you.

JULIE: I want to relax, and play around, and have some fun.

WOLFE: Fun! Fun is work! It's work that's fun. You've had more fun in the last twenty years than any woman in America. And let me tell you, Julie, the theatre is just beginning in this country. It used to be London—Paris—Berlin. Now it's New York. I tell you, a fine actress to-day—there's nothing she can't do. And the finest one of them all, that could do the biggest things of them all, she says she wants to have fun.

JULIE: Oh, Oscar, there are lots of actresses, and so many good ones. (*Cross right*)

WOLFE: Yes, good, but not for this play.

JULIE: What play?

WOLFE: Not even any of these young one that are coming up. Gwen maybe. A little young, but she could do it. Only—(*A gesture of helplessness*)—she's gone, too.

JULIE: Oscar, what play? What are you talking about?

WOLFE: Julie, I've never been one of these artistic producers—you know—The Theatre of The Future. Way back when I was a call boy at Daly's Theatre for two dollars a week I made up my mind show business was good place to make money in, and so I went into it, and I had been in it forty years, and I haven't got a nickel. Mind you, I've done a few good plays, too, but always I had an idea they would also make a few dollars. But this time it's different. I have got, I tell you, a play I am so crazy to produce it I don't care how much I lose on it.

JULIE: Really, Oscar! What is it? Who wrote it!

WOLFE: A new fellow you never heard of. Gunther his name is—a college professor out in Idaho. You wouldn't believe a college professor could know so much. He sits out there in that desert, mind you, and he writes this play and he doesn't know himself how good it is.

JULIE: What's it about?

WOLFE: That doesn't matter—it's how he does it. It's going to bring in a whole new kind of playwriting. They've never seen anything like this! God, what a play!

JULIE: Oscar! How exciting?

WOLFE: Exciting, yes. If I can do it right. But how am I going to do it. You gone. Gwen gone.

JULIE: You'll find someone. You're sure to.

WOLFE: All right. Never mind. Go ahead and relax—relax, when you could be making history. I do the play anyhow. Not so perfect maybe—but I do it. I do it because I want to be known as the man who produced this play.

JULIE: But if it's as good as that it would run years and years, wouldn't it?

WOLFE: No. A month—two months—I don't give it more than that. The first one's like this—they got to get used to them.

JULIE: I couldn't, Oscar. I couldn't.

WOLFE: All right. Get married and be a bazaar patroness. Mark my words, you'll come back again.

JULIE: They don't always come back. Look at Gwen. And Tony! He's been away a year.

(The sound of the opening of the outer door, and a gay call from GWEN*)*

GWEN: *(Off)* Yoo-hoo!

JULIE: Gwen! *(Meets* GWEN *up right.* GWEN *and* PERRY *enter.)*

GWEN: *(Greets* JULIE*)* Oh, how nice! Hello there! *(Crosses to* OSCAR*)*

WOLFE: Hello, children! And how's the mama?

JULIE: *(Greets* PERRY. *A line shot through the greetings)* Where's the baby?

PERRY: Hello, everybody!

(Oscar crosses, shakes hands with PERRY *and then goes down right. Attracted by the sound of* GWEN'S *voice,* FANNY, *followed by* DEAN *and* KITTY, *enter from library.* DEAN *pops a final bite of cake into his mouth. Dusts his hands briskly)*

FANNY: So it is . . . Hello, there . . . and Perry.

DEAN: How are you! How are you!

KITTY: Hello! Hardly ever see you people.

GWEN: *(Crossing to* FANNY*)* How are you, Grandma, dear? You look wonderful . . . Hello, Kitty!

FANNY: I'm fine. How's Aubrey?

KITTY: Where is he? Where's the baby?

JULIE: Don't tell me he isn't coming? *(*PERRY *crosses to piano.)*

GWEN: Oh ye, Miss Peake's bringing him. She makes him rest two minutes before his bottle or three minutes after—I never can remember. We didn't wait . . . Where' s Gil? I thought he'd be here.

*(*PERRY, *still with an air of detachment from the group, is up at the piano, leaning over it, his back partly turned to the others. He is glancing idly at the pages of a book, without seeming really to be interested in it.* FANNY *is sitting in chair left of sofa.)*

JULIE: He'll be here soon.

GWEN: Oh, fine!

WOLFE: Soon enough he'll be here. All the way from South America he's got to come to ruin my business. And Perry here—he couldn't pick out a nice girl from Park Avenue some place. It's got to be a Cavendish. Huh?

PERRY: How's that? *(Emerges briefly from his book.)*

WOLFE: I say you couldn't marry a good Junior League actress, huh? Instead of my Gwen.

PERRY: Oh . . . uh . . . yeh.

GWEN: Now, Perry!

JULIE: The boy friend's a little upstage today, isn't he?

GWEN: No, he isn't. Are you, Perry?

PERRY: I didn't think I was. Gosh, I want to do whatever . . . *(Comes down, slowly)* Why don't you tell them about it? See what they think. *(Crosses up to secretary)*

JULIE: Why, what's up? *(Cross to sofa, sits. KITTY goes back of sofa.)*

FANNY: What is it?

GWEN: Well—it's me. *(Sits on sofa)* Now, this is the way it is. The baby's two months old, and he's the darlingest baby that ever lived, but he doesn't do anything but sleep all the time, and, according to Miss Peake's schedule, you can only play with him about four minutes a day. Of course, when he gets older, it'll be different, but just now he doesn't need me at all. I'm in the way.

PERRY: How can you be in the way! *(Comes down)*

GWEN: I am in the way. She glares whenever I pick him up. I thought there'd be all kinds of things to do for him, but there aren't. So here I am with absolutely nothing to do until he gets so he kind of knows me. And on top of that, here's Perry going away on a business trip. He'll be gone about four weeks, anyway.

PERRY: I may be back in three.

GWEN: The whole thing's only five . . . Now, this is what happened.

JULIE: Well, thank God.

GWEN: They've got this Hungarian play and they've offered me a simple marvelous part—

JULIE: Who has?

GWEN: The Theatre Guild.

FANNY: Theatre Guild!

DEAN: What? What?

GWEN: It only means every other week, because they're going to alternate with Shaw's play.

FANNY: You're going on again.

GWEN: No. It's only for the subscription period, unless it turns out to be a great hit, and this can't.

KITTY: Well!

(On JULIE'S *face there is a look which is not altogether happy. There is something of shock in* GWEN'S *news, and, for her, something of apprehension. Somehow, this makes* JULIE'S *leaving the stage a little less agreeable.)*

WOLFE: Hold on a minute. Let me understand this. You're going back on the stage? Is that it?

GWEN: *(Cross to* OSCAR*)* No. Nothing like that. It's only of these few weeks, and just because it's a marvelous part. She's a slavey in this Budapest household—the kind of thing I've always been crazy to play—apron and cotton stockings and my hair pulled back tight . . . Oh, Perry, it would be such fun!

KITTY: Well, this is news!

FANNY: And about time!

DEAN: Nice little organization—the Theatre Guild.

PERRY: Gosh, Gwen! I don't mind a few weeks if it's going to make you as happy as that.

GWEN: Oh, Perry! *(Throws her arms about him. Kisses him)* Isn't he a darling!

KITTY: It's really thrilling, to think of Gwen going back. Aren't you thrilled, Julie?

JULIE: Why—I should say—I am! *(Rises, goes to* GWEN*)* Gwen, darling, I'm very happy—*(Then goes up)*

GWEN: I'm as excited as if I'd never been on the stage before! My, it'll be funny to see my picture in the papers again. To tell the truth, I've sort of missed it.

FANNY: How soon are you going to open?

GWEN: About a month, I guess. We go into rehearsal next week.

DEAN: That'll be a first night!

KITTY: I should say so.

(DOOR BELL)

GWEN: It's really a terrific part. She carries the whole play. I'm scared pink, but of course if I can do it it'll put me where I can—it'll be dandy! *(A little embarrassed laugh. The outer door bell rings.)*

JULIE: Yes, Won't it!

WOLFE: Five weeks, eh? *(Thoughtfully)* That means you are through with it early in February.

GWEN: *(Puzzled)* What? *(WOLFE pats Gwen's hand and chuckles with delight.)*

(DELLA enters, right, goes to answer door. JO follows almost immediately, right, carrying tray of cocktail shaker and glasses.)

DEAN: Ah! *(JO puts tray on table, left.)*

GWEN: Perry, you do feel all right about it, don't you? Because if you don't, I just won't do it, that's all.

PERRY: Well, of course you'll do it. What do a few weeks matter!

(They cross to bench in front of window. DEAN strolls up toward the cocktails. JO, at his approach, begins to shake them, genially. He pours one for DEAN.)

DELLA: *(At door, off)* Welcome back, Mr. Marshall.

GILBERT: *(Also heard off)* Thank you,

DELLA: How are you?

JULIE: It's Gil.

> *(GILBERT enters from the alcove. He pauses a moment on the threshold. Seeing that others are present, he contents himself with kissing JULIE'S hand. Then he greets the others. The following lines are said in unison.)*

FANNY: Well, at last!

DEAN: Ah, Marshall!

GWEN: It's Gil!

KITTY: Well—well——

GILBERT: Julie, dear!

JULIE: Gil!

GILBERT: It's good to see you—to be back.

> *(There is a general handshaking—greeting—business of welcome, with, perhaps, two shaking his hands at the same time.)*

DEAN: Hello, there, old fellow.

KITTY: Welcome back, Mr. Marshall.

GWEN: Hello, there. How brown you are!

> *(GILBERT shakes hands with GWEN and PERRY.)*

GILBERT: Think so? And how's the little mother?

PERRY: Hello, Marshall. Glad to see you.

WOLFE: Mr. Marshall.

GILBERT: *(To WOLFE)* How do you do? *(To FANNY, goes center)* How well you're looking.

FANNY: Never was better. How are you, Gil?

GILBERT: Fine, thanks——*(To KITTY)* And how are you?

KITTY: Fine. *(DELLA exits right.)*

GILBERT: Well! It's nice to find you all gathered here like this. I'm going to assume it's all in my honor, too.

KITTY: Indeed, yes!

DEAN: Cocktail, Marshall? *(Offers glass)*

GILBERT: Uh—no, I don't believe I will. I'm used to a different kind of stuff, down there. I'm a little afraid of the New York brand.

FANNY: I'll take one, Bertie.

(DEAN *hands* FANNY *a cocktail, then gets one for himself.* JO *takes off silver service in library.)*

JULIE: How was the trip, Gil? How many knots an hour, and all that sort of thing? *(Sits on a sofa)*

GILBERT: *(Stands center)* Oh, about as usual. Pretty hot when we started, but cooled off when we came up north.

DEAN: *(Down left)* How long does that trip take, anyhow? Three weeks, isn't it? (OSCAR *crosses up and sits on chair right.)*

GILBERT: Eighteen and a half days, as a rule, with fair weather. Let me see—yes, we made it in eighteen and a half days, this time.

GWEN: Oh, what a trip! I'd be bored to death, wouldn't you? *(To* JULIE*)*

JULIE: Why—I don't know. No. The boat might be full of dashing young Brazilians, or one or tow of the Horsemen of the Apocalypse——

GILBERT: As a matter of fact, there was a very representative crowd on board this trip. Some of the biggest planters in South America. Zamaco. Manolo. Berlanga.

FANNY: Really?

GILBERT: *(A sudden recollection)* Oh, here's something that'll interest you folks. *(Crosses left.)* There was a theatrical troupe on board. American. They'd been down in Buenos Aires trying to play in English. Ridiculous, of course! Poor devils! Didn't even have enough to pay their passage. There they all were, on the dock. Of course we couldn't see them stranded. So we got together enough to see them home. I guess I felt sentimental about them on account of you people.

JULIE: Oh! *(A second's rather terrible pause)*

FANNY: Really!

GILBERT: Seems the manager skipped out with the money. You know the way those fellows are. *(Crosses to center)* Think they'd be down-hearted, but they were carefree enough, once they got on the boat. Turned out to be a very decent lot. *(Sits on sofa)* Couple of them were married—uh—lived in Jersey some place—had—uh—— *(JO has entered during this speech.)*

(This speech of GILBERT'S *has been received with a mannerly but stony silence on the part of the* CAVENDISH *family.)*

FANNY: I'll go in and finish my tea. *(To* JULIE *and* GILBERT.*)* . . . Jo, some hot water. Put a log on the fire.

(She goes toward library as she speaks. Exits library. JO *exits right.* GIL *and* PERRY *rise.* DEAN *and* KITTY *exit in* FANNY'S *wake.)*

GWEN: *(Rather breathlessly)* Is is true that it's winter in South America when it's summer in New York?

GILBERT: Yes. The seasons are just the opposite from yours.

GWEN: How funny? *(Crossing to left)* But then I suppose they think we're funny.

GILBERT: No. You see, they travel a great deal—understand how it is.

GWEN: Oh. *(Indicates to* PERRY *to come along)*

GILBERT: Well! And so you've got a family now, h'm? How is she? Am I going to see her?

PERRY: She's a boy. *(Crossing left to* GWEN*)*

GILBERT: Well, that was a boner, wasn't it! Anyhow, I imagine you're the busy little wife and mother nowadays. No more of this theatrical business, h'm?

GWEN: Well——

JULIE: Gwen is going to into a new play. *(Rise, goes right)*

PERRY: Yes.

GILBERT: A new play! Why, how old is your child!

GWEN: Not old enough to miss me—is he, Perry? . . . Come on, let's have some tea.

(GWEN *exits into library.* PERRY *looks at* GILBERT. *There is a foolish little grin on his face. Exits after* GWEN)

WOLFE: I hope to see you again, Mr. Gilbert Marshall. *(Exits library)*

(The door closes part way as he draws it behind him on leaving. GILBERT *acknowledges this with a little formal nod. He waits for the library door to close partly. Turns eagerly await her)*

GILBERT: Julie! Julie! How I've missed you! *(Goes to her)*

JULIE: Gil! How could you!

GILBERT: What!

JULIE: How could you talk like that! Didn't you see how they—— Oh Gil!

GILBERT: What do you mean? What did I do!

JULIE: You—Oh, never mind. It doesn't matter.

GILBERT: But Julie, if you'd just tell me. What was it!

JULIE: No . . . Tell me about your . . . trip, Gil. Did you have a nice time? *(Crosses to sofa—sits)*

GILBERT: The trip didn't matter. It just meant reaching you. You're looking just lovely, Julie. I've never seen you so beautiful. *(She turns a cheek to him, coldly. There is nothing else she can do.)* It's been the longest six months of my life. When you finally wired that the end was in sight—that the play was actually closing— do you know what I did? I gave everybody on the place a holiday with double pay.

JULIE: I'm very—honored.

GILBERT: *(Sits on arm of sofa, right)* They're like a lot of children, down there. It's a great country, Julie.

JULIE: It must be.

GILBERT: It's as different from the life up here as you can imagine. You'll love it. At Cordoba I was in bed every night at ten o'-clock, for four months. Up at six, in the saddle eight hours a day.

JULIE: Oh! Yes?

GILBERT: Julie. It's so beautiful—and peaceful—and big! And you'll meet real people. None of your . . . Solid! Substantial! The kind that make a country what it is. This man Zamaco who was on the boat. He's my nearest neighbor, you know. Has the next estancia.

JULIE: Oh, yes. You told me.

GILBERT: Yes, indeed. You'll see a lot of the Zamacos. He's a Spaniard of the highest type—very big cattle man. She was a Kansas City girl—Krantz—you know—daughter of Julius Krantz—the packer.

JULIE: Oh! Julius Krantz.

GILBERT: Very fine woman, and most entertaining.

JULIE: I'm sure.

GILBERT: They're stopping at the Ritz. I thought we'd dine together Sunday night—the four of us—they're getting tickets for a concert some place—she used to be quite a harpist, you know.

JULIE: No, I didn't.

GILBERT: Of course it'll be wonderful for you—having her only thirty miles from us. She'll be company for you while I'm off at the mines.

JULIE: Mines?

GILBERT: Though for that matter, you'd be perfectly safe alone. There are fifteen house servants and most of them have been there for years. Old Sebastian, for example. Do you know what he'll do, if necessary? He'll sleep on the floor outside your door all night.

JULIE: Oh, no—really, I'd rather he didn't. You see, I'd start getting sorry for him, and I'd give him one of my pillows, and then a blanket, and pretty soon I'd be out there and he'd be in the bed.

GILBERT: *(A mirthless laugh)* But the place you'll love—is England, Julie. The absolute quiet of it—you know English people— they never intrude. I don't see any of the country people except Hubert Randolph. He and Lady Randolph have the Wyckhamshire place. Isn't a finer man in England, to my way of thinking. And very amusing. Anybody who says the English haven't got a sense of humor doesn't know Randolph. He'll stand there, sober as a judge—you won't think he's going to say a word—suddenly he'll get off something that'll make you laugh every time you think of it.

JULIE: Such as what?

*(*DOOR BELL*)*

GILBERT: Oh, I don't know. It isn't what he says, so much as the way he says it. He's a great fellow. One thing I've found, Julie, is that for real people you've got to go to——*(Door bell rings.)*

JULIE: *(Relieved at the interruption)* Oh, that's the baby, I guess. Gwen! I guess this is the baby!

*(*GILBERT *and* JULIE *go right.)*

GILBERT: Huh! Oh! Gwen's baby. *(*JO *enters door left. Goes to outer door)*

JULIE: Where do you want him, you people? Here's the baby!

*(*WOLFE *and* GWEN *enter, the former with his arm about* GWEN'S *shoulder. She is smiling up at him, he looking down at her. They have evidently been having a chummy conversation.)*

WOLFE: *(On the entrance)* . . . and I know what I'm talking about.

JULIE: Say, what are you two so chummy about?

WOLFE: We two? We got our secrets. *(To* GWEN*)* Ain't we?

GWEN: Big guilty ones.

WOLFE: You bet we have! You go ahead—relax. We get along.

*(*JO *has opened the outer door. There is heard a bedlam of barking—*

more than one dog, certainly. Sounds of voices—"Quiet there! Down! Shut up! What's the matter with you.")

JO: *(A voice off)* Well, who'd of thought . . . What! . . .

JULIE: Good heavens! What's that! What is it!

(There appears in the hallway two HALLBOYS laden with baggage—bags—boxes—a sun machine and a monkey in a cage—next the tall, sinister figure of GUNGA. He is an East Indian, wearing his native costume, with turban. On his shoulder is a brilliant-hued bird as large as a parrot. He stands silent after his entrance. This figure is greeted with a little involuntary shriek of terror from JULIE.)

JULIE: Oh! What's that!

GWEN: Oh, look at him!

WOLFE: Say, what in God's name! . . .

GILBERT: What's going on?

(TONY enters. Ahead of him, straining at the leash, are two huge police dogs. TONY wears a dashing top coat of camel's hair, and a light felt hat with a brush or feather in it, of the sort one sees in the Austrian Tyrol. On his entrance he is admonishing the dogs.)

TONY: Here, here! Where're you going? Not so fast!

JULIE: Tony! Tony!

WOLFE: Tony! Is it you!

GWEN: Why, Tony!

(FANNY enters. DEAN, KITTY and PERRY follow in the background. Following close on TONY is JO. The luggage is of surprising size, quantity and richness.)

TONY: *(Casually)* Hello, Sis! How've you been? . . . Hi, Gwen . . . Oscar . . . Say, Jo, got any beefsteak? *(Indicates dogs)*

JULIE: Tony, where have you come from? Why didn't you let us know?

(JO takes the dogs from TONY and goes off right with them. DELLA

*comes running on, right. There now follows a babel of greetings, ex-
clamations.)*

FANNY: Tony! For God's sake!

KITTY: How did you get here?

DEAN: Of all the surprises!

GWEN: Why didn't you radio?

TONY: Hush, my pretties! Tell you all about it in a minute. All the
fascinating facts. *(He turns to the Indian servant)* Gunga!

GUNGA: Waguha!

TONY: Mem singha salah ronhamar. Pondero mulah giva. Salah
Singha Ronhamar. Gahlef! Della, show him where to go, will
you?

DELLA: *(Awed)* Yes, sir.

*(Jo re-enters at right. Helps with the luggage. During the next few
speeches, DELLA, GUNGA and the HALLBOY and JO carry everything upstairs. Exit center of balcony. TONY gives his coat and hat
to JO as he passes.)*

FANNY: Is he going to stay in the house?

TONY: Gunga? He saved my life over in India. Another minute and
the tiger'd have had me.

JULIE: Tony, what do you mean by doing a thing like this! Bursting
in on us this way! Why didn't you let us know!

TONY: I was afraid to let you know. That's why I came by way of
Canada. I landed in Canada.

FANNY, DEAN, GWEN, KITTY: Canada!

JULIE: Why?

TONY: Because Albania and Schlesingen were going to declare war
on each other. I knew if I got out she'd marry him and everything would be all right.

JULIE: Who'd marry whom!

FANNY: What's that!

DEAN: What's he talking about?

GWEN: He's making it up.

TONY: It's been in the papers! Natalia broke off her engagement with Rupert of Schlesingen. Then the Albanians . . .

JULIE: Wait a minute!

GWEN: Hold on.

KITTY: Who is she?

DEAN: Natalia!

WOLFE: Natalia! Natalia!

FANNY: Who's Natalia?

TONY: Natalia's the Princess of Albania. She's a nice kid, but God! I didn't mean anything serious. That's the trouble with those princesses. Sheltered lives. Dance with 'em a couple of times and they want to elope with you. Of course, when she broke off with Rupert, and the Prime Minister sent for me——

JULIE: Oh! I'm beginning to understand. You've started a European war.

(PERRY *during this speech joins* GILBERT, *right.*)

TONY: Oh, I don't think they'll fight. She'll get over it . . . Anyhow, that isn't why I came home. Oscar, listen! I was cruising around the Bayer-strasse in Koenigsberg one night, and I happened to pass a little theatre. Stuck away in a courtyard. There was a poster of this thing outside. I started to read it—I don't know, I got a hunch about it, and went in. (GILBERT *and* PERRY *find their interest in this narrative flagging. They stand a little apart from the group, hands in pockets, thoughtful.*) Well, say!

WOLFE: Good, huh?

TONY: Good? It's the God-damnedest play I ever saw in my life, and I bought it. You're to write 'em three thousand dollars tomorrow. American money.

WOLFE: You bought it?

FANNY: What for?

JULIE: Yes, what for?

TONY: What for? I'm going to act in it, of course.

GWEN: Really?

FANNY: Well, that's fine. *(Rises, goes to* TONY*)*

DEAN: I'm glad of that, Tony.

WOLFE: You don't say. *(He turns to see the effect of this revelation on* JULIE. *She is mildly stunned.)*

JULIE: Tony, you don't mean pictures? You're going back on the stage?

KITTY: Of course. *(To* TONY*)* Don't you?

TONY: Do I? Wait till you see this play, Oscar. Reinhardt's going to do it in Berlin, and Pitoeff's got the French rights.

WOLFE: Well, what's it all about? What's so wonderful?

TONY: Look! I'll show you. *(As this account gets under way,* GILBERT *and* PERRY *withdraw a little further from the group. Presently their eyes meet; there is a flash of understanding between them. In a moment they are deep in conversation. For the present, however, they are drowned by* TONY'S *voice.)* If this doesn't bowl you over, I'll go back to the Ganges. *(He is pulling a pile of assorted papers out of his pocket. He turns* FANNY'S *chair back to audience, placing his papers on it. Quickly selects the one he wants; lets the others drop to the ground.)* Where the devil—oh, yes. *(Spreads one of them out. They all crowd around.)* Now here's the scene plan. Of course you can't make anything out of this, but I'll show you how it works.

KITTY: What's that there?

TONY: In the first place, they use this new constructivist scenery— grouping the actors on different levels and playing on scene up there and another one down here.

DEAN: Oh, my God!

GWEN: That new German stuff!

TONY: You don't enter or exit in the ordinary sense—you just slide, or else let down by wires. Schwenger, the fellow that does it in Koenigsberg, fainted six times the first night. When they want to show a different scene all they do is switch off the lights down here, switch them on up here. In goes this level, out goes that! It's got every trick of the motion pictures, plus another dimension. Now here's the big kick. See that? Where my finger is?

DEAN: Yes?

KITTY: Yes!

(As they all crane their necks there is just an instant's complete silence. The voice of GILBERT, *talking to* PERRY, *comes up.)*

GILBERT: And that way we cut our overhead fourteen per cent.

TONY: *(As he picks up again, the voice of* GILBERT *is once more drowned.* GILBERT, *in another second, ends his talk with* PERRY, *waits with some impatience for a chance to have a word with* JULIE.*)* That swings the whole thing around—the audience becomes the actors and the actors become the audience.

JULIE: Serves 'em right.

TONY: I tell you it's a knock-out. Of course the great thing about this play is it takes two nights to do it.

FANNY: Two nights!

DEAN: Tony, my boy!

KITTY: I never heard of such a thing.

WOLFE: Only two?

GWEN: You're cuckoo, Tony.

TONY: Now wait a minute. You don't understand what this thing is. It's a modern version of the Passion Play.

WOLFE: *(Fearfully)* And you play—what?

TONY: The lead, of course. It's pure blank verse, and the incidental music—listen. *(He dashes up to the piano, followed by the eager group. Seats himself)* There's a sacrificial motif runs right through—tear your heart out—(He strikes a single chord. Is about to proceed when* GILBERT *breaks in)*

GILBERT: Ah—Tony—Julie, before you start—

JULIE: Huh? . . . Wait a minute, Tony . . . Yes, Gil?

(TONY stops playing. They all pay polite but impatient attention.)

GILBERT: If you people don't mind—I'm awfully sorry—I've got to break away, Julie . . . Glad you're back, Tony, but I've got about an hour's business.

JULIE: Oh, must you go, Gil? I——

GILBERT: Well, I'll be right back. Later, I thought, perhaps we could-

PERRY: Gwen, I think I'll have to go, too . . . seeing this fellow . . . you'll be home, huh?

GWEN: Of course, Perry.

PERRY: Well, then, I'll——

GILBERT: Good-bye, everybody. Good-bye. *(A chorus of heedless good-byes from the group.)* Good-bye . . . Oh, Julie. Where would you like to dine?

JULIE: Huh!

GILBERT: Where would you like to dine?

JULIE: Oh, Gil, I don't think I'll go out to dinner to-night. I'd think I'd better—Tony here—if you don't mind——

GILBERT: I understand. That's all right. I'll call for you at the theatre at eleven. *(GILBERT and PERRY exit outer door.)*

JULIE: *(As he goes)* Uh—yes . . . *(She stands apart from the rest, thoughtful, silent.)*

TONY: *(Picking it up on high)* Now here's the way this thing goes. *(He plays a few impressive chords.)* Then when he comes down from the mountain there's a stunning passage——*(He goes into something subdued and wistful.)*

(He plays for a moment. FANNY, DEAN, KITTY, and GWEN are leaning over the piano. WOLFE stands a little apart from the others, down center, but his head is turned toward TONY, and his attention is on him. JULIE comes down right of WOLFE, puts his hand on his arm to attract his attention. WOLFE turns to JULIE, slowly.)

JULIE: Oscar——

WOLFE: *(Rather absently)* Huh?

JULIE: Why don't you let me read the play?

WOLFE: What?

JULIE: That play by your college professor——Why don't you let me read it?

WOLFE: What do you mean, read it? What for?

JULIE: Why, I just thought I'd like to, that's all. To sort of get an idea of the part.

WOLFE: I'll send you up a manuscript this evening. *(The music ceases; there is a chorus of exclamation and admiration from the group.)*

GWEN: Oh, that's thrilling!

FANNY: Gives me goose-flesh.

DEAN: Very nice—very nice, indeed!

KITTY: Goes right through you!

TONY: But the biggest kick of all comes in the fire-worship scene in the eighth act. They've got a religious procession there, lasts twelve minutes, and, believe me, it's pretty pagan! Oscar, if you can get by with that and not be padlocked——*(Strikes a chord or two. Sings "Boom! Boom!"* DELLA *enters, goes to door.)*

(DOOR BELL)

(MISS PEAKE, the nurse, enters from outer door with the baby in her arms. DELLA *follows and crosses left.)*

JULIE: It's the baby! Look! It's the baby!

(The group breaks. They leave TONY *and the piano and surround the baby. There is a good deal of clucking and kitzakitzing and those strange noises with which adults seek to divert the helpless infant. Overlap these speeches)*

KITTY: Isn't he darling?

JULIE: Tony, look! You've never seen him before!

BERT: Well, what do you think of him?

FANNY: Give him to me. Give him to me. (*He is passed over to her*) Well! There you are! (*Comes center*)

KITTY: He is cute!

TONY: (*Rises from piano*) I think he's terrible. (*Sits as before*)

FANNY: (*Standing the baby in one arm. Indicates the portrait of* AUBREY CAVENDISH *on the wall*) Do you know who that is, young man? You were named for him. Aubrey Cavendish Stewart, and, and see that you live up to it . . .

JULIE: Mother, do you think you ought to hold him?

FANNY: Now, now! I guess I can hold a baby!

WOLFE: Here you are. Sit down. (FANNY *sits in her chair, her back to audience.*)

KITTY: Ooooooo! Who you staring at, ooo big eyes! Ooo great big eyes sing!

GWEN: Miss Peake, don't you want to take his coat off?

MISS PEAKE: I think it's a bit chilly in here, Mrs. Stewart.

KITTY: Oh, he can't keep his coat on.

JULIE: Let's take him in by the fire.

DELLA: (*At tea table*) Another cocktail, Mr. Dean. (DEAN *crosses and takes cocktail.*)

GWEN: We've got to take him in by the fire, people.

WOLFE: (*Stooping to survey the baby*) Say, that young fellow is a Cavendish, all right! He can't deny that!

DEAN: By Jove, Fanny! He does look like Aubrey!

KITTY: Do you think you'll be an actor?

WOLFE: Say, he shouldn't be an actor! Look at him! (*A sudden idea. A snap of the fingers*) Here's an idea!

GWEN: Yes? What?

WOLFE: Listen, show folks! I got a great new play I'm going to pro-duce—(*A side look at* JULIE)—and in it they talk all the time about a baby. Why shouldn't we have a scene where the baby is carried on, and—(*A gesture toward the baby.* DELLA *comes center with tray of cocktails.*)

GWEN: You're crazy, Wolfey! Perry wouldn't hear of it.

JULIE: Gwen, he'll have to start some time.

FANNY: Certainly will!

DEAN: (*Holding up his cocktail glass and signalling the others to join him*) Here's to Aubrey Cavendish Stewart! (*A chorus of assent from the others. A little rush for the cocktails.*)

ALL: Yes! Yes! Aubrey!

TONY: (*Gives a glass to* FANNY) Here you are, Fanny! (*Holds aloft his glass*) To the kid!

FANNY: (*The child in her arm. Takes the glass in her hand. Holds it aloft*) To Aubrey Cavendish!

GWEN: Stewart!

FANNY: That won't stop him! He's a Cavendish, and he's going to carry on! We always have, and we always will. "When one drops out there's always another to take his place. When one drops out there's always been another" . . .

JULIE: Now, mother . . .

FANNY: To the future greatest actor of his day! Aubrey Cavendish Second! (*They all drink.*)

MISS PEAKE: I really think, Mrs. Stewart——

GWEN: (*Takes the child from* FANNY) Yes. All right, Miss Peake. Come on, everybody. He's got to go in where it's warm.

(*A general movement toward the library door. More clucking and hubbub over the child. "Look! He's laughing! . . . Here we go! . . . He knows what it's all about . . ."*)

TONY: Wait till you hear the ballet music, you people! How's this piano?

JULIE: Come on, mother dear.

(*All except* FANNY *exit into library. The noise goes on from there, fainter, of course, but still heard, very merry.* TONY *is playing some gay strains on the off-stage piano.* FANNY *has remained in her chair. As the others have passed into the next room, she now attempts to rise, her cane falls from her hand and she sinks back in the chair.)*

DELLA: *(When the cane falls.* DELLA *counts eight and enters)* Isn't he the cute one, though? *(She exits into library.)*

(After DELLA *exits,* FANNY, *slowly lifts the glass to the picture of her late husband,* AUBREY CAVENDISH. *She again attempts to rise, but the glass falls to the floor and the hand that held it drops to the side—and her head falls forward. There is a moment's pause. The voices from the next room come up, high and gay, and there is laughter, and chirping to the baby.)*

GWEN: *(Voice from the library)* Where's Fanny?

JULIE: Where's Mother? . . . Mother, come on in. See what he's doing now! Mother, where are you? *(Appears in library doorway.)* Mother, come on in. He just did the cutest——*(Stops, startled, at something queer in the figure huddled in the chair. Comes quickly, fearfully, crosses to the chair, one hand outstretched. Comes around in front of chair. Touches* FANNY. *Calls)* Gwen! Tony! Oscar!

(At the note in her voice they come, streaming in slowly, talking a little, perhaps, in a subdued tone, and rather apprehensive. At look in JULIE'S *face they are warned. Their faces take on a stricken look. Awed, fearful, they tiptoe toward the still form in the chair.)*

CURTAIN

DINNER AT EIGHT

GEORGE S. KAUFMAN
AND EDNA FERBER

Copy of program of the first performance of "DINNER AT EIGHT" as produced by Sam H. Harris at the Music Box, New York, with the following cast:

MILLICENT JORDAN	Ann Andrews
DORA	Mary Murray
GUSTAVE	Gregory Gaye
OLIVER JORDAN	Malcolm Duncan
PAULA JORDAN	Marguerite Churchill
RICCI	Cesar Romero
HATTIE LOOMIS	Margaret Dale
MISS COPELAND	Vera Hurst
CARLOTTA VANCE	Constance Collier
DAN PACKARD	Paul Harvey
KITTY PACKARD	Judith Wood
TINA	Janet Fox
DR. J. WAYNE TALBOT	Austin Fairman
LARRY RENAULT	Conway Tearle
THE BELLBOY	Robert Griffith
THE WAITER	James Seeley
MAX KANE	Sam Levene
MR. HATFIELD	William McFadden
MISS ALDEN	Ethel Intropodi
LUCY TALBOT	Olive Wyndham
MRS. WENDEL	Dorothy Walters
JO STENGEL	Frank Manning
MR. FITCH	George Allson
ED LOOMIS	Ham Robert

FROM THE SOCIETY COLUMN OF THE
NEW YORK TIMES

. . . who will sail for Bermuda on the tenth.

Mr. and Mrs. Oliver Jordan, of 927 Park Avenue, entertained at dinner last night in honor of Lord and Lady Ferncliffe. Their guests included Miss Carlotta Vance, Mr. and Mrs. Daniel Packard, Dr. and Mrs. J. Wayne Talbot, and Mr. Larry Renault. Following the dinner Mr. and Mrs. Jordan and their guests attended a musical comedy.

The list of patronesses for the Riverdale House benefit will include Mrs. G. Orton Stanhope. . .

DINNER AT EIGHT
STORY OF THE PLAY

Mrs. Jordan, of the fashionable New York Jordans, is responsible for this many-sided episode in New York life. Lord and Lady Ferncliffe, bound for New York, have accepted by wireless an invitation to dine at her house. Whereupon she sits down to the telephone to invite as guests the people who are eligible, and the flurry of organizing a dinner gets under way. "Dinner At Eight" goes skipping around the city to reveal the background of each of the invited guests. At dinner they will be an immaculate gathering revealing nothing of themselves. But while Mrs. Jordan is absorbed in the turmoil of organizing a dinner you acquire information of which she is quite unaware. She does not know, for example, that her husband is failing in business and that he is stricken with heart disease that is numbering his days. She does not know that the flamboyant Dan Packard, whom she is inviting, is secretly acquiring the old family business that pays for her dinner, nor that Mrs. Packard has been relieving the boredom of her footless existence by a secret amour with Doctor Talbot. Nor does Mrs. Jordan know that the famous movie star, Larry Renault, is her daughter's lover, or that Renault, for all his pompous grandeur, is penniless and on the brink of suicide. She knows nothing of the tragic drama that is going on at that moment in her servants' hall. All this hidden anguish which touches her vitally and gives her guests strange relationships, Mrs. Jordan has neither the time nor the ability to comprehend.

At the last moment Lord and Lady Ferncliffe break their engagement and remove the only reason there can be for such an imposing assembly. In the concluding-scene, set in the Jordan drawing-room, all the guests save one dutifully gather, hear the news of the nobility's defection, chatter innocuously and drift off to the dining-room.

THE SCENE

ACT ONE

SCENE I: Upstairs sitting-room in the New York house of Mr. and Mrs.Oliver Jordan. Ten AM.

SCENE II: Oliver Jordan's office. Two-thirty PM.

SCENE III: The home of the Packards. Four-thirty PM.

SCENE IV: The Jordan sitting-room. Five-thirty PM.

ACT TWO

A Week Later

SCENE I: Larry Renault's apartment in the Hotel Versailles. Four PM.

SCENE II: Dr. Talbot's office. Five PM.

SCENE III: Butler's pantry in the home of the Jordans. Five-thirty. PM

SCENE IV. The sitting-room. Six PM.

ACT THREE

SCENE I: The Packard home. Seven-thirty. PM

SCENE. II: Larry Renault's apartment. Seven forty-five. PM

SCENE III: The Jordan drawing-room. Eight PM.

DESCRIPTION OF CHARACTERS

MILLICENT JORDAN: She is a pretty, rather vapid woman of thirty-nine.

DORA: A maid, young and attractive.

GUSTAVE: The butler, is about thirty-five, of light complexion and good-looking in a vaguely foreign way.

OLIVER JORDAN: A man in his early forties; quiet, well-bred, sensitive. You are rather surprised to learn that he is in business.

PAULA JORDAN: Nineteen, modern, chic.

RICCI is a tall, Saturnine Italian; slim, graceful and a little sinister.

HATTIE LOOMIS: MRS. JORDAN'S sister. A few years older than MILLICENT, and attractive-looking in spite of a harassed and rather bitter expression.

MISS COPELAND is a spare and spinsterish forty eight.

CARLOTTA VANCE is a battered beauty of, perhaps, fifty-three. She cannot be said to be faded, for there still is about her a magnificent vitality and zest. Her figure is gone, for she likes good living, and in the past twelve or fifteen years has given up the struggle. There clings to her, intangibly, much of the splendor, the success, the elan of the old days when she was a famous theatrical beauty and the mistress of millions.

DAN PACKARD is one of those big, vital men; bellowing, self-important, too successful. His clothes are noticeable. He seems never to sit down, ramps and gesticulates as he talks, and he talks a great deal. He is always in the midst of a big deal, and curiously enough it really is a big deal. Every now and then, in his talk or in his manner, there crops up a word or gesture reminiscent of his western mining-days.

KITTY PACKARD: A pretty woman of twenty-nine; the slightly faded wild- rose Irish type. She was Kitty Sheehan before her marriage. There is, in her face, the petulance of the idle and empty-headed wife.

TINA: A somewhat hard-faced, capable and shifty girl of twenty-five or six.

DOCTOR TALBOT is happy in the possession of a good figure, a conventionally handsome face, a dark neat mustache, a reassuring bedside manner. Perhaps forty-six.

LARRY RENAULT is a handsome man in his early forties, with the perfect profile that so gracefully lends itself to a successful motion picture career. His figure still passes, but about the whole man there are the unmistakable marks of middle-age, abetted by pretty steady drinking, increasing failure, and disappointment. It is a vain and weak face, but not unappealing.

EDDIE: The bellboy.

MAX KANE: A small, tight, slim, eel-like man in his thirties; swarthy, neat, and very Broadway. He is unmistakably Jewish, but he does not talk with an accent, unless it is the accent of the Cockney New Yorker.

MR. HATFIELD: A suave figure in a cutaway coat and striped trousers.

MISS ALDEN: She is about twenty-seven, poised, capable without being bustling, intelligent, and attractive in her white uniform.

LUCY TALBOT: She a wren-like, somewhat faded little figure, but possessed of a quiet power, too, as well as poise and gentle breeding.

MRS. WENDEL is Swedish, but with no trace of accent. She is an ample woman in her mid-fifties. Her natural amiability is clouded at the moment by a bad tooth, and her face is tied up in a great toothache bandage.

JO STENGEL is about sixty. His hair is well grayed. He is kindly looking. Time has refined his features. His eyes are shrewd, his manner quiet, yet there is about him the indefinable air of the showman.

FITCH: In his business suit and eyeglasses, is the solid man of affairs.

ED LOOMIS would be one of those insignificant, grayish-looking men if it were not that he is distinguished a trifle by his air of irascibility, due probably, to faulty digestion and the world in which he finds himself.

ACT ONE

SCENE I

Upstairs sitting-room in the OLIVER JORDANS' *home. A door down Right leads to the hall. Above it is a small table on which is a lamp; above that a fireplace over which hangs a Cezanne landscape. In the Center of the back wall, three large windows, curtained, draped, and with Venetian blinds which, though drawn, admit brilliant sunshine. In front of the window, a long table on which are two lamps, books and magazines. A sofa down Right, an upholstered chair Left of Center. A door leading to* MILLICENT'S *bedroom up Left. Down Left, against the wall, is a desk and small chair. Right of the chair is a breakfast table. Altogether, it is a luxurious and rather feminine room.*

It is ten o'clock of a bright November morning. MILLICENT *is breakfasting in a negligee. She is a pretty, rather vapid woman of thirty-nine. She is dividing her attention between her orange juice and the letter in her hand. A folded copy of the "Herald-Tribune" is on the chair L.C.*

As the Curtain rises, DORA, *a maid, young and attractive, comes from the bedroom, L., a dress thrown over her arm. She crosses and goes into the hall, R. As she reaches Center, the butler enters R. from the hall.* GUSTAVE *is about thirty-five, of light complexion, and good-looking in a vaguely foreign way. He brings a silver pot of coffee.*

MILLICENT: *(Feeling the side of the coffee-pot)* I hope it's hot this time.

GUSTAVE: Very hot, madam. *(He turns to leave. Her voice halts him.)*

MILLICENT: *(Pouring coffee)* I shan't be home to lunch. Mr. Jordan and I are out to dinner. I don't know about Miss Paula. I'll have to ask her.

GUSTAVE: Very good, Madam.

MILLICENT: Tell Ricci I want to see him before he takes Mr. Jordan to the office.

(RICCI *nods; exits R.* MILLICENT *has poured her coffee; starts to drink it as* OLIVER JORDAN *enters R. A man in his early forties, quiet, well bred, sensitive. You are rather surprised to learn that he is in business. His topcoat is over his arm, his hat in hand. He has just popped in to say good-morning and goodbye)*

OLIVER: *(Hat and coat on couch)* Hello, darling. You're early!

MILLICENT: Oh, hello.

OLIVER: We could have had breakfast together if I'd known. Unless you think people might talk. *(He stoops for a perfunctory kiss. She, her eye.still on the letter in her hand, presents a cool, wifely cheek. He catches sight of a plate of thimble-size popovers on the table. Begins to nibble one)* Mm! They didn't give me any of those.

MILLICENT: *(Absently, busy with her mail)* I shouldn't have them, either. *(Dashes a printed card into the waste-basket)* Join Cooper Union!

OLIVER: How'd you sleep? Better? *(Sits on arm of chair L.C., glancing through newspaper.)*

MILLICENT: Never closed an eye. Then the minute I dropped off the fire-engines woke me up.

OLIVER: Where do they go every night? I've never seen a fire in New York. I think they go around looking for them.

MILLICENT: *(Who has opened another letter)* Well! This is too shocking! (OLIVER *looks up from paper.)* Peggy Mainwaring is starting a night club in her lovely old house in Sutton Place.

OLIVER: Really?

MILLICENT: *(Still reading)* "Opening attraction—Schnozzle Levine."

OLIVER: Old Lady Mainwaring must be whirling in her grave.

MILLICENT: *(Tosses letter into waste-basket)* Well, at least it'll keep Peggy out of Harlem.

OLIVER: *(Rises. About to go)* What's on for tonight? We're home, I hope.

MILLICENT: Oh, now, darling, you know perfectly well tonight's the Hilliards' costume party.

OLIVER: Oh, look here, Millicent. D'you mean I have to go as something?

MILLICENT: Oh, you'll love it. I got you Richard the Conqueror, and I'm a Floradora Girl. *(Returns to her letters.)*

OLIVER: Makes an ideal couple.

MILLICENT: I wanted Tarzan for you, but it's so draughty at the Hilliards'!

OLIVER: Look here—it's a late affair. We can have dinner at home, h'm?

MILLICENT: We're dining with the Cartwrights and going on-from there.

OLIVER: And I have to go through dinner in that armor! *(GUSTAVE enters R., carrying radiogram on small tray; crosses to MILLICENT)*

MILLICENT: *(A soothing smile)* Well, we're home tomorrow night.

OLIVER: Thank God!

MILLICENT: The Martins are coming in for bridge. *(His look says "And you call that an evening at home!" picks up his topcoat; starts to put it on.)*

GUSTAVE: This just came, Mrs. Jordan. *(GUSTAVE goes out R.)*

MILLICENT: Oh, good! Wait a minute, Oliver. *(Opens and reads radio to herself, mumbling a word or two as she deciphers its meaning)* "Delighted. Friday———" Listen to this, Oliver. I've got the Ferncliffes

OLIVER: *(Momentarily arrested)* What?

MILLICENT: Lord and Lady Ferncliffe. They get in this morning on the Aquitania. I sent them a radio last night, and they're coming to dinner Friday. Wasn't that bright of me?

OLIVER: Yes—if you want the Ferncliffes.

MILLICENT: Want them! Why, you know everybody'll pounce on them. Besides, we've got to have them, They entertained us in London.

OLIVER: *(Sits arm of L.C. chair)* Yes, and very dull it was, too.

MILLICENT: Oh, I don't know. I like those formal English dinners.

OLIVER: Not that one. All family portraits and Australian mutton and fox-hunting and Lloyd George. And the guests! A lot of people who had been buried for years, and who got up just. for that dinner.

MILLICENT: Don't be American, Oliver. It's a great coup for me to get them Friday. That gives me just a week.

OLIVER: Friday!—I was taking Paula to the opera.

MILLICENT: Huh? I thought just a small dinner. What do you think? Ten's a nice number.

OLIVER: *(Overcome)* Oo! Fascinating number.

MILLICENT: Of course it's terribly short notice. I thought I'd ask the Talbots—the Doctor and Lucy. The Ferncliffes and you and I are six. And your precious Carlotta Vance. Would you like me to ask her?

OLIVER: Oh, fine! I haven't seen her.

MILLICENT: I think it's sweet of me. *(Thoughtfully)* Of course, she's never met the Ferncliffes. She goes with a much faster crowd over there.

OLIVER: Carlotta! She knows everybody in Europe.

MILLICENT: Not the Ferncliffes. She's too flamboyant. Now let me see. I'll need just one more couple, and an extra man. *(Rummaging through her address book)* I'll be all morning telephoning. Talbot—Talbot, Butterfield eight six-three-twofive. *(Scribbles it on a slip of paper.)*

OLIVER: *(Who has been turning something over in his mind, rises)* Look here, dear. If you're looking for another couple—

MILLICENT: *(Her eye still on the slip)* Butterfi— what?

OLIVER: If you need another couple I wish you'd ask Dan Packard and his wife.

MILLICENT: You're joking!

OLIVER: I know it sounds funny, but there's a reason.

MILLICENT: But with the Ferncliffes!

OLIVER: They'll like him. Over there they like that two-fisted Western stuff.

MILLICENT: And what about her! I suppose they'll like her, too!

OLIVER: They'll think she's very refreshing. Look here, Millicent, I wouldn't ask this if it weren't important to me. You know that Packard's become a big man in the last year or so. I don't want to go into details, but it's—damned important.

MILLICENT: *(Realizing his earnestness, and weakening slightly)* Oh, Oliver.

(PAULA JORDAN enters R. Nineteen, modern, chic. She is dressed for the street.)

PAULA: *(Pulling on her gloves)* Off to the marts of trade. Hello, Mother! Dad, what're you lolling in boudoirs for? What's become of the shipping business? *(Kisses him on cheek.)*

OLIVER: What indeed! Mm! Don't you look smart!

PAULA: Next year's style. I won't be home for dinner, Mother. Ooh, I'm late! *(DORA enters R. with fresh linen over her arm; crosses to bedroom)*

MILLICENT: What about this afternoon, Paula? Where am I meeting you?

PAULA: Hm?

OLIVER:. *(Has picked up hat and coat. Looks at MILLICENT.)* Look here, Millicent, you'll do that for me, won't you?

PAULA: Do what?

MILLICENT: Well, if it's as important as you say.

OLIVER: Believe me it is.

MILLICENT: Oh, well—

OLIVER: That's my brave girl! Thanks— Drop you, Paula?

PAULA: *(With a shake of the head)* Walking. *(OLIVER exits R.)*

MILLICENT: *(Calls after him)* I want to see Ricci before you go.

OLIVER: *(From down the hall)* Right!

PAULA: Mother; I can't meet you this afternoon. I simply can't.

MILLICENT: Paula, you've put it off time after time. The mono-gramming takes months. When do you expect to get things?

PAULA: It can't be today, We're giving a tea at the office for Chanel.

MILLICENT: If that silly magazine is more important to you—After all, I'm not the one that's being married.

PAULA: But there's loads of time.

MILLICENT: There's not loads of time. You're being married in three months and not a stitch of trousseau.

PAULA: I'm not the girl to gloat over a linen closet. All tied up with little pink bows. *(A vicious gesture)* I'll get everything when the time comes.

MILLICENT: Well, for an engaged girl you're certainly casual. Do you act like that with Ernest?

PAULA: Ernest says I'm a flawless fiancée.

MILLICENT: Oh, by the way, what was all this last night?

PAULA: What?

MILLICENT: Ernest called up this morning in a perfect dither. When you weren't up he asked to talk to me.

PAULA: Oh, yes.

MILLICENT: "Did I know how you were feeling, and were you any better?" I told him I didn't know there was anything the matter with you, and he said he brought you home at ten last night with a terrible headache.

PAULA: Yes, I did have. But I'm all right now. *(Starts R.)*

MILLICENT: I distinctly heard you come in at four this morning.

PAULA: *(A trifle dashed)* Oh! Yes! Well I went out again. *(Great frankness)* I took three aspirins, and my headache vanished, and there it was, only eleven o'clock, and some of the crowd called up and said there was a marvelous party going on so I went out again.

MILLICENT: Well, I hope you've got charm enough to explain that to Ernest. Where was the party?

PAULA: Oh—around. We went over to Twenty-One and look, darling, I've just got to run. I'll be home before dinner. I'm going out with Ernest. Will you be here?

MILLICENT: I suppose so. (DORA *appears in. L. doorway.)*

PAULA: Bye! *(Goes out R. quickly.)*

DORA: Mrs. Jordan, do you want the pink to go?

MILLICENT: What?

DORA: I didn't pack the pink because I don't think it needs cleaning.

(GUSTAVE enters R.)

MILLICENT: Oh, I thought it did. I'll look at it. *(Disappearing through L. door, her voice coming out from the next room)* I've worn it five times and I'm sure it must be filthy.

DORA: *(Whispers)* Hello. *(Comes down to GUSTAVE. GUSTAVE draws DORA to him; takes her in his arms. DORA, pleased, but fearing discovery; points toward MRS. JORDAN in bedroom; whispers)* I've got to go. *(She leans close to him.)*

MILLICENT: *(Off stage)* Dora! (DORA *scoots. GUSTAVE picks up the laden tray; goes out R. The voices of MILLICENT and DORA are heard from the bedroom)* Oh, no, Dora. I think it looks dreadful. Pack it in with the others. Really, pink is almost as extravagant as white. It's so hard to keep clean.

DORA: It looks lovely on you.

MILLICENT: I wish I looked well in black. It isn't very good on me. I think I'll wear the beige today. Get it out, will you, Dora? I imagine it needs pressing.

(As the voices are heard in the bedroom, the figure of RICCI the

chauffeur, appears in the R. doorway. He stands a moment, hears the voices of MILLICENT *and* DORA, *and takes a step or two into the room, his eyes on the bedroom doorway.* RICCI *is a tall, saturnine Italian; slim, graceful and a little sinister. He is wearing his chauffeur's uniform, cap in hand.)*

DORA: It probably does.

MILLICENT: Goodness, yes! Take it right down. Have you got everything there for Ricci? I wonder what in the world's keeping him.

DORA: *(Comes in L. the beige dress over her arm. She is walking quickly; sees* RICCI, *who stands regarding her steadily. She starts to go past him. He tries to block her way. She evades him, then calls)* He's here now, Mrs. Jordan.

MILLICENT: *(Off)* Send him right in, will you? *(Their eyes hold a second.* DORA *makes herself very small and aloof as she disdainfully turns from him.* RICCI *straightens his coat as he goes toward L. door.* DORA *exits R.)*

RICCI: Yes, Madam.

MILLICENT: *(Still unseen in the bedroom)* Ricci, after you've taken Mr. Jordan to the office *(She appears in the bedroom doorway at this point with box)*—take this box to Charvet—you know you've been there before—East Fifty-fifth Street. And then you're coming back here for me in time for lunch. Is that clear?

RICCI: *(Takes the box; turns to go R.)* Yes, madam.

MILLICENT: And oh, yes! Stop at Cartier's and see if my stationery is ready. *(He half turns, as if for further orders.)* That's all—Oh, my goodness! I nearly forgot. *(Goes quickly to her desk. Writes a few words on a card as she continues talking)* As soon as you drop Mr. Jordan, go up to Thorley's and get two dozen Talisman roses—long-stemmed. And remember Talisman.

RICCI: Talisman.

MILLICENT: That's right. *(Has finished the card. Is addressing the envelope)* And don't have them sent. Take them over yourself to *(Writing)*—Lady Ferncliffe—Where's that radio *(Searches her*

desk. Finds the radio) Waldorf-Astoria. *(Writes "Waldorf Astoria")*
They'll know. They get in this morning. Is that clear?

RICCI: Perfectly.

MILLICENT: *(A little abstracted)* I think that's all. *(RICCI goes out R.*
MILLICENT sighs deeply. Shuffles a few papers; finds the one she is
seeking. With an eye half on this paper she dials the telephone num-
ber) Is this Doctor Talbot's home?—Is Mrs. Talbot there? This
is Mrs. Oliver Jordan. I want to speak to Mrs. Talbot *(She is*
turning the pages of her own private address book, hunting down cer-
tain telephone numbers as she waits.) Lucy!—This is Millicent.
How are you?—Oh, I'm fine— Listen, Lucy dear, I'm giving a
little dinner for Lord and Lady Ferncliffe. You know they're
here from England. I want you and the Doctor to come. A week
from tonight—Friday—-that'll be lovely. I'm only asking a few
people whom I know they'd like. I'm inviting you informally
like this because the time's so short, and anyway it's just a small
dinner—Yes, that's right. Friday, the twenty-third, at eight o'-
clock. *(HATTIE LOOMIS, MILLICENT'S sister, appears in the R.*
doorway. A few years older than MILLICENT, and attractive-looking
in spite of a harassed and rather bitter expression. Her clothes are
modish enough, but not too new. She is not shabby; neither can she be
called smart. As usual, she is carrying a smallish lumpy brown paper
parcel. MILLICENT sees her; waves a hand) We'll probably see a
play afterward, I think they'd like that, though there's nothing
to see That'll be fine—Goodbye!

HATTIE: What's that? Covers for thirty again?

MILLICENT: No, no. Only ten. The Ferncliffes are over here and
I've just got to entertain them. They gave a dinner for us in
London.

HATTIE: That's fair enough—Listen, Millie, can I have a look at
that blue flat crepe of Paula's remember?—that you promised
me for Joan? Everything's got capes this year and I had this
piece of blue velvet—*(Sits, R. sofa, beginning to open her paper*
parcel)—that I thought might do. But if it's the wrong shade I'll
have to pick up something else.

MILLICENT: Do you have to have it right now? I'm simply—

HATTIE: Don't you bother. I'll tell Dora. I saw her as I—*(Up to hall doorway quickly. Calls)* Dora! *(Back into the room a step or two)* Because if it doesn't match I want to get right down. Everything gets picked over. *(DORA appears in doorway.)*

MILLICENT: Dora, will you go to Miss Paula's room and get that blue crepe dress of hers? You know?

DORA: The evening one?

MILLICENT: Yes. I want to show it to my sister.

(DORA goes out R.)

HATTIE: *(Crossing to L.C. chair)* I hope it's right. Oh, well. When's your dinner?

MILLICENT: A week from tonight.

HATTIE: Just ran into Oliver downstairs. I thought he looked a little underdone. *(Sits L.C., the piece of velvet in her hand, draping it over her arm.)*

MILLICENT: *(Absently. She is at her desk)* What?

HATTIE: As if he could stand a few violet-rays.

MILLICENT: *(Fishes from a desk pigeonhole an impressive announcement card with two colored tickets attached by clips)* Oh, Hattie, what are you doing—*(Consulting card)*—next Monday afternoon?

HATTIE: *(Cagily)* I don't know. Why?

MILLICENT: That Russian Prince of Alison Cruikshank's is giving a talk against Communism in the Rose Room of the Park Lane.

HATTIE: Sorry. I've got to see a man about a dog.

MILLICENT: *(As she turns back to her desk)* Well, I just thought you might use the tickets if you weren't doing anything.

HATTIE: *(One of those indrawn society laughs)* Thank you!

MILLICENT: I wish now I'd never started this miserable dinner. *(In inspiration)* Tommy Van Veen!

HATTIE: What about him?

MILLICENT: My extra man

HATTIE: He's nothing extra.

MILLICENT: If I can only get him. He'd fit in so—(*Turns to her sister*) What do you think? Now, here's the list. (*Reaches for her slip of paper*) I've got the Ferncliffes, of-course—that's what makes it so difficult you see, she's so deaf you have to yell your head off, and all he knows is Parliament and grouse.

HATTIE: Gives you a nice start.

MILLICENT: That isn't the worst. Oliver's got some business thing up his sleeve and insists on my asking those Packards. You know who they are. All the money in the world, and bellows at the top of his lungs.

HATTIE: (*Brightly*) Put him next to Lady Ferncliffe.

MILLICENT: And as for Mrs. Packard! They say she was a checkroom girl, or something. Commonest little piece. She's his second wife—years younger. Of course, it was his money.

HATTIE: It gets better and better. Tell me more about her.

MILLICENT: I met her at the races once. She was beautifully dressed. But the bracelets and the perfume and the makeup—they gave her away at fifty yards. And when she opened that little rosebud mouth well, she spoke pure spearmint.

HATTIE: Ferncliffe'll be crazy about her. He'll probably divorce the old girl.

MILLICENT: There's one good thing—I've got the Talbots. They are sweet. And a doctor always fits in. I think I'll put him next to Carlotta Vance.

HATTIE: Oh, when did she come over?

MILLICENT: A few days ago. I ran into her at The Colony. Of course, I think she's poisonous, but I've got to have her here some time. When I think of the way she behaved that summer at Antibes. You'd think a woman of her age—

HATTIE: Why; she can't be so old.

MILLICENT: Oh, Hattie!

HATTIE: How old was she when she played "La Vailliere? Remember how beautiful she was, and how thrilled we were!

MILLICENT: Well, she doesn't thrill me now, but I've got to have her. We were in and out of her house all that summer. Everybody was. Sunning on her rocks and sprawling on her terrace. It's really astonishing, the people she gets around her over there. Michael Arlen and Willy Maugham and Charlie Chaplin—even Shaw came in one day. I've got to have her.

HATTIE: Yes, have her—if you're sure you don't like her. She just fits in.

MILLICENT: Oliver's fond of her. She was one of his college crushes. He says she's a child about business and advises her. If you ask me, I think she's a man-eating shark. Look at the fortune she got out of old Stanfield. And that theatre named after her. It's hers, you know.

HATTIE: I wish somebody'd name a theatre after me—The Hattie Loomis.

MILLICENT: You know, way down deep I'm really glad to have her. I want to show her there are some people she could never hope to meet over there, but that she can meet in my house.

HATTIE: I see. Who has the choice of weapons?

MILLICENT: (Reaches for the telephone directory under her desk) I don't suppose that Packard woman would be up at this hour.. Oh, dear, when I think of that voice.

HATTIE: Wouldn't it be wonderful if they couldn't come?

MILLICENT: (Running a finger down the P's in the directory) Pablo— Pacific—Packard—

HATTIE: Sometimes I think there are compensations in being a poor relation.

MILLICENT: (At the number now. Writing it on her pad) El-do-ra-do. E-L-five

DORA: (Enters R., carrying the blue dress) It was in with her summer things. I had to find it.

HATTIE: (Rises; crosses as DORA enters. Snatches up piece of velvet) Oh, no It's a million miles off. *(Takes the dress from* Dora *)* I'll have to go down. Thanks, Dora. *(* Dora *goes R.)* It's lovely, though, Millie. *(Holding up the blue dress)* Joan'll look sweet in it.

Millicent: I never liked it much. *(Consults phone pad. Lifts receiver)* Eldorado-five—

Hattie: Joan'll love it. I'll have to run. *(Wraps dress, velvet, in a bundle, hastily)* How I hate matching things.

Millicent: Are you going to stay down for lunch? *(About to start dialing. Abandons it.)*

Hattie: Oh, no, I have to be home.

Millicent: Hattie, if I pick you up, say quarter to three, will you go with me to just to places and look at some stuff for Paula? You're so good at that. She won't do anything about it.*(Starts to dial.)*

(Warn Dim Out)

Hattie: I was going to start this little cape for Joan. She wants to wear it tomorrow night.

Millicent: *(With a gesture that says, "Wait a second a second. I'm busy." Finishes dialing her number. Turns now to Hattie)* You can do it tonight, Hattie. You know you can. You're so quick.

Hattie: I don't like to sit and sew when Ed's home. He hates it. *(Crosses to sofa.)*

Millicent: Oh, he won't mind. Tell him to go to a movie. I'll pick you up at quarter to three. *(In telephone)* Could I speak to Mrs. Packard please? This is Mrs. Oliver Jordan. Is Mrs. Packard up yet?

Hattie: Listen, Millie, I—

Millicent: *(Waiting, receiver in hand)* Please, darling. Ed won't mind. How is Ed? *(Very absent)*

Hattie: He's got the bubonic plague.

Millicent: *(Concentrates on the phone)* That's fine. (Hattie, *with a grim smile, goes out R.* Millicent *has not noticed her departure. Keeps on talking into the phone)* Mrs. Packard? This is Mrs.

Oliver Jordan. How are you? *(Removes receiver a few inches from her ear, with a wry look, as that voice comes over the telephone)* I hope I didn't wake you. Well, I thought this might be a strange hour, for you. Mrs. Packard, Mr. Jordan and I are giving a small dinner for Lord and Lady Ferncliffe, two very dear friends of mine from England. We would like so much to have you and Mr. Packard come. *(She sets her teeth)* Oh, that'll be lovely. I'm so pleased. Well, I'm delighted. Don't you want to know the date? It's a week from tonight. Friday, the twenty-third. I'm inviting you informally like this because the time's so short, and anyway, it's just a small dinner. Friday, the twenty-third. Dinner at eight. *(The LIGHTS start to dim out.)* I thought we'd all go to the theatre afterward, and see a play. Though perhaps you and Mr. Packard would prefer a musical comedy.

THE LIGHTS ARE OUT.

SCENE II

The private office of OLIVER JORDAN, *head of the Jordan Line. It is on the fifth floor of an old-fashioned red brick office build-ing on State Street, facing the Battery. The structure dates back at least fifty years, and now is almost surrounded by modern skyscrap-ers. With the possible exception of a flat-topped desk C., the fur-nishings of the room are those of the day of old Oliver Jordan, grandfather of the present head of the steamship line. Even the chair and a good deal of watch-chain and collar, which, hangs over a black slate mantelpiece with a coal-burning grate. For the rest, there is a wooden filing cabinet; up Right, a decrepit and scuffed leather chair Left of the desk, whose stuffing is oozing here and there. The chair is placed alongside the desk for callers. Another smaller chair is at the back, another Right of the desk. An ancient safe whose door is ornamented with a faded painting of a maritime scene, with ships, scrolls, festoons and border, up Left. There is a wooden door, down Left, with a hatrack above it, and a large win-dow down right, through which can be seen the harbor and bay.*

As the lights go up, MISS COPELAND *is at the files, a sheaf of documents in her hand. Phone.* MISS COPELAND *is a spare and spinsterish forty eight. As the* LIGHTS *go up, the* TELEPHONE *sounds from the desk. It is not the shrill insistent ring one usually hears, but a faint simple tinkle. The connection has come from the outer office. She goes to the telephone.*

MISS COPELAND: Hello! Who? Yes, put him on. I'll talk to him. Yes, Mr. Kingsberry. No, he isn't. Yes, he's always back by this time. He must have gone some place else after lunch. (OLIVER *enters L. puts his coat, hat and stick on the coat-tree in the corner. There is plainly something on his mind.*) Just a minute, Mr. Kingsberry. He just came in. (*To* OLIVER) Mr. Kingsberry on the telephone.

OLIVER: All right. I'll talk to him. (MISS COPELAND *starts to go L.*) When Mr. Packard gets here show him right in.

MISS COPELAND: Yes, sir. (*Goes out L.*)

OLIVER: (*At desk, into telephone*) Yes? Oh, hello, Mr. Kingsberry! I see. Oh, they are? I see. Um..Well, no, I'm not prepared to buy it right now, but you can tell Miss Satterlee and her sister for me that the Jordan stock is just as good today as it was when their father bought it.. allowing, of course, for these times. I'm sure that if Mr. Satterlee had lived he'd have advised them to. Well, the stockholders' meeting is a week from Monday. I wish you'd ask them to hold off until that time. After all, their father and my father were friends for half a century. I think they'd regret any hasty action. Thank you very much for your courtesy. Goodbye. (OLIVER *hangs up the receiver, rises, walks slowly toward the window.* MISS COPELAND *enters L. as he gets to window.*)

MISS COPELAND: (*With great impressiveness*) Miss Carlotta Vance is here to see you.

OLIVER: Carlot—here! Outside! Carlotta! (*Rushes to L.door.*)

(CARLOTTA VANCE *is not one to wait outside. She is already on the threshold, her hands dramatically outstretched to meet his. As they meet,* MISS COPELAND, *lost in admiration, backs out of L. door, her eyes on* CARLOTTA *until the door is closed.* CARLOTTA VANCE *is a battered beauty of, perhaps, fifty-three. She cannot be said to be faded, for there still is about her a magnificent vitality and zest. Her figure is gone, for she likes good living, and in the past twelve or fifteen years has given up the struggle. There clings to her, intangibly, much of the splendour, the success, the elan of the old days when she was a famous theatrical beauty and the mistress of millions. Her dress is rich, careless, and somewhat fussy, what with scarfs, veils, chains, furs, muff. She moves and sits with consciousness of herself. Her speech is racy, biting. She is very much on to herself. There is a little babble of greetings, cooings, exclamations.)*

CARLOTTA: Oliver! Ducky! How are you! How simply marvelous to see you! I never was so glad to see anyone in all my life! *(Kisses him dramatically, on one cheek, then on the other, embracing him.)*

OLIVER: *(At the same time)* Well, for God's sake, Lotta! This is a surprise! What brings you down here! How've you been? I heard you were over here. You're looking marvelous!

CARLOTTA: Do I? I do, don't I? And you! You're actually handsomer than ever. Oh, oh, Oliver! *(Just touches the grey at his temples)* Distinguished!

OLIVER: *(Takes her hand)* This is great! Let me look at you.

CARLOTTA: *(Describes a sweeping circle about the room, for his inspection, but the little parade ends with her rather shrewd eye encompassing the outmoded and shabby surroundings in which she finds herself)* My God, what a hole! Is this what I own stock in? Why I thought it would be all platinum and plush. What do you make down here? Worm holes?

OLIVER: Well—good enough for my father—Gosh, but I'm glad to see you again! I read you'd landed. What're you doing over here?

CARLOTTA: *(Sinks into the depths of the old leather chair L. of desk)* Trying to mend the shattered fortyune.

OLIVER: You picked a good day for it. And the right part of town, too. *(A gesture toward the window)* There are all our financiers, sitting on those benches. Now, who did you come way down to the Battery to see? Not me. *(Sitting on front of desk.)*

CARLOTTA: *(Opening her handbag, fishing a paper from among the debris)* Well, sir, not to deceive you, I came down to see *(Gropes a moment; adjusts her lorgnette carefully. Reads from letter)* United States Customs' Inspector Isidore J. Greenbaum—the son of a bitch! *(Looks up)* Why shouldn't I own six fur coats?

OLIVER: Perfectly reasonable.

CARLOTTA: And then, right in front of the Customs, what did I sight but Jordan Line? And I says to meself, maybe the old gentleman is in. And here you are.

OLIVER: I'm very grateful to Mr. Greenbaum.

CARLOTTA: I told him, I said, "I didn't come to this country to bring money. I came to take it out." Oliver darling, I'm as flat as a mill-pond. I haven't a *sou*.

OLIVER: Oh, now, come, Carlotta! How about all those gilt-edged securities? And your theatre! Why, that theatre alone ought to bring you enough to live on

CARLOTTA: That's my chief reason for coming over. To try to get rid of that rat trap.

OLIVER: What's the matter with it?

CARLOTTA: May I take you for a stroll down Forty-second Street and a little look at the Carlotta Vance Theatre? It's between the Flea Circus and a Hamburg-and-Onion Eatery. It's had six weeks of booking in the past two years. And what were they? Special matinees of a Greek actress named Maria Koreopolous playing Sophocles' "How Are You" in the original Greek. That filled a long-felt want. Then there was a movie week. A big educational film called "The Story of Evolution; or, From Ooze to Hoover," in ten reels. It then swung back to the legitimate with a little gem entitled "Papa Love Mama." Three days. For the past six months they haven't taken the lock off the door. It's now known as the spiders' rendezvous, but you can't collect rent from them!

OLIVER: Well! Then it's not bringing in a cent.

CARLOTTA: So my little problem is to find somebody I can sell it to. Though I don't know what they'd do with it, unless they flood it and use it for swimming pool. *(A sudden thought)* I wonder if I couldn't sell it back to the Stanfield estate. There's an idea. You know, when he gave me that theatre I thought it was pretty magnificent of the old boy. I wish now I'd taken a sandwich.

OLIVER: Oh, now, Lotta, you always exaggerated. I'll bet you're rolling in wealth.

CARLOTTA: What've I got? Railroads, oil, cotton. That's what they gave you in my day. I could only take what they had. You know what's happened to those things.

OLIVER: Well, you are down to cases. "International Beauty Returns To Stage"?

CARLOTTA: Never. I'll have my double chins in privacy. I've seen too many hardened arteries dragged out to make a first-night holiday. Though I must say I saw Julie Cavendish last night and she looked wonderful. Forty-five, if she's a day.

OLIVER: Look here, Carlotta. Your stuff must bring you in a little something. It can't cost you an awful lot to live over there.

CARLOTTA: Oh, no but you saw what it was like in Antibes—you and Millicent. Ten and twenty for lunch—cocktails—most of them stay for dinner. And the house in London. They drop in there Noel and Winston, and now and then the Prince. I've really done pretty well for a little girl from Quincy, Illinois, but it runs into money. And unless you've salted down your million! Look at Lily Langtry! Not half my looks, but she got her Edward. I picked the wrong period. Too young for Edward and too old for Wales. I feel right between princes

OLIVER: Why don't you live over here for a while? Get a little apartment; simplify everything.

CARLOTTA: Oliver, I've been back in New York four days. It's the first time I've been back in ten years. I'm lost already. Everything's changed I'd die here. I belong to the Delmonico period. A table by the window, facing Fifth Avenue, with the flower boxes and the pink lamp shades and the string orchestra. Oh I don't know—willow plumes and Inverness capes, dry champagne and snow on the ground—God, they don't even have snow any more.

MISS COPELAND: *(Enters. A little timid at interrupting)* Pardon me.

OLIVER: Yes, Miss Copeland?

MISS COPELAND: *(A few steps into the room)* Mr. Eaton is on the phone. He's taking a train, and—

OLIVER: All right, I'll talk to him. Hello, Archie! *(To back of desk. In phone. MISS COPELAND is edging off L., with a lingering glance of admiration at CARLOTTA VANCE. CARLOTTA looks up from the depths of her chair with a friendly smile.)*

MISS COPELAND: *(Thus encouraged)* Oh, Miss Vance—I just want to tell you—I hope you won't mind—I can't help telling you how exciting it is, seeing you right here.

OLIVER: *(At telephone)* Yes?

CARLOTTA: Sweet of you

MISS COPELAND: I'll never forget—I saw you in "Trelawney"—oh, you were wonderful.

CARLOTTA: Oh yes. That was the last thing I did.

OLIVER: *(Still at telephone)* I understand.

MISS COPELAND: I remember it as plainly as if it was yesterday. Though I was only a little girl at the time.

CARLOTTA: *(Smile stiffens)* How extraordinary!

MISS COPELAND: *(Backing toward L. door)* Well, I'm glad I had the chance to tell you. It's wonderful seeing you like this. *(MISS COPELAND goes out L.)*

OLIVER: *(At telephone)* That'll be Tuesday? All right. *(He hangs up. Comes front of desk. To CARLOTTA)* Sorry.-You have to work occasionally, even in business. Well, see here, Lotta, I wish there was something I could do to straighten this tangle out for you. I don't think any of my friends need a theatre right now. And as far as your stocks are concerned—those things are still good. And, incidentally, so is your Jordan stock. You're not thinking of selling that, I hope?

CARLOTTA: I don't know, Should I?

OLIVER: Much rather you wouldn't.

CARLOTTA: But, after all, ladies must live.

OLIVER: It's like this, Carlotta. Jordan stock has never been on the market. It's held very closely. Only six or seven people in all. Of course, you've got a very small block. What did you pay for it, anyway? Remember?

CARLOTTA: Sixty-one thousand two hundred and fifty dollars.

OLIVER: *(Amused)* Carlotta, you're wonderful!

CARLOTTA: No. I remember because it's the only stock I ever paid for myself. You said it was a good thing, and it has been, too, for twenty years. Of course, in the last year or two—You wouldn't want to buy it back yourself, would you?

OLIVER: I'd like to, but it would be pretty difficult, just now.

CARLOTTA: Why, I've always thought of you as having all the money in the world.

OLIVER: I thought so too, for a few years.

CARLOTTA: When I think of Oliver Jordan, 3d!

OLIVER: I dropped that long ago.

CARLOTTA: Oliver Jordan at twenty-one! New York was full of gilded youths, but the gold was encrusted on you.

OLIVER: *(Sits on desk)* I suppose I was what they called a stage-door Johnny—though you will admit I never carried a bouquet.

CARLOTTA: You always sent me roses—those deep velvet roses, hundreds and hundreds of them. And not a pearl necklace in a carload.

OLIVER: And you let me read my plays to you, remember? I was going to be a playwright in those days and the hell with the shipping business.

CARLOTTA: Dear Oliver, you were sweet! And so serious and respectful. I was very fond of you, Oliver.

OLIVER: I was very much in love with you, Carlotta. You were the most divine creature in the world. I was at your feet, but so was all New York. If you took supper at a restaurant, it was made. If you wore a certain hat, it became the rage.

CARLOTTA: I was rather gorgeous, wasn't I? Remember, they named everything after me—cigars, and race-horses, and perfumes, and battleships.

OLIVER: How thrilled I was the first time you went out with me. I remember waiting for you, all chills and fever, hoping everyone knew I was meeting Carlotta Vance. Supper at Martin's "There's Carlotta Vance! There's Carlotta Vance!"—a hansom through the Park, with a moon like a silver platter. You let me kiss you, Carlotta. Remember?

CARLOTTA: Did I? One thing I'll never forget. It was the day you were twenty-one, Oliver. And you asked me to marry you.

OLIVER: What a young fool you must have thought me!

CARLOTTA: I thought it was sweet of you. Remember, I was thirty-ish. I even went home and wept a little. They didn't often ask me to marry them.

OLIVER: It broke my heart when you refused me, Carlotta. I took my revenge on the theatre. None of my plays should it have! So I went back to Papa Jordan and the shipping business.

CARLOTTA: *(She looks around the office)* And here you are.

OLIVER: *(Rises)* Yes. Here I am.

MISS COPELAND: *(At door L.)* Mr. Packard is here now.

OLIVER: Oh! Yes. Send him right in. *(Turning to* CARLOTTA *as* MISS COPELAND *goes)* Do you mind? Dan Packard. Quite a fellow. Big western stuff—Used to be a miner.

CARLOTTA: I'm just going.

PACKARD: *(Voice is heard booming off before he enters)* That's no elevator—that's a bird-cage! Hey, Jordan, what kind of a dump—I beg your pardon.

(He enters L.; stops abruptly as he sees CARLOTTA. MISS COPELAND, *unable to precede him in his rush, has followed fussily behind. She now withdraws, closing the door.* DAN PACKARD *is one*

of those big, vital men, bellowing, self-important, too successful. His clothes are noticeable. He seems never to sit down; ramps and gesticulates as he talks, and he talks a great deal. He is always in the midst of a big deal, and curiously enough it really is a big deal. Every now and then, in his talk or in his manner, there crops up a word or gesture reminiscent of his western mining days.)

OLIVER: Lotta, this is Dan Packard, Miss Carlotta Vance.

PACKARD: *(As Carlotta rises and acknowledges the introduction with a nod)* Miss Vance, I—wait a minute! Vance! You don't mean Carlotta Vance. *(He does not stop for her confirmation)* Why, I know you! Jordan, you old son of a gun!

CARLOTTA: *(To JORDAN, Grimly)* Saw me when he was a boy.

PACKARD: Why, your picture was up on the wall of every mining shack in Montana, right longside of John L. Sullivan. Bunch of us rode forty miles into Butte just to see you. Sutton's Opera House. What was that piece you were in? You wore pants, I remember. *(A quick glance at her present contour)* Say!

CARLOTTA: *(Hastily)* That's an exit cue. *(Starts toward L. door.)*

OLIVER: *(Following her)* When'll I see you, Lotta? Soon?

PACKARD: *(To R. of desk)* Don't go on my account.

CARLOTTA: I'm at the Barclay.

OLIVER: I'll call you. Look here—you're dining with us next week. Friday, isn't it?

CARLOTTA: Am I?

OLIVER: Of course you are. *(Over his shoulder, to PACKARD)* So are you, Dan. But I'll see you before that. What did you say? The Barclay?

CARLOTTA: Righto! Goodbye, Oliver. *(Then, to PACKARD)* Goodbye, Lochinvar! *(She goes out L.)*

PACKARD: What'd she call me?

OLIVER: Sit down, Dan. How're you been? *(As he crosses to his desk.)*

PACKARD: *(Taking off coat)* Only stay a minute. Running down to Washington, five-thirty. (PACKARD *puts his coat on desk)* Got to drop up home, pick up a bag. Bunch of us going down. *(Pulls chair over to desk)* I'll tell you in confidence what it's about. Seems the President wants to get right down to the bottom of things. So he asked a little crowd of us to run over. Jim Thorne, Whitaker, couple of others. Breakfast at the White House, gab for a while, jump right back again. Not so bad. Private car, plenty of stuff, poker game.

OLIVER: That sounds grand. Dan, the reason I asked you to come in—

PACKARD: Holy smoke, I almost forgot! What time is it? *(Delves for his watch)* Mind if I use your phone? *(He is already reaching for it; receiver in hand, he turns inquiringly to* OLIVER *)*What kind of a—

OLIVER: Just tell my operator, she'll call you.

PACKARD: *(Into phone—on his feet)*-Get me Ashland-four-six-one-seven-nine, will you, girlie? Say my secretary, Miss Brice. Snap it up!*(As he talks into the telephone his eye travels appraisingly over the room—wanders toward window)* Say, who put up this building, Peter Stuyvesant? This isn't an office; it's a museum.

OLIVER: Not exactly modernistic. But it was the last word when the old gentleman built it. *(A gesture to the portrait)* I suppose it's sentimental of me, but I don't believe I'd want to change it. Been like this for seventy-five years.

PACKARD: I hope those tubs of yours don't date with the office— *(*TELEPHONE *rings.* PACKARD *leaps to it.* OLIVER *rises, puts* PACKARD'S *hat and coat from desk to chair L.)* Hello! That you, Miss Brice? I won't be in. What's that directors' meeting? Monday morning. Wait a minute. *(His quick eye sweeps the desk; he snatches a piece of paper which is an important-letter; begins to make notes on it.* OLIVER *instinctively flings out a hand to salvage. it. Too late.)* Coast State Waterways. Oh, yeh. Did you send that South American cable? Good. Did the Governor call me? Tell him I can't see him. And get me ten good seats for that Vanities show tomorrow night. And you know-I don't want to sit back of the second row. Now! I want you to send a case of Scotch, with my compliments, to District Attorney Michael G. Slade,

Presbyterian Hospital. Cancel my seats for the fight tonight. And get this, this is important. Call up the stables down in Maryland and tell O'Rourke I'm changing the feed on Streak-o'-Lightning. Tell him to try half bran mash from now on, Bran mash! Mash. That's all. *(Hangs up. Turns to* OLIVER*)* Now, then, Jordan, what's on your mind?

OLIVER: I'm not intruding?

PACKARD: That's all right. What's troubling you? Kind of up against it?

OLIVER: Not quite that. You probably know about our business. We're strictly freight carriers. New York and Southern Coast— Havana, Port au Prince. I needn't tell you what's happened to trade down there—sugar, coffee. Of course it isn't going to last forever. But what I want to know is, if it does take a little longer than we figure, would you be in a position-you and your associates—to sort of tide us over?

PACKARD: *(Shifts his position as he thinks this over)* H'm.

OLIVER: I realize I might have to turn over some of my holdings. I'd rather not disturb any of the other stockholders. Not many in it. Most of them have had it for years. Inherited.

PACKARD: Well, I'll tell you. Of course I don't know anything about your business, but it looks to me as if it's gone to seed. Only have to look around this office. All those old fogies out there. As far as that Southern trade's concerned, I don't see much future in it. Tell you the truth, Jordan, I don't think you've got much to offer.

OLIVER: *(With some indignation)* Just a minute, Packard! You know nothing about my business. The Jordan Line is one of the best known in the shipping world. Our boats have traveled the ocean for a century. We started with clipper ships. And we're not going to stop now. We're not through–not by a damn sight!

PACKARD: Gosh, Jordan, I didn't mean anything. You know—I'm a business man—I may have put a little—you know how it is these days—everybody after you—I apologize.

OLIVER: *(His hand absently rubbing his chest, as though to still a discomfort there)* That's all right.

(WARN Dim Out.)

PACKARD: Tell you what I'll do. You get together some figures on this thing. Can you do that?

OLIVER: Why—I could.

PACKARD: Balance sheet, assets—total tonnage, and when the boats were built, list of stockholders—not many of them, you said?

OLIVER: No, no. It's held quite closely.

PACKARD: Well, let me have a list of them. Now, when do you want to send this to me?

OLIVER: Oh—it won't take long. You understand, Packard, this is confidential.

PACKARD: Sure! Sure!

OLIVER: Another thing. We've got a stockholders' meeting on the twenty-sixth. That's a week from Monday.

PACKARD: You give me that dope early next week, and I'll let you have an answer in a few days.

OLIVER: That's very kind of you. *(Again the vague rubbing of the chest.)*

PACKARD: What's the matter there—got a pain? *(Imitating gesture.)*

OLIVER: No, no. Little indigestion.

PACKARD: Juice of half a lemon. I get it all the time. Half a lemon in hot water. *(A hasty glance at his watch. Has hat and coat from chair)* Jumping Jupiter! I've got to travel. You'll send me that stuff? Do what I can for you, anyway. God knows!

OLIVER: Thanks. (PACKARD *goes.* OLIVER *stands a moment in front of the desk. His hand passes once more over his chest, absently. Then, slowly, he starts to walk around to his chair. As* PACKARD *slams the door—)*

THE LIGHTS DIM OUT.

SCENE III

KITTY PACKARD'S *bedroom in the* PACKARD'S *apartment. It is a rather startling room, done in the modernistic manner by the newest and most fashionable modern decorator. The color is white— all the shades of white from cream, through ivory to oyster.* KITTY *has just had it done, and finds she doesn't like it very well. It isn't, she thinks, becoming to her. There is a large and luxurious bed in the upper Left corner of the room, a dressing table down R. bearing bottles, brushes, mirrors, jars; a bedside table, a modernistic upholstered chair. There are two doors, one leading into* DAN PACKARD'S *room, down L., the other into the hall, up R. It is half-past four in the afternoon.* KITTY PACKARD *is in bed. She has been in bed all day. A pretty woman of 29, the slightly faded wild rose, Irish type.*

She was KITTY SHEEHAN *before her marriage. There is, in her face, the petulance of the idle and empty-headed wife. She is sitting up among her pillows and is wearing a charming bed-jacket over her nightgown. Her hair is arranged as carefully as though a more formal occasion. All about her, on the bed, on the table, and even on the floor, are the odds and ends that have accumulated for her amusement during the long day. On the bed are a game in a pasteboard box, a nail buffer, a hand mirror, and a movie magazine. On the bed table is a movie magazine, on top of which is a large candy box, which, in turn, supports a tray on which are a chocolate pot, cup, saucer and spoon, cream pitcher, sugar bowl and a small bowl of whipped cream. A powder puff is also on the table. Strewn around the bed, on the floor and on the dais are three movie magazines, one of which is open, and two brightly bound detective story novels, one of which lies open. Under the bed, unseen, is a large and imposing volume. On the dais, leaning against the foot of the bed, is a Pierrot doll. Near it is a tabloid newspaper. Another doll, a Pierrette, is in the chair Center, and a third doll reclines on the dressing table bench. Over the doll is carelessly thrown a feathery bed jacket. On the dressing table are a clock, an elaborate case of toilet articles, a cigarette box, an atomiser, a hairbrush, a mascara box, a powder jar and puff, a comb, and a jewel case, open, in which are a rope of pearls and a number of jeweled bracelets. All of the dress-*

ing table fittings are in white, or black and white. At the rise of the Curtain, KITTY *is to be seen working over the puzzle held balanced in her hands. Her whole attention is concentrated on it. She fails to make it come right, tosses it aside pettishly, looks about for amusement, takes up a motion picture magazine, flips its pages idly, throws that aside.*

KITTY: *(Calls)* Tina! Tina! (TINA *enters the hall.* TINA *is* MRS. PACKARD'S *personal maid. A somewhat hard-faced, capable and shifty girl of twenty-five or six. She is wearing a smart maid's uniform.)*

TINA: Yes, Mrs. Packard? *(Crosses to her.)*

KITTY: What time is it now?

TINA: *(Glances at clock on dressing table)* Half past four.

KITTY: What did Doctor Talbot say? What time's he coming?

TINA: He didn't say exactly. He asked were there any symptoms, and I said, no, I didn't think so, so he said all right then, some time this afternoon.

KITTY: *(Annoyed)* I've got a cold and my legs ache all over.

TINA: Oh, well—you didn't tell me to say that, Mrs. Packard.

KITTY: Well, you should have known it! What'll I do from now until . . . Where'd that puzzle get to? *(Her eye travels about the bed and bedside; falls on the chocolate tray)* Oh, take that all away. Wait a minute! *(Reaches swiftly for the spoon, dips it into the whipped cream, licks it with a lingering tongue.* TINA *picks up the tray. Goes to R. door.)* Get me that other candy box, the big one. *(Looks about at her assortment of pastimes. A deep sigh. Picks up the discarded puzzle, and again tries to concentrate on this.)*

TINA: *(Returns with the candy box, an enormous affair of pink satin and gold lace. She comes up the bedside, stands, box in hand, watching a moment to see if* MRS. PACKARD *is really going to perform the trick this time. After an absorbed second)* If you tip it up this way *(A gesture with her hand)*—you can get the blue in.

KITTY: *(Throws the puzzle across the room)* Oh! *(*TINA *hastily places the candy box on the bed, goes to retrieve the puzzle, puts it on bed table,* *straightens things on table,* KITTY *turns over on her side; her glance encounters the candy box; she opens it and begins greedily to inspect its contents,. Selects a chocolate, begins to nibble it. Nibbling the chocolate, her eye roaming the room)* I don't like this room. It's all done, and I don't like it. Do you?

TINA: *(Gazing about).* I don't understand it. Is it finished?

KITTY: I think I'll have'em do it again, not modernistic.

TINA: I liked it the old way, with the pink satin.

KITTY: Yeah, that's what I'll do-I'll change it back again Was the dog out?

TINA: I don't know for sure.

KITTY: Well, find out, and have John take him. *(As* TINA *exits R.)* He's got to have his walk. *(Left to her own devices,* KITTY *picks up buffer, starts to polish her nails, tires of it, picks up a largish hand mirror and surveys herself in it, tipping it at various angles, peering at a tiny blemish on her skin, smoothing her eyebrows, widening her eyes, and performing like antics to which women are given when alone with a mirror. Takes a large fluffy powder puff from the bedside table; pats her face with it.)*

TINA: *(Returns with a very gay hatbox, ornamented with a brilliant bow)* Your hat's come.

KITTY: Ooh!

TINA: And Mr. Packard's just come in

KITTY: Give it here. *(Sits up eagerly. Between them she and* TINA *opens the box. The hat emerges a modish winter thing with an ornament and a little nose-veil)* Looks cute, doesn't it?

TINA: Mm.

KITTY: *(Hands* TINA *the mirror)* Here! Hold this! *(Adjusts the hat to her head. Peers at the effect in the mirror held by Tina)* No; higher. There! Now let me have it.*(Takes the mirror, holds it herself, still looking at her reflection in the glass.* TINA *steps back a few paces, the better to see. The booming of* DAN PACKARD'S *voice is heard down the hall as he approaches.)*

PACKARD: *(Entering R. He is in topcoat and is wearing his hat)* Oh, hello—You in bed again? What's the matter?

KITTY: I don't feel good. *(TINA goes out R.)*

PACKARD: *(Notes her hat)* What's the idea of the hat? Going out? *(Has been making straight for the closed door of his own bedroom L. Opens the door. Shouts)* Hey! John! You know what I want. Just overnight.

VOICE: *(Off)* Yes, Mr. Packard.

PACKARD: *(Glances at watch. To* KITTY*)* Got to get right out. *(Throws hat and coat on bed)* Why don't you get up! Do something!

KITTY: You don't care what I do.

PACKARD: *(As the scene progresses he takes off his hat and coat, which he tosses onto the bed; looks at himself in her dressing table mirror to see if he needs a shave; unfastens his tie; vanishes into his own room for a second; emerges with a tie of another color)* Look at me! Never sick a day in my life. And why! I get out, and do things, keep going. Hey, John! I don't want any dinner clothes. *(Again to her)* That's the reason.

KITTY: *(Looking at herself in the mirror)* That's because you're an extravert and I'm an introvert.

PACKARD: A what?

KITTY: Doctor Talbot says you're an extravert and I'm an introvert, and that's why I have to be quiet a good deal and have time to reflect in.

PACKARD: Reflect in! What have you got to reflect about? I've got to think and act at the same time! Do you know why I'm going to Washington tonight? Because the President wants to consult me about the affairs of the Nation! That's why!

KITTY: What's the matter with them?

PACKARD: Everything's the matter with them! That's why he's sending for me! And I'll tell you something else, if you want to know. It wouldn't surprise me a bit if he offered me a Cabinet job, and what do you know about that?

KITTY: *(Busy with her own thoughts)* Where'd that buffer get to?

PACKARD: *(Goes off L.)* You ought to be married to some of the guys that I see. That'd give you something to reflect about. *(He comes on)* Why, I went into an office this afternoon—fellow begging me to—and it turns out he can't even keep a little bit of a business going! I juggle fifty things and he can't handle one! And *(He goes off L.; reappears immediately)*—here's the blow-off! I've been trying to get hold of just his kind of layout for the last two years, and the damn fool hands it to me! Only he don't know it. *(Disappears)* I give him a song and dance—he's sending me a full list of stockholders. I buy up what I need and it's all over but the shouting! *(He returns)* Little Dan Packard owns the best shipping line between here and the Tropics, and Mr. Oliver Jordan is out on his ear.

KITTY: *(Bringing that fine mind of hers to bear)* We're going there for dinner next Friday, and I'm going to wear my new pink.

PACKARD: We are what?

KITTY: Mrs. Oliver Jordan called me up, and they're giving a swell dinner, and we're invited.

PACKARD: *(Putting on tie)* Oh, that's what he was driving—We're not going.

KITTY: The hell we ain't! Why not?

PACKARD: I can't go and eat his dinner! If he's a sucker, that's his funeral. Business is business, but I can't go walking into his house!

KITTY: No! Presidents and Washington, and all those rummies, but you can't go anywheres with me! Once in our life we get asked to a classy house, and I've got a new dress that'll knock their eye out, and we're going!

PACKARD: We are not going!

KITTY: *(Now on her knees in the bed, the hat still on her head. In high rage)* We are so! You big crook, you pull a dirty deal and it ruins my social chances! Well, you can't get away with it!

PACKARD: Oh, go lay down! You tell me what I can do! Well, we're not going, and that's all there is to it. *(Exits L.)* Come on, now, John, snap into it!

KITTY: *(Still on her knees, expresses her hatred for the absent DAN with a series of hideous and unadult facial contortions, reminiscent of her past. That finished with, she realizes that she needs a new method of attack. She sinks back among her pillows, taking the hat off as she does so; draws up the covers very thoughtfully, and arrives at her plan of campaign)* Dan-ny! *(A honeyed voice)* Danny! Ple-ease! Kitty wants to go. Kitty wants to see all the dreat bid—*(She is now in baby talk of the most revolting kind)*—lords and ladies in the big booful house. *(No sound from the other room. The baby talk is followed by a dirty look)* Danny! It's for Lord Ferncliffe and Lady Ferncliffe. Danny!

PACKARD: *(His head through the L. doorway; his gaze very intent on her)* What did you say?

KITTY: It's for Lord and Lady Ferncliffe, from England.

PACKARD: *(Emerging)* Who says so?

KITTY: She did.

PACKARD: Why the hell didn't you tell me in the first place?

KITTY: Because you were mean to poor little Kitty.

PACKARD: Ferncliffe? You know who he is, don't you? He's one of the richest men in England.

KITTY: Oh, goody! Then you'll go?

PACKARD: Why—I've been trying to meet him for years.

KITTY: See? And Kitty did it for you

PACKARD: Ferncliffe, eh? Well, I'm not going to miss him, Jordan or no Jor—Do you know what I'll do? *(Thinking it out swiftly as he talks)* I'll buy up that Jordan stock through dummies. I'll use Baldridge and Whitestone—fellows like that. Keep my name out of it.

KITTY: Out of what?

PACKARD: Oh, for God's-

TINA: *(Enters R.)* Doctor Talbot's come.

KITTY: Doctor Talbot? Good!

PACKARD: *(Grabs his hat and coat; a quick "goodbye")* He'll fix you up all right! Ferncliffe! God, what a break! Bye, Kitten! See you tomorrow. Stick that in the car, John! S'long, Kitten. *(He is gone off R.)*

KITTY: *(Through* PACKARD'S *speech, chiming in on "Bye, Kitten")* Goodbye! Goodbye! Yes, that's fine! Goodbye! *(She barely gives* DAN *time to get out of the room)* Tina, Quick! Get me the other bed-jacket. *(As* TINA *goes to the dressing table* KITTY *slips off her bed-jacket and hurls it across the bed, holding out her arms for the new one)* Get me my pearls out of the case! Don't let him come in till I tell you. Get the things off the bed! Fix it up a little! *(Mirror in hand,* KITTY *applies powder puff, lipstick and comb)* Give me that book! The big one!

TINA: *(with a wild look around)* Where is it?

KITTY: Look around ! It fell down! *(TINA drops to her hands and knees and begins looking around the bed)* Hurry up. It's there some place!

TINA: *(Bringing up a brightly bound detective story)* Is this it?

KITTY: No, no! That Dr. Talbot gave me! It's a big thick one and it says, "Aspects of the Adult Mind." *(She manages the two-syllable words with difficulty.)*

TINA: *(Fishing under the bed)* I got it!

KITTY: Give it to me!

TINA: *(Her lips move silently for a second as she reassures herself about the title)* Yeah, this is it!

(WARN Dim Out.)

KITTY: *(Taking the book)* All right now! *(She dismisses* TINA *with a wave of the hand.* TINA *gathers up candy boxes, kicks a magazine under the bed, scurries out R. A final preening on* KITTY'S *part—a patting of the pillow. She opens the book at random. but decides that she really ought to be further along than that. She slaps over another hundred pages; then, inserting a finger as though to mark her place, she closes the book. She is very much the invalid, interrupted while reading, as the* DOCTOR *enters.* DR. TALBOT *is happy in the possession of a good figure, a conventionally handsome face, a dark neat mustache, a reassuring bedside manner. Perhaps forty-six.* TINA *has followed him into the room.)*

TALBOT: *(His is a quiet, soothing voice)* Well! Hello! What's all this?

KITTY: *(Suddenly weak)* Hello, Doctor! *(TINA crosses to L; closes door.)*

TALBOT: Just ran into your husband downstairs. Tells me he's going to see the President.

KITTY: Yes, he's going to help him fix things. *(TINA picks up magazines from the bed.)*

TALBOT: *(Seats himself on the side of the bed. A finger on her pulse)* Well, What's the trouble with the little lady?

KITTY: Well. Doctor, I don't know. I kind of ached all over ,and felt funny and you've got to be so careful about flu—*(TINA exits R.)* and I thought maybe if I stayed in bed—*(The door closes behind TINA, As she departs, Kitty's voice trails off into nothingness. She is listening intently, as she talks, for the sound of TINA's retreating footsteps. DR. TALBOT's finger is still on her pulse.)* You don't ever come unless I send for you.

TALBOT: I'm very busy, Kitty. You know how busy I am.

KITTY: But I'm so lonely, Wayne. And you know how I need you. *(Her arms go about his neck. A trifle reluctantly, he responds to her embrace.)*

THE LIGHTS DIM OUT QUICKLY.

SCENE IV

The JORDAN *sitting room. Late afternoon of the same day. A tea table, with a lace cloth, stands before the chair C. The Venetian blinds are half raised. Otherwise the room is as before. Three shaded lamps are lighted.* DORA *is lighting the lamp L. of table as the scene begins. Takes a last look around to see that everything is in order. Satisfied that it is, she goes off.*

Immediately GUSTAVE *enters R. Over one arm he carries, neatly folded, a pair of newly pressed trousers, from which dangles a pair of suspenders. As he enters he peers toward the bedroom, having caught a vanishing glimpse of* DORA

GUSTAVE: *(Enters as* DORA *exits)* Psst! *(She does not hear him. He puts trousers on back of chair C. goes to L. door)* Psst!

DORA: *(Enters; comes to* GUSTAVE *)* Darling!

GUSTAVE: My little princess! *(A long embrace and a kiss.)*

DORA: You ought to be downstairs. She'll be home to tea any minute.

GUSTAVE: There is yet time. *(Kisses her again. Withdraws a little so that she is very near as she now talks to him.)*

DORA: Oh, Gustave, I only feel safe when I am with you like this. That Ricci!

GUSTAVE: Has he been bothering you again—that snake!

DORA: He tries to grab hold of me. And he says things, in Italian like this—*(She hisses these last two words)* I don't know what they mean.

GUSTAVE: How could you ever like him, that *flugter hund*!

DORA: I didn't. Besides, that was before you came here.

GUSTAVE: Ma petite! *(He tries to draw her to him. This time she repulses him definitely.)*

DORA: No, no. I'm not going to kiss you any more.

GUSTAVE: Not going to kiss me! What it have I done?

DORA: Why should I let you kiss me? We're not engaged or anything.

GUSTAVE: What are you saying? You know I am mad for you! All night long I cannot sleep! My Dora! *(Another gesture towards her)* I love you! Why are you so cold to me? At night why do you lock your door, always? You know how much I love you!

DORA: *(In a panic)* No, no, Gustave! No! *(Pulls herself together a little)* I couldn't be like that! I couldn't!

GUSTAVE: You do not love me-!

DORA: I do! I do! But—you come from Europe. You don't understand. I waws brought up strict. If anybody loves me like that they would want me to marry them.

GUSTAVE: Marry! Oh, but Dora! To marry takes so much money. I have been in America only a year.

DORA: *(Almost crying)* You don't want to marry me!

GUSTAVE: I love you! I love you!

DORA: *(Breaking in on his speech)* You don't love me! You were only fooling with me! You're as bad as Ricci. I hate you! I'm going away, that's what I'm going to do! I'll get another place and you'll never see me again! I hate you! *(A WHISTLE from down the hall, followed by PAULA'S voice, calling. GUSTAVE snatches trousers from chair, hangs them over his arm.)*

PAULA: *(Enters from hall.)* That you, Mother? *(PAULA enter R.)* Oh, I thought I heard—Mother isn't home yet, huh?

GUSTAVE: Not yet, Miss Paula. I believe she'll be in soon.

PAULA: Oh! Tell her I'm home. *(Goes off R. to her room down the hall whistling a fragment of a popular tune. The sound of her whistling dies away.)*

GUSTAVE: Dora, don't talk like that! I will do anything for you. I have never been like this—never!

DORA: If you loved me you would marry me. Goodbye. *(Turns to go R.)*

GUSTAVE: Wait-*(she halts.)* I will marry you.

DORA: *(In joyful unbelief)* Gustave! When?

GUSTAVE: *(Evasively)* Ah. Soon.

DORA: But when?

GUSTAVE: Well—when we can.

DORA: Thursday! We'll both be off.

PAULA: *(Heard off, from her bedroom down the hall)* Gustave!

GUSTAVE: *(A move toward R. door)* Yes, Miss Paula. *(Pulling himself together.)*

PAULA: *(Still heard in the distance)* I wonder if I could have a cup of hot tea in my room?

GUSTAVE: Very good, Miss Paula. *(In a cautious undertone to)* But, remember—no word of this. It must be a secret.

DORA: *(Very low)* All right. And we won't tell Ricci. He might do something.

GUSTAVE: *(A whisper)* That's right. Only us.

DORA: Thursday. *(A fond gesture in* DORA'S *direction.* GUSTAVE *goes out R. With* GUSTAVE'S *departure a little look of triumph comes over her face. She has achieved what she wanted. She stands for a moment in contemplation of her victory, her pleasure visibly mounting. Humming a bit of gay song, she trips into the bedroom L., highly pleased with herself. The voices of* OLIVER *and* RICCI *are heard approaching down the hall.)*

RICCI: I would stop here and rest if I were you, sir.

OLIVER: I'd rather go to my bedroom.

RICCI: I'd sit here for just a minute and get your breath. *(*OLIVER *and* RICCI *enter R.*OLIVER *is being half-supported by* RICCI *and seems to be breathing with a little difficulty. He sinks on sofa. Obviously he is not well.* RICCI *behind sofa)* Here we are, sir. I'll see if Mrs. Jordan—*(Looks toward L door.)*

OLIVER: *(Rising, hastily)* No, no, no! Mrs. Jordan mustn't—*(The quick movement of rising has been too much. Gasping a little, he sinks back into sofa.* RICCI *returns quickly to his L. side. As* OLIVER *sits,* DORA *appears in L. doorway, drawn by the men's voices. Comes forward in some alarm.)*

DORA: What's the matter? Mr. Jordan!

OLIVER: I'm all right. I'm all right.

DORA: Anything I can do, sir? What should I get? *(To* RICCI*)* What's the matter with him?

RICCI: You must not get up, sir. You should lie back. The head down. *(To* DORA *)* Has Mrs. Jordan come in?

DORA: No, she hasn't. What should we do?

OLIVER: *(Rising again, but cautiously)* Not so much fuss. Please! *(With an effort, pulls himself together)* I'm quite all right. I'm going to my own room. *(RICCI attempts again to assist him)* What happened, Ricci?

RICCI: You were stepping out of the car, sir. You—you stumbled.

OLIVER: That's—funny. I didn't fall? H'm?

RICCI: No, no. I caught you. You did not.

OLIVER: *(Thoughtfully)* I'm much obliged to you, Ricci. Remember, both of you. Nothing about this to Mrs. Jordan. *(Goes out R.)*

DORA: Do you think he's all right?

RICCI: *(Goes to R. door, looks after the retreating figure. Turns)* Sure. He's all right. *(Comes toward DORA. His whole attention suddenly concentrating ominously on her.)*

DORA: You keep away from me, Tony Ricci! *(Backs away from him.)*

RICCI: My little darling Dora, why are you frightened of me? Why do you always run away from me? Tell me, my pretty little Dora. Why? Him? *(with a swift movement he seizes her wrist in a tight grip.)*

DORA: *(Tries to free herself)* Let me go!

RICCI: *(Pulls her closer to him. Holds her in a vise)* Listen to me! You were sweet enough to me before he came here. And you think now you can spit on me for that Alsatian pig!

DORA: *(Breaking in)* You crazy fool! Let me go! *(Vainly pulls and tugs away from him.)*

RICCI: *(pulls her closer to him)* I show you who is the pig.

DORA: You let me go! I'll scream!

RICCI: Oh, no, you won't. *(A glance over his shoulder at R. door. DORA begins to pound his chest with her free fist. RICCI twists the wrist he is holding. DORA opens her mouth to scream. RICCI claps a hand over her mouth. In a flash she twists loose and sinks her teeth in his hand. With a curse he frees her other hand and deals her a hard, vicious slap in the face. RICCI turns and goes out R. quickly. DORA has staggered a little under the blow, crouched a little, her hand to her face. Stands, a bundle of fear and misery, whimpering a little. The voices of* MILLICENT *and* HATTIE *are heard from the hallway.)*

MILLICENT: *(Off)* Oh, well, come in long enough to have a cup of tea. I'll send you home with Ricci.

HATTIE: I ought to be home now. (DORA, *hearing their voices, arranges her attire, smoothes her hair. Darts to the table up C. Fusses with the books and magazines.)*

MILLICENT: *(Entering R. She is in street attire, as is* HATTIE, *who follows her in.* MILLICENT *crosses straight to her bedroom L., which she enters, talking as she goes.)* Nonsense. Cup of tea'll be good for you. I'll die if I don't have one in a minute. *(In a higher pitch, from the bedroom)*-There's nothing in the world wears me out like shopping. I hate it.

HATTIE: Hello, Dora.

DORA: Good afternoon, Mrs. Loomis. *(Her hand on the injured cheek.)*

HATTIE: What's the matter . . . neuralgia?

DORA: *(A nod and a gulp)* Yes, madam. *(She gets out R. as quickly as possible.)*

MILLICENT: *(From the bedroom)* Well, this settles it. I am not going to kill myself for Paula. If she doesn't care enough to come along she can be married like a shop-girl for all of me. (GUSTAVE *enters R., bringing the tea things. He arranges them on the table.)*

HATTIE: Remember that lovely trousseau poor Mama got for me? All lace and embroidery?

MILLICENT: *(Still in the next room)* You've probably still got it, I know you.

HATTIE: Those fifteen-foot tablecloths? I sold them to Ringling Brothers for a tent.

MILLICENT: *(Hearing the clink of china)* Is that the tea? I'll be right in.

HATTIE: *(Sauntering over to the table and peering into a sandwich)* M'm. What's this, Gustave? *(Pours tea.)*

GUSTAVE: I believe that's watercress, madame. With mayonnaise. *(Starts to go R.)*

MILLICENT: *(Entering. Has taken off her hat and furs)* I am simply dead. Maybe this'll pick me up. Any messages, Gustave? *(Taking cup of tea which HATTIE has poured.)*

GUSTAVE: Oh—yes, madam.... Mr. Townsend regrets very much that he cannot come to dinner on Friday, the twenty-third. He will be out of town.

MILLICENT: Oh, damn!

GUSTAVE: *(Very quietly)* Yes, madam. *(Goes out R.)*

MILLICENT: *(Crosses to desk. Sits)* Well, I've got to begin all over again. I'll bet if I called one man this morning, I called ten. Would you believe it? There just isn't an extra man in all New York!

HATTIE: *(Sits at table)* I never could understand why it has to be just even—male and female. They're invited for dinner, not for mating.

MILLICENT: Don't be bohemian, Hattie, I've got to have a balanced table. *(Indicating a list on the desk)* Now, there are the good ones. I've tried them all.

HATTIE: I know. It's like one of those boxes of candy. You begin with those luscious chocolate creams and at the finish you're down to candied violets and spit-backs. What becomes of all the men, anyhow? You see men on the street. Do they set them out in the morning and take them in at night?

MILLICENT: Well, I don't know what I'm going to do. There just isn't anybody, that's all. *(Takes cup back to tea table. Returns to desk. Sits.)*

HATTIE: Why don't you try a little new blood? They don't have to be those same old set pieces. Don't you know any prize-fighters or politicians or playwrights? Get somebody that'll go with Carlotta. Give her a little fun. Get an actor, or something.

MILLICENT: *(Thoughtfully)* An actor. Of course it would have to be one that's not acting. Let me see.

HATTIE: A movie star! Aren't there any movie stars around?

MILLICENT: *(Snaps her fingers in triumph)* Larry Renault! He'd be marvelous. I wonder if he's still in town.

HATTIE: He was yesterday.

MILLICENT: How do you know?

HATTIE: Ed. Ed, the movie-hound. Read me an interview with him in last night's Telegram. He's leaving pictures and going into a play.

MILLICENT: I wonder where he's stopping. Did it say?

HATTIE: *(A great effort of memory)* Yes, it did. Let me see. It's one of those hotels in the Fifties-they all stop at it. Now, just—it'll come to me—

MILLICENT: *(Busy with her own thoughts, while* HATTIE'S *recollecting)* You know, he knows Carlotta. We met him three years ago, in Antibes. He was simply a sensation. He'd just made that big picture-Sins of something—and he was absolutely mobbed wherever he went. The Casino crowds just gaping, and the girls fighting to get into his car. And on the beach! I must say I never saw such a figure. He wore even less than the girls.

HATTIE: Ed doesn't like him since the talkies. He says he seems different. You can't fool Ed about the movies. He remembers Flora Finch, and Mae Marsh, and Henry B. Walthall

MILLICENT: Of course, I don't even know if he'd know me now. We met at a dozen dinners. I wonder who'd know where he's stopping.

HATTIE: *(Suddenly)* Versailles! That's it. Hotel Versailles.

MILLICENT: *(Reaches for the telephone book)* Oh, good! Are you sure?

HATTIE: Yes, I remember the whole interview. He was wearing a black moire lounging robe with a white monogram.

MILLICENT: *(Hunting the number)* I don't suppose people like that are ever home.

HATTIE: What's the name of that play he's going to be in?

MILLICENT: *(One finger marking her place, she looks up at* HATTIE.*)*

I'll put him next to Carlotta, and then give her Doctor Talbot on the other side. Let's see next to Doctor Talbot the Packard woman—h'm—Talbot and the Packard woman no, they'd never get on together.

HATTIE: See if you can get him first and let nature take its course.

MILLICENT: *(Consulting the book again)* Plaza three—*(Scribbles the number on her note pad; starts to dial.)*

HATTIE: *(Jumping up; pulling on her gloves)* Well, I make you a present of it, darling. At least that's one trouble I haven't got. Three rooms and a kitchenette eliminates the extra-man problem.

PAULA: *(Enters R.)* Hello, Aunt Hattie. I didn't know you were here.

HATTIE: Hello, Paula. Pour you a cup of tea?

PAULA: I had some in my room, I've been sleeping.

MILLICENT: *(Has finished dialing; the receiver to her ear)* I thought you were at the office, that tea for Chanel.

PAULA: *(Nibbling a sandwich)* Oh, she was an awful bust. She wore pearls with a sport suit—ropes of 'em.

MILLICENT: *(Into the phone)* Hotel Versailles? *(The word catches PAULA'S attention)* Is Mr. Larry Renault stopping there?

PAULA: *(A little startled)* Who?

MILLICENT: Larry Renault. You know, the movie actor. I'm giving a dinner and I thought it'd be fun if he came.

HATTIE: See you soon, Millie. I've got to be going.

MILLICENT: *(Carelessly)* Oh, don't be in a hurry.

HATTIE: Yes; got to. Ed's sort of an old-fashioned husband. He thinks wives ought to be home before dinner. *(Goes out R.)*

MILLICENT: *(At the telephone)* Hello! I'm waiting for Mr. Larry Renault. (GUSTAVE *enters with the evening paper, which he places on table up C.)*

PAULA: How did you happen to think of him?

MILLICENT: *(Turns)* What? Oh, Gustave, has Mr. Jordan come in yet? He's late, isn't he?

GUSTAVE: He's been in quite some time, madam. He's in his room.

(WARN Curtain.)

MILLICENT: Really! Does he know I'm home?

GUSTAVE: I'm not sure, madam. I believe he's lying down. I understand he has a slight headache.

MILLICENT: Oh—I didn't know. Tell him I'll be right in. *(Into the phone as GUSTAVE departs)* Hello! Can't you get—Is this Mr. Renault? Mr. Renault, this is Mrs. Oliver Jordan. I don't know if you remember me. Yes! Antibes! Why, you're wonderful! Mr. Renault, I'd like it so much if you could come to a little dinner I'm giving a week from tonight. Just a tiny dinner. Lord and Lady Ferncliffe are coming, and Carlotta Vance—of course, you know Carlotta-Well, that's so nice. Friday, the twenty-third, at eight o'clock—that's right. What? My daughter? Well, what a memory! *(To PAULA)* He remembers you, Paula. *(Into phone)* She's right here, and very flattered. Oh, no, she won't be at the dinner. She isn't invited. But she's quite grown up now. Wait a minute. Won't you say hello to her? I know she'd be thrilled to death. *(To PAULA)* Here, Paula go ahead. Don't be silly. *(Turns the receiver over to PAULA.)*

PAULA: *(Reluctantly takes the receiver)* Hello! Yes, this is Paula Jordan. Indeed I do. Well, people don't forget you, do they? Now, you're just being whimsical, Mr. Renault.

MILLICENT: *(As she flutters off R. In a loud whisper)* Be nice to him. I want to see how Dad is.

PAULA: *(Telephone)* Oh, no, I'm not.

MILLICENT: *(As she goes into the hallway)* Oliver, I didn't know you weren't feeling well. *(Exits R.)*

PAULA: *(Very intense. Into the telephone)* You're insane! You can't come here. No, she's gone. No, I can't. I tell you I can't tonight. I've got to go out with Ernest. No, it won't work again. He's furious about last night. Larry, you've been drinking. Listen, I'll call you later on another phone. Of course I love you. Of course. Goodbye.

(The Curtain starts to descend. Hangs up quickly. Takes a darting look to see if anyone could have been within earshot. Sits a little huddled figure in the chair at desk.)

THE CURTAIN FALLS

ACT TWO

SCENE 1

A week later.

LARRY RENAULT'S *apartment in the Hotel Versailles. It is a rather smart hotel in the East Fifties, of the type patronized by successful actors and motion picture people. Its style of furnishing is modern French in excellent taste. The employees' uniforms are very chic, and a shade too spectacular.*

The room which we see is the sitting room. It is bright, tastefully arranged, comfortable. A door at the Left leads into a bedroom, unseen. At the back. there is a fireplace, furnished with gas logs. On either side of the fireplace are narrow French windows leading to minute twin balconies. There is a second door at the Right, which leads, to the outer corridor.

There is a low armchair below the door Right, and a small desk and chair above it. On the desk, prominently displayed, is a photograph of PAULA JORDAN, *this in a heavy silver frame: Beside it, in a larger leather frame, is a photograph of* RENAULT *himself in one of his favorite, (and more youthful) poses. There is a large, comfortable chair R. of Center, with a bridge lamp above it. Up Right, at right angles to the footlights, is a commode on which there is a lamp; above it is a mirror. Opposite, at Left, is another commode and lamp with a picture above. There is a small couch down Left, with detachable cushions and two pillows; an end table beside it on which is a telephone, an empty whiskey bottle and a glass. There a large rug in the Center of the room, and small throw rugs at each door*

There is no one on the stage at the rise the Curtain. The sound of the BUZZER *at the outer door off R. is heard. A slight pause.* LARRY RENAULT *enters from the bedroom.*

He is a handsome man in his early forties, with the perfect profile that so gracefully lends itself to a successful motion picture career.

*His figure still passes, but about the whole man there are the un-
mistakable marks of middle age, abetted by pretty steady drinking,
increasing failure, and disappointment. It is a vain and weak face,
but not unappealing. He is wearing the black moire dressing gown
mentioned by* HATTIE. *The initials "L.R." in white form an impressive monogram on the left side. A white silk shirt with a soft collar, dark trousers and black patent-leather lounging slippers
complete his costume. He is slightly unshaven, as he means to shave
before dressing to go out to dinner. It is now about four o'clock in the
afternoon. As he crosses room the* BUZZER *sounds for the second
time. As he opens the R. door* EDDIE, *the bellboy, steps into the
room. He is carrying a bottle of whiskey rather carelessly wrapped.*

LARRY: Oh, it's you..Where've you been so long?

EDDIE: *(Gives him the bottle)* Come as quick as I could. *(Turns to go.)*

LARRY: Hey! Wait a minute! *(Boy stops.)* Where's my change?

EDDIE: Had to go to a new place. Cost half a dollar more.

LARRY: Who told you to go to a new place? *(The Boy has not stopped.
He is out the door before* LARRY'S *last word is finished. The door
slams behind him.* LARRY *stands looking after him for a second, then
heads for the couch, unwrapping the bottle as he crosses. Takes paper
off bottle, throws empty bottle from table into waste basket, opens bottle, and starts to pour drink. The* PHONE *rings. The bottle still in
hand, he answers the phone)* Hello. *(A bit eagerly, as he recognizes
the voice)* Oh, hello, Max Yeah, I'll be here. Why? Can't you tell
me over the phone? All right I'll be waiting for you. *(Hangs up;
takes up drink.* BUZZER *sounds. An annoyed glance, then puts the
bottle on the table and goes to the R. door. It is* PAULA JORDAN *who
enters. There is about her the unnatural vivacity of one who has secret and important news.)* Paula!

PAULA: Mr. Renault! *(Whirls into the room)* Not Mr. Larry Renault!
Not the great motion picture actor! *(Runs to him. Is in his arms.
They kiss.)*

LARRY: Crazy little darling!

PAULA: *(Not stopping)* How've you been and how are you and I want
to know how you are! And do you love me?

LARRY: You know I do! *(They kiss.)*

PAULA: Well, I just thought I'd ask. *(Throws muff and fur piece on chair as she crosses L. Takes off hat; throws it on couch.)*

LARRY: What's happened to you? Why all the animal spirits?

PAULA: Oh, nothing. Just girlish vivacity. And hunger.

LARRY: Hunger!

PAULA: Would you give a girl a cup of coffee? Nothing else.

LARRY: Of course. *(Reaches for the phone)* What's the matter? Didn't you have any lunch?

PAULA: Well I had a sort of liquid lunch.

LARRY: *(In phone)* Room service, please. *(Turns to her)* Did you say coffee? Don't you mean tea?

PAULA: I do not mean tea.

LARRY: Well, if you—*(Then into phone)* Room service? This is Mr. Renault, in Nineteen Hundred. Will you send up a pot of coffee, please? *(Turning to PAULA)* Anything else?

PAULA: Toast.

LARRY: *(In phone)* Toast. *(To PAULA)* Buttered?

PAULA: *(Sits on couch)* Buttered.

LARRY: *(In phone)* Buttered. That's all. Right away, please. *(Hangs up; sits R. of her)* Now, what's got into-you?

PAULA: I had lunch in a speakeasy. I had lunch in a speakeasy with Ernest. I had three double Martini cocktails and Ernest had double lamp chop with spinach a dollar fifty.

LARRY: That sounds like a quarrel.

PAULA: Well—yes. You can get pretty nasty on spinach. Larry, I can't face him again, tonight. Listen, darling, let's go somewhere together, you and I. Let's get a car and drive up the river, and have dinner.

LARRY: Look, Foolish, this is the night I'm having dinner at your mother's.

PAULA: Oh, Lord! Yes, we can't do that to poor Millicent . . .

(LARRY *rises; gets drink*) You're the Extra Man . . . A great big glamorous figure to—(*A sudden thought*) Larry.

LARRY: What?

PAULA: Don't drink tonight. At Mother's, I mean.

LARRY: Now, Paula, don't get maternal. (*Puts down drink.*)

PAULA: I know. (*Rises*) But I want them to see you at your best.

LARRY: (*An impatient step away*) Oh; for God's sake, Paula!

PAULA: (*Comes to him*) All right, all right!Let's talk about something else. Tell me what you've been doing. Tell me everything you've done since yesterday. Did you see Baumann? When d'you go in rehearsal? I want to know everything. Only first I want to be kissed, and kissed, and kissed.

LARRY: (*Takes her in his arms*) My sweet! My marvelous little girl!

PAULA: You love me, don't you, Larry? I know but say it.

LARRY: You know I worship you. I adore you!

PAULA: Oh, Larry! Darling! Wouldn't it be lovely if we could just stay here all evening. We'd pretend it was our house. We'd order up dinner, and pretend I'd cooked it, and we'd light the gas logs and pretend they were real, and we'd sit together in the firelight, you with a movie magazine, and me with a bit of sewing—doesn't it sound terrible! (*A note of laughter from her; gets handbag from couch.*)

LARRY: It sounds very charming.

PAULA: Just a home boy. (*Opens her handbag to glance at herself in her mirror*) Oh, what a sight! (*Powder; her curls*) Larry, what about the play? Do tell me about it. When do you start rehearsing? Monday?

LARRY: (*Wanders over to the whiskey bottle*) Yes, I think so. Just had a call from Max Kane. He's coming right over. I suppose everything's settled (*Takes up his drink; tosses it off.*)

PAULA: (*Trying not to notice the size of* LARRY'S *drink*) That's—fine.

LARRY: I suppose it's a wise thing—Max seems to think so. He may be right. A season in the legitimate, before I go back to pictures. Let them see me—they like that sort of thing.

PAULA: He's a funny little man, isn't he? I never met anyone like that. *(Has finished with lipstick and powder-puff. A look at her hair in pocket mirror)* May I use your comb? *(wanders into the bedroom. Her voice comes up from there, as she disappears)* But he's amusing. I like that kind of person.

LARRY: Oh, Max is all right. I let him talk. But this play thing is a good notion—I've been thinking about it quite a while.

PAULA: *(Re-enters, sits on couch)* I'm crazy to see you in it. It's such a romantic part.

LARRY: Oh, the play's not much, but the part is very interesting. It's practically the only male part in the play.

PAULA: There's the beach-comber.

LARRY: Oh, that doesn't amount to anything—

(Is about to pour himself another drink)

PAULA: Oh,Larry! Please don't.

LARRY: *(Putting glass down with a bang)* God! Are you going to keep on—I can't even—I do wish you'd mind your own business.

PAULA: Don't you talk to me like that!

LARRY: Then why don't you leave me alone!

PAULA: *(Rises)* Oh, darling, let's not quarrel. I couldn't stand another. I've been through the most dreadful scene with Ernest.

LARRY: *(Coming to her)* I'm so sorry. Why didn't you tell me? What's the matter?

PAULA: *(Faces him squarely)* Ernest is being sent to London. He expects me to go with him.

LARRY: London! You mean right away!

PAULA: I don't know. Soon. He was so excited about it, and happy. He began telling me how wonderful it would be—we could run over to Paris in the Spring. I tried but it only sounded—then he got angry. Finally he said I didn't love him. I wanted to scream, no, I don't! I don't!

LARRY: You didn't do it!

PAULA: *(Not stopping)* And when I think that I've got to see him again tonight. Tonight! *(Laughs a little hysterically.)* You'll be at Mother's dinner. *(Laughs again, a high little cracked laugh.)* "Tell me about your work. Is Hollywood really.." *(Turns away, trailing off into something like a whimper.)*

LARRY: *(His arms around her)* Paula, stop that! Pull yourself together! Stop it!

PAULA: *(Facing him)* Oh, Larry, what are we going to do? I've got to tell him.

LARRY: But you mustn't. *(The door BUZZER SOUNDS)* Come in! It's your coffee.

PAULA: I'd forgotten all about it.

(The WAITER enters R. with a portable table balanced on his shoulder. On it is service for one.)

LARRY: Right over here, waiter. This will fix you up.

WAITER: *(Has put the table down C.)* Is everything all right, sir?

LARRY: Yes, I think so. *(The WAITER stands, check in hand.)* Oh. *(Takes the check; signs it. A little futile slapping of the pockets in search change. None is forthcoming.)* Paula, have you got a quarter? I don't seem to.

PAULA: What? *(A gesture to bag on couch)* Help yourself.

WAITER: Shall I pour it for you, sir? *(LARRY assents "Yes."'' LARRY opens the bag; takes out a quarter; gives it to the WAITER.)* Thank you. *(He goes out R. PAULA, who has been detached in mood from all this, now swallows down a cup of coffee, black.)*

LARRY: Hay! You must have needed that.

PAULA: Larry, let me tell Ernest. It's so rotten not to. Poor Ernest, he's a dear. *(A sigh. Hand passed over her forehead)* Why, less than a month ago I thought I was in love with him. And you were just one of those million dollar movie stars. Only a month ago!

That was another girl—a different person. What a very young person!

LARRY: Now listen to me, Paula.

PAULA: *(Pacing up and down.)* I know, I know. Ernest is just the sort of man I ought to marry. And you're the sort that girls are always warned against. I know all the things you've done. I know all the times you've been married-

LARRY: But I'm still married.

PAULA: I don't care! I'm sick of hiding my love for you—What do I care about my prim little life—Miss Hickson's-on-the-Hudson-"One two three turn, One two-" I want to give it up! I hate it! *(A gesture of helplessness from* LARRY*)* Do you think I could still love Ernest after all this! Oh Larry! *(Comes to him)*

LARRY: Paula, I've reproached myself a thousand times. If only I'd never touched you.

PAULA: Oh Larry, don't talk to me as though I were the little country girl ruined by the city slicker. I knew what I was doing. I'm proud of it.

LARRY: *(Crosses to C. before speaking)* Paula, for the first time in my life I'm thinking of the other person. *(PAULA turns away with a look of impatience.)* You don't know anything about me. Not a thing. You've read about me in the papers. We met at a cocktail party. You've known me a month.

PAULA: But Larry, how can—

LARRY: I know. It's been a beautiful month. But you don't really know me. You know less about me than—the waiter who just went out of this room.

PAULA: We've been together every day.

LARRY: Yes—as lovers. But we've hardly spoken a sensible word to each other. You know that I don't like pink, and I eat my oysters without cocktail sauce. But that isn't me.

PAULA: All right. Tell me you murdered a man in Alaska

LARRY: That's what I mean. You're not even grown up. You're a kid of nineteen. You're nineteen and I'm forty-t- I'm almost forty.

PAULA: All the more reason. College boys in coonskin coats
them.

LARRY: It isn't just age—it's everything. You've never known anything but Park Avenue, and butlers, and Pierre's—

PAULA: *(Sits on couch)* That's not true. I've got a job. I go to work
every day.

LARRY: It's the fashion to have a job in your crowd. You don't know
what it means to to be up against it. To be fightin'em every second.

PAULA: *(Sits on couch)* But Larry! What's that got to do with it.
What's that got to do with our love!

LARRY: Love—! Do you want to know the truth, Paula? *(Sits R. of
her)* I love you. As much as I can love—any woman. But at my
age it isn't real love any more. There's been too many. I've been
in love a hundred times. *(Crosses R.)* I've been married to three
wives. Would you like to know about them.

PAULA: No!

LARRY: Well, there was Violet. She was a vaudeville hoofer, and still
is. I bet she hasn't changed her act in twenty years. It was a hell
of a marriage—rooming houses and dirty kimonos and fried
egg sandwiches. We used to fight like wildcats. Then I broke
into pictures, and I left her. *(Sits R. of her)* I made three pictures—Sinners in Eden—King of the Desert—Desert Love.
Then I married Edith. She was crazy about my profile. Always
talking about it. She was society. Good deal like you, Paula.
Funny, I never thought of that before. Anyhow, we were happy
for about six months. Then Hollywood got her. Parties—
drinks—they were pretty rough in those days. Then one
night—you know the rest of it—out in her car alone, drunk as
the devil—over the cliff.

PAULA: You were really in love with her, weren't you, Larry?

LARRY: As for Diana well, you know her. Biggest draw of any
woman in pictures. Ambitious! Anything to get on, and knife
me to get there. Always saying some day she'd be bigger than I
was and now—*(He catches himself as he realizes that he has said too*

much- rises; crosses R.) Well, there they are, the three of 'em. Pretty picture, isn't it? I won't tell you about the others. They swarmed on me—every kind and age and description. And I— Oh, what the hell do you want with *me!*

PAULA: *(Rises; comes to him)* I love you, Larry.

LARRY: You're young and fresh. I'm burned out. For God's sake, Paula, this is the first decent thing I ever did in my life. Listen to what I'm telling you-.

PAULA: I won't listen. I love you. Ernest and London and Mother and Dad—I love you, Larry! Nothing else matters in the whole-world!

LARRY: Paula, don't say that!

PAULA: *(Breaking in)* Larry, it's no use. Nothing you can say will make any difference. I'm going to tell them! Now! Today! Tonight! *(Starts for her hat. He holds on to her.)*

LARRY: *(Breaking in)* I won't let you! D'you understand! I won't let you smash-up your life.

PAULA: I'll smash it up if I want to! *(Gets hat from couch)* I'm going straight home and tell Mother and Dad! And tonight I'm going to tell Ernest!

LARRY: You're not!

PAULA: I am!

LARRY: I tell you—you're not! *(A noisy, prolonged and patterned* BUZZ *at R. door announces the impending entrance of* MAX KANE. *It has come insistently in the midst of their argument. The noise quiets them, finally. They stand a moment.)* That—that's Max. *(He glances toward R. door; back to* PAULA.) Paula, I want you to promise me

PAULA: *(Very low and determined)* No. *(*MAX, *fearful that* LARRY *is asleep, begins rattling the door.)*

LARRY: *(Turns between answering the door and getting a promise of silence from)* Paula, for God's sake!

PAULA: It's no use, Larry. My mind is made up.*(knocks on the door. They stand, facing each other.)*

(LARRY *goes to the door.* PAULA *picks up her bag, her gloves.* MAX KANE, *whom* LARRY *now admits, is a small, tight,. slim, eel-like man in his thirties; swarthy, neat, and very Broadway. He is unmistakably Jewish, but he does not talk with an accent, unless it is the accent of the Cockney New Yorker. His clothes are extreme in pockets, haberdashery and cut.*)

MAX: Don't you ever get up? *(He sees* PAULA*)* Oh!

LARRY: *(Ill at ease)* You know Mr. Kane. Miss Jordan.

MAX: Oh, sure! How's the little lady?

PAULA: I'm splendid, thank you. And you?

MAX: Top-of the bottle!

PAULA: I'll telephone you, Larry—later.

LARRY: Please think of what I said.

MAX: Am I butting in?

PAULA: No, I was just going. Goodbye. *(At the R. door)* Goodbye, Larry.

LARRY: *(Their eyes meeting)* Goodbye.

MAX: *(Has again placed his hat on his head. It now is perched well back, at a precarious angle. He has a habit of talking through the cigarette in his mouth)* Well, how's the Great Profile! Been out today, or just sticking around here?

LARRY: *(Going over to the table on which the whiskey stands)* No, I wasn't feeling very well, and I slept kind of late. I'm going out to dinner. *(Is pouring his drink.)*

MAX: Why'n't you go up to McDermott's and get a workout every day? Take some of that blubber off you. *(Lifts cover off of toast dish)* What's this? Toast? *(Polishes off a slice.)*

LARRY: I'm all right. Once I go into rehearsal I'll get in shape. *(Tosses off a stiff drink..)*

MAX: *(A gesture toward the drink)* Just keep on with that. That'll fix you.

LARRY: What's up? Did you see Baumann?

MAX: Yeah. Uh, look, Larry, I got a little disappointing news for you, kind of.

LARRY: What's the matter?

MAX: You know how Baumann is—this way, that way—you never know when you got him. Well—

LARRY: For God's sake, come out with it!

MAX: I'm telling you. I go in there this afternoon. He's sitting there—a face like this—*(A gesture)* I start in talking about the play, and what does he do, he says he's got to go South next month. He's sick.

LARRY: *(Sets down his glass)* What's that mean?

MAX: Well, there you are. He's got to go South—and you can't do a play if you're South.

LARRY: Why, he's got to do it. Everything was settled.

MAX: Well, it was talked over, but it wasn't really—you see, in the theatre, unless you got it down in black and white—and then sometimes it's no good.

LARRY: *(Pacing)* Well, that's a hell of a—We'll take it away from him. He's not the only producer. The cheap crook.

MAX: Sure, Baumann's no good. That's how he got where he is. But that ain't the point. What does he do, he goes and turns the play over to Jo. Stengel.

LARRY: Jo Stengel! I thought he did nothing but highbrow plays—Ibsen.

MAX: Yeah, he likes to do those kind, but right now he needs a little money and he figures this thing sort of looks like box-office.

LARRY: Yes—of course with my draw. Stengel, h'm? He understands I'm to be starred, of course?

MAX: Well, that's just it.

LARRY: What?

MAX: Look, Larry—I don't want you to blame me for this—I been plugging you for months—

LARRY: *(Fixes* MAX *with a glare of suspicion)* What the hell are you trying to tell me?

MAX: Now, don't go up in the air about it. Because there's sure to be something else.

LARRY: *(Ominously)* Do you mean I'm out! You double-crossing bastard! Do you mean I'm out!

MAX: God, Larry, could I help it?

LARRY: Help it! Why, you dirty little swine-

MAX: Now, hold on! All right. I'm a this and I'm that. But there wasn't any way I could stop it. It was all done before I knew anything about it.

LARRY: *(Paces a step or two back and forth, trying to get control of himself)* Who's going to play the part?

MAX: Cecil Bellamy.

LARRY: Ha! That piffing little—why, he's English, in the first place.

MAX: Well, the part says English explorer.

LARRY: All right! *(Glares)* I can be English! I can be as English as. anybody. *(Pacing in his annoyance; speaking from time to time, throwing lines over his shoulder)* I've waited for this play for six weeks. I could have had a million things.

MAX: Sure. Sure you could. And you can get 'em yet. Larry. Only—

LARRY: Only what? Go on say it, you little squirt

MAX: No, only you been a long time away. And you know the public. Besides, there's a bunch of 'em want to work on the stage again—picture names.

LARRY: Well, good God, you're not going to compare me!—

MAX: No—no! But you see, you're not a talkie name—

LARRY: I was in talkies. I made some of the first talking pictures that were made.

MAX: Yeah. But—Trouble is, they forget. They forget overnight. You got to get to work again. Get out there and act. Let 'em see you.

LARRY: All right. That's what I got you for. You've got to dig something up. And none of your four shows a day in vaudeville.

MAX: You could have got twenty weeks with that act if you'd behaved yourself.

LARRY: What about those radio people? Didn't you hear from them?

MAX: Well, I'm watching that. The fella's out of town.

LARRY: And the personal appearances—what did you do about that?

MAX: Mm—for personal appearances you got to be right in the limelight. That's my point. They forget about you. The best thing would be a part in a play.

LARRY: All right. But where's the vehicle?

MAX: Well—now—don't jump down my throat again. But I got an idea.

LARRY: What kind of an idea?

MAX: I was thinking about this play again. You know Larry, I never said anything, but I never did think that was such a hot part for. you. *(Fixes* LARRY *now with a finger)* Do you know the part I would be crazy to play if I was an actor?

LARRY: What?

MAX: That beach-comber.

LARRY: Beach-comber! You're asking me to go on—*(Pounds his chest in outraged vanity)*—and play a part that—Get the hell out of here! Go on! Get out! Get out, you miserable little—

MAX: *(Soothingly)* Now Larry, don't make a mistake.

LARRY: *(Between his teeth)* Get out! Get out before I kick you out!

MAX: *(A shrug. Quietly adjusts his hat)* Have it your own way. *(A gesture with the hand. A last furtive look to see if he means it. He opens the door.)*

LARRY: Wait a minute! *(MAX stands motionless, his hand on the door)* Shut the door! *(MAX does so.)* What makes you think the other part isn't right for me?

MAX: *(Crossing quickly to* LARRY*)* It's no good. They'll get tired of him. But this other fellow! Comes on, once—hell of a scene—goes off they keep waiting for him to come back, and he never does! What a part!

LARRY: Of course his one scene is very nice.

MAX: It's the high spot of the show. You know what'll happen? At the finish this What's-His-Name'll be trying to take bows, and they'll all be yelling "Renault! Renault!"

LARRY: *(Not unpleased)* You think so, huh?

MAX: A pushover! Now what do you say? *(A quick consulting of his watch)* I'm seeing Stengel right away—he's an old friend of mine—*(Starting to go.)*

LARRY: Well, wait a minute. Don't let on you've talked to me yet. Just say maybe you can get me to play it.

MAX: Sure! Leave it to me.

LARRY: Of course—I'd be—featured?

MAX: Maybe it'd be smart not to. Sneak up on 'em

LARRY: But after all, I'm a star. I got eight thousand a week in pictures. Everybody knows that.

MAX: Mm—that was quite a while ago. And this is the theatre. I'll tell you what—It's quarter to five. I'll run right down to Stengel's office; get you in before he leaves there today. I'll call you right back. *(Gets coat.)*

LARRY: Hold on a minute. He mustn't think I'm after this part. Make him come to me.

MAX: Now, Larry, it ain't done that way. You're the actor, and—

LARRY: I'm Larry Renault! I don't go to managers with my hat in my hand. He'd expect to get me for nothing. But if he comes up here, sees this place—

MAX: God, Larry—bringing managers to actors! *(A shrug)* Well, maybe he'll do it as a favor to me. You know, I used to be Jo's office boy.—How long you going to be here?

LARRY: Oh a long time. I'm not dining till eight.

MAX: *(Prepares to leave)* Well! If I can do it, I'm good. Look, Larry—*(One arm in his coat sleeve, he pauses to give these final instructions)*—if he comes up here, you want to watch your step. We can't afford to let this part get away from us.

LARRY: *(A slight pause while LARRY paces, nervously, turning the whole thing over in his mind. Suddenly he wheels)* Max, I can't do it.

MAX: *(Very low.)* You've got to do it.

LARRY: Larry Renault can't go on and play a mere character part. I won't do it. I won't humiliate myself.

(The sound of BUZZER. LARRY goes slowly to R. door. MAX drifts thoughtfully upstage, so that he is not seen from the hall doorway. MR. HATFIELD, the assistant manager of the Hotel Versailles, is seen at R. door. He comes a step or two into the doorway, a suave figure in cutaway coat and striped trousers. He goes through the form of bowing deferentially from the waist.)

HATFIELD: *(Professionally cheery)* Good afternoon, Mr. Renault!

LARRY: Oh! How-do-you-do?

HATFIELD: Beautiful day, isn't it?

LARRY: *(Uneasily)* Yes—ah—

HATFIELD: I've taken the liberty of bringing up your bill again, Mr. Renault. *(A quick warning look from LARRY. An apprehensive look over his shoulder toward MAX, he starts speaking and pushing HATFIELD out of the door)* Our cashier would like to balance his books, so if—*(MAX, as he catches the drift of what is going on, comes cautiously forward a few steps for a look at the proceedings.)*

LARRY: Oh, yes, yes. *(Hurriedly takes the envelope from HATFIELD's hand)* I'll send you down a check. I've someone here now. Thank you very much. *(Quickly closes the door. Stuffs the envelope into the pocket of his dressing gown)* Damned impertinence!

MAX: *(With a great show of cheerfulness)* Well! I'll bustle on down, get hold of Stengel—*(On his way, LARRY stops to give two or three heartening slaps on the back)* Come on! Snap out of it This time next year you'll be riding the high waves!

LARRY: *(With a false air of agreement)* I'm all right.

MAX: Sure! You're swell! Well—goodbye!

LARRY: Oh—Max!

MAX: Huh?

LARRY: *(A transparent attempt at lightness. He even manages a cackle. of laughter)* Here's. a funny thing! I wonder if you could let me have five dollars. Taxi fare. I didn't get out to the bank-I'm going to this dinner—and what do you think I've got! *(Plunges his hand in his pocket, brings out a little scattering of coins, at which he glances, very amused)* Seventeen cents! Ha-ha!

MAX: Say, I got just enough to get to the office. I'll bring it to you when I come back. *(He goes out R. hurriedly.* LARRY *stands alone, crosses to C., jingling the coins in his palm. He tosses them on the end table. As he throws them,* BUZZER *sounds.)*

LARRY: Come in! *(The* WAITER *has entered R., using his pass key, as calls to him. He leaves the door open.)*

WAITER: Can I take the table?

(WARN Dim Out.)

LARRY: Yes. *(The* WAITER *comes over, picks up the table, hoists it to his shoulder, turns to leave.)* Oh, waiter!

WAITER: Yes, sir?

LARRY: I' just remembered I haven't had a thing to eat all day. I'm not dining till eight. I'll tell you what. Bring me a cup of coffee, good and strong, and let me see—I think I'll take a caviar sandwich.

WAITER: Yes, sir. *(Hesitates.)*

LARRY: *(Dismisses him with a wave of the hand.)* That's all.

WAITER: I'm sorry, Mr. Renault, but were you going to sign for it?

LARRY: What?

WAITER: Well, excuse me, but my orders are that if you sign for it, I can't serve any more food here.

LARRY: What's that! Not serve!—*(Rushes to the telephone)* You get that order up here! I'll tell that manager—You get that order—

WAITER: Yes sir. *(He goes out R., closing the door gently behind him.)*

LARRY: *(Just as the* WAITER *is vanishing. In phone)* Hello! Hello! *(Then very quietly puts hand on hook, then replaces receiver. Immediately the* PHONE *rings.)* Hello! No, I didn't call. No. Wait a minute. Yes, I did. Send up a bellboy, will you? To go on an errand. *(An afterthought)* Listen. I want Eddie—Eddie, the one that always comes up here. *(Hangs up. A look around the room, searching for something. The silver frame containing* PAULA JORDAN'S *picture. He goes quickly to it, removes the photograph, props the picture precariously up against the leather frame containing his own picture, brings the silver frame over to the table. Another look around. Notices his cuffs. Removes one link, tosses it on the table with the frame. As he starts to remove the other—)*

THE LIGHTS DIM OUT.

SCENE II

DOCTOR TALBOT'S *office. There is a door at the back, leading into the laboratory and examination rooms. The door at the Left opens on the reception room; the door at the Right connects with the* TALBOTS' *house proper.*

The room is pine-paneled, restful, simply and tastefully furnished as a doctor's consulting room. In a niche over the door at the back there is a bust of Hippocrates. Built-in book shelves extend to the ceiling. The doctor's flat-topped desk is at the Right, turned slightly at an angle, with chairs R. and L. of it. On it, in addition to the usual desk furnishings, are two telephones, and a large photograph of the doctor's wife and his fourteen-year-old son. A comfortable chair for patients is at the side of the doctor's desk. A revolving bookcase and small bench is at the Left of the stage. There is a clock above door L., a barometer above door R.

As the curtain rises MISS ALDEN, *the nurse attendant, enters from the laboratory. She is about twenty-seven, poised, capable without being bustling, intelligent, and attractive in her white uniform. She goes into the reception room.*

As the curtain rises MISS ALDEN *gets C., the* CLOCK *strikes five. A clear and pleasing sound. A brief moment of silence.* DR. TALBOT *enters R. He is wearing his topcoat and hat. His whole aspect is that of a man wearied almost to the point of exhaustion.*

He has an hour of consultation work ahead of him. He glances at his desk pad; presses his desk BUZZER. *It is heard sounding in the reception room, off L. He drops into his chair.*

MISS ALDEN *enters immediately. Between* DR. TALBOT *and* MISS ALDEN *there is a friendly professional understanding. They convey to each other, with a look or a brief sentence, the entire history of a patient's case.*

MISS ALDEN: *(There is a slip of paper in her hand. She goes directly to* DR. TALBOT'S *desk and places the slip of paper before him.)* There are six in the waiting room. And Mr. Parker telephoned. It's his sinus again, but he can't get here till seven. He wants to know if you'll see him.

DR. TALBOT: *(Wearily)* Oh, I suppose so.

MISS ALDEN: Did you see Mrs. Talbot as you came through? She wanted to talk to you.

DR. TALBOT: *(Rather distractedly. Rises, removes coat)* No, No, I didn't.

MISS ALDEN: You look all in. It must have been tougher than you thought it would be.

DR. TALBOT: Fierce! Carcinoma of the head of the pancreas. On the table an hour. It was a beautiful operation.

MISS ALDEN: *(Taking* TALBOT'S *coat and hat)* You must be limp as a rag. Don't you want a cup of coffee?

DR. TALBOT: *(As he rises he takes off his suitcoat and goes toward C. door)* No, I'll be all right.

MISS ALDEN: *(An afterthought)* Oh, how's the patient? Did he live?

DR. TALBOT: Yes, he's fine. *(Exits C. The* PHONE *rings. It is his private wire, and the ring is rather fainter than that of the ordinary phone.)*

MISS ALDEN: *(Coat and hat on her arm. Goes to the phone)* Doctor Talbot's office. Who is it, please? Well, who is it? I'm sorry, but I have to have the name. *(A little knowing smile)* Oh, yes, Mrs. Packard. He's in. Just a minute. *(Goes to the door C., which is slightly open)*

DR. TALBOT: Yes?

MISS ALDEN: *(With no little delight)* Call on your private wire.

TALBOT: Who is it?

MISS ALDEN: *(A little smile)* Mrs. Packard.

TALBOT: *(Quickly)* I'm not here!

MISS ALDEN: *(With devilish elation)* I'm awfully sorry. *(Is going toward L. door, very pleased with herself)* I've already told her you're in. *(Goes out L.)*

DR. TALBOT: *(Off)* Oh, for God's—! *(He enters. He has changed his suit coat to a roomier older coat. He strides into the room, halts a moment and stands glaring at the waiting telephone. With resignation he goes to his desk; sits R. of it; speaks into phone)* Hello. Now Kitty—Kitty! But there's no occa—No, I can't come over! You know perfectly well these are my office hours. I've got a whole roomful of—there's nothing the matter with you—take an aspirin—well, I've been busy. I'll see you tonight at the Jordans—of course, you can go. There's nothing the matter with you. Other women!

(LUCY TALBOT enters quietly R. She does not mean to overhear the telephone conversation, but she finds herself in the midst of it and must stand a moment before she is impelled to make her presence known. She is a wren-like, somewhat faded little figure, but possessed of a quiet power, too, as well as poise and gentle breeding. Her dress is dark, almost prim, relieved with white collars and cuffs, very simple and delicate. TALBOT, rather frantic at the telephone, does not see her. His hand is pressed to his forehead) Of course there's no other woman. Kitty, you're driving me absolutely—*(Lucy, in order to*

let her husband know that she is in the room, shuts the door behind her firmly enough to attract his attention. She advances a few steps into the room as he rather, blunderingly goes on with his conversation, changing its tone completely, or attempting) I think you'd better rest for an hour, and then take a mild bromide—say an aspirin. Well, I have patients in the office. There's no cause for alarm. *(He hangs up quickly. Then, with a great assumption of ease, he turns to his wife, rising)* Hello, Lucy!

LUCY: *(In the same tone)* Hello, Jo!

TALBOT: How are you, dear?

LUCY: I'm fine. And you?

TALBOT: I'm all right.

LUCY: Anything new?

TALBOT: *(Very airily. Sits R. of desk)* No. No.

LUCY: Just the same old thing, h'm?

TALBOT: What?

LUCY: I mean—unreasonable women patients.

TALBOT: Oh—yes—she's not really sick. I just prescribed a sedative. She doesn't need anything.

LUCY: *(Sits L. of desk)* How about an apple a day?

TALBOT: *(Startled)* What's that?

LUCY: Don't bother, dear.

TALBOT: Huh?

LUCY: Don't bother. Because I know all about it.

TALBOT: Why—uh—what are you talking about?

LUCY: Please, Jo! I'm not going to make a scene. You know I never do, do I? Remember how nicely I behaved about the others? Mrs. Whiting, and the Dalrymple girl, and that Ferguson woman, and Dolly, and—*(A swift look around)*—where do you keep your files?

TALBOT: *(With great dignity)* I tell you, you are quite wrong about this woman.

LUCY: *(Rises)* Now, Jo. I knew when it started, and I knew when you began to tire of her. They came at about the same time, didn't they? And now she's at the insistent stage. It's a great bore, isn't it, darling. *(He turns his eyes away from her, and with that gesture admits the truth of what she has said)* Don't think that I don't mind, Jo. I pretend not to—but I do. But I can't let it tear me to pieces the way it did that first time. It was just before Wayne was born—remember? I thought the world had come to an end. The noble young physician was just a masher.

TALBOT: Surely, a little more than that.

LUCY: A great deal more, Jo. That's what makes it so pathetic. You are really two people. One is so magnificent, the other so shoddy.

TALBOT: *(His fingers drum nervously for a moment on the table. Then slowly, painfully, he speaks of himself)* I suppose it's natural enough. Son of a railroad brakeman—what can you expect?

LUCY: Mm. I'm sure he blew the whistle for every hired girl between here and Albany. I wonder how your mother felt about that.

TALBOT: Don't.

LUCY: She's that other side of you the—lovely side, Jo.

TALBOT: Perhaps if she had lived I'd have been different. *(A gesture that breaks the introspective mood)* I don't know why you've stayed with me all these years. Why did you?

LUCY: *(To above desk)* A very foolish reason, Jo. Because I'm still in love with you. Isn't that funny? You'd think I'd have more pride.

TALBOT: I'm in love with you, Lucy. It's never been otherwise. Those other women—it's like gambling or drinking or drugs. You just keep on.

LUCY: No Jo, that isn't it at all. Do you know what I think? I think you're still the little boy living over on Tenth avenue, a little in awe of the girl from Murray Hill. The little boy who thinks that sex is something to be ashamed of. And that's why—forgive me, Jo—all these women in your life have been a little common ,a little bit Tenth avenue, too. I know you love me, Jo. Try to think of me as a woman, too.

TALBOT: *(His hand tightening on hers)* Lucy, darling, I feel closer to you now than I have in years.

LUCY: I'm glad, Jo.

TALBOT: I never want to see that woman again as long as I live.

LUCY: Nonsense! See her as often as you like. You're seeing her tonight, aren't you? Isn't she going to the Jordans'?

TALBOT: Good God, yes! I forgot. If only we could stay home tonight, just the two of us.

LUCY: I'd like to, too, Jo. But we've got to go.

TALBOT: Why do we have to go?

LUCY: Now, Jo!

TALBOT: Why did you ever accept it?

LUCY: What could I do? Say we had an engagement? They'd only ask us some other night.

TALBOT: But why do they ask us at all? What's it all about?

LUCY: Because we had them for dinner. And before that they had us for dinner, and that's why we had them. (A little light laugh from the two of them.)

MISS ALDEN: *(Enters hurriedly L. Though she makes no undue commotion, it is evident that she is disturbed)* Doctor!—Oh, I'm sorry. *(Seeing MRS. TALBOT)*—Mr. Oliver Jordan is outside, and he seems quite ill. I think you'd—

TALBOT: Have him come right in. *(MISS ALDEN goes out L. quickly. TALBOT'S head comes up. He pulls himself together. He is at once the professional man.)*

LUCY: *(Speaks on "Oliver Jordan is outside")* I'll go. *(She goes out R. immediately. TALBOT has risen. He crosses quickly to R. door, which has stood open. As he stands at the door MISS ALDEN voice is heard, off.)*

MISS ALDEN: You're fine now. Here let me help you. *(OLIVER JORDAN enters, assisted by MISS ALDEN. Obviously he has had an accute attack, from which he is just emerging.* Talbot *supports him as he comes through the door.* Miss Alden, *with her free hand, closes the door behind her.)*

Talbot: *(Breaking in)* Why, what's this, Oliver? Come over here and sit down. Take it easy. That's right.

Oliver: *(Being assisted toward the chair L. of desk. His hand held over the region of the pain)* It's right here.

Talbot: *(Quickly, to* Miss Alden*)* Nitrate of amyl—quick! *(*Miss Alden *vanishes into the laboratory. As* Oliver *drops into the chair,* Talbot *quickly undoes his tie, unbuttons his shirt and undershirt.* Miss Alden *returns immediately with the amyl, gives it to* Talbot, *who quickly breaks the covering, holds the drug to* Oliver's *nose)* Sniff that! *(Almost immediately, under the influence of the strong drug,* Oliver *revives.* Miss Alden *leaning over him, her hands resting lightly on his shoulders)* There! That's better! *(*Talbot *takes his stethoscope from his inner coat pocket, applies it over* Oliver's *heart.)*

Oliver: *(A feeble gesture of protest)* I'm all right now. *(Heedless of protest, concentrates on the examination. At its conclusion he straightens, stands completely still for a second; looking down at There is a quick exchange of glances between* Talbot *and* Miss Alden.*)*

Talbot: *(Crossing to behind desk)* Yes, of course you are.

Oliver: *(Relieved. Smiles wanly)* I've got no business doing this. What's the matter with?

Talbot: *(Sits. As* Miss Alden *exits C. Closes door)* How long has this been going on? Have you had it before?

Oliver: *(Buttoning his shirt)* Why, no, not like this. I started to walk home from the Athletic Club and suddenly I felt funny. I managed to get into a taxi, and—here I am. What is it, anyhow?

Talbot: Oh, probably a little indigestion. *(A gesture that vaguely points in the direction of the heart)* What have you been eating? What did you have for lunch?

Oliver: Why, nothing that would upset me. A little fish -

Talbot: If I were you, I'd watch my diet. Simple food, and not too much of it.

OLIVER: Well, if that's all—

TALBOT: I'd like to have you come in again in a day or two. More thorough examination. How's tomorrow?

OLIVER: Tomorrow—that's Saturday. I'd rather make it next week some time.

TALBOT: Now pretend this is a business appointment. Tomorrow— what time? When do you leave your office?

OLIVER: *(Good-naturedly humoring the doctor)* All right, all right! How about two-thirty?

TALBOT: I'm at the hospital until four. Make it four-fifteen?

OLIVER: Four-fifteen. (TALBOT *makes a note of this on his pad; seeing* OLIVER *rise,* TALBOT *also rises)* Well! *(Finds himself surprisingly steady. Looks about in mild triumph)* Why, I feel great! I may fool you and not come in at all tomorrow.

TALBOT: You show up here. Broken appointments are charged double.

OLIVER: You boys certainly clean up. What did I get for my money today? A whiff of smelling salts.

TALBOT: Look here—what're you doing tonight?

OLIVER: Huh? Why, you're coming to dinner, among others.

TALBOT: Can you sneak out early, and go to bed?
(WARN Dim Out.)

OLIVER: Why—I think we're all going to theatre.

TALBOT: *(A slow cross to C.)* I wouldn't do it, if I were you. Take it easy for a while. Avoid any excitement, or emotional strain. Stop worrying. Stop thinking about business.

OLIVER: What does that mean? The old pump out of order?

TALBOT: No, no. (MISS ALDEN *enters C. with card index box. Busies herself at desk)* But it's bound to feel the effect of any physical disorder. That's all.

OLIVER: *(A pause. Thoughtfully)* I—see.

TALBOT: *(Heartily)* Well, see you later, h'm? Dinner at eight?

OLIVER: *(Starting L.)* Yes, I believe so. Goodbye.

TALBOT: Goodbye, Oliver–

OLIVER: *(At door L.)* I'm—I'm not fooled. *(Exits.* TALBOT *stands motionless, looking after* OLIVER*)*

MISS ALDEN: *(Comes down to* TALBOT *)* How bad is it?

TALBOT: Coronary artery. Spasm.

MISS ALDEN: How long will he live?

TALBOT: A few months—weeks—days, even. *(Walks slowly to his desk.)*

MISS ALDEN: You're sure?

TALBOT: Positive. You can tell it like—*(Snaps his fingers)*—that.

MISS ALDEN: Poor fellow.

TALBOT: *(Sits R. of desk. Assents, almost unintelligibly)* Yes.

MISS ALDEN: *(Assumes again her professional manner)* Ready? *(*TALBOT *nods.* MISS ALDEN *goes to the L. door, opens it, stands looking into the other room.)* All right. Mrs. Beveridge *(She remains at the door, waiting for the new patient to enter. The Doctor still sits thoughtfully at his desk. His head comes up, his face assumes the professional look for the next patient.)*

THE LIGHTS DIM OUT.

SCENE III

The butler's pantry at the JORDANS'. *It is a rectangular room, its walls, woodwork and curtains in a pale yellow, very cool and agreeable. It is a workmanlike place, equipped for serving. There is a door Left.*

Right Center, between sink and Frigidaire, is large cupboard, its shelves filled with plates, cups, saucers, glassware; flower vases on the top most shelves; compote dishes. Underneath are drawers. Just above these is a broad shelf for laying out plates, etc.

In the lower Right of the room is a sink, to which is attached, at one end, a drainboard. In the back wall, C., is a very large built-in Fridgidaire icebox with a solitary green bottle of Kalak water on top of it.

Against the Left wall, just next to the kitchen door and above it, is a second-cupboard with a serving shelf. A little to the Left of Center is a kitchen table, its narrow end turned toward the audience. Two chairs are alongside this table.

There is a small portable radio on the cupboard shelf at the Right. The time is about five-thirty.

At the Rise, the RADIO *is going full tilt—a popular tune played by one of the hotel tea dance orchestras.* DORA, *the only occupant of the pantry, is preparing for tonight's dinner. As she works she hums happily in compliment to the radio's music, and occasionally tosses in a few words of the lyric—when she she knows them. She has been wiping glasses. There are already eight of them—champagne glasses—on the table. She finishes the last two, puts them with the others. Brings down ten dinner plates from a shelf, puts them on the serving shelf.*

There is about her a certain elation and bloom, the reason for which now becomes apparent. She holds out her hand, on which is her new wedding ring. Holds the hand, thus ornamented, up to her own enchanted gaze.

Enter L. MRS. WENDEL *the cook.* MRS. WENDEL *is Swedish, but with no trace of accent. She is an ample woman in her mid-fifties; is dressed in white, and wears a large apron. Rolled up sleeves. Her natural amiability is clouded at the moment by a bad tooth, and her face is tied up in a great toothache bandage. Her left arm encircles a yellow mixing bowl, which rests on one broad hip. In the hand that holds the bowl she grasps an envelope containing a letter. With the other hand she busily stirs the mixture as she talks. She drops the letter on the table, goes to the icebox. Relinquishing her spoon for a time, she opens the icebox, deftly removes the top from a milk bottle, pours a little milk into the mixture within the bowl, replaces the milk bottle, slams the icebox door.* DORA, *in the mealtime, having got the necessary number of plates from the R. cupboard, is now occupied in scanning them to see that they are properly shining. Occasionaly, she rubs one with a tea cloth, or runs hot water from the tap over a cloudy looking plate*

MRS. WENDEL: *(At the icebox)* I put a letter there for Gustave. It just came.

DORA: What?

MRS. WENDEL: A letter came for Gustave. Turn that lower *(indicating radio.* DORA *modifies the* RADIO *music. Drifts over to the table to look inquisitively at the letter)* It's from that place he came over from in Europe

DORA: *(Reads the postmark)* Lu-cerny. S-u-i-s-s-e. *(Spelling it)* Where's that, Mrs. Wendel?

MRS. WENDEL: *(Coming down to peer over Dora's shoulder)* It's what they call Switzerland. I got one too, today.

DORA: It looks like a woman, the writing.

MRS. WENDEL: Mine was from my brother. He wants fifty dollars.

DORA: *(Tucks the letter in her apron pocket. Going to the sink)* Letters from your folks is always money. *(Fills a glass with water, turns, stands sipping it, her gaze on Mrs. Wendel, who is briskly beating her mixture at table)* How's your tooth, Mrs. Wendel? Any better?

MRS. WENDEL: I put essence of cloves on it, but it keeps jumping. I wish I could get to the dentist. Only for this dinner I could have.

DORA: Yeah, it had to be just today, or else we could have had a celebration. *(Again* DORA'S *gaze fastens itself upon the new ring.)*

MRS. WENDEL: I have to laugh the way you thought you could fool me. The minute I looked at your face I knew you was married.

DORA: Remember, don't you tell a living soul. I better take my ring off. *(Speaking as she removes her ring, knots it again in the hand-*

kerchief, tucks the handkerchief into her pocket) If that Ricci sees it, I wouldn't put nothing past him.

MRS. WENDEL: I wouldn't breathe it to him. *(A sudden thought)* It don't seem hardly right, getting married yesterday and coming right back to work today.

DORA: It was fun, though. I was all excited and laughing, but Gustave, he was so scared you'd think he was getting hung.

MRS. WENDEL: The men are always like that.

DORA: He was all right, though, after. When we had dinner. You ought to go to that place, some time, where we ate. For a dollar you get choice of crab meat or soup, and then there's fish, and then choice of pork chops with applesauce, prime ribs of beef au jus, or chicken a la Calcutta. We took that.

MRS.WENDEL: I got chicken for them tonight. I'm glad because it don't take much fixing. I was two hours on the lobster aspic—they're such a job—and then they'll eat it up in five minutes.

DORA: It's good, though. I hope there's some left over.

MRS. WENDEL: I made the big one so there would be. Wait till you see it.

DORA: They got a lord and lady coming, haven't they? I wonder how she'll look.

MRS.WENDEL: They look just like anybody else—only homelier.

DORA: I think they're having mostly old people. Miss Paula won't be there. She's going out with Ernest.

MRS. WENDEL: When they get married, that'll be a lot of cooking.

DORA: If you ask me, I don't think she's going to marry him. He's always calling up and she's always making excuses.

MRS. WENDEL: I don't like him. I peeked in at him once through the door. He hasn't any It. (GUSTAVE *enters L., bearing a tray and the remains of a depleted tea.)*

DORA: Oh, hello!

GUSTAVE: *(Puts down the tray with something of a thump)* Thought she'd never get through. Sip. Sip. (*He is at* DORA'S *side R.C. as soon as he can get there; kisses her tenderly.*)

MRS. WENDEL: (*With a fondly deprecatory gesture*) Oh! (*Exits L.*)

DORA: I thought you were never coming back. I was going to go up there and get you.

GUSTAVE: (*A final kiss. Removing his coat and hanging it over the back of a chair back of table*) I was wishing she'd choke. All I could think of was getting back to my little Dora. (*He takes from a hook a long apron designed for protection in rougher work. Ties it around his waist.*)

DORA: I wish this dinner was over.

GUSTAVE: (*Placing tray on shelf L.*) We'll serve 'em fast. Take the plates away from them. What's the meat course?

DORA: Chicken. (*Putting chair near door L.* GUSTAVE *takes from the shelf a long and vicious looking carving knife, together with a knife sharpener. He proceeds to wield the two with expert strokes.* DORA *goes back R. to polishing her plates*) I had my ring on again. I wish I could keep it on all the time. (*Puts her hand in the apron pocket. Encounters* GUSTAVE'S *letter*) Oh, here's a letter came for you. From Switzerland. (*Holds out the letter.*)

GUSTAVE: (*Puts the knife and sharpener down on the table a shade too calmly. Takes the letter, barely glances at it*) Oh! Yes. It will be from my sister. (*Puts it in his pocket. He turns away; goes to the cupboard L.*)

DORA: Why don't you read it?

GUSTAVE: (*Busy with reaching down the glasses*) It will be the same story. They must buy a new plow—my brother-in-law is sick— there is another baby coming.

DORA: I'd like to see what Europe is like. I bet it's interesting. You been all over, haven't you?

GUSTAVE: A good butler should be a cosmopolitan. I have worked in France, in Germany, in England—even one winter I was in Cairo.

DORA: Oh, how I'd like to go traveling and see all those things with you. Gustave! Couldn't we go! Couldn't we save our money, both of us, and maybe go next summer?

GUSTAVE: You would not like it. Anyway it is finished over there. Kaput!

DORA: I would so like it! And I could meet your folks. Maybe you're ashamed of me!

GUSTAVE: (*Comes quickly over to her. He has the glass and towel in his hands, she the plate and towel in her hands*) No, no, my darling! My darling Dora. (*They kiss.*)

DORA: My wonderful husband! How does it happen some other girl didn't grab you?

GUSTAVE: I was waiting for you, my beautiful Dora. (*Kiss.*)

DORA: Oh, Gustave, I never been so happy. I would be just perfectly happy, only if it wasn't for that Ricci.

GUSTAVE: Don't be a silly child! What can he do! (*MRS. WENDEL enters L. In triumph she is carrying the aspic, an imposing structure in a great platter. The aspic is in the form of a hollow ring. Inside the ring are piled the chunks of lobster. In one hand, though both are grasping the platter, MRS. WENDEL carries a very large three-pronged fork, the center prong protruding beyond the other two. The handle is a foot long.*)

MRS. WENDEL: God be thanked, this is finished. (*Depositing it on the C. table.*)

GUSTAVE: Look out for those glasses.

MRS. WENDEL: (*Fork in hand, she steps back and surveys her handiwork*) And it's the best one I ever made, if I do say so. Here it is, almost six, and I've been working on it since three. She couldn't get another cook in New York to do what I've done to-day with a toothache killing me. They'd say, "I'm sick and you can cook your own dinner." (*At the Frigidaire, gets some parsley. She has been gesticulating with the fork during this speech. She now leans over the dish, distributing the parsley.*)

DORA: It's just beautiful, Mrs. Wendel.

GUSTAVE: A good thing for the toothache is to hold a little brandy like this. *(Tips his head to one side, to illustrate holding a mouthful of brandy.)*

MRS. WENDEL: I'm afraid to take anything with the dinner to cook.

GUSTAVE: *(Goes to cupboard L., brings forth a decanter of brandy)* Nonsense! A mouthful won't hurt you. Just a schluck. *(Reaching for one of the frail glasses standing on the table.)*

MRS. WENDEL: Well, all right. I'm half crazy. *(GUSTAVE pours her a drink.)* You take one, too— and Dora. We'll drink a toast. The bride and the groom!

GUSTAVE: That's fine! Heh, Dora? *(Pouring two more drinks.)*

DORA: All right. I'll turn on the wedding march.

MRS. WENDEL: Yes, that's right. (Crosses R.) I'll stand up for you.

DORA: *(She goes to RADIO; turns it up so that the orchestra comes up loudly)* Oh, that's good! Come on, Gustave! *(Takes his arm.)*

MRS. WENDEL: *(Very much in the spirit of the thing, her voice high above the music. They join MRS. WENDEL at R.)* To the bride and groom. Skoal!

GUSTAVE and DORA: *(In unison)* Skoal! *(A little excited giggle from DORA. The three of them execute a little march. The kitchen door flies open. It is RICCI. He takes one dramatic step into the room and stands, a menacing figure, confronting the three.)*

DORA: *(A. terrified half-whisper)* Gustave!

RICCI: You lying little bitch! *Porco di madona!*

DORA: *(Breaking in)* Gustave! I'm scared!

GUSTAVE: *(A gesture to quiet her)* I tend to him.

MRS. WENDEL: Get out of my kitchen

RICCI: *(Advances a step or two, crouchingly)* So! You sneak off and get married, eh?

DORA: No, we ain't! No such thing!

MRS.WENDEL: *(Breaking in)* You're crazy They ain't married!

RICCI: Oh, no! Then why do you tell Josephine next door, who tell the chauffeur, who tell me, that they go to City Hall—

MRS. WENDEL: I did not, you lying Wop! *(Quickly, to* DORA*)* I didn't breathe it!

DORA: Oh! Oh!

GUSTAVE: *(On* MRS.WENDEL'S *speech)* Oh, Mrs. Wendell!

RICCI: *(Also on* MRS.WENDEL'S *speech)* So! It is true! *(Another step forward.)*

DORA: *(Continuing)* No! No! *(Cowering behind* GUSTAVE*)*

RICCI: *(Continuing)* It is true!

(He is at the table. His fist comes down on the table with a crash. It encounters the handle of the big knife which GUSTAVE *has recently sharpened. He grips it and brings it up slowly into view.)*

(WARN Blackout.)

DORA: *(Hysterically)* Oh, my God!

MRS. WENDEL: *(At the sight of the knife)* Og, Hedon!

GUSTAVE: *(Shoves the two* WOMEN *behind him, protectingly)* Put down that knife! *(Dora is whimpering with terror.)*

RICCI: *(Knife in hand, he pushes back his sleeve as he talks, preparing for battle)* If Ricci not have her, then no one will have her!

DORA: Oh, God! Oh, God!

GUSTAVE: Put it down, I tell you! *(A wild glance around. Sees the great fork which* MRS. WENDEL *has in her hand. Seizes it as a desperate weapon)* Put it down!

DORA: No, no! Gustave!

MRS. WENDEL: *Gud hjalp mig!*

RICCI: So you think you can stop me, eh? First you want me to take care of you! *(Eyes fixed on his adversary, knife poised, he begins a stealthy advance, around the end of the table.* GUSTAVE, *fork in hand, is crouched to meet his advance. There is a bit of jockeying for position.* GUSTAVE *retreats a step, shakes off the restraining hands of the* WOMEN.*)*

DORA: Gustave! He'll kill you! He'll kill you! Don't fight him!

Don't fight him! Ricci! Oh, my God! Oh, my God! Oh, my God!

MRS. WENDEL: *(Simultaneously)* Stop them! Stop them! Get the missus! Somebody stop them! Oh, min Gud!

(For a second there is complete silence, broken only by the music over the RADIO . . . *a gay and lilting tune. Then the moment arrives.* GUSTAVE, *seeing his opportunity, makes an unexpected lunge, which surprises* RICCI, *who had meant to make the attack. Stepping quickly backward to avoid* GUSTAVE'S *weapon, he comes into violent contact with the laden table, which overturns with a crash. Down go wine-glasses, plates, aspic.* GUSTAVE *follows up his offensive. The two men grapple on the floor, knife and fork flashing. Screams from the* WOMEN *as the table is overturned. A particularly terrifying scream from* DORA *as the* MEN *roll on the floor. The* MUSIC *is gayer than ever.)*

MRS. WENDEL: *(As the table overturns)* The aspic! *(The table crashes.)*

BLACKOUT

SCENE IV

Upstairs sitting room at the JORDAN'S. *Six o'clock. The lamps are lighted.* MILLICENT JORDAN, *in a negligee, is at the telephone.*

MILLICENT: Yes, that will be all right. No, I only want those four. I want the ones that played at Mrs. Post's last week. No, no, it isn't for dancing. I explained all that on Monday. It's just music through dinner. And be sure to give me the one with the black mustache that plays the violin. And tell him he's not to come into the dining room and start playing at us. He's to stay where he is, with the others. Now, they'll wear their red coats, won't they? They're so romantic. And I don't want anything but Hungarian music. That gypsy stuff, or whatever you call it. *(attempts the word without much assurance)* Czigane. Yes. *(DORA enters R. She is plainly still agitated by the events that have just taken place below stairs)* And they'll be here no later than quarter to eight. You know the address? That's it. Goodbye. *(Hangs up.)*

DORA: Madam—

MILLICENT: Yes, Dora?

DORA: *(Comes to R. sofa. In considerable embarrassment)* Cook wants to know if she can come in. *(A gesture toward the hall)* She wants to speak to you a minute.

MRS. WENDEL: Why yes. Tell her to come in. *(Wordlessly and a little apprehensively, DORA summons MRS. WENDEL from the hall. DORA retreats a step or two, but cannot bear to withdraw until she has caught at least a bit of the scene to follow. MRS. WENDEL advances to front of sofa, a figure of portent. The bandage has been removed, but occasionally, as she talks, her hand goes to the aching face)* Yes, Mrs. Wendel?

MRS. WENDEL: It's the lobster aspic.

MILLICENT: The aspic? What about it?

MRS. WENDEL: It didn't turn out right. I think it must have been the gelatine. It didn't set.

MILLICENT: What do you mean? You can't use it?

MRS. WENDEL: No ma'am. It's no good.

MILLICENT: *(Rises and crosses to C.)* Do you mean to tell me at this hour!—Why, it's six o'clock—What do you mean, you can't use it?—Let me see it. *(Makes as though to accompany MRS. WENDEL to the kitchen. Dora makes her escape R.)*

MRS. WENDEL: It's no use. I threw it away. It was like water.

MILLICENT: This is inexcusable. I particularly wanted this dinner to be—You can use the lobster, can't you? *(Pacing R. and L.)*

MRS. WENDEL: No, ma'am. It's—uh—I've never seen lobster like it. I don't think it's good.

MILLICENT: Well, this is a fine state of things! Where's my dinner? What are we going to do?

MRS. WENDEL: I thought maybe we could send for some crab meat, all ready, and I'd cook it Newburg.

MILLICENT: But the aspic was so dressy! It looks so smart when it's served.

MRS. WENDEL: Yes ma'am. But this one wouldn't have.

MILLICENT: *(A gesture of accepting the inevitable)* All right. Send for some crab meat. I'll tell, you what you do. Is Ricci here?

MRS. WENDEL: *(Hesitatingly)* Yes, ma'am.

MILLICENT: Have him drive over to Schultz's, on Lexington, and bring it right back.

MRS. WENDEL: Ricci isn't feeling very good.

MILLICENT: What's the matter with him?

MRS. WENDEL: He hurt himself. He slipped and fell and there was a thing there, and he—hurt himself. *(A gesture indicating an injury to the face.)*

MILLICENT: Where? When did this happen?

MRS. WENDEL: It was the swinging door. I don't know much about it. I wasn't there.

DORA: *(Enters R.)* Excuse me. Miss Carlotta Vance is calling on Mr. Jordan.

MILLICENT: On the telephone?

DORA: No, ma'am. She's downstairs.

MILLICENT: Downstairs!

MRS. WENDEL: I'll call Schultz up, Mrs. Jordan, and have them send it right over.

MILLICENT: Yes, do that. Tell them I want it right away. It's an emergency. *(MRS. WENDEL exits R.)* Dora, what do you mean— downstairs? Miss Vance is coming to dinner at eight. Are you sure?

DORA: Yes, ma'am. She's calling on Mr. Jordan.

MILLICENT: How did you happen to go to the door? Where's Gustave?

DORA: He isn't feeling very good.

MILLICENT: This is fantastic! What's the matter with him?

DORA: He hurt himself.

MILLICENT: I must be going mad! What's the matter with this

household? Why, I never in all my life—*(CARLOTTA'S voice from off R.)*

CARLOTTA: Yoo-hoo! Millicent! Where are you?.

MILLICENT: Oh, dear! *(Below her breath. Then raising her voice)* In here, Carlotta! *(A gesture indicating that DORA is to show her the way. But CARLOTTA does not wait to be ushered. DORA exits L.)*

CARLOTTA: *(Entering R. with a rush)* Hello, Millicent darling!

MILLICENT: Carlotta, dear!

CARLOTTA: Oh, what a ducky little room! You don't mind my rushing up, do you? I just popped in to see Oliver.

MILLICENT: Really! How nice! But I don't think he's-

CARLOTTA: Well, I'll wait. Anything to be out of those streets. *(Sinks into sofa)* Whew!

MILLICENT: *(Appalled to see CARLOTTA loosen her furs and make preparations for something of a stay)* Perhaps it's something I could tell Oliver. Sometimes he stops at the club—Dora!

CARLOTTA: *(Breaking in)* No, it's business. I'm afraid I've done something rather naughty. I've come to confess.

MILLICENT: *(As DORA re-enters L.)* Dora, Mr. Jordan hasn't come in, has he?

DORA: No, madam, he hasn't. *(DORA makes as though to go out L.)*

CARLOTTA: Oh could I have a whiskey and soda? Millicent, do you mind? I'm dying!

MILLICENT: Why, of course. Dora, a whiskey and soda for Miss Vance. *(DORA exits R.)*

CARLOTTA: I'm absolutely cracked up. I'm simply depleted. I've been in every office building between the Battery and the Bronx. Do you mind if I take my shoes off?

MILLICENT: *(Sits chair L.C.)* No please do. *(CARLOTTA slips her feet halfway out of her pumps, one foot on the floor, the heel out, her knees crossed so that the slipper of the other foot dangles from her toe as she talks.)*

CARLOTTA: Oh! *(A sigh of relief)* What a city! I left the hotel at eleven this morning, a young and lovely girl, and now look at me! An old woman! I took on ten years just trying to get from the Barclay to Times Square. Then, when we reached my building there was a crowd outside worse than Bank Holiday. It took me five minutes to fight my way through it, and it turned out to be a man selling rubberless garters at two for a quarter. I told the taxi driver to wait, and he said, "Lady, I ain't got time to wait—I got three children." Then I had a nice, restful luncheon with four lawyers—it was up on the seventy-eighth floor of the Whatsis Building—the Sky Club—a cloud floated right into my soup.

MILLICENT: Isn't it awful? But we get used to it.

CARLOTTA: The minute I've seen Oliver I'm going fight home and pop myself into bed and not get up until noon tomorrow. Thank God I don't have to go to some dreadful dinner tonight.

MILLICENT: (*In a tone of ice*) Why—you're coming here.

CARLOTTA: Am I? So I am. How simply enchanting! Why, of course—the Ferncliffes. That means a cozy little game of bridge. Well, I can always stay awake for that.

MILLICENT: But we're going to the theatre.

CARLOTTA: Oh, how delightful! I always enjoy a new play. What are we seeing?

MILLICENT: We're going to see "Say It With Music."

CARLOTTA: Oh . . . charming! I thought it was so amusing.

MILLICENT: You've seen it?

CARLOTTA: Oh, I don't mind seeing it again. He's very funny—(*A vague gesture*) with the cigar.

DORA: (*Enters R., carrying a large florist's box whose contents are so long that the stems protrude from one end. The cover has been removed; one sees a profusion of roses. She goes to* MILLICENT) These just came, Mrs. Jordan.

MILLICENT: (*Takes the box*) How lovely! (*Tips them toward* CARLOTTA) Talisman roses.

CARLOTTA: Exquisite!

MILLICENT: *(Picking up the card envelope)* It's my favorite rose. *(Reads the card)* From the Ferncliffes. *(Patronizingly)* Lord and Lady Ferncliffe. How thoughtful of them!

CARLOTTA: Not Bunny! Flowers from Bunny!

MILLICENT: Bunny?

CARLOTTA: Bunny Ferncliffe. All his friends call him Bunny. He does look like a rabbit.

MILLICENT: *(A trifle dashed)* Why—I didn't know you knew them.

CARLOTTA: To think of Bunny loosening up for flowers! Why, nobody in London will believe it. Once he dropped a shilling down the grating and he made them dig up Piccadilly to get it.

(GUSTAVE enters R. carrying a tray with the whiskey and soda. Down his right cheek and over left eye are two very noticeable strips of adhesive tape. To offset this his bearing is more magnificent than usual. Goes to table L. of sofa. Puts tray on table.)

MILLICENT: Dora, put some water in that tall vase. *(Hands her the flowers)* And— let me see— I think they'd look well on the console in the dining room.

DORA: Yes, ma'am. *(Goes to the table up C. Places the box on the table for the moment; picks up the tall vase.)*

MILLICENT: Why, Gustave! What's happened to your face! *(DORA, arrested by the question, stands nervously awaiting its outcome. At MILLICENT'S tone, CARLOTTA, too, glances with curiosity at GUSTAVE'S face.)*

CARLOTTA: Why, Gustave! It's my Gustave! Gustave, when in the world did—He was my waiter for weeks at the Bauer-au-lac in Lucerne. When was it, Gustave? Two winters ago? No—three.

GUSTAVE: *(With an uncomfortable little cough)* Ah—yes, madam.

MILLICENT: How interesting!

CARLOTTA: How is your darling wife and those lovely children? *(Turns to MILLICENT)* He's got three of the most—Have you seen them? And his wife—*(The vase drops from DORA'S hands with a thud.)*

MILLICENT: *(Reprovingly)* Dora!

DORA: *(Crushed)* Excuse me—madam. *(She rushes blindly out R.)*

MILLICENT: Why, what's the matter with her? Gustave, see if anything's the matter.

GUSTAVE: Yes, madam. *(He picks up vase; starts to go R.)*

CARLOTTA: Gustave! Bringing those Continental customs over here! *(OLIVER enters R.)*

GUSTAVE: Oh, no, madam! *(Exits R.)*

OLIVER: *(Throws a little puzzled backward glance his shoulder, having passed the fleeing DORA in the hall. Sees CARLOTTA. Comes to her)* Why, Carlotta! *(to MILLICENT)* hello, dear.

MILLICENT: Hello, darling.

CARLOTTA: Well, I've found out about you Big Business Men. Leave your offices at four. What have you been up to for the last two hours?

OLIVER: *(Wanly)* All sorts of mischief.

MILLICENT: *(Goes to OLIVER)* Darling, you're all mussy. Look at your tie! Been playing squash?

OLIVER: No. No.

MILLICENT: Why don't you try to get a rest before dinner? Oh, Carlotta wants to talk to you.

CARLOTTA: *(Pouring herself a drink, and mixing it)* I shan't be a minute, Oliver dear.

MILLICENT: I'll be tactful and vanish. *(Exits L. OLIVER goes to the tray; pours himself a stiff drink; takes it.)*

CARLOTTA: *(Watching this in some surprise)* Mm! Hard day at the office, h'm? I tried to get you there. Did they tell you?

OLIVER: *(Crosses L.)* No. I left early.

CARLOTTA: Then I called up here. They said you'd be in about six, so I took a chance.

OLIVER: What's the matter? Something wrong?

CARLOTTA: Oliver, ducky, you won't be cross with Carlotta, will you? I wanted to ask you first, and I told him, but the man said it had to be today there was some sort of meeting and you weren't at your office, so I went ahead. And then I got sort of worried, about it—

OLIVER: What are you trying to tell me?

CARLOTTA: Well Oliver sweet, poor Carlotta was so stony,and it was such a chance—*(In a rush)*—so I sold my Jordan stock. I hope you don't mind.

OLIVER: *(A moment of blank pause. Then* OLIVER'S *mind begins to work, rapidly)* Who'd you sell it to?

CARLOTTA: *(Fumbling in her handbag)* His name was—he was really quite a sweet fellow—such a charming manners—*(Fishes out the check; scans it)* Mr. Baldridge James K. Baldridge.

OLIVER: What'd he look like?

CARLOTTA: Well, do you know, he was really quite handsome. He looked a good deal like Reggie Traymore—you know—around the eyes. You must remember Reggie. *(*OLIVER *strides quickly to the desk. Takes notebook out of pocket; feverishly finding his number.)* I hope I didn't do wrong. I did try to reach you. I called the office three times.(*OLIVER *starts to dial his number, his gestures quick and terribly decisive.* CARLOTTA *talks as he dials.)* You said you didn't want to buy it yourself, and there was this nice Mr. Bainbridge with all that beautiful money fight in his hand. It's certified.

OLIVER: *(Into the phone)* Is Mr. Kingsberry home? Mr. Oliver Jordan.

CARLOTTA: Oh, dear, you are cross with me. I'm just devastated. I never would have done it. I would have gone barefoot and hung rather than—

OLIVER: *(Sharply into the phone)* Hello! Is that you, Kingsberry? This is Jordan. Sorry to bother you at home. *(A deep breath. A hand passes over his head. He pulls himself together, reaches for the properly self-controlled opening)* Did you—uh—have the Satterlee sisters sold their Jordan stock? You sold it this afternoon. May

I ask who bought it? Whitestone? Whitestone. Thank you. Thank you very much! *(Hangs up. Stays a moment, motionless.)*

CARLOTTA: *(Rises. A little uncomfortably)* Well, I'll be trotting along. I'm-seeing you at dinner. *(Raises her voice)* Goodbye, Millicent.

MILLICENT: *(Off L.)* Goodbye.

OLIVER: What?—Oh—I'll take you downstairs, Carlotta. *(The* TELEPHONE *rings.* OLIVER *makes a half turn.)*

CARLOTTA: Oh, don't bother, *(*MILLICENT *appears from L.)* Toodle-oo!

MILLICENT: *(On the phone ring, speaks, enters)* I'll go, dear. It's probably for me. See you later, Carlotta.

CARLOTTA: *(To* MILLICENT*)* Goodbye—*(Going toward R. door, with* OLIVER*)* Now, Oliver, you shouldn't take business so seriously. Smile! Don't be so American, really you never used to be . . . *(They are gone.)*

MILLICENT: *(At the telephone)* Yes? This is Mrs. Jordan. Lord Ferncliffe's secretary? Yes. Yes? What's that! But you must be— But they can't. *(In an absolute frenzy)* But they can't go to Florida! They're coming here to dinner. But it's not possible. I'm giving the dinner for them. They've gone! When? But people don't do things like that! But letting me know at this hour —I don't care how sudden it was, you should have let—*(*PAULA JORDAN *enters R. She is wearing the costume in which we have seen her at* LARRY RENAULT'S *apartment. She takes off her hat with a little gesture of something like defiance. Stands, tense, waiting for her mother to finish at the telephone)* Well, all I can say is, I never heard of such a thing in my life! Never! *(Bangs the receiver on the hook.)*

PAULA: *(Coming C.)* Mother, I want to talk to you!

MILLICENT: What!

PAULA: It's about Ernest and me! I want to talk to you! I can't—

MILLICENT: *(Pacing up and down)* Paula, don't bother me now! For pity's sake, don't bother me! I don't want to listen to your silly little—

PAULA: But Mother, you don't understand! This is terribly important! Ernest—
(WARN Curtain.)

MILLICENT: Paula, shut up! Shut up, I tell you! *(Her hand pressed to her head)* Let me think! *(PAULA is stunned into momentary silence by her mother's tone and words. MILLICENT stands, seething, her thoughts concentrated on her own problem. Into this brief pause OLIVER enters quietly R. to front of sofa.)*

OLIVER: Millicent, dear, do you mind if I don't go to the theatre? I'm feeling pretty rotten. If I could just go to bed—

MILLICENT: *(As though unable to believe her ears)* What's that you're saying?

OLIVER: I say, I'm feeling pretty rotten—*(His hand on his chest)*— and I'm up against a business thing that—

PAULA: *(Sympathetically)* Oh, Dad, I'm-*(Crossing to him.)*

MILLICENT: *(In mounting hysteria)* Business thing! At a time like this you talk about a business thing! And feeling rotten. This is a nice time for you to say you're feeling rotten! You come to me with your—*(Turning to PAULA)* and you, whimpering about Ernest! Some little lovers' quarrel! I'm expected to listen to Ernest and business and headaches when I'm half out of my mind! Do you know what's happened to me? I've had the most hellish day that anybody ever had! No aspic for dinner—and that Vance woman coming in—and Gustave looking like a prize-fighter—and sending for crab meat—crab meat—and now, on top of everything, do you know what's happened! *(Quivering breath of rage and bafflement as she prepares to launch her final thrust)* The Ferncliffes aren't coming to dinner! They call up at this hour, those miserable cockneys—they call up and say they've gone to Florida! Florida! And who can I get at this hour! Nobody! I've only got eight people! Eight people isn't a dinner. Who can I get? And you come to me with your idiotic little—I'm the one who ought to be in bed! I'm the one who's in trouble! Trouble! You don't know what trouble is either one of you! *(Storms out of the room to L. OLIVER and PAULA stand in silence, their eyes following her.)*

CURTAIN.

ACT THREE

KITTY PACKARD'S *bedroom. The time is 7:30.*

DAN *and* KITTY *are dressing for the* JORDANS' *dinner.* KITTY *is at her dressing table.* DAN *is in his room L. The door is open. The conversation is going on between the two as they dress.*

KITTY'S *dressing table is littered with bottles, jars, atomizers, brushes, toilette articles. Her throat and arms are bare, as she is clad in a chemise and dressing gown. On her feet are mules. She is almost at the point where her dress may be carefully plain that she has spent much time on the details of her toilette. She is marcelled, facialed, manicured, massaged, within an inch of her life.*

Carefully spread out on the bed is the dress she is to wear at dinner. Vivid satin evening slippers, to be worn with her gown, stand near the chair, side by side.

At the rise of the curtain, KITTY *is giving to her face those last detailed touches—mascara, lipstick, eyebrow pencil. She uses a hand mirror for these operations, but occasionally glances in the larger mirror of the dressing table, in order to get the full effect of her efforts.*

From the adjoining room comes DAN'S *cheerful whistle while dressing. After a moment he appears briefly in the doorway. He, too is only half-dressed for the evening. He has on the trousers of his evening clothes, a shirt, patent leather shoes, collar. White dress-suspenders dangle behind him. His hair is rumpled. He is wiping his hands on a towel, having just finished shaving.*

PACKARD: *(As he pops in)* How you coming, Kitten? (KITTY, *intent on darkening her eyelashes with mascara, does not answer)* Huh? How you coming?

KITTY: *(Turns, furious, her pencil poised)* I've told you a million times not to talk to me when I'm doing my lashes.

PACKARD: O.K. Then don't talk to me when I'm shaving. *(He disappears into his bedroom. Immediately* TINA *enters R. She is carrying a small florist's box. From the depths of this she is holding up, for her own admiration, a large cluster of orchids.)*

TINA: I think these are the handsomest ones you ever bought.

KITTY: *(Turning her glare upon Tina)* Will you take those back? I'll tell you when I want 'em.

TINA: Yes'm. *(Goes out R. quickly.)*

KITTY: *(Loudly, after* TINA *has disappeared)* Put 'em back in the icebox, you nitwit! *(Resumes her carefully detailed work with the eye pencil. In the adjoining room,* DAN *now bursts into loud song. He is in high spirits. The sound enrages* KITTY, *who suspends her work an instant to glare in the direction of the voice. The song, after its first height, drops a little as* DAN *reappears at L. door. He is putting on his tie. Crosses to* KITTY.*)*

PACKARD: Yes, sir, I'd give a thousand bucks to see Jordan's face when he walks into that meeting Monday. There'll be Whitestone and Baldridge each with a big hunk of stock in their fists, and when they begin to count noses-*(A gesture and a whistle indicating that all is over)*-little Oliver can go buy himself a rowboat and start all over again.

KITTY: I guess this is the last time we'll be invited there to dinner. We'd better eat a good one.

PACKARD: How do you mean?

KITTY: He'll be pretty sore, won't he, when he finds out you double-crossed him?

PACKARD: Huh? Jordan'll never know. Didn't I tell you? I stick in Whistestone for president and Baldridge is the treasurer; my name never appears. We can go there to dinner as long as there is something to eat. *(TINA enters R. She is carrying, suspended from its hanger, a magnificent ermine evening ermine evening wrap. This she places over the back of the chair.)*

KITTY: You're so smart you're going to land in jail someday. Tina, where the hell are my slippers? *(TINA scrambles hastily for the slippers at chair up C.; dashes back, kneels at* KITTY'S *feet, removes the mules, puts on the slippers.* KITTY *is trying on her bracelets, and is holding up her arm to get the effect of the first two or three.)*

PACKARD: Well, they got to go some to get Dan Packard. They've been laying for me ever since the old Montana days. But I got hold of the Copperhead, and I got the Big Emma, and I came to New York and put it over on'em, and whose got bigger bracelets than you've got?

KITTY: *(To* TINA*)* Oo! Look out, will you? What are you trying to do? Slice my heel off!

PACKARD: And I'm just beginning, Tootsie. Just beginning. Remember what I told you last week?

KITTY: *(Turning her back to her dressing table)* I don't remember what you told me a minute ago.

*(*TINA *goes out R.)*

PACKARD: Washington. Don't you remember that? How'd you like to be a Cabinet member's wife, mingling with all the other Cabinet members' wives, and Senators' wives and Ambassadors', and even the President's wife? What'd you think that? Huh!

KITTY: Nerts!

PACKARD: You don't know what you're talking about. There isn't a woman living wouldn't break her neck to get in with that bunch.

KITTY: *(With definite defiance in her tone)* Yeah! You don't drag me down to that graveyard. I've seen their pictures in the papers those girlies. A lot of sour-faced frumps with last year's clothes on. Giving medals to Girl Scouts, and rolling Easter eggs on the White House lawn. A hell of a lot of fun I'd have! You go live in Washington. I can have a good time right here.

PACKARD: Listen, Stupid, if I get this appointment, I'm going to Washington. And if I go to Washington you're going, too. Understand!

KITTY: *(Rising slowly)* Do you mean you're really going to get it?

PACKARD: You're right, I am!

KITTY: *(At bay)* I won't go!

PACKARD: Oh, yes, you will!

KITTY: I will not! I won't go 'way from New York! All my friends are in New York!

PACKARD: You'll go if I go!

KITTY: Oh, no, I won't! You can't boss me around! I can yell just as loud as you can.

PACKARD: (A snarl of rage) Oh-h-h-h! *(Plunges off L. KITTY stands, victorious, glaring after him. She picks up the buffer from her dressing table, burnishes her nails with vicious energy, glares again after him, seats herself before her mirror, drops the buffer with a little clatter. Sits, doing nothing, thinking a way out of her situation. DAN re-enters buttoning his vest. One finger pointing menacingly, he gestures toward KITTY. KITTY in queenly contempt following her victory, picks up her hair brush, ignoring DAN. Begins to smooth her hair. DAN stands at threshold a second)* You've been acting damn funny lately, my fine lady. And I'm getting good and sick of it.

KITTY: Yeah? And so what?

PACKARD: I'll tell you what. I'm the works around here. I pay the bills. And you take your orders from me. *(Crosses to C.)*

KITTY: *(Rising, brush hanging idle in her hand)* Who do you think you're talking to? That first wife of yours out in Montana?

PACKARD: You leave her out of this!

KITTY: *(Continuing)* That poor mealy-faced thing, with her flat chest, that never had the guts to talk up to you!

PACKARD: Shut up, I tell you!

KITTY: *(Not stopping. Crossing to him)* Washing out your greasy overalls, cooking and slaving for you in some lousy mining shack! No wonder*(Together)* she died!

PACKARD: God damn you!

KITTY: *(Still continuing. Gesticulating with the hair brush)* Well, you're not going to get me that way! You're not going to step on my face to get where you want to go—you big windbag!

KITTY: *(A purr of pure malice)* Don't you wish you knew?

PACKARD: *(Seizes her wrist.* KITTY *screams)* Tell me who it is!

KITTY: I won't!

PACKARD: Tell me, or I'll break every bone in your body!

KITTY: I won't! You can kill me, and I won't!

PACKARD: I'll find out. *(Drops her wrist)* Tina! Tina!

KITTY: She don't know. *(There is a moment during which the two stand silent, waiting for the appearance of* TINA. *There comes slowly into the doorway and a step or two into the room a* TINA *who, in spite of the expression of wondering innocence on her face, has clearly been eavesdropping. She comes forward so that she stands between the two silent figures.)*

PACKARD: Who's been coming to this house?

TINA: Huh?

KITTY: You don't know, do you, *(Together)* Tina?

PACKARD: Shut your face, you slut! *(Turns again to* TINA*)* You know, and you're going to tell. What man's been coming to this house?

TINA: *(A frantic shake of the head)* I ain't seen nobody.

PACKARD: *(Grasps her shoulder. Gives her a little shake)* Yes, you have! Come on! Who's been here? Who was here last week? Who was here when I went to Washington?

TINA: Nobody. Nobody—only the doctor.

PACKARD: No—no! I don't mean that. What man's been coming here behind my back.

TINA: I ain't seen a soul.

KITTY: Hah! What did I tell you?

PACKARD: *(Looks at her as though trying to find a way of worming the truth out of her. Decides it is hopeless. Gives her a push toward the R. door.* TINA *exits.)* Get the hell out of here! *(*KITTY *stands waiting to see what turn events will take.* PACKARD *paces a step this way and that. Wheels suddenly)* I'll divorce you, that's what I'll do. I'll divorce you, and you won't get a cent. That's the law for what you've done.

KITTY: You can't prove anything. You've got to prove it first.

PACKARD: I'll prove it. I get detectives to prove it. They'll track him down. I'd like to get hold of that guy just once. How I'd like to get my fingers around his neck. And I will, too. I'll get him! I'll kill him, and I'll throw you out like an alley cat.

KITTY: Yeah? You'll throw me out. Well, before you throw me out you'd better think twice. Because me, I don't have to get detectives to prove what I've got on you.

(WARN Dim Out.)

PACKARD: You've got nothing on me!

KITTY: No? So you want to go to Washington, do you? And be a big shot, and tell the President where to get off? You want to go in politics. *(Her tone becomes savage)* Well, I know about politics. And I know all about the crooked deals you bragged about. God knows I was bored stiff—but I was listening. Stealing from Delehanty, and the Thompson business, and gyping old man Clarke, and now this Jordan thing. Skinning him out of his eye-teeth. When I tell about those it'll raise a pretty stink! Politics! You couldn't get into politics. You couldn't get in anywhere. You couldn't get into the men's room at the Astor!

PACKARD: You snake you! You poisonous little rattlesnake. I'm through with you. I've got to go to that dinner, but after tonight we're through. And I wouldn't go there with you, except that meeting Ferncliffe is more important to me than you are. I'm clearing out tonight, get me? Tomorrow I send for my clothes. And you can sit here and get flowers from your soulmate. We're through. (PACKARD *stalks off L. Slams the door.*)

KITTY: *(Stands looking sullenly after him. Then she drifts over to her dressing-table, drops into the chair, regains a measure of composure, picks up her powder-puff, dabs at her face with little angry dabs, glances down at her right arm, and misses the absent bracelet)* Tina! Tina!

TINA: *(Enters R., too promptly)* Yes'm.

KITTY: *(Her tone strangely dulcet)* Tina, would you mind picking up that bracelet? It fell.

TINA: *(Glancing around, sees it; goes to it; picks it up; looks at it admiringly as she brings it to* KITTY. *She holds it too long, so that* KITTY *reaches toward it. But* TINA, *instead of relinquishing it, brings it closer to her own gaze)* My, it's pretty, ain't it?

KITTY: *(A little uneasily.)* Give it to me.

TINA: Look it just fits me.

KITTY: Give it here, will you!

TINA: You've got so many bracelets, I don't see how you can use 'em all.

KITTY: What are you driving at?

TINA: *(Looking down at it, then up at* KITTY *with a hard and meaningful eye)* Nothing. Only I thought with you having so many, maybe you might want to give me one.

KITTY: Here, powder my back, will you? *(Hands her the powder-puff. Quickly* TINA *picks up the powder-puff; begins busily to powder* KITTY's *back, the bracelet still in her left hand.)*

THE LIGHTS DIM OUT

SCENE II

LARRY RENAULT'S *apartment in the Hotel Versailles.*

It is a quarter to eight.

The room is in considerable disorder—a disorder reflecting the befuddled mind and uncoordinated movements of its occupant. The garments in which we have last seen LARRY *are now strewn over the room—his trousers on the floor near the bedroom, his shirt seen on the floor of the bedroom, his shoes in widely separated spots. The black moire dressing-gown is in a heap on the floor C. His evening topcoat, folded so as to reveal the glistening black silk lining, is also flung over the sofa. Two sections of the evening paper are thrown about the room.*

The whiskey bottle, now empty, is on the table by the sofa, and near it an overturned glass. The cushions on sofa and chairs are awry, and one of them has fallen to the floor. The drapes on the window are drawn.

(LARRY RENAULT *himself, in full evening dress—tails, white waistcoat, white tie, silk hat on the side of his head—is walking up and down the room impatiently. About his walk is a sort wavering uncertainty that denotes a degree intoxication. Pushes up his left sleeve an inch or two to look at his wrist watch; sees that it is not there; remembers why. Makes for the telephone to ascertain the time.)*

LARRY: *(His speech is slightly slurred)* Hello!—Hello!—What time is it?—Time—time! Time! Seven forty-five. Thanks. *(Hangs up noisily. Paces the room with increased impatience. Encounters a pillow on the floor; kicks it savagely so that it lands near the French window R.C. As he kicks pillow, the* TELEPHONE *rings. Eagerly he removes the receiver)* Hello! Yes, this is Mr. Renault—Yes, I got it—Listen, my good fellow. I'm not accustomed to being dunned for hotel bills. I'm a very busy man—my secretary usually attends to those things—but he's in California, at the moment. You'll get your money—You'll get it when it suits my convenience. *(Hangs up. The sound of the door* Buzzer *comes immediately. He wheels in the direction of R. door. Shouts)* Come in!

(MAX KANE *comes nimbly into the room, with* JO STENGEL *following slowly some paces behind him.* JO STENGEL *is about sixty; his hair is well grayed; he is kindly looking; time has refined his features; his eyes are shrewd, his manner quiet; yet there is about him the indefinable air of the showman.)*

MAX: Liberty Hall, eh?

LARRY: Where the hell have you been! I told you I was—*(warns him with a gesture of the right hand as, with the left, he impressively ushers in* JO STENGEL.)

MAX: I brought up Mr. Stengel, Larry. (JO STENGEL *enters.*) Meet Larry Renault, Mr. Stengel.

LARRY: *(A complete change of manner)* Oh—how are you, Mr. Stengel?

STENGEL: *(They shake hands)* Mr. Renault.

LARRY: Well, this is quite an occasion. (STENGEL *glances at* Max.) Meeting of two celebrities. We ought to have the newsreel men here. (MAX *is removing his coat.*)

STENGEL: Yes. *(His eye takes in* LARRY'S *costume, including the high hat, which is still on his head)* Of course, I didn't realize it was a full dress affair. I just came as I was.

MAX: *(Appreciates this with a laugh which breaks off rather sharply as his quick eye spots the empty whiskey bottle. He edges unobtrusively toward it, talking as he goes, with a fine air of carelessness)* Mr. Renault's got a date with some of his Park Avenue friends. *(Picks dressing gown from floor; puts it on sofa; furtively picks up the bottle, shielding it behind his back; gets rid of it behind the convenient sofa)* These big picture boys, they're pretty social. *(Having accomplished his purpose, he turns upon the other two a radiantly glassy smile.)*

STENGEL: Yes. I've heard.

LARRY: They'll wait. Sit down, Mr. Stengel. Don't you want to take your coat off?

MAX: *(Trots hastily over to* STENGEL.) Sure he does. Take your coat off, Mr. Stengel.

STENGEL: *(Sitting)* Well no—I've only got a minute. I got a classy dinner date too—I got to meet a hamburger, with onions, at Dinty Moore's. (STENGEL *safely seated, chair R.C.,* MAX *stands upstage, between them.* LARRY RENAULT *stays on his feet, pacing as he talks.* MAX *laughs his sycophantic laugh.)*

LARRY: I don't care much for those chop-house places. Matter of fact, there isn't a decent restaurant in New York. *(A look from* STENGEL *to* MAX. LARRY'S *drunkenness is apparent)* Take this hotel—class of people they've got, you'd think—but it's terrible. I'm not going to eat here any more.

STENGEL: You don't say?

LARRY: *(Warming to the subject)* You really have to go to Europe for good cooking. Paris! There's a little place on the Left Bank—nobody knows about it. The way they cook kidneys—their rognons aux beurre are absolutely marvelous! *(Wafts a kiss into the air, very Gallic, in memory of that delectable meal)* But the most exquisite food I ever ate was—*(To* STENGEL*)*—guess where?

STENGEL: *(Very promptly)* I give up.

LARRY: A little place called Ming Chow's, in Peking. Better than when I dined with the Emperor—I want to tell you about that, some time.

STENGEL: Maybe. Some other time. *(Starts to rise; gives up as* LARRY *continues; sinks back into chair.)*

LARRY: Of course, most of the time, I carried my own chef. That's really the only way to travel.

STENGEL: *(Rising)* Well, look, Mr. Renault, I haven't got an awful lot of time—

MAX: Yeah, Larry. Suppose we get down to brass tacks.

LARRY: All right, my good fellow—Well, Stengel, you' re going to produce this play, h'm? And you want me to act in it?

STENGEL: *(A bit taken aback)* Well, I—*(His alarmed eye goes to* MAX.*)*

MAX: *(Hurriedly)* This is just getting acquainted, Larry. *(With his spurious good-nature, to* STENGEL*)* You see, he's crazy to play the part.

LARRY: Just a minute! Let's get this straight. *(Hurling his silk hat up-stage)* I understood from Mr. Kane, here, that you wanted to know if I would be willing to portray the beach-comber in this thing.

STENGEL: Wait a minute! Not so fast, there.

MAX: *(Comes quickly between the two, breaking in)* Now, now! What's the difference which one is—he wants to do it—and you want him to do it—so what's the difference—

LARRY: A lot of difference.

MAX: Now, Larry!

LARRY: In the first place, if I decide to accept this part—and I don't say I will—it'll have to be built up.

MAX: There's the actor for you! No matter how good the part is, right away they want it built up.

STENGEL: Built up! The fella's got one scene, and they find him dead on the beach. This ain't a spiritualism play.

LARRY: No? Well, you're forgetting one thing, Stengel. Don't forget I'm Larry Renault.

MAX: Larry, for God's sake!

LARRY: Shut up! Now listen, Stengel. I'm a Name, and I know it. And so do you. And I'm not going to go on and play second fiddle to any cheap English ham.

MAX: *(In a frantic half-whisper)* Larry!

LARRY: *(Waving Max away)* Eight thousand a week—that's what I got. And I was going to get ten—only the talkies came in. So don't think you're doing me a favor, giving me a part in your ratty little play—because I'm doing you one. *(Max, desperate, turns away.)*

STENGEL: I think maybe we're keeping you from your dinner, Mr. Renault. *(Turns to depart.)*

MAX: *(Over to* STENGEL*)* Listen, Jo, he doesn't mean anything—he just means—

LARRY: Oh, yes, I do. And just because it's Mr. Jo Stengel doesn't mean a thing to me. I'm still good. I'm better than I ever was. See that! *(Runs his hands down his slim flanks)* And that! *(Indicates the famous profile)* Give me the right part and you'll have the biggest hit that even Mr. Jo Stengel ever produced.

STENGEL: *(Quietly and conclusively)* Good night, Mr. Renault.

MAX: Listen, Jo—!

LARRY: Oh, I see. You're doing a second-rate show. You don't want real artists. *(*STENGEL *starts to go.* LARRY *crosses to him)* Well, your English ham will give you what you want. *(Grabs his arm)* Listen to me, old-timer. I'm drunk, and I know I'm drunk.

MAX: Larry—

LARRY: But I know what I'm saying. *(STENGEL breaks from grasp.)*

MAX: *(Whirling LARRY around)* For God's sake; Larry!

STENGEL: It's all right, Max. I'll see you tomorrow.

MAX: I'll take you to the elevator. *(STENGEL exits R., followed by MAX.)*

LARRY: *(Who has continued to talk through the Others' speeches)* I wouldn't be in your rotten show! I didn't come to your office, did I! Not Larry Renault! You came to see me. And d'you know why! Because I'm an important artist, and you're a cheap pushcart producer! *(Turns away, then back to R. door, and leans through the door to shout his final insult)* Pushcart! *(For a second LARRY hangs precariously in the doorway, glaring after the departing figures down the hall. Sways a little, then lurches back into the room, coming to a wavering halt at about the middle. He is muttering a little to himself. As MAX re-enters, LARRY is looking toward the door. MAX comes in swiftly; slams the door behind him; fixes LARRY with an eye of utter fury. There is a moment's silence as the two MEN stare at each other.)*

MAX: You—drunken—fool! Ha! I bring him up here! I go down on my hands and knees to do it. And you!—God, I can't believe it! I can't believe that any man—*(Mutters "God damn fool" under his breath as he turns to go)* Well, that's that! *(Snatches up his coat from the chair.)*

LARRY: *(As MAX goes toward R. door)* Just a minute! I've got something to say to you, too! Telling him I was crazy to play that part! Yessing him all over the lot! You know what I think! It's you got the play away from Baumann and gave it to Stengel! It's you did me out of the part! You double-dealing Kike! You're in with the managers! You've been taking my money and working for them!

MAX: *(Very low—in a cruel level tone)* You don't say! Working for the managers, eh? And taking your money? Me! That you're into

for five hundred bucks—in touches. All right. If yc
been lying to you all this time, you're going to get the truth
now. *(A deprecatory wave of the hand from* LARRY; *a sneering sound
and a half turn away)* Renault, you're through.

LARRY: *(Turns slowly toward him)* Get out of here.

MAX: I'll get out. And stay out. But get this first. *(Crossing over to
LARRY)* I never worked so hard to put anybody over as I did
you. You think I told you all the things I tried! No. Because I
couldn't come to you and tell you what they said. I was too
sorry for you.

LARRY: *(A little fearfully)* Sorry for me!

MAX: Vaudeville! Why, every time I walked into the booking office
they leaned back and roared. Called me "Maxie, the grave-
snatcher." And the radio—remember I told you I hadn't seen
the right fellow! I saw him. Only he saw me first. Last night I
sent-a wire to Hollywood. I knew it was no use, but I sent it
anyway. Do you want to see the answer? *(Drawing it out of his
pocket.)*

LARRY: *(Backing away, as though from something dreadful)* No.

MAX: *(Reads)* "When we are in the market for extras we will let you
know." *(Crushes the telegram into a ball; throws it at* LARRY'S *feet.)*

LARRY: Trying to throw a scare into me.

MAX: No. I'm just telling you the truth. What the hell, you never
were an actor, but you did have looks. Well, they're gone. And
you don't have to take my word for it. Look in the mirror. They
don't lie. Take a good look. *(Comes closer to him, while* LARRY *retreats)* Look at these pouches under your eyes. Take a look at
those creases. You got wattles under your chin. *(His taunting
hand is up, pointing at this, at that.* LARRY *slaps it down like a
frightened child.)* You sag like an old woman. *(A gesture indicates
the face of the man before him)* Get a load of yourself. What's the
matter? Afraid? You ain't seen nothin' yet. Wait till you start
tramping round looking for a job. No agent'll handle you. Wait
till you start sitting in ante rooms, hours and hours. Giving
your name to office boys who never heard of you. You're
through, Renault. You're through in pictures, and plays, and

vaudeville and radio and everything! You're a corpse, and you don't know it. Go get yourself buried. (*Exits R., closing the door decisively behind him.*)

(LARRY *stands as though dazed, swaying a little. He passes a hand over his head. He looks about the room vaguely. His eye falls on the wall-mirror. He lunges swiftly toward it; stands before it, peering intently at the reflection of his own face. Tries to smooth away with his fingers the bags under his chin and beneath his eyes. There they are. He turns away with something like a shudder. He advances heavily a step or two; stands. With his handkerchief he wipes the cold sweat from beneath his chin, from his upper lip, from his clammy brow. He espies the crumpled telegram on the floor. Lunges toward that; picks it up; smooths it. A quick look. Throws it down, as though sickened. A noisy rapping of knuckles on R. door. As* LARRY *half turns toward the sound* EDDIE, *the bellboy, enters. He is carrying the silver frame, wrapped in its newspaper, an untidy bundle.* EDDIE'S *walk is a scuffling swagger that carries with it unmistakable disrespect. He tosses his bundle onto the first chair handy. At the same time he plunges his hand in his pocket; brings out the cuff links, which he throws on the table.*)

EDDIE: They don't want this junk. They wouldn't give me nothing on it.

LARRY: (*Dazedly, crossing to* EDDIE) What?—Why—that's a silver frame! Those links are solid platinum.

EDDIE: All right—you take 'em. I lugged 'em to every pawnshop on Sixth Avenue. (*Starts to slouch out of the room.*)

LARRY: You little liar! You never took them any place!

EDDIE: (*Turns, his expression ugly*) Say! Who are you calling liar? What do I get out of all this—you down-and-out ham?

LARRY: You filthy little rat, how dare you talk to me like that?

EDDIE: (*Contemptuously*) O.K.! (*A wave of the hand. He turns to leave.*)

LARRY: No, no! Wait! I didn't mean that. I didn't mean to call you that. I'm sorry. Listen! I've got to have some liquor. I'm sick. You lay it out for me, and I'll pay it back to you.

EDDIE: What kind of a sucker do you think I am?

LARRY: No, no! I've got to have it! I've got to! I'll pay you back. I'll pay you back tomorrow.

EDDIE: You won't be here tomorrow.

LARRY: What?

EDDIE: Aw, boloney! *(He goes out. Closes R. door.)*

(LARRY stands. Then, desperate for a drink, he searches the corner for the bottle. He finds it where MAX has tucked it behind the couch; eagerly holds it up in the hope of finding just a mouthful remaining. There is nothing. He drops the bottle to the floor. The sound of the door BUZZER. LARRY wheels in terror.)

LARRY: Who's that!

(The sound of a key in the lock. FITCH, the hotel manager, and HATFIELD, the assistant manager, come into the room. FITCH, in his business suit and eyeglasses, is the solid man of affairs. HATFIELD, garbed in the assistant's uniform of cutaway and striped trousers, defers to his superior. HATFIELD carries a sheaf of cards, one for each floor, on which are specified the hotel rooms and their occupants. In the other hand is a pencil. The two advance well into the room, as though taking possession, though their manner is, to the end, polite.)

FITCH: How do you do, Mr. Renault? I haven't had the pleasure of meeting you before. Though you've been with us for some time. I'm Mr. Fitch, the Manager.

LARRY: *(Vaguely)* Oh, yes.

FITCH: I believe you know my assistant, Mr. Hatfield?

LARRY: *(Wets his lips)* Yes.

FITCH: *(A little apologetic laugh)* Mr. Renault, we find ourselves in an awkward predicament. We've just had a communication from some very old clients of ours—Mr. and Mrs. Sherman Montgomery—possibly you know them. They've been making this their home for many years—every winter. And have always occupied this particular suite. They say it's like home to them.

Now, we've just been notified that they're coming in tomorrow. Tomorrow—is that right, Mr. Hatfield?

HATFIELD: Yes, sir. Tomorrow afternoon.

FITCH: Well, there you are. Under the circumstances I am afraid we must ask you for these rooms.

LARRY: Oh! Well—what other rooms have you got for me?

FITCH: That's just the trouble. We're terribly full up. The Horse Show, and—Mr. Hatfield, is there any place we can put Mr. Renault?

HATFIELD: (A great show of consulting his slips) I'm—afraid—not, Mr. Fitch (A little embarrassed laugh) It looks as though everything is taken.

FITCH: (Echoes HATFIELD'S laugh) I'm sorry, Mr. Renault—but of course old customers have to be taken care of.

LARRY: That's—that's all right. Funny, I was just about to tell your office I was leaving. (FITCH and HATFIELD exchange looks.) Some friends of mine—Palm Beach—private car—When do you want me to—

FITCH: No hurry. Shall we say—tomorrow morning?

LARRY: (Thickly) All right.

FITCH: We'd be very glad to have one of our people come in and pack your things tonight. You're probably pretty busy.

LARRY: No. No, I'll—I'll tend to it.

FITCH: Shall we say—noon tomorrow, Mr. Renault? (LARRY merely nods his assent.) Thank you very much. So sorry to have inconvenienced you in this way. (Clears his throat. They give the effect of a little procession as they leave R., FITCH first, HATFIELD following. LARRY stands in the C. of the room, a sagging figure. He takes a step, kicking the empty whisky bottle as he does. He notices the seventeen cents on the table. Looks at it; laughs; sweeps it off the table.)

(WARN Dim Out.)

LARRY: Seventeen cents! (He has swept the coins upstage toward the fireplace. His gaze encounters the gas logs. An idea is born in his *mind. He lurches to them, looks fixedly at the gas logs and the little knob which serves to turn on the gas. Swiftly he stoops and tries it. There is heard the hiss of escaping gas. He turns it off, in a kind of triumph. A quick look around the room. Runs to the R. door; turns the lock; looks at the, crack under the door; whips off his dress-coat, stuffs it and rug hurriedly under the crack. He now runs to the L. door; closes it; finds his afternoon trousers on the floor; spreads them and rug close to the crack beneath the door. A look at the windows. Uses his evening top-coat and pillows to plug up one of these, a few cushions for the other. Strips the heavy seat-cushions off the couch as he needs them. Gazes around; sees the telephone; dashes to it. His voice a croak)* Hello!—I don't want to be disturbed for a while— I'm busy—*(Summoning his forces again, surveys all the work he has done. Finds it good. His vanity asserts itself. He must make a good exit. Doesn't like the idea shirt-sleeves. His coat is serving as stuffing for a door. He picks his dressing-gown as the thing to wear; dons it; ties it; looks at himself. Backs to the chair, still looking at himself, turning his head this way and that to decide which side of his famous profile is more nearly perfect. Pulls floor lamp out of his way; places chair facing fireplace so that floor lamp is shining on it. It isn't quite right artistically, he decides. He turns out all the* LIGHTS *except the floor lamp, which throws a glow over the chair in which he is to sit. There. That is better. A last summoning of courage. You see him pulling together the remnants of his manhood. A deep inhalation and exhalation. A rush to the gas-fixture. The sharp hiss as it is turned on. He settles himself in the armchair. The chair is so turned that we see the back of his head, a glimpse only of the famous profile, one arm over the side of the chair, as he has previously rehearsed his position.)*

THE LIGHTS DIM OUT SLOWLY

ACT THREE

The Jordan drawing-room, eight o'clock. It is a large, gracious and rich room, well balanced and furnished with that distinction which comes of the combination of the best of the old and the new. At R. is a window. Up R. and up L. two semi-cylindrical niches in which stand twin vases holding graceful sprays of flowers. The opening at the back, C., is a large arched doorway opening into a foyer. Two steps lead up from the drawing-room to the foyer. Double doors down L. to the dining-room—closed.

Against the back wall of the foyer, facing the drawing-room, can be seen, through the archway, the figures of three HUNGARIAN MUSICIANS *in their red coats.*

As the Curtain rises the MUSICIANS *are near the finish of their first number, though no one is in the room to hear them. The dinner guests have not yet begun to arrive. The host and hostess are not yet downstairs.*

(After a moment MILLICENT JORDAN *enters C. from L. She is in evening dress, and in her haste is fastening and adjusting her pearl necklace, her arms upraised as she appears. She glances at the* MUSICIANS *she passes them grouped in the foyer, nods her recognition, and stands on the top step leading down to the drawing-room, surveying the scene with the critical eye of the hostess. She comes down into the room; moves an ashtray here, a cigarette box there; adjusts a flower spray at a more pleasing angle; moves a chair an inch or two. She turns back to the foyer just as the* MUSICIANS *are finishing their selection; stands a moment awaiting the concluding bars. The* Leader *of the* MUSICIANS; *violin and bow in hand, rises and bows. The other* Two *follow his example.)*

MILLICENT: That's very nice. But do you mind—not quite so loud? You see, the people will be right in here—*(Indicates the drawing-room)*—talking. After we've gone down to dinner you can play louder. *(The* LEADER *bows his assent. The other* Two *nod. They sit again.* MILLICENT *exits C. to L. Before they begin their next number there is the usual preliminary violin-bow scraping, adjusting of chairs, mopping of brows, clearing of throats. They begin another number, softly. For a few seconds the music goes on while the room is again empty.)*

(HATTIE LOOMIS *appears C. from R. She gives an interested little glance over her shoulder at the* MUSICIANS *as she passes into the drawing-room.)*

HATTIE: *(After a little survey of the room, looks back toward the entrance C. to R.)* Ed! Ed! Where are you? *(Comes down R.C.)*

ED: *(Speaking as he appears in the doorway)* I'm coming. (ED LOOMIS *would be one of those insignificant, grayish-looking men if it were not that he is distinguished a trifle by his air of irascibility, due, probably, to faulty digestion and the world in which he finds himself. He is wearing a dinner coat and black tie—the one man, it later turns out, who is not in full evening dress.)*

HATTIE: She's got music.

ED: *(Very cross. To L. of her)* I hear it.

HATTIE: Now, Ed! Are you going to be like that all evening! You ought to be glad to help Millie out. It isn't going to be so terrible.

ED: Not so terrible! Calling up at quarter to seven, just when we're sitting down to dinner—and I got to get into this uniform and come over here and meet a bunch of fatheads I don't want to know, and eat a lot of fancy food I can't digest, and miss that Garbo picture I've been waiting two months for up at Eighty-sixth Street!

HATTIE: You can see that any time.

ED: *(Pacing R. and L.)* I can not! I waited all this time because it was two dollars downtown, and it's only at the Eighty-sixth one night, and God knows where it'll be tomorrow night.

HATTIE: Don't you want to meet Larry Renault? That's better than going to a movie.

ED: Larry Renault! That has-been!

HATTIE: And Carlotta Vance!

ED: And Jenny Lind—is she coming?

HATTIE: Now, Ed, Millie does a lot of things for us—Besides, who can you get at quarter to seven but relatives?

ED: All right. I'm a relative and I'm here.

(Reaches in pockets for cigarette.)

HATTIE: *(Going up C.)* Wonder why she isn't down. I think I'll run up and see her.

ED: *(Lifting the cover of a cigarette box)* I don't suppose they've got a Lucky Strike.

HATTIE: *(As she goes out C. to L.)* Oo-ooh! Where are you, Millie? Upstairs?

ED: *(Goes from cigarette box to cigarette box, lifting each lid, inspecting the contents, and slamming the lid down again with increasing irritation. Failing in his search, he turns to the Orchestra)* One of you boys got a Lucky? *(One of the MEN, without breaking his rhythm, tosses him a package of Luckies. ED removes one cigarette, tosses the pack back, and comes back down R.C. into the room, lighting his cigarette as he does so. MILLICENT and HATTIE re-enter. MILLICENT's voice is heard just moment before the two women actually appear.)* Thanks!

MILLICENT:—and then, on top of everything, the Ferncliffes not coming I never had such a day in all my life!—Hello, Ed— It's all I can do to stand up. *(Crosses to sofa.)*

HATTIE: I can imagine. *(Crosses down R.)*

ED: Where's Oliver? *(Enter GUSTAVE C. from R.)*

MILLICENT: He'll be down. He's got a headache, or something.

ED: Me, too.

GUSTAVE: Mr. and Mrs. Daniel Packard. *(Exits R.)*

(DAN and KITTY PACKARD appear C. from R. They give the effect of being in full panoply. DAN's linen seems more expansive, more glistening, his broadcloth richer, than that ordinarily seen. KITTY's dress is the ultimate word in style and a bit beyond that in cut. When later she has occasion to turn her back one modifies one's

first impression of the front décolletage, which now seems almost prudish.)

MILLICENT: *(In that exaggerated tone of the very social hostess)* How nice! It's so lovely to see you!

PACKARD: How-d'you-do, Mrs. Jordan? *(Coming down into the room.*KITTY *has taken his proffered arm)* This is indeed a pleasure. You know Mrs. Packard, I believe?

MILLICENT: Of course I do. So pleased to meet you again, Mrs. Packard. So sweet of you to come.

KITTY: *(Who has learned the right answer)* So—uh—so nice of you to have me.

PACKARD: *(To* KITTY*)* See! We're on time, Sugar! *(To* MILLICENT*)* She thought we were going to be late.

KITTY: No, I didn't, sweetheart.

MILLICENT: *(Who has been hovering on-the verge of the necessary introductions)* Mrs. Packard, may I present my sister and my brother-in-law—Mr. and Mrs. Loomis. This is Mr. and Mrs. Packard.

KITTY: *(Surveying room. Crosses to front of sofa)* I'm pleased to meet you.

PACKARD: *(Crosses R. to* ED *and shakes hands)* Hello, there! Glad to know you!

HATTIE: How do you do?

ED: *(Simultaneously)* How are you?

PACKARD: *(Without stopping)* Y'know, for a minute there I had you wrong. I figured maybe you were Ferncliffe.

Ed: You were close. I'm pinch-hitting for him. *(*HATTIE*, standing next him, gives him a vicious nudge.* KITTY *sits sofa.* ED *turns to glare at* HATTIE *over his shoulder)* What's the matter?

MILLICENT: *(Coming C. a shade too glibly, even for an experienced hostess, and casting on brother-in-law* ED*, meanwhile, a fleeting but malevolent glance)* Yes, isn't it too bad? Lord Ferncliffe was taken desperately ill late this afternoon. Neuritis. The doctors said he must have sunshine.

PACKARD: Say, that's too— (He gets the full import of her remark), Wait a minute! Do you mean he's not coming?

MILLICENT: Oh, impossible. They rushed him right down to Florida on a special train.

KITTY: (A high shriek of malicious laughter, in single note, as she hears PACKARD thus defeated) Ha! (Immediately smothers the sound with her palm against her mouth, PACKARD wheels on her in soundless rage. The OTHERS, startled, look at her inquiringly. KITTY turns the sound into a patently false cough.)

MILLICENT: (Crossing to KITTY) Would you like a glass of water? (KITTY shakes her head in refusal.)

PACKARD: (Taking cigarette from table L. Of chair R.C.) She don't need anything.

HATTIE: (Coming to the rescue, crossing to back of sofa) I don't care for Florida, do you? Have you ever been to Florida, Mrs. Packard?

KITTY: Oh, sure.

MILLICENT: I love it—but we're not going down this winter. (To the PACKARDS) Are you?

KITTY: (In a coo) No, I don't think we are. (To PACKARD) Are we going to Florida this winter, sweetheart? (Rise.)

PACKARD: (Meaningly) I wouldn't count on it if I were you.

HATTIE: Oh, isn't that too bad.

MILLICENT: I shall miss it so. It's so wonderful, not to think about anything, just to lie all day in the sun. (PACKARD is lighting cigarette.)

KITTY: But you got to look out you don't blister. My skin's awful delicate. I don't dare expose it. (Turns, as she speaks this. line, so that the extremely low cut back of her gown is in full view for the first time. ED casts a comprehensive look at the view.)

MILLICENT: Who is going down this winter, I wonder?

PACKARD: Nobody, I guess. Looks as though the sailfish are going to get the vacation this year. *(There is a ripple of polite laughter at this little sally. Under cover of the merriment* OLIVER JORDAN *enters C. from L., stands for a moment on the top step, and then comes down to the room. There is about him an air of detachment— he seems to be no part of the room and its occupants. For a moment he is unnoticed by the* OTHERS.*)*

MILLICENT: Yes, we've fallen upon queer ways, haven't we? Goodness knows where any of us will be this time next year.

PACKARD: Oh, America will come out on top.

Ed: Hello, Oliver.

PACKARD: *(Continuing)* Why, here's Oliver! *(Goes to him C. with a great show of heartiness and good-fellow-ship)* Well,-how's the boy? Say, I've been wanting to call you up!

OLIVER: Hello, Hattie. How are you?

HATTIE: I'm fine.

OLIVER: *(Continuing)* Hello, Ed.

MILLICENT: *(Through these greetings)* You've met my husband, haven't you, Mrs. Packard?

OLIVER: Yes, indeed It's delightful to see you again.

KITTY: Yeah.

PACKARD: *(To* OLIVER*)* You're looking great! How've you been? How's that pain of yours? *(enter* GUSTAVE *C. from R.)* Better? Did you take that lemon juice?

GUSTAVE: Doctor and Mrs. Talbot. *(Exits R.)*

OLIVER: Yes. Fine—fine!

*(*DOCTOR TALBOT *and* LUCY *enter C. from R., crossing to* MILLICENT*)*

MILLICENT: Hello! Darlings! So glad to see you. Lucy, what a sweet dress!

LUCY: Hello, dear.

TALBOT: *(Simultaneously)* Millicent! You're looking very lovely.

MILLICENT: *(Looking about to see where introductions are in order)* Let me see—

LUCY: *(Not stopping. Catching sight of familiar faces)* Hello, Hattie.

HATTIE: Hello, Lucy.

LUCY: How are you, Oliver?

OLIVER: I'm fine. *(At the same time DR. TALBOT and ED have briefly greeted each other.)*

MILLICENT: *(Continuing, performing the necessary introductions)* Lucy—Mrs. Packard. This is Mrs. Talbot, Mrs. Packard. Mrs. Packard, I don't believe you've met Doctor Talbot. *(Lucy crosses to ED and OLIVER)*

TALBOT: Yes, we've met.

KITTY: *(Simultaneously)* Yes, I know Doctor Talbot.

PACKARD: *(Simultaneously)* Go on! He's her father confessor. Hello, Doc! *(Goes to him; grasps his hand; claps him on the shoulder)* How's the old medico! Haven't seen you round my house lately. What's the matter? Patient get well on you?

TALBOT: Yes, she's getting along very well without me—aren't you, Mrs. Packard?

KITTY: I get along better when you're looking after me.

LUCY: *(Not unkindly)* You mustn't become too dependent on Jo. He might fail you. *(The party now starts to break up into three groups: PACKARD and DR. TALBOT, C., engage in conversation which is dominant in tone. In the second group, L., are ED, MILLICENT and KITTY; in the third, R., LUCY, HATTIE and OLIVER)*

PACKARD: Hey, Doc! Saw your name on the members' list out at my golf club. I didn't know you belonged.

TALBOT: Oh, I've been a member there for years. Don't get a chance to play much.

PACKARD: We ought to have a game some time. What d'you go round in?

TALBOT: I'm not very good. Lucky to break a hundred.

PACKARD: Say, that's just about my speed! How about tomorrow afternoon?

TALBOT: Afraid I haven't the time for golf. If I have an hour or two I generally jump on a horse—do a little riding.

PACKARD: Ride! Say! I'll ride with you! You're talking to an old cowboy! Well, what do you think of that? *(Turning to the other* GROUPS, *with his genial roar)* I've found a buddy here! Hey! Mrs. Talbot! *(In the second group, made up of* ED, MILLICENT *and* KITTY, *the conversation has been simultaneous, with the* PACKARD-TALBOT *talk.)*

MILLICENT: *(Speaks on "member there for years." Sits on sofa L.)* Well, Mrs. Packard, and what have you been doing with yourself lately?

KITTY: Oh, I don't know. Nothing much.

MILLICENT: Have you seen any of the new plays?

KITTY: Sure. I go to all the shows.

MILLICENT: We're taking you to see "Say It With Music" tonight. I hope you haven't seen it.

KITTY: I saw it twice.

ED: *(Who has been drifting aimlessly, pricks up his ears at this and joins the two women.)* Where'd you say we're going tonight?

MILLICENT: "Say It With Music." They say it's so amusing.

(In the third group, composed of LUCY, HATTIE *and* OLIVER, *the conversation has again been simultaneous.)*

HATTIE: *(speaking on "didn't know you belonged")* Lucy, I never see you any more. Why don't you call me?

LUCY: Why, I love being with you, Hattie. I always think everybody's busier than I am.

OLIVER: Isn't it insane? We never see the people we want to in this New York. The weeks go by, and—

HATTIE: Remember those grand days in that big Murray Hill house of yours?

LUCY: We did have fun when we were kids.

HATTIE: It's positively frightening. You can see life getting the best of you.

OLIVER: Give it the best. What's the difference?

LUCY: *(As* PACKARD, *ending his conversation with* DR. TALBOT, *says* "Hey! Mrs. Talbot!") Yes, Mr. Packard?

PACKARD: *(The groups now quiet)* Just discovered your husband and I have a lot in common.

LUCY: So I understand. *(Moving toward* PACKARD, *C., as she talks.* TALBOT *crosses to* OLIVER *)* Why don't you and Mrs. Packard have dinner with us next week? How would Thursday suit you? There's an idea! I want you all to come to dinner at our house next Thursday. *(*ED *crosses R. to* HATTIE *.)*

MILLICENT: That'll be lovely.

KITTY: We'd be delighted

ED: *(Has crossed to* HATTIE, *under cover of this general outburst. Speaks on* "How would Thursday suit you." *With more than his usual irritability)* We're going to see "Say It With Music"

HATTIE: Well?

ED: We saw it!

HATTIE: All right. *(Crosses to behind sofa.)*

LUCY: *(Not stopping)* And the Ferncliffes! I'd love to ask the Ferncliffes. Where are they, Millicent?

MILLICENT: My dear, didn't I tell you? Poor dear Bunny—that's what we call Ferncliffe—was taken desperately sick this afternoon, and they had to whirl him down South—*(Enter* GUSTAVE *C. from R.)*—to save his life. *(A mildly surprised look from* OLIVER.*)*

GUSTAVE: Miss Carlotta Vance! *(*KITTY *rises.)*

LUCY: Why, how ghastly!

TALBOT: *(Simultaneously)* What was the trouble? *(*GUSTAVE *exits C. to L.)*

(CARLOTTA VANCE appears C. from R. A resplendent figure. And then, for good measure, a Pekinese dog, which she carries under one arm. She comes straight on in to C., talking as she appears.)

CARLOTTA: Millicent darling, do forgive me.

MILLICENT: Carlotta—!

CARLOTTA: I am so sorry. He wouldn't stay home. He cried and cried. I just had to bring him. He's so spoiled since I brought him to America. Aren't you, Mussolini?

MILLICENT: Isn't he sweet? Carlotta, have you met—

CARLOTTA: What do you think of Ferncliffe! Isn't Bunny a swine! Running off to Florida and ruining your whole dinner! *(A sweeping gesture that tosses the other guests into the discard.)*

MILLICENT: Darling—

CARLOTTA: You know, I left here, and went straight to my hotel, and there was his telegram—"Off on a fishing trip—I love your America—never felt so well in my life Won't you join us. Bunny." *(LUCY and HATTIE plunge valiantly forward to cover MILLICENT'S discomfiture. Their voices are high and clear. They speak simultaneously. An embarrassed laugh from MILLICENT.)*

LUCY: *(Crossing C. in the general direction of PACKARD and ED at R.)* Have you seen that wonderful German picture at the Europa? Really, they have the most marvelous way of doing things, and their attention to detail—no matter how small the part.

CARLOTTA: *(Crossing to. him at R.C. chair)* Oliver, darling, here you are. Aren't you glad to see me?

OLIVER: *(Gracefully)* Carlotta, you know I love you.

CARLOTTA: Then you're not cross with me? *(Turning to PACKARD)* You'd have thought I'd done something terrible. *(ED starts over L., stopping C. a brief moment to give groups a disgusted survey, then continuing to L. of sofa.)* Just because I sold my Jordan stock. I was stony broke, and a man came along and made me the most wonderful offer, right out of the blue—well, I grabbed it! That wasn't so terrible, was it?

OLIVER: What do you think, Packard? Was that so terrible? *(His gaze is fixed on* PACKARD.*)*

PACKARD: Well, business is business. Every fellow's got to look out for himself. That's the kind of world it is. (GUSTAVE *and* DORA *enter C. from L.)*

CARLOTTA: It must be wonderful to be a sheltered woman. A man to look after you so that you never have to worry for yourself.

PACKARD: Say, I should think that ought to be a cinch for you! *(Laughs at his own witticism.)*

LUCY: The trouble with a shelter is that in a store it sometimes falls down around your ears.

OLIVER: I suppose we all dream of being something we're not. There was a time when I thought I was Bernard Shaw. *(He trails off as* GUSTAVE *appears with cocktails.)*

HATTIE: (TALBOT *joins group at sofa. Making her leap in the direction of* TALBOT*)* Do you know I'd rather go away in the winter than in the summer. I love New York in the summer. Everybody's out of town and you can just have the city to yourself. *(Joins* MILLICENT *and* KITTY *below the sofa. The conversation is simultaneous with that of the other group.)*

TALBOT: Matter of fact, New York is healthier in the summer. Though it's all one to me—I have to work the whole year round.

MILLICENT: I've never been in New York in the summer. I don't think I could stand it. Those buildings must be like ovens.

TALBOT: In time I think every building will be artificially cooled, just as it's now artificially heated. After all, why not? There's no reason why we should be more uncomfortable in the summer than we are in the winter, simply because of the elements. We protect ourselves against the cold—why not against the heat?

KITTY: I like it here in the summer. I've had some swell times on pent-house parties.

HATTIE: Oh, all my life I've wanted to be pent-house girl, like one of Arno's pictures in The New Yorker.

ED: Yeah. You'd do well at that. *(A little laugh from the others.)*

MILLICENT: Of course the ideal life is to be in New York just about three months in the year.

TALBOT: Wait a minute! What about us doctors? What have we got to do—follow you around? *(Again a laugh.)*

MILLICENT: Well, of course then we won't need doctors. *(More light laughter.)*

(In both groups the conversation has simmered down to polite nothingness. As it nears this stage the figures of DORA and GUSTAVE stand a moment, and slowly approach the guests. DORA is carrying the canapés, GUSTAVE the cocktails. DORA is deathly pale, her eyes are red-rimmed from weeping, her whole face a mask of tragedy. GUSTAVE, too, is pale, his, expression stricken and guilty. The adhesive tape bandages are still on forehead and cheek. The pace of BOTH is leaden, funereal. DORA goes first to MILITANT group, GUSTAVE goes to OLIVER'S. In each group there are little murmurs of comment or appreciation as the trays are passed. As DORA offers the canapés)

KITTY: Oh, aren't they pretty! What do you suppose this is?

HATTIE: Be careful! They're hot.

KITTY: Mm—caviar!

TALBOT: I know I'm going to eat too many of these.

MILLICENT: Nonsense, they can't hurt you. There's nothing to them. *(As GUSTAVE offers the cocktails to the other group the conversation is simultaneous with that of the first group.)*

PACKARD: Ah, here we are! Well, I certainly needed this—What's in them?

OLIVER: I think Gustave generally uses rum. I don't like gin in my cocktail.

LUCY: *(Doesn't drink)* Oh, aren't they good!

CARLOTTA: This is the kind you get in Cuba, isn't it? *(Simultaneously GUSTAVE and DORA, having served their respective groups, move toward the opposite group, GUSTAVE to L; DORA to R.*

As they try to pass each other they come face to face; stop for one second as their eyes meet, DORA'S *accusing,* GUSTAVE'S *beseeching. For one second the air is charged with emotion, then they cross and resume their serving.)*

PACKARD: *(His voice breaking the* GUSTAVE-DORA *tension)* Hey! Don't go far away with those! *(The two groups now break and drift about a little. There is a little desultory conversation.)*

MILLICENT: Let me see We're all here except Mr. Renault. I hope he hasn't forgotten.

CARLOTTA: Oh, he'll be here. He's just staging an entrance. *(*ED *snaps fingers for cocktail.* CARLOTTA *sits on sofa.* PACKARD, OLIVER *and* LUCY R. *above chairs R.C.* MILLICENT *and* TALBOT *C.* HATTIE, KITTY *and* ED L. GUSTAVE *down L.)*

KITTY: Oh, I'm crazy to see him. I think he's gorgeous!

PACKARD: Where's that shaker? I want another one of these.

*(*PAULA *appears C. from L. Being on her way out to dinner with Ernest, she is in evening clothes, with an evening coat. She stands on the top step, her eyes searching the* GROUP*)*

TALBOT: I'm going to break a rule and have another one myself.

MILLICENT: You all know my daughter, Paula. *(A little murmur of acknowledgment from the group.)*

OLIVER: Hello, there! Where's your young man?

MILLICENT: Yes, where's Ernest?

PAULA: He's outside in the car. He turned shy on me, and wouldn't come up. I like this party. I may stay here.

LUCY: Hello, Paula dear! How's the future bride? When are you going to be married?

PAULA: Huh?—Oh, I—Where's Mr. Renault? Wasn't he going to be here?

MILLICENT: Yes, he's coming. He's not here yet.

PAULA: Oh! *(A little fleeting look of anxiety crosses her face.)*

PACKARD: She's hanging around to see the movie star. The rest of us don't stand a chance. (GUSTAVE *refills* PACKARD'S *glass.* DORA *crosses to group down L. A little laugh from the group, in which* PAULA *joins half-heartedly.)*

CARLOTTA: Oh, Larry's always late. He makes a point of it

MILLICENT: Well, we'll, wait a few minutes. He can't be long now. *(Attempts to start the conversational ball rolling)* Of course, with traffic what it is, it's a wonder anybody gets anywhere. *(The company has broken up into three groups, busy with chit-chat. In one group down L. are* CARLOTTA, ED *and* TALBOT. *In a second group up L.C.,* OLIVER, KITTY, HATTIE. *In the third, down R. which* MILLICENT *now joins, are* PACKARD *and* LUCY. GUSTAVE *and* DORA *move about with the cocktails and canapés. During all this* PAULA *is restlessly glancing toward the door off R., never giving her full attention to any one person in the room. Bits of conversation come up; one hears a fragment from this and that group. It is all recognizable as something one has heard many times before.)*

PAULA: Don't know what New York's coming to. Traffic getting worse and worse. Keep on putting up high buildings. What happens! (KITTY *laughs loudly.* OLIVER *and* HATTIE *join in politely.* PAULA *asks* GUSTAVE *for cocktail.)*

TALBOT: But if, Germany can't pay—what then? You can't get blood out of a stone.

ED: That's what I say.

KITTY: They say it's getting warmer every winter. It's on account of the Gulf Stream. They say there'll be palm trees growing where the Empire State is.

OLIVER: Well, that'll be nice. (DORA'S *at group down R.)*

MILLICENT: Of course, I don't get a minute to read. The only time is when I go to bed at night, and then I'm so sleepy—

TALBOT: That's very true.

ED: The first thing they've got to do is cut salaries. Look at what they pay their stars! (PACKARD *laughs.* GUSTAVE *to* TALBOT *and* ED *to refill glasses.)*

LUCY: But the trouble with children today is that they're blasé at fourteen. They've been everywhere. They've seen everything.

They've done everything. (GUSTAVE *takes tray; collects glasses from* CARLOTTA'S *group.* DORA *is above group down R.*)

OLIVER: But most people don't go to the opera for the music.. They go to be seen.

CARLOTTA: Oh, I know! You become just as attached to them as if they were human beings.

HATTIE: It's just steak and lamp chops over and over again I wish somebody would invent a new meat. (*The* ORCHESTRA *starts the last number.*)

MILLICENT: (*Speaking to the* GUESTS *as a whole*) I don't think we'll wait for Mr. Renault. He must have been delayed.

CARLOTTA: (*Rises and crosses. to C.*) Yes, let's have dinner. I'm starving. And so is Benito. (*Turns to the Pekinese in her arms*) Aren't you, Mussolini?

MILLICENT: (*To* GUSTAVE) All right, Gustave. You may serve dinner. (GUSTAVE *bows, opens doors L. and exits. Dora goes off up L.*) I hope Mr. Renault won't be offended (KITTY *comes to* CARLOTTA; *pets dog.* TALBOT *starts out. They* ALL *start to move toward the L. door.*)

(*WARN Curtain.*)

PACKARD: (*Following* MILLICENT *with* LUCY.) Last come, last served. That's the way we used to do out in Montana. We used to swarm around that cook shack like a bunch of locusts. And the way those beans and biscuits vanished—boy! The guy who was late was out of luck. He could eat grass.

TALBOT: I didn't get a bite of lunch. Reached the hospital at ten o'clock and was there until nearly five. Then I found an office full of patients, and I never did come up for air.

(PACKARD *and* TALBOT *are off L., following* MILLICENT *and* LUCY.)

LUCY: *(Speaking on "Didn't get a bite of lunch")* Millicent, I hope you haven't got too good a dinner, or mine will suffer by contrast.

MILLICENT: My dear! I'm having just the simplest meal in the world. I couldn't have less. *(They are off L.)*

ED: *(Looking at his wrist watch)* Half-past eight. We won't get to the show till the second act.

HATTIE: I thought you didn't want to see it.

ED: If I've got to go I don't want to get there in the middle. *(They are off L.)*

KITTY: *(Comes down to* CARLOTTA*)* Isn't he cute! I've had a lot of Pekineses, but I don't have any luck with them. They die on me. *(*CARLOTTA *snatches the dog away from* KITTY; *starts toward L. door.)*

OLIVER: *(Coming down to* KITTY*)* Ladies!

OLIVER: *(As* KITTY *and* CARLOTTA *are about to go L.)* You know what they do in Vienna?—they eat their dinner after the theatre instead of before.

KITTY: In Madrid they eat dinner at ten o'clock, and the shows don't begin until midnight. *(She is off L.)*

CARLOTTA: Really! What time is sunrise? Noon? *(She exits L.* PAULA *remains the sole occupant of the room, nervous, distrait, looking toward the foyer in the direction from which the late guest would come.)*

OLIVER: *(Comes back to her)* What's the matter, Paula? Something wrong?

PAULA: *(Pulling her wrap up about her shoulders)* No, no. I'm just going, Dad.

OLIVER: *(Kisses her cheek tenderly, just a touch; passes a hand over her hair)* Good-night, my dear. *(*OLIVER *goes out L.)*

(The GUESTS *being out of the room, the* MUSIC *slowly comes up in volume.* PAULA, *on the steps, turns and peers fixedly out in the di-*

rection from which LARRY *would come, C. from R. Turns a step or two toward the room. Sees a cocktail on the table R.; goes quickly to it; snatches up a full glass; drains it. Turns, wavers with indecision, then, with a rush, goes out C. to R. Through this we have heard faintly the* CONVERSATION *and* LAUGHTER *of the* GUESTS *on their way to the dining-room. Now a burst of* LAUGHTER *comes up at some special sally. For some fifteen or twenty seconds, while the stage is empty, the* MUSIC *plays on, a romantic, throbbing. Hungarian waltz.)*

THE CURTAIN FALLS

STAGE DOOR

GEORGE S. KAUFMAN
AND EDNA FERBER

CAST OF CHARACTERS

Olga Brandt

Mattie (COLORED MAID)

Mrs. Orcutt (ELDERLY WOMAN)

Frank (COLORED HOUSEMAN)

Young Women

Mary Harper (BIG MARY)

Mary McCune
   (LITTLE MARY)

Bernice Niemeyer

Madeleine Vauclain

Judith Canfield

Ann Braddock

Terry Randall

Kaye Hamilton

Linda Shaw

Jean Maitland

Bobby Melrose

Louise Mitchell

Susan Paige

Pat Devine

Kendall Adams

Tony Gillette

Ellen Fenwick

Young Men

Sam Hastings

Jimmy Devereaux

Business Men:

Fred Powell

Lou Milhauser

David Kingsley (IN HIS 30'S)

Keith Burgess (YOUNG MAN)

Mrs. Shaw (MIDDLE-AGED
   WOMAN)

Dr. Randall (MIDDLE-AGED MAN)

Larry Westcott (PUBLICITY MAN)

Billy (PHOTOGRAPHER)

Adolph Gretzel
   (MIDDLE-AGED MAN)

ACT I

Scene 1. Footlights Club (Main Room). Somewhere in the West Fifties, New York.

Scene 2 One of the Bedroom. A month later.

ACT II

Scene 1. Again the Main Room. (Same as Act I, Scene 1.) A year later.

Scene 2 Two months later. (Same.)

ACT III

Scene 1. The following season. (Same.) A Sunday morning.

Scene 2. About two weeks later. (Same.) Midnight.

ACT ONE

SCENE 1:

The Footlights club. A club for girls of the stage

It occupies an entire brownstone house in the West 50's, New York. One of those old houses whose former splendor has departed as the neighborhood has changed. The room we see is the common living room. It is comfortably furnished with unrelated but good pieces, enlivened by a bit of chintz. The effect is that of charm and livability, what with the piano, a desk, a fireplace with a good old marble mantel. Prominently is a copy of a portrait of Sarah Bernhardt, at her most dramatic. There is a glimpse of hallway with a flight of stairs. The lower part of the arch leading to hall is two low bookcases. The one L. stage holds the phone, the one R. stage holds mail, messages, papers, an occasional hat is thrown there. It is an October evening, just before the dinner hour. The girls are coming home from matinees, from job hunting, they are up and down the stairs, and presently they will be out again on dinner dates, playing the evening performances, seeing a movie.

Two girls are in the room at the moment, one at the piano up L., the other at a writing desk up R.

The girl at the piano, OLGA BRANDT, *is dark, intense, sultry-looking.* BERNICE NIEMEYER, *at the desk, is a young girl definitely not of the ingenue type. This is at once her cross and (in her opinion) her greatest asset as an actress. For a moment nothing is heard but the music. The girl at the piano is playing beautifully, and with exquisite technique, Chopin's Nocturne in F minor. A girl,* SUSAN PAIGE, *comes in from street door, stops for a quick look through the mail, tosses a "Hi!" into the room, and goes on up the stairs.*

The piano again.

BERNICE: *(To* SUSAN*)* Hello. *(Rises, crosses to* OLGA*)* What's that you're playing?

OLGA: *(Her Russian origin evident in her accent)* Chopin.

BERNICE: How did you learn to play like that?

OLGA: Practice. Practice.

BERNICE: How long did it take you?

OLGA: *(Out of patience)* Oh! *(A little discordant crash on the keys)*

BERNICE: Well, I was just asking.

> *(The phone rings as* MATTIE, *the maid, is descending the stairs, a little pile of towels over her arm.* MATTIE *is colored, about 30, matter-of-fact, accustomed to the vagaries of a houseful of girls and tolerant of them.)*

MATTIE: Hello! Yes, this the Footlights Club. . . *(To the girls in the room)* Miss Devine come in yet? *(A negative shake of the head from* OLGA, *and a muttered "uh-uh" from* BERNICE.*)* No, she ain't *(She hangs up.)*

BERNICE: *(To* MATTIE*)* Was it a man?

> *(Meanwhile voices are heard as street door opens.)*

BIG MARY: Oh no, let's have dinner here and go to a movie.

LITTLE MARY: Well, all right.

BERNICE: *(Pursuing her eternal queries)* Who's that? *(Moves to R. of arch)*

OLGA: *(A shade of impatience)* Big and Little Mary.

> *(*BIG *and* LITTLE MARY—MARY HARPER *and* MARY MCCUNE—*come into view in doorway from hall up R. There is a wide gap in stature between the two. One comes about to the other's elbow.)*

BIG MARY: What time is it? Dinner ready yet?

BERNICE: Where've you been? Seeing managers?

LITTLE MARY: *(Drooping)* Yeh. We're dead.

> *(The two* MARYS *in C. of arch)*

BIG MARY: We've been in every manager's office on Broadway.

(OLGA *stops playing.*)

BERNICE: Is anybody casting?

BIG MARY: How do we know? We only got in to see one of them

BERNICE: Which one? Who'd you see?

LITTLE MARY: Rosenblatt.

BERNICE: What's he doing?

BIG MARY: Take it easy. It's all cast. *(Her tone implies that this is the stereotyped managerial reply)*

LITTLE MARY: All except a kid part ten years old.

(BIG *and* LITTLE MARY *start upstairs.* OLGA *starts playing again.)*

BERNICE: *(Eagerly)* I could look ten years old. *(She becomes a dimpled darling)*

LITTLE MARY: No. Big Mary had the same idea and she's littler than you are.

BIG MARY: You're almost as tall as Little Mary.

BERNICE: *(Crossing to* OLGA*)* Listen, why is the little one called Big Mary and the big one Little Mary?

OLGA: *(Stops playing)* Nobody knows. Will you for heaven's sake stop asking questions?

BERNICE: Oh, all right

MADELEINE: *(enters R.)* Hello!

BERNICE: Where've you been? *(The last remark is addressed to a new-comer who stands in doorway. She is* MADELEINE VAUCLAIN, *a languid beauty, who runs through a sheaf of letters to discover if there is any mail for her. Phone rings.* BERNICE *picks it up.)* Footlights Club! . . . *(Another girl has come in street door and dashes upstairs pulling off coat as she goes up. She is* BOBBY MELROSE, BERNICE *to the girls.)* Terry Randall come in? *(As they shake their heads in negative.)* Not yet. *(Hangs up)*

MADELEINE: *(Drops down R. C.)* I saw her sitting in Berger's office. I guess she gives up hard.

BERNICE: *(Alert at once)* Is Berger doing any casting?

MADELEINE: Listen, why don't you try making the rounds once instead of sitting on your bustle and writing letters—

BERNICE: *(Up the stairs)* I make the rounds, but all you see is the office boys.

MADELEINE: Well, who do you think sees the letters?

BERNICE: *(Stops on stairs a moment)* Well, if they won't see you and won't read the letters, where do you go from there? *(Exit up stairs.)*

MADELEINE: *(Calling after her)* If you find out I wish you'd tell me.

MATTIE: *(In dining room doorway)* Either you girls eating home?

MADELEINE: I'm not.

MATTIE: Anyhow, it's ready. *(Goes, leaving doors open)*

OLGA: *(Continues playing)* Yes, yes.

MADELEINE: Look, you don't want to go out tonight, do you? I've got an extra man.

OLGA: *(A shake of the head)* I am rehearsing.

MADELEINE: Tonight?

OLGA: *(With bitterness)* Tonight. I play the piano for a lot of chorus girls to sing and dance. *(She goes into it, plays about eight bars of a very cheap tune, ends with discord. She rises furiously.)* That's what I am doing tonight and every night! For that I studied fifteen years with Kolijinsky! *(Storms into a dining room L.)*

MADELEINE: *(Moves L. after her—mildly astonished at this outburst)* Well, look, all I did was ask you if you wanted to go out tonight. *(A new figure appears in doorway. It is* JUDITH CANFIELD, *hard, wise, debunked. She has picked up a letter from hall table)*

JUDITH: *(With dreadful sweetness as she drops down C.)* Oh, goody, goody, goody! I got a letter from home.

MADELEINE: Hello, Judith!

JUDITH: *(Averting her gaze from letter as she opens it, brings herself to look at it with a courageous jerk of the head.)* Mmmm! Pa got laid off.*(Turns a pale)* My sister's husband has left her. *(Her eye skims a line or two. Turns another page)* And one of my brothers slugged a railroad detective. I guess that's all. *(She moves R. to couch and sits)* Yes. Lots of love and can you spare fifty dollars.

MADELEINE: Nothing like a letter from home to pick you up. . . Look, Judy, what are you doing tonight?

JUDITH: *(Who has dropped into a couch, whisked off her pump, and is pulling out toe of her stocking)* I don't know. Why?

MADELEINE: I've got an extra man.

JUDITH: *(Brightening)* You mean dinner?

MADELEINE: Yes. Fellow from back home in Seattle. He's in the lumber business. He's here for a convention.

JUDITH: Sounds terrible.

MADELEINE: No, he isn't bad. And he's got this friend with him, so he wanted to know if I could get another girl.

JUDITH: Is the friend also in the lumber business?

MADELEINE: I don't know. What's the difference!

JUDITH: He'll be breezy. "Hello, Beautiful!"

MADELEINE: If we don't like it we can go home early.

JUDITH: Well *(Weighing it)* do we dress?

MADELEINE: Sure!

JUDITH: Okay. I kind of feel like stepping out tonight.

MADELEINE: *(Going toward stairs.)* Swell. We'd better start. It's getting late.

JUDITH: *(Tugging at her stocking)* I'll be ready,

MADELEINE: Hello, Ann

ANN: Hello. (MADELEINE *disappears.* JUDITH *wriggles her cramped toes, sighs. Still another girl,* ANN BRADDOCK, *has come downstairs and goes toward dining room. She wears a hat and carries her coat, which she tosses onto piano as she passes.)* Going in to dinner?

JUDITH: Got a date.

ANN: Well, that's all right for you—you're not working. But I can't go out to dinner, and run around, and still give my best to the theatre. After all, you never see Kit Cornell dashing around. *(Righteously, she goes into dining room L., sits at head of table.)*

JUDITH: *(Mutters at first)* Kit Cornell!*(Rises. Then raises her voice as portrait on wall gives her an idea.)* What about Bernhardt! I suppose she was a home girl!

(From above stairs and descending stairway, the voice of MRS. ORCUTT, the House Matron is heard.)

MRS. ORCUTT: Yes, I'm sure you're going to be most comfortable here. Both of your roommates are lovely girls. Now if you'll just *(Sees JUDITH)* Oh! *(MRS. ORCUTT is a woman of about 46. In manner and dress you detect the flavor of a theatrical past. Her dress is likely to have too many ruffles, her coiffure too many curls. She is piloting a fragile and rather wispy girl whose eyes are too big for her face. We presently learn that her name is KAYE HAMILTON.)* Uh this is Judith Canfield, one of our girls. I'm so sorry, I'm afraid I didn't—

KAYE: Kaye Hamilton.

MRS. ORCUTT: Oh, yes. Miss Hamilton is planning to be with everything uh she'll room with Jean and Terry, now that Louise is leaving.

JUDITH: That'll be swell. Excuse me. *(Shoe in hand, she limps toward stairs and up)*

MRS. ORCUTT: *(A little gracious nod)* Now, that's our dining room. *(A gesture)* Dinner is served from six to seven, because of course the girls have to get to the theatre early if they're working. Now, let me see. You're in the same room with Terry and Jean, so that's only twelve-fifty a week, including the meals. I suppose that will be all right?

KAYE: Yes, thank you.

MRS. ORCUTT: Now, about the reference—*(She looks at a piece of paper she has been holding)* I'll have that all looked up in the morning.

KAYE: Morning? Can't I come in tonight?

Mrs. Orcutt: I'm, afraid not. You see—

Kaye: But I've got to come in tonight. I've got to.

(A girl comes in at street door, runs through hallway and rapidly upstairs, humming as she goes: Pat Devine. Halfway up we hear her call 'Yoo-hoo!')

Mrs. Orcutt: *(After the interruption)* Well—uh—it's a little irregular. However . . . Did you say your bags were near by?

Kaye: Yes. That is, I can get them.

Mrs. Orcutt: *(Reluctantly)* Well, then, I suppose it's all right .... Now,-we have certain little rules. As you know, this is a club for stage girls. I assume you are on the stage?

Kaye: Yes. Yes. I'm not working now, but I hope . . .

Mrs. Orcutt: I understand . . . Now about callers—men callers, I mean

Kaye: There won't be any men.

Mrs. Orcutt: Oh, it's quite all right. We like you to bring your friends here. But not after eleven-thirty at night, and—of course only in this room.

Kaye: I understand.

Mrs. Orcutt: I try very hard to make the girls feel that this is a real home. I was one of them myself not many years back, before I married Mr. Orcutt. Helen Romayne? Possibly you remember?

Kaye: I'm afraid I don't.

Mrs. Orcutt: That's quite all right. I think that covers everything. If you wish to go, and get your bags. Mattie! *(Peering toward dining room)* Will you come here a minute?

Mattie: *(In dining room)* Yes, ma'am!

Mrs. Orcutt: *(She gently pilots Kaye toward doorway)* Now, each girl is given a door-key and there's a little charge of twenty-five cents in case they're lost. So you see it's to your own interest not to lose it. Well, good-bye, and I'll expect you in a very short time.

(As MATTIE *has appeared in dining room doorway* BERNICE *comes downstairs, crosses living room toward dining room.)*

BERNICE: What have we got for dinner, Mattie?

MATTIE: We got a good dinner.

BERNICE: *(As she disappears, sits on* ANN'S *L.)* Smells like last night. Is it?

(Sound of front door closing. MRS. ORCUTT, *very businesslike, returns)*

MRS. ORCUTT: Now, Mattie, there's a new girl coming in as soon as Louise Mitchell leaves. You'll only have a few minutes to get that room straightened up.

MATTIE: Yes, ma'am.

MRS. ORCUTT: Let's see, Terry Randall isn't in yet, is she?

MATTIE: No, ma'am.

MRS. ORCUTT: Well, if I don't see her be sure to tell her there's a new girl moving in with her and Jean Don't forget fresh paper in the bureau drawers, and—

(Down the stairs like an angry whirlwind comes LINDA SHAW, *clutching a dressing gown about her. Her hair is beautifully done, she is wearing evening slippers, obviously she is dressed for the evening except for her frock.)*

LINDA: *(Up C.)* Mattie, isn't my dress pressed yet?

MATTIE: *(Starting toward* LINDA) Oh! Was you wanting it right away?

LINDA: Right away! When did you think I wanted it?

MATTIE: Well, I'll do it right this minute.

LINDA: Oh, don't bother! I'll do it myself! *(Storms out in hallway up L.)*

MATTIE: *(After her)* You never give it to me till pretty near half-past five.

(Phone rings. MRS. ORCUTT *answers.)*

MRS. ORCUTT: I'll go. *(To Mattie who exits up L.)* Footlights Club!
. . . Yes, she is . . . The Globe Picture Company?.. Mr. Kingsley
himself? . . . Just a minute, *(Impressed)* I'll get her right away ...
(Calls toward stairs) Jean! Oh, Jean!

JEAN: *(From above)* Yes.

MRS. ORCUTT: *(In hushed tones)* Mr. Kingsley of the Globe Picture
Company wants to talk to you.

JEAN: Oh, all right.

MRS. ORCUTT: *(Back to phone)* She'll be right down. *(She lays down
receiver with a tenderness that is almost reverence, and takes a few
steps away, looking toward stairway. As* JEAN *appears,* MRS.
ORCUTT *affects an elaborate nonchalance and exits into dining
room.)*

*(*JEAN MAITLAND *is a beautiful girl in her early 20's.; She is, perhaps, a shade too vivacious. A better actress off than on. Her hair is
blond, and that toss of her head that shakes back her curls is not
quite convincing. An opportunist: good-natured enough when
things go her way, she has definite charm and appeal for men.* JEAN
throws her all into her voice as she greets the man at the phone.)

JEAN: Hello! Mr. Kingsley! How perfectly—*(Obviously she is met by
a secretary's voice. Dashed by this, her tone drops to below normal)*
Yes, this is Miss Maitland. Will you put him on pleas⌣? *(Again
she gathers all her forces and even tops her first performance.)* Hello!
Mr. Kingsley! How wonderful! . . . Yes, I know you said that,
but in your business you must meet a million beautiful girls a
day . . . Well, anyhow, half a million . . . *(Coyly)* . . . Dinner! You
don't mean tonight! Ohm... Yes, I did have, but it's nothing I
can't break. . . Oh, but I want to. I'd love to . . . What time?
Yes, I'll be ready. I suppose we're dressing? . . . Yes, I'd love to.
All right. Good-bye.

*(As she hangs up receiver, figures pop out of the vantage points from
which they have been listening.* BERNICE *and* ANN *come out of dining room with* MRS. ORCUTT; *cloppity-clop down the stairs come*
BIG *and* LITTLE MARY *and* BOBBY MELROSE. BOBBY *is a soft
Southern belle, fluffy, feminine. At the moment she is in a rather
grotesque state of nettle hair curlers, cold cream and bathrobe.)*

BIG MARY: *(A squeal of excitement)* Jean!

BERNICE: I'm dying!

LITTLE MARY: Tell us all about it!

ANN: Yes, do!

BERNICE: What time is he coming?

MRS. ORCUTT: *(Entering)* Well, Jeanie, does this mean we're going to lose you to pictures?

(OLGA, too, appears in dining room doorway, and stands there absorbing the scene.)

BOBBY: Aren't you palpitating?

BERNICE: How soon is he coming? Can I see him?

JEAN: Now listen you girls, no fair hanging around when he comes.

LITTLE MARY: Aw!

JEAN: You've got to promise me—no parading.

(The girls have come down C.)

BIG MARY: Big-hearted Bertha!

BERNICE: I'll bet you'll let Terry meet him.

JEAN: Well, Terry's different.

ANN: All this fuss about a man! I wouldn't lift my little finger to meet him. *(She stalks into dining room, sits head of table.)*

LITTLE MARY: She is over-sexed!

MRS. ORCUTT: David Kingsley! You know, he was Al Woods' office boy when I played "The Woman in Room 13."

BERNICE: *(Off hand)* Really.? *(To JEAN)* What are you going to wear?

JEAN: I wonder if Pat'll let me have her rose taffeta.

BERNICE: Sure she would!

JEAN: And I'll wear Kendall's evening coat.

MRS. ORCUTT: When he became a producer he wanted me for his first play. But by that time I had married Mr. Orcutt—

(From above-stairs comes the sound of singing: "Here Comes the Bride." Other voices take it up. The group in the room at once knows what this means, and their attention is turned towards stairs.)

BIG MARY: Oh, here's Louise!

BERNICE: Louise is going!

BOBBY: Oh, my goodness! I promised to help her pack!

LITTLE MARY: Let's get some rice and throw it!

BIG MARY: Oh, for heaven's sake, that's silly

(ANN enters L. FRANK, the houseman, comes downstairs laden with bags. MATTIE'S husband 35 or so. Close on FRANK'S heels comes LOUISE MITCHELL in traveling clothes, wearing a corsage of gardenias. She is accompanied by 3 girls. One is SUSAN, a student at an acting school. The others are PAT DEVINE, a night-club dancer, and KENDALL ADAMS, of the Boston Adams'. MATTIE, broadly grinning and anticipatory, comes to dining room doorway. LOUISE is ushered into room on a wave of melody.)

MRS. ORCUTT: Well, my dear, and so the moment has come. But when you see how saddened we are, you will realize that parting is sweet sorrow, after all.

(JUDITH comes downstairs, followed by MADELEINE. Both in deshabille.)

JUDITH: *(As she drops down R.)* Well, Mitchell, you're finally getting the hell out of here, huh?

MRS. ORCUTT: Judith! That seems to me hardly the spirit.

JUDITH: Sorry.

LOUISE: Judy doesn't mean anything.

FRANK: *(In hallway)* Shall I get you a taxi, Miss Louise?

LOUISE: Oh, yes, thank you, Frank. *(FRANK exits up R. with bags. The moment of departure has come. She looks about her for a second.)* Well, I guess there's no use in my trying to—Why, where's Terry? I thought she was down here.

KENDALL: Isn't she here?

SUSAN: No.

JEAN: She hasn't come in yet.

LOUISE: Oh dear, I can't go without seeing Terry.

BERNICE: What's she up to, anyhow? I haven't seen her for days.

JEAN: I don't know. She's gone before I'm awake in the morning.

LOUISE: Well, anyhow, I guess I'd better get out of here before I bust out crying. You've all been just too darling for words, every single one of you (LINDA, *having retrieved her dress, flashes through hall from up L. and makes for stairs.*) Who's that? Oh good-bye, Linda. I'm going. (LINDA, *no part of this, tosses a "good bye" over her shoulder as she goes upstairs.*) And no matter how happy I am, I'll never forget you, and thanks a million times for the perfume, Pat, and you, Susan, for the compact, and all of you that clubbed together and gave me the exquisite night-gown.

BERNICE: Oh, that's all right.

LOUISE: So I hope I'll make a better wife than I did an actress—I guess I wasn't very good at that—

BIG MARY: You were so!

KENDALL: Yes.

LITTLE MARY: You were swell.

LOUISE: I guess I wasn't very swell or I wouldn't be getting mar—(*Catches herself*) that is, any girl would be glad to give up the stage to marry a wonderful boy like Bob—anyway, I certainly am. Goodness, when I think that for two whole years he's waited back there in Appleton, I guess I'm pretty lucky.

BIG MARY: Yes.

(The faces about her, while attentive, do not reflect full belief in her good fortune)

LOUISE: Well, if any of you ever come out that way with a show, why, it's only a hundred miles from Milwaukee. Don't forget I'll be Mrs. Robert Hendershot by that time, and Wisconsin's per-

fectly beautiful in the autumn—the whole Fox River valley—
it's beautiful *(It's no use. She cannot convince even herself, much less
the rather embarrassed young people about her)*

*(The situation is miraculously saved by the slam of the street door
and the electric entrances of a new and buoyant figure.* TERRY
RANDALL *has the vivid personality , the mobile face of the born actress. She is not at all conventionally beautiful, but the light in her
face gives to her rather irregular features the effect of beauty. High
cheekbones, wide mouth, broad brow.)*

TERRY: *(Breathless in hallway)* LOUISE!

SUSAN: Here's Terry.

TERRY: *(As she drops down C. to* LOUISE*)* Darling I was so afraid
you'd be gone. I ran all the way from Forty-sixth Street.
Nothing else in the world could have kept me—look—what do
you think! I've got a JOB!

*(This announcement is greeted with a chorus of excited exclama-
tions.)*

BOBBY: You haven't!

BERNICE: Who with?

PAT: Tell us about it.

SUSAN: Terry, how wonderful!

BIG MARY: Tell us all about it!

TERRY: I will, afterward—Louise, what a darling crazy hat! I just
love it on you.

LOUISE: Oh, Terry, have you really got a job! What in?

JEAN: Who is it? Berger?

TERRY: Yes.

BERNICE: I thought he was all cast.

TERRY: He was, all except this. It's got one marvelous scene—you
know one of those gamuts.

(With three attitudes and a series of wordless sounds one denuncia-

tory, one tender, one triumphant— she amusingly conveys the range of her part.)

(From among the group)

SUSAN: It sounds marvelous!

PAT: Terry, you'll be wonderful!

FRANK: *(In hallway)* Taxi's waiting, Miss Louise.

GIRLS: Oh!

LOUISE: *(A glance at her wristwatch)* Oh, dear, I can't bear to go. How'll I ever hear the rest of it? I've got to go.

JEAN: Oh dear.

GIRLS: Oh!

LOUISE: Terry, baby!

TERRY: Be happy, darling!

(LOUISE *throws her arms about* TERRY, *kisses her. General embracing and good-byes.)*

LOUISE: Jean! Kendall! *(She kisses* JEAN *her other roommate.)* Good-bye, good-bye! (LOUISE *is hurrying from room, others streaming into hallway to speed her.)*

KENDALL: Don't forget us!

MADELEINE: Send us a piece of wedding cake!

JUDITH: We want the deadly details.

(A chorus of good-byes from the girls.)

MRS. ORCUTT: I hope you'll be very happy, dear child. Good-bye.. good-bye..good-bye!

(LOUISE *is gone. The girls stream back into room.)*

KENDALL: When do you go into rehearsal, Terry?

OLGA: Yes when?

TERRY: *(As she drops down L. to armchair)* Right away!

BERNICE: Gosh, Terry, you certainly got a break. Berger wouldn't even talk to me.

LITTLE MARY: Berger's an awful meany. How'd you get to him, anyway?

TERRY: I just stood there outside his door for a week.

PAT: And it did the trick?

BIG MARY: I tried that.

BOBBY: It never helped me any.

JUDITH: Me neither. I laid there once for a whole afternoon with "Welcome!" on me.

TERRY: I've had a longer run outside his office than I've had with most shows. This was my second week. I was just going to send out for a toothbrush and a camp chair *(Rises)* when suddenly he opened the door. He was going. I said, "Mr. Berger!" That's practically all. I've said for two weeks "Mr. Berger." *(She gives four readings of "Mr. Berger," ranging from piteous pleading to imperious command.)*

LITTLE MARY: What did he do?

SUSAN: What happened?

TERRY: He never even stopped. Suddenly I was furious. I grabbed his arm and said, "Listen! You're a producer and I'm an actress. What right have you got to barricade yourself behind closed doors and not see me! And hundreds like me! The greatest actress in the world might be coming up your stairs and you'd never know it."

KENDALL: Terry! What did he say!

TERRY: He said, "Are you the greatest actress in the world?" I said, "'Maybe." He said, "You don't look like anything to me. You're not even pretty and you're just a little runt." I said, "Pretty-! I suppose Rachel was pretty. And what about Nazimova! She's no higher than this." *(Indicates a level)* "But on a stage she's any height she wants to be."

JUDITH: P. S. She got the job.

TERRY: Yes. *(A deep sigh that conveys her relief at the outcome)*And when I walked out on Broadway again it seemed the most glamorous street in the world. Those beautiful Nedick orange stands, and that lovely traffic at Broadway and Forty-fifth, and those darling bums spitting on the sidewalk—*(Doorbell rings. Instantaneously the group is galvanized. The girls realize the lateness of the hour. TERRY glances at her watch.)* Oh my!

MADELEINE: A suitor!

KENDALL: My word, it's late! *(Runs for stairs)*

BIG MARY: Come on, let's eat.

(To dining room with LITTLE MARY, ANN, OLGA and BERNICE)

BOBBY: Oh, it's my new young man. Mattie, tell him I won't be a minute. *(Dashes upstairs)*

(Meanwhile MADELEINE and JUDITH are dashing for stairs.)

MADELEINE: Wait a minute, Mattie. Give us a chance to get upstairs.

JUDITH: Yes, Mattie. We don't want to give him the wrong idea of this house.

JEAN: *(As she starts for stairs with TERRY.)* Terry, I couldn't be gladder.

TERRY: Me neither.

JEAN: Terry! What do you think's happened to your little girlfriend? I'm having dinner with David Kingsley tonight.

TERRY: Jean, how marvelous. Did he say anything about a picture test?

JEAN: *(As they go upstairs)* Not yet, but it must mean he's interested. Now look, when he gets here I want you to come down and meet him, because you never can tell.

(MATTIE, having waited until the coast was clear, now goes to front door. Sound of a man's voice. HASTINGS: "Is Miss Melrose in?" MATTIE'S reply: "Yes, she is. Come right in." A young man stands in doorway, a trifle ill at ease in these unfamiliar surroundings. He

hasn't the look of a New Yorker. There is about him the rather graceful angularity and winning simplicity of the Westerner.)

MATTIE: You all can wait in there.

YOUNG MAN: Oh, thanks. Just tell her Sam Hastings is calling for her.

MATTIE: *(As she goes to dining room door)* I think she knows about it—she'll be down directly.

(SAM HASTINGS mutters a thank-you as MATTIE passes into dining room, closing doors behind her. Left alone, SAM makes a leisurely survey of the room, rather getting in the way of his own big frame as he turns. He decides, unfortunately, on the least substantial chair in the room up L. and sits gingerly on its edge. At once there is a short sharp crack of protesting wood. He is on his feet like a shot. He prowls the room a bit. From above stairs a snatch of popular song Swift footsteps are heard descending stairs. He turns expectantly but it's not his girl. It is KENDALL, who is humming a bit of song as she comes. Stops on stairs to fix stocking. She stops abruptly as she sees a stranger. With a glare at the embarrassed SAM she goes into dining room. Doorbell rings. Then a peremptory voice shouts from upstairs)

JEAN: Judy. *(Followed by three sharp raps on a door)* You going to stay in the johnny all night?

(He clears his throat and looks away, though there's nothing to look away from. BERNICE comes out of dining room. Closes door behind her. Her eye brightens as she beholds the young man.)

BERNICE: *(Summoning all her charm)* Oh, pardon me. You're not Mr. David Kingsley!

SAM: No, my name's Hastings.

(With a syllable of dismissal, "Oh!" BERNICE goes on her way, and up the stairs. By this time MATTIE is opening front door. A voice {DEVEREAUX} inquires:)

DEVEREAUX: Miss Paige in?

MATTIE: Yes, come right in. *(The boy who appears is even younger than*

SAM. *Perhaps 19. Slight, graceful, dark-haired, rather sensitive looking.* MATTIE *calls from foot of stairs.*) Miss Susan

(SUSAN'S *voice from upstairs—"All right, Mattie"* MATTIE *exits up L. The two boys confront each other rather uncertainly. The newcomer in the doorway ventures a mannerly:*)

DEVEREAUX: *(Over L. C.)* How do you do?

SAM: Howdy-do?

(A little awkward pause)

DEVEREAUX: My name is Devereaux.

SAM: Mine's Hastings.

DEVEREAUX: Yes, I recognized you. I saw you in that Keith Burgess play last month.

SAM: *(Over R.)* You sure must have looked quick.

DEVEREAUX: I liked that part. You did a lot with it. Too bad the play flopped.

SAM: I don't rightly recall you. Have you played anything lately?

DEVEREAUX: Last month I played Emperor Jones, and I'm cast now for Hamlet.

SAM: Hamlet?

DEVEREAUX: I'm at the New York School of Acting. This is my last year.

SAM: Oh! And then what?

DEVEREAUX: Then I'm going on the stage.

SAM: Did you ever try to get a job on the stage?

DEVEREAUX: Not yet.

SAM: That's more of a career than acting. I've been in New York two years. I'm from Texas. Houston Little Theatre. We came up and won a contest, and I stayed. I've had two weeks work in two years. Don't ask me how I live. I don't know.

DEVEREAUX: You could go back to Texas, couldn't you?

SAM: Go back! Oh, no! I'm an actor.

(SUSAN *runs down stairs, in street clothes*)

SUSAN: Hello, Jimmy!

DEVEREAUX: Hello, Sue. Do you know Mr. Hastings?

SUSAN: How-dy do?

DEVEREAUX: Miss Susan Paige. She's up at the school, too. She's going to do Hedda Gabler.

SAM: Well, you have to start somewhere.

SUSAN: *(Laughingly)* Yes.

(DEVEREAUX *says "good-bye." There is a word of farewell from* SAM *and* SUSAN *as doorbell rings.*)

DEVEREAUX: *(As he and* SUSAN *go into hall)* Where do you want to eat?

SUSAN: *(Going off up R.)* How much money have you got?

DEVEREAUX: Sixty-five cents.

SUSAN: I've got thirty. That's ninety-five. *(As the open door the are accosted by a hearty masculine voice, subsequently identified as that of* FRED POWELL. *"This the Footlights Club?")* Yes. Won't you just—Mattie Somebody at the door.

(MATTIE *having appeared in hallway*)

MATTIE: Yes'm, Miss Susan .....You gentlemen calling on somebody?

(FRED POWELL *and* LOU MILHAUSER *come into view. They are two over-hearty Big Business men out for a holiday. Their derby hats and daytime attire will be a shock to the girls, especially* JUDITH)

POWELL: Yes, we're calling for Miss Madeleine Vauclain.

MILHAUSER: And her friend.

MATTIE: *(At foot of stairs)* Miss Madeleine!

MADELEINE: *(Upstairs)* Yes.

MATTIE: Couple gentlemen down here say they calling for you and somebody.

MADELEINE: Coming down!

MATTIE: She's coming down.

(They come into living room, and finding another man there, offer a recitative greeting, a smile and wave of the hand. Then they look the room over.)

MILHAUSER: What'd you say this place was? A Home for Girls?

POWELL: Yeh, all actresses. A whole bunch of 'em live here.

MILHAUSER: Kind of a handy place to know about.

POWELL: Yeah.

MILHAUSER: *(Whisks from his pocket two cellophaned cigars)* Smoke?

POWELL: Thanks.

(As they light up, MILHAUSER, having tossed crumpled cellophane jackets to a nearby table, sends a glance of half-inquiry at SAM. Hastily, in order to divert any further advances, SAM opens his cigarette case and lights a cigarette.)

MILHAUSER: Certainly is a funny place, New York. Now, you take a layout like this. Wouldn't find it anywhere else in the world.

POWELL: Bet you wouldn't, at that.

MILHAUSER: I always thought actresses lived in flats or—uh—hotel rooms.

POWELL: Lot's of 'em do.

MILHAUSER: *(Struck by a new thought)* What about men actors- Where do they live?

POWELL: I don't know—Lambs' Club, I guess.

MILHAUSER: Oh, yeah.

(SAM shifts his position a little, throws them a look. BOBBY, finally, coming downstairs, saves the situation. She is at her most Southern.)

BOBBY: *(From stairs)* Hello there, Texas!

SAM: *(Gathering up his coat and hat)* Oh, hello

BOBBY: Ah hope Ah didn't keep you waitin'.

SAM: No! No!

BOBBY: One thing about me, Ah'm always prompt.

(Outer door closes. They are gone off up R.)

POWELL: That was a cute little trick.

MILHAUSER: Yeah....Look! What about this one you've got on the fire for me? She any good?

POWELL: Sure, sure. You leave it to Madeleine.

MILHAUSER: Oh, well, as long as she's good-natured.

(There is a rustle of silk on stairway. "Ah!" exclaims POWELL *in anticipation and relief.* MADELEINE *and* JUDITH *descend stairs in full evening regalia, gathered from the richest recesses of the club— furs, silks, gloves, jewelry.)*

MADELEINE: *(Furiously, as she catches sight of the men's attire)* Well, is this what you call dressing?

POWELL: Huh?

MADELEINE: Why didn't you come in overalls!

POWELL: Now, now, baby. We got snarled up in a committee meeting, didn't we, Lou?

MILHAUSER: Sure. Sure.

POWELL: This is Lou Milhauser, girls. Miss Madeleine Vauclain and—uh—

MADELEINE: *(Sulkily)* This is Miss Canfield

MILHAUSER: Hello, Beautiful! *(Very jovial. He crosses to* JUDITH, *takes her arm.)* How about it? Shall we step out and go places?

JUDITH: Yes, let's.

MILHAUSER: Now, don't be like that. We're going to have a good time.

POWELL: Sure we are! The works ! *(He is piloting* MADELEINE *out to hallway)* Come on, boys and girls Where do we want to eat?

MILHAUSER: *(As he starts off with* JUDITH*)* I got an idea. How about a little Italian place?

JUDITH: Little Italian nuts. I want a decent dinner.

(A slam at door. They are gone.)

OLGA: *(Entering and speaking to* KENDALL *as latter enters living room from dining room)* Kendall, are you going to your show? I am rehearsing at the Winter Garden, if you want to walk down.

*(*OLGA *crossing to C.)*

KENDALL: It's too early for me. We don't go up till eight-fifty.

(The TWO MARYS *enter from dining room.)*

OLGA: The Winter Garden! The star pupil of Kolijinsky at the Winter Garden! *(She stalks out street door up R.)*

LITTLE MARY: Bellyaching! And she's got a job! Look at me. Edwin Booth and I retired from the stage at practically the same time.

KENDALL: *(As she starts for stairs.)* Oh, dear, I think I'll take a rest before the night show. Matinee days are frightfully tiring. *(She goes up to her room.)*

BIG MARY: Frightfully tiring! Why doesn't she go back to Boston where she belongs! That'd rest her up.

LITTLE MARY: There ought to be an Equity law against society girls going on the stage. "Miss Kendall Adams, daughter of Mr. and Mrs. Roger Winthrop Adams."

BIG MARY: "Of Boston and the Lucky Strike ads."

*(*PAT *and* ANN *come out of dining room, The tinkle of china and silver. The doors are shut by* MATTIE. *Dinner is over.)*

ANN: What's it like out? It looked rainy when I came in.

BIG MARY: *(At window)* No, it's all. right . . . Oh, girls, look! There's the Cadillac again for Linda Shaw.

LITTLE MARY: Is he in it?

BIG MARY: No just the chauffeur, same as always'

PAT: Who's the guy, anyhow? Anybody we know?

LITTLE MARY: He doesn't ever come. Just sends the car.

PAT: Well, nice work if you can get it.

ANN: *(Righteously)* I think it's disgraceful. A nice girl wouldn't want a man to send for her that way. And if you ask me, it gives the club a bad name

(A warning gesture and a "pss-s-stt" from LITTLE MARY *as* LINDA *descends stairs.* LINDA *is beautifully dressed for the evening. She is wearing the dress whose pressing had annoyed her, her evening cape is handsomely furred. Enormous orchids)*

BIG MARY: Oo, Linda! How gorgeous!

LINDA: *(Pausing reluctantly)* Oh, hello.

LITTLE MARY: Come on in. Let's see you.

BIG MARY: What a marvelous coat, Linda!

PAT: Yes, and a very nifty bit of jack rabbit, if I may say so. *(Her finger outlines a collar in the air)*

LINDA: Oh, that! Mother sent it to me. It used to be on a coat of hers.

LITTLE MARY: It's lovely.

PAT: *(Mildly)* Oh mother has a nice taste in orchids, too.

LINDA: Yes. Don't you wish you had a mother like mine? *(She sweeps out)*

(The TWO MARYS *dart to window.)*

PAT: What would you two do without that window? Why don't you pull up a rocking chair?

ANN: Linda Shaw's comings and goings don't interest me. Girls make such fools of themselves about men! *(She goes out up R.)*

BIG MARY: Say, what do you know about Jean? Having dinner with David Kingsley.

LITTLE MARY: Some girls have all the luck. Where'd she meet him anyhow?

BIG MARY: Oh, at some cocktail party.

PAT: I wish I could meet him. He can spot picture material like that. He's got an eye like a camera.

LITTLE MARY: Yeah, he picked three stars last year. Nobody ever heard of them before he sent them out there

PAT: *(Yawning and stretching)* Well, I'll never meet him . . . Oh, what to do till eleven o'clock! Except sleep.

LITTLE MARY: Anyhow, you've got something to do at eleven. Look at us!

BIG MARY: Yeah, you're working.

PAT: I hate it. Hooting in a night club for a lot of tired business men. The trouble is they're rot tired and there's no business.

(Doorbell rings)

BIG MARY: *(At window)* I think it's David Kingsley! It looks like him.

PAT: Kingsley? Are you sure?

LITTLE MARY: *(Peering)* Yes, that's him. Look, we'd better get out of the way, hadn't we?

BIG MARY: Yes I guess so.

(PAT, mindful of her pajamas, also gathers herself together. BERNICE runs down stairs with rather elaborate unconcern.)

BERNICE: *(Too polite)* Oh, pardon me, I just want to speak to— Frank—about something *(Exits dining room)*

(PAT stands looking after BERNICE for a second. Then, as MATTIE crosses hallway to answer door PAT makes her own decision and darts up stairs. A man's voice at door.)

KINGSLEY: *(In hall)* Miss Maitland, please.

MATTIE: Yessuh. Come right in.

KINGSLEY: Tell her, Mr. Kingsley. (DAVID KINGSLEY *enters. Perhaps 36 or 37. A man of decided charm and distinction, wearing evening clothes. You see his white muffler above the dark topcoat.)*

MATTIE: If you'll just rest yourself, Mr. Kingsley, I'll go right up.

(MATTIE *goes up stairs with a stateliness that indicates her apprecia-*
tion of the caller's importance.)

(KINGSLEY *glances about the room a bit.* He opens cigarette case,
lights a cigarette. BERNICE *comes out of dining room. Her face is*
turned toward someone in the room she has just left, and it is this
person she is addressing, apparently all unaware that anyone, cer-
tainly not KINGSLEY, *is in the living room*)

BERNICE: Yes, Mattie, an actress's life is such an interesting one; if
you could only see the different types that I do in the course of
a day, Mattie. For example, an English actress came into an office today. (*Goes suddenly very English*) "My dear Harry, how
definitely—ripping to see you. Definitely ripping!" And then,
Mattie, a little girl from Brooklyn came in. "Listen, I did write
for an appurntment. You got a noive" (*She turns, and to her ob-*
vious embarrassment there is MR. KINGSLEY. *She is a picture of*
pretty confusion.) Oh, I am so sorry! I didn't dream anyone was
here.

KINGSLEY: (*Politely amused*) That's quite all right.

BERNICE: (*Following up her advantage*) I'm—Bernice Niemeyer.
(KINGSLEY *bows slightly, murmurs her name.*) Well. I just
thought. (*She is dangling at the end of her rope.*)

(*Here she is mercifully interrupted by* PAT'*s descent of the stairs and*
singing. The jacket of PAT'*s pajama suit is missing. Her slim figure*
is well revealed in the trousers and scant short-sleeveless top. Her
low-heeled scuffs have been replaced by pert high-heeled mules.)

PAT: I wonder. (*Makes a slow turn toward* BERNICE— *a turn which by*
a strange chance serves at the same time to reveal the best points of
her figure to the waiting KINGSLEY.) You—you didn't see my
book anywhere around here, did you?

BERNICE: (Sourly) What book? (*She goes upstairs.*)

(PAT *flutters in her quest to a table, goes to bookshelf, selects a vol-*
ume, ruffles its pages to make sure the book meets her mood, then
gives a little sigh of delight, clasps book to her breast and trips up-
stairs, turns to show her bare back and is off. KINGSLEY *barely has*
time to recover himself again before another aspirant for his ap-

proval appears from the dining room. It is MRS. ORCUTT *who has shed her workaday dress for something very grand in the way of a black silk dinner gown.)*

MRS. ORCUTT: *(Crossing C. to him—outstretched hands)* David Kingsley! Little David Kingsley.

KINGSLEY: *(A little bewildered, rises to meet the emergency)* Why—how do you do! *(As he shakes hands)*

MRS. ORCUTT: *(Coquettishy)* Surely you remember me.

KINGSLEY: *(Lying bravely)* Of course I do.

MRS. ORCUTT: Who am I? *(He has an instant of panic)* Helen—

KINGSLEY: Helen.

MRS. ORCUTT: Helen who?

KINGSLEY: Helen—

MRS. ORCUTT: Ro—

KINGSLEY: *(Catches desperately at this straw)* Ro—

MRS. ORCUTT:—mayne! Helen Romayne!

KINGSLEY: *(Repeating it just the barest flash behind her)* Helen Romayne. Why, of course! Well, what a charming surprise. Imagine your remembering me! A scrubby little kid in the office.

MRS. ORCUTT: But that little office boy became one of the most brilliant producers in the theatre. Those beautiful plays! I loved them all.

KINGSLEY: So did I. But something happened to the theatre about that time. It was sort of shot from under us.

MRS. ORCUTT: But you've gone right on. You've risen to even greater triumphs in the pictures.

KINGSLEY: *(Quietly ironic)* Yes, even greater triumphs.

(A step on the stair. MRS. ORCUTT turns.)

MRS. ORCUTT: *(As she starts for dining room)* Well it was lovely seeing you. I hope you'll be coming again.

KINGSLEY: I hope so, too.

(MRS. ORCUTT *makes her escape as* JEAN *appears on stairs, resplendent in her borrowed finery,* PAT's *green taffeta, and* BOBBY's *evening wrap.*)

JEAN: *(As she shakes hands)* So glad to see you, Mr.Kingsley.

KINGSLEY: I'm glad you managed to be free.

JEAN: I guess girls generally manage to be free when you invite them.

KINGSLEY: You don't think maybe my being in the motion picture business has got something to do with it?

JEAN: Why, Mr. Kingsley, how can you say such a thing!

KINGSLEY: You think it's all sheer charm, huh?

JEAN: Of course . . . Look, would you mind awfully if I *(Calls upstairs)* Terry! Come on Terry! *(From above)* I'm coming.

JEAN: That's Terry Randall, my roommate. Did you see

"Cyclone"? Or "The Eldest Son"?

KINGSLEY: Oh, yes. In "Cyclone" she was—

JEAN: It was just a tiny part. She came into the drugstore.

KINGSLEY: Oh, yes. Just a bit, but she was good—Yes, she was excellent!

JEAN: Wasn't she?

(TERRY *comes down stairs.* TERRY *is still wearing the plain dark little dress in which we have previously seen her. If it were not for the glowing face she would seem rather drab in comparison to the dazzling* JEAN.)

TERRY: *(With great directness)* Well, if you will come calling at a Girls' Club, Mr. Kingsley, what can you expect?

KINGSLEY: I didn't expect anything as charming as this.

TERRY: Mm! You are in the moving picture business, aren't you?

KINGSLEY: I am, Miss Randall. But my soul belongs to God.

JEAN: Don't you think she'd be good for pictures, Mr. Kingsley? Look. (*Turning* TERRY'S *profile to show to best advantage*)

TERRY: I think I'd be terrible.

JEAN: Don't talk like that. Of course she's rehearsing now in the new Berger play. That is, she starts tomorrow.

KINGSLEY: Good! I hear it's an interesting play.

TERRY: Do you know the first play I ever saw, Mr. Kingsley?

KINGSLEY: No, what?

TERRY: It was your production of "Amaryllis."

KINGSLEY: "Amaryllis!" You couldn't have seen that! That was my first production. Ten years ago.

TERRY: I did, though. I was eleven years old, and I saw it at English's Opera House in Indianapolis. My mother took me. She cried all the way through it, and so did I. We had a lovely time.

KINGSLEY: But "Amaryllis" wasn't a sad play.

TERRY: Oh, we didn't cry because we were sad. Mother cried because it brought back the days when she was an actress, and I cried because I was so happy. You see, we lived seventy-five miles from Indianapolis, and it was the first time I'd ever been in a theatre.

JEAN: Now, really, I don't think it's tactful to talk about the theatre to a picture man.

TERRY: I'm afraid I'm kind of dumb about pictures. Mother used to say the theatre had two offspring: the legitimate stage and the bastard.

JEAN: (*Taking* KINGSLEY *by the hand and pulling him from the room*) Come on! And forget I ever introduced her to you.

(*He goes, calling, "Good-bye, Miss Randall."*)

TERRY: (*Calling after him*) Oh, I hope I didn't—

KINGSLEY: (*As door closes on them*) It's all right. I forgive you.

(Left alone, TERRY *suddenly realizes she has had no diner. As she goes toward dining room she calls.)*

TERRY: Mattie! Mattie! *(Opens dining room doors)* Oh, dear, is dinner over?

MATTIE: *(In dining room)* Yes. I'm just clearing away.

TERRY: Oh, Mattie, darling, could you let me have just anything? Champagne and a little caviar?

MATTIE: *(In dining room)* Well, I'll fix you a plate of something.

TERRY: You're an angel.

(As TERRY *turns away from dining room* KENDALL *is coming down stairs, dressed for the street. At sight of* TERRY *she pauses to chat.)*

KENDALL: Isn't it splendid, Terry, about your getting a job!

TERRY: It seems pretty dazzling to me, after six months. I only hope it's as big a hit as yours.

KENDALL: It's queer about being in a hit. You go through everything to get into one, and after a few months you're bored with it. It's like marriage. *(Doorbell rings—calls)* It's all right, Mattie, I'll answer it . . . Going out, Terry?

TERRY: Not tonight.

KENDALL: *(At street door)* See you later.

(A voice at the door: "Hello, there! Who are you?" KENDALL'S *voice, a film of ice over it: "I beg your pardon." The man's voice explains, "I'm looking for Jean Maitland."* KENDALL *calls, "Mattie!" and goes on her way. The call is unheard by* MATTIE. KEITH BURGESS *appears in archway. He is the kind of young man who never wears a hat. Turtle-necked sweater, probably black, pressed tweed suit, unshaven)*

KEITH: *(Comes in to C.)* Where's Jean Maitland?

TERRY: *(Seated, chair L. C.)* In a taxi with a big moving picture man.

KEITH: She can't be. She had a date with me.

TERRY: Sorry. It isn't my fault.

KEITH: Who are you?

TERRY: Who wants to know?

KEITH: *(D. C.)* Are you an actress?

TERRY: Are you dizzy in the morning? Do you have spots before the eyes?

KEITH: My name is Keith Burgess.

TERRY: Is it?

KEITH: Don't you know who I am?

TERRY: Yes. You're a playwright, and you wrote a play called "Blood and Roses" that was produced at the Fortieth Street Theatre, and it ran a week and it wasn't very good.

KEITH: It was the best goddamn play that was ever produced in New York! And the one I'm writing now is even better.

TERRY: Mm. Maybe two weeks.

KEITH: *(Vastly superior)* I don't think in terms of material success. Who cares whether a play makes money! All that matters is its message!

TERRY: But if nobody comes to see it who gets the message?

KEITH: I write about the worker. The masses! The individual doesn't count in modern society.

TERRY: But aren't the masses made up of individuals?

KEITH: Don't quibble!

TERRY: I'm so sorry.

(Doorbell rings)

KEITH: I ask nothing as an individual. My work, my little room— that's all.

TERRY: No furniture?

(FRANK crosses hall.)

KEITH: A table, a chair, a bed. My books. My music.

(The voice of KAYE at door.)

KAYE: (Offstage R.) I'm Miss Hamilton, Kaye Hamilton.

(KEITH *moves D.R.*)

FRANK: Oh, yes, I think Mrs. Orcutt's expecting you.–

(MRS. ORCUTT *appears in hallway from up L., just in time to greet the new arrival who enters up R.*)

MRS. ORCUTT: Glad to see you again, Miss Hamilton. Everything's in readiness for you. Frank, take Miss Hamilton s things right up. Oh! *(As she sees* TERRY *in living room)* Terry, this is Kaye Hamilton, who's going to share the room with you and Jean. Terry Randall.

(TERRY *rises, goes U. L.C.*)

KAYE: I'll try not to be in the way.

TERRY: Oh, don't start that way. Grab your share of the closet hooks.

KAYE: Thank you.

MRS. ORCUTT: *(As she shows* KAYE *upstairs)* Now, if you'll Just come with me I'll show you where everything is.

TERRY: *(As they start up)* Let me know if I can be of any help.

MRS. ORCUTT: *(Talking as they ascend)* If you have a trunk check Frank will take care of all that for you.

KAYE: No, no, I haven't got a trunk.

(They are gone, KEITH *throughout has been observing* TERRY *with an old-fashioned eye of appreciation)*

KEITH: Hey! Turn around! *(She does so, rather wonderfully.)* You shouldn't wear your hair like that. It hides your face. *(Moves to L. C.)*

TERRY: *(Moves R. to couch)* Oh, do you notice faces? I thought you were above all that.

KEITH: I notice everything. Your head's too big for the rest of you. You've got pretty legs, but you oughtn't to wear that kind of dress.

TERRY: (*Sits L. arm of couch*) I suppose you're known as Beau Burgess! What the Well-Dressed Man Will Wear!

KEITH: Oh, you like snappy dressers, eh? Monograms and cuff-links.

TERRY: No, I don't meet very many monograms.

KEITH: (*Steps in. His gaze roaming around the room.*) What do you live in this place for? Do you like it?

TERRY: I love it. We live and breathe theatre, and that's what I'm crazy about.

KEITH: Are you? So am I. What do you want to do in the theatre? What kind of parts do you want to play?

TERRY: I want to play every kind of part I'm not suited for. Old hags of eighty and Topsy and Lady Macbeth. And what do I get? Ingenues—and very little of that.

KEITH: Don't take 'em. Wait till you get what you want.

TERRY: (*Rises. Moves D. R.*) Well, it's a nice idea. But did you ever hear of this thing called eating?.

KEITH: (*Eases down after her*) You mustn't think of that. Why, I've lived on bread and cocoa for days at a time. If you believe in something you've got to be willing to starve for it.

TERRY: (*Below couch*) I am willing. But you don't know what it is to be an actress. If you feel something you can write it. But I can't act unless they let me. I can't just walk up and down my room, being an actress.

KEITH: It's just as tough for a writer. Suppose they won't produce his plays! l write about the iron-worker and they want Grand Dukes, I could write pot-boilers, but I don't. The theatre shouldn't be just a place to earn a living in. It should be thunder and lightning, and power and truth. (*Steps L.*)

TERRY: (*Eases L.*) And magic and romance!

KEITH: (*Turns R. to her*) No, no! Romance is for babies! I write about today! I want to tear the heart out of the rotten carcass we call life and hold it up, bleeding, for all the world to see.

TERRY: *(Steps in to* KEITH*)* How about putting some heart into life instead of tearing it out all the time?

KEITH: *(Eases R.)* There's no place for sentiment in the world to-day. We've gone past it.

TERRY: I suppose that's why you never hear of Romeo and Juliet.

KEITH: That's a woman's argument. *(Turns L.)*

TERRY: Well, I'm a woman.

KEITH: *(Eases R.)* Why haven't I run into you before? Where've you been all the time?

TERRY: I've been right here, in and out of every office on Broadway.

KEITH: Me, too. But I'm going to keep right on until they listen to me. And you've got to keep on, too.

TERRY: I will! I'm going to!

*(*MATTIE *appears in dining room door.)*

MATTIE: You all want your dinner now, Miss Terry? It's ready.

TERRY: Oh, Mattie, I'd forgotten all about it.

KEITH: Never mind, Mattie. How about dinner with me? We'll go to Smitty's and have a couple of hamburgers.

TERRY: With onions?

KEITH: Sure—onions! *(going)* Say, what the hell's your name, any-how?

(Curtain cue. They go out U.R. The TWO MARYS *come downstairs arguing about Clark Gable and Spencer Tracy as curtain falls.)*

CURTAIN

ACT I

SCENE 2:

One of the bedrooms. A pleasant enough but rather cramped room, with 3 beds, 3 dressers, 3 small chairs. There is a bathroom door down L., a window C. A door up L. leads to hall.

Each dresser reflects something of the personality and daily life of its owner. Stuck in the sides of the mirrors are snapshots, photographs newspaper clippings, telegrams, theatre programs. It is night, and through the window we get a glimpse of the city's lights with electric sign through window one quarter up.

At the beginning the room is unoccupied.

KAYE *comes into the room from bathroom with towel and comb, closes door. She is wearing a bathrobe over her nightgown, goes to chair, puts towel over back, then to window— pulls down shade— the electric sign blacks out.* KAYE *goes to her dresser, which is conspicuously bare of ornament, souvenirs, or photographs. She opens top drawer, takes out her handbag, removes her money from a small purse and counts it, a process which doesn't take long. Two dollars and sixty cents.There is a knock at the door.*

KAYE: Yes?

JUDITH: *(As she opens door up L.)* Can I come in? Where's Terry?

KAYE: She isn't back yet.

(Judith is wearing sleeping pajamas and she is in the process of doing her face up for the night. A net safeguards her curls)

JUDITH: *(As she crosses R.)* Look, do you think she'd mind if I borrowed some of her frowners? I forgot to get some.

KAYE: I think there's some in her top drawer.

JUDITH: *(As she pulls open drawer.)* Thanks . . . You don't go out much evenings, do you?

KAYE: *(As she puts lingerie on back of chair in bureau)* No.

JUDITH: Any sign of a job yet?

KAYE: No, not yet.

JUDITH: Something'll turn up. It always does. *(She waits a moment for KAYE's answer, but there is none.)* You know, you're a funny kid. You've been here a month, and I don't know any more about you than when you came in. The rest of us are always spilling our whole insides, but you never let out a peep. Nobody comes to see you, no phone calls, never go out nights, you haven't even got a picture on your dresser. Haven't you got any folks? Or a beau or something? *(No sound from KAYE. JUDITH turns to glance at her.)* Sorry. My mistake.

(The voices of BIG and LITTLE MARY are heard in the hall. BIG M.: "Mm, somebody's cooking something." LITTLE MARY: "Smells like a rarebit." The TWO MARYS in hats and coats, stick their heads in at door.)

LITTLE MARY: Who's cooking? You?

JUDITH: No Madeleine. Where've you been? Show?

BIG MARY: We saw the Breadline Players in "Tunnel of Death."

LITTLE MARY: *(Sourly)* Come on, lets get some rarebit before it's all gone.

(They disappear down hallway.)

JUDITH: *(Sits arm of chair R.)* Terry's late, isn't she? It's half-past eleven. And she isn't in the last act.

KAYE: She'll be here in a minute. Have you seen the play?

JUDITH: I haven't had time yet. I'm going tomorrow night.

KAYE: I didn't like it very much, but Terry's awfully good. Just a little part, but you always knew she was on.

(PAT appears in doorway. She is wearing a tailored suit and hat.)

PAT: *(Peering round)* Anybody in here? Well, off to the mines.

JUDITH: Oh, hello, Pat! Going to work?

PAT: Yes, the night shift with a hey-nonny-nonny and a swiss on rye. (*Does a little floor-show dance step, and goes*)

KAYE: I wonder what it's like working in a night club. I wish I'd learned to dance.

JUDITH: Well, with your looks you'll get along all right. (KAYE *is silent. By this time* JUDITH *has wandered over to* KAYE'S *dresser on other side of room up L. still continuing her beauty treatments.*) Where's your hand-mirror? Why, where's the whole set?

KAYE: I haven't got it any more.

JUDITH: (*A little too casually*) It was gold, wasn't it?

KAYE: Uh huh.

JUDITH: Got any folks you have to support?

KAYE: (*Quietly*) No I haven't any folks.

JUDITH: (*To* JEAN'S *bureau up R.; starts creaming her hands.*) Well, if you want some, I'm the girlie that can fix you up. Five brothers and four sisters, and you couldn't scare up a dollar eighty among the lot. I've got a little sister named Doris. Fifteen, and as innocent as Mata Hari. She's coming to New York next year to duplicate my success.

KAYE: (*Somewhat wistfully*) I think it would be rather nice, having a little sister with you.

JUDITH: Yeh, only she won't be with me much. Two weeks and they'll have her in the Home for Delinquent Girls.

(TERRY *enters, a drooping figure. A glance at the two occupants of the room. Her back to door, she slowly closes it behind her and slumps against it.*)

KAYE: Hello!

JUDITH: Hello, Terry.

TERRY: Young lady, willing, talented, not very beautiful, finds herself at liberty. (*As she starts R.*) Will double in brass, will polish brass, will eat brass before very long. Hi, girls!

KAYE: Terry, what's the matter?

TERRY: We closed. Four performances and we closed.

KAYE: Terry, you didn't!

JUDITH: Tonight! But it's only Thursday!

TERRY: *(Sitting in chair R.)* Well, it seems you can close on Thursday just as well as Saturday—in fact it's even better, it gives you two more days to be sunk in.

JUDITH: But it didn't get bad notices. What happened?

TERRY: We just got to the theatre tonight, and there it was on the call-board. "To the Members of the Blue Grotto Company: You are hereby advised that the engagement of the Blue Grotto will terminate after tonight's performance. Signed, Milton H. Schwepper, for Berger Productions, Incorporated."

KAYE: Terry, how ghastly!

JUDITH: Just like that, huh?

TERRY: Just like that. We stood there for a minute and read it. Then we sort of got together in the dressing rooms and talked about it in whispers, the way you do at a funeral. And then we all put on our make-up and gave the best damned performance we'd ever given.

JUDITH: Any other job in the world, if you get canned you can have a good cry in the washroom and go home. But show business! You take it on the chin and the paint up your face and out on the stage as gay as anything. "My dear Lady Barbara, what an enchanting place you have here! And what a quaint idea, giving us pig's knuckles for tea."

TERRY: Yes, it was awfully jolly. I wouldn't have minded if Berger or somebody had come back stage and said, "Look, we're sorry to do this to you, and better luck next time." But nobody came around—not Berger, or the author, or the director or anybody. They can all run away at a time like that, but the actors have to stay and face it.

JUDITH: You'll get something else, Terry. You got swell notices in this one.

TERRY: Nobody remembers notices except the actors who get them.

KAYE: The movie scouts remember. What about your screen test?

JUDITH: Yes, how about that? Have you heard from it?

TERRY: *(Rises and up to bureau R.)* Oh, I'm not counting on that. They might take Jean. She's got that camera face. But they'll never burnup the Coast wires over me.

JUDITH: Jean can't act. You're ten times the actress that she is.

TERRY: *(Throwing herself across bed)* Oh, how do you know who's an actress and who isn't! You're an actress if you're acting. Without a job and those lines to say, an actress is just an ordinary person, trying not to look as scared as she feels. What is there about it, anyhow? Why do we all keep trying?

BERNICE: *(Enters with mourning veil hat, followed by* MADELEINE *who has a dish in her hand.)* How do I look?

KAYE: Marvelous.

JUDITH: What are you?

BERNICE: I'm seeing the Theatre Guild tomorrow. They're going to revive "Madame X." *(Exit)*

MADELEINE: Anybody want some chop suey? Terry? Kaye?

TERRY: No, thank you.

KAYE: No, thanks.

JUDITH: *(Tempted by this)* Chop suey? I thought it was rarebit.

MADELEINE: We didn't have any beer, so I'm calling it chop suey. *(She goes)*

JUDITH: Certainly sounds terrible. *(Crossing L. to door turns with a hand on door)* Look, I guess you want this closed, huh?

TERRY: Yes, please.

(Door closes. KAYE *and* TERRY *are alone. With a sigh* TERRY *again faces reality. Listlessly she begins to undress.* KAYE *is almost ready for bed. As she turns back bedclothes she pauses to regard* TERRY.*)*

KAYE: I know how sunk you feel, Terry. It's that horrible letdown after the shock has worn off.

TERRY: The idiotic part of it is that I didn't feel so terrible after the first minute. I thought, well, Keith's coming around after the show, and we'll go to Smitty's and sit there and talk and it won't seem so bad. But he never showed up.

KAYE: Terry, I shouldn't try to advise you where men are concerned. I haven't been very smart myself—but this isn't the first time he's let you down. Don't get in too deep with a boy like Keith Burgess. It'll only make you unhappy.

TERRY: I don't expect him to be like other people. I wouldn't want him to be. One of the things that makes him so much fun is that he's different. If he forgets an appointment it's because he's working and doesn't notice. Only I wish he had come tonight. *(She is pulling her dress over her head as she talks and her words are partly muffled until she emerges.)* I needed him so. *(Suddenly her defenses are down.)* Kaye, I'm frightened. For the first time; I'm frightened. It's three years now. The first year it didn't matter so much: I was so young. Nobody was ever as young as I was. I thought., they just don't know. But I'll get a good start and show them. I didn't mind anything in those days. Not having any money, or quite enough food; and a pair of silk stockings always a major investment. I didn't mind because I felt so sure that that wonderful part was going to come along. But it hasn't. And suppose it doesn't next year? Suppose it never comes?

KAYE: You can always go home. You've got a home to go to, anyhow.

TERRY: *(Rises)* And marry some home-town boy—like Louise?

KAYE: I didn't mean that, exactly.

TERRY: I can't just go home and plump myself down on Dad. You know what a country doctor makes! When I was little I never knew how poor we were, because mother made everything seem so glamorous, so much fun. *(Starts L. for bathroom all this time TERRY has continued her preparations for bed: hung up her dress, slipped her nightgown over her head.)* Even if I was sick it was a lot of fun, because then I was allowed to look at her scrap-book. I even used to pretend to be sick, just to look at it and that took acting; with a doctor for a father. (*Exits and makes rest of change off stage continuing dialogue*) I adored that scrap-book. All those rep company actors in wooden attitudes I remember a wonderful picture of mother as Esmeralda. It was the last part she ever played, and she never finished the performance.

KAYE: What happened?

TERRY: She fainted, right in the middle of the last act. They rang down and somebody said, "Is there a doctor in the house?" And there he was. And he married her.

KAYE: Terry, how romantic!

TERRY: Only first she was sick for weeks and weeks. Of course the company had to leave her behind. They thought she'd catch up with them any week, but she never did.

KAYE: Didn't she ever miss it? I mean afterward.

TERRY: (*Coming back into room, crosses R. to bureau*) I know now that she missed it every minute of her life. I think if Dad hadn't been such a gentle darling, and not so dependent on her, she might have gone off and taken me with her. I'd have been one of those children brought up in dressing rooms, sleeping in trunk trays, getting my vocabulary from stage-hands. (*As he creams her face*)

KAYE: That would have been thrilling.

TERRY: But she didn't. She lived out the rest of her life right in that little town, but she was stage-struck to the end. There never was any doubt in her mind I was going to be an actress. It was almost a spiritual thing, like being dedicated to the church.

KAYE: I never thought of the theatre that way. I just used it as a convenience, because I was desperate, and now I'm using it again because I'm desperate.

TERRY: Oh, now I've made you blue. I didn't mean to be gloomy. We're fine! We're elegant! They have to pay me two weeks' salary for this flop. Eighty dollars. We're fixed for two weeks. One of us'll get a job.

KAYE: I can't take any more money from you. You paid my twelve-fifty last week.

TERRY: Oh, don't be stuffy! I happened to be the one who was working.

KAYE: I'll never get a job. I'm—I'm not a very good actress.

TERRY: Oh, now!

KAYE: And there's nothing else I can do and nobody I can go back to. Except somebody I'll never go back to.

TERRY: It's your husband, isn't it?

KAYE: *(Looks at* TERRY *a moment, silently)* I ran away from him twice before, but I had to go back. I was hungry, and finally I didn't even have a room. Both times, he just waited. He's waiting now.

TERRY: Kaye, tell me—what is it? Why are you afraid of him?

KAYE: *(Turns her eyes away from* TERRY *as she speaks)* Because I know him. To most people he's a normal attractive man. But I know better. Nights of terror. "Now, darling, it wouldn't do any good to kill me. They wouldn't let you play polo tomorrow. Now, we'll open the window and you'll throw the revolver at that lamp-post. It'll be such fun to hear the glass smash." And then there were the times when he made love to me. I can't even tell you about that. *(She recalls the scene with a shudder.)*

TERRY: Kaye, darling! But if he's as horrible as that, can't you do something legally?

KAYE: *(A desperate shake of her head)* They have millions. I'm nobody. I've gone to his family. They're united like a stone wall. They treated me as though I was the mad one.

TERRY: But, Kaye, isn't there anybody—What about your own folks? Haven't you got any?

KAYE: I have a father. Chicago. I ran away at sixteen and went on the stage. Then I met Dick—and I fell for him. He was good-looking, and gay, and always doing sort of crazy things— smashing automobiles and shooting at bar-room mirrors. I thought it was funny, then.

TERRY: And I've been moaning about my little troubles.

KAYE: You know, I'd sworn to myself I never was going to bother you with this. Now, what made me do it!

TERRY: I'm glad you did. It'll do you good.

KAYE: Yes; I suppose it will.

TERRY: (*As she takes counterpane off bed*) Well, we might as well get those sheep over the fence. Maybe we'll wake up tomorrow morning and there'll be nineteen managers downstairs, all saying, "You and only you can play this part."

KAYE: I suppose Jean'll be out till all hours.

TERRY: (*At window, puts up shade—electric sign comes on one quarter up.*) There's a girl who hasn't got any troubles. Life rolls right along for her (*Puts up window*) Well, ready to go bye-bye?

KAYE: (*Switches off all lights except bed lamps—electric sign to one-half*) I suppose I might as well. But I feel so wide awake.

(*As* TERRY *opens window a blast of noise comes up from the street. A cacophony made up of protesting brakes, automobile horns, taxi drivers' shouts, a laugh or two.*)

1ST VOICE: (*Off*) Hey, buddy, back her up a bit, will you?

2ND VOICE: (*Off*) O.K., Bill.

(*From her dresser* KAYE *takes a black eyeshield and adjusts it over her eyes after she is in bed.* TERRY *does same, then shouts a Good night! loudly enough to be heard above the street din.* KAYE'S *good night is equally loud. Simultaneously they turn out their bed lights. For a second but only a second the room is in darkness. Then the reason for* TERRY'S *eyeshade becomes apparent. A huge electric advertising sign on an adjacent roof flashes on, off, on, off full up alternately flooding the room with light and plunging it into darkness.*)

TERRY: (*Shouting*) Funny if we both did get jobs tomorrow!

KAYE: Huh?

TERRY: (*Louder*) I say, it would be funny if we both got jobs tomorrow!

KAYE: Certainly would.

(*A moment of silence. The door bursts open.* JEAN *comes in, bringing with her a quiver of excitement. She is in dinner clothes.*)

JEAN: (*Turns on light full up except bed lamps and bureau lamp. Electric sign dims one-half.*) Terry! Wake up!

TERRY: What's the matter?

JEAN: (*Slams window down—street noise stops*) We're in the movies!

TERRY: What?

JEAN: Both of us! We're in the movies! They just heard from the Coast.

TERRY: Jean! How do you know? What happened?

JEAN: Mr. Kingsley just got the telegram. They liked the tests, and we're to go to the office tomorrow to sign our contracts. We leave for the Coast next week! Terry! Can you believe it!

KAYE: Oh, girls, how exciting!

TERRY: (*Bewildered*) Yes. Yes. You mean right away?

JEAN: Of course we'll only get little parts in the beginning. But there's that beautiful check every week, whether you work or not. And the swimming and the sunshine and those' little ermine jackets up to here. No more running around to offices and having them spit in your eye. And a salary raise every six months if they like us. So at the end of three years it begins to get pretty good, and after five years it's wonderful, and at the end of seven years it's more money than you ever heard of.

TERRY: Seven years! What do you mean. Seven years!

JEAN: Yes, it's a seven-year contract. that is, if they take up the options.

TERRY: But what about the stage? Suppose I wanted to act?

JEAN: Well, what do you think this is juggling? Motion picture acting is just as much of an art as stage acting, only it's cut up more. You only have to learn about a line at a time and they just keep on taking it until you get it right.

TERRY: (*Staring at* JEAN. *A stricken pause. Then she shakes her head slowly. Her decision is made.*) Oh, no.

JEAN: What?

TERRY: I couldn't.

JEAN: Couldn't what?

TERRY: That isn't acting, that's piecework. You're not a human being, you're a thing in a vacuum. Noise shut out, human response shut out. But in the theatre, when you hear that lovely sound out there, then you know you're right. It's as though they'd turned on an electric current that hit you here. And that's how you learn to act.

JEAN: You can learn to act in pictures. You have to do it till it's right.

TERRY: Yes, and then they put it in a tin can, like Campbell's Soup. And if you die the next day it doesn't matter a bit. You don't even have to be alive to be in pictures.

JEAN: I suppose you call this being alive! Sleeping three in a room in this rotten dump. It builds you up, eh?

TERRY: I'm not going to stay here all my life. This is only the beginning.

JEAN: Don't kid yourself. You've been here three years, and then it's three years more, and then another three and where are you? You can't play ingenues forever. Pretty soon you're a character woman, and then you're running a boarding house like old Orcutt. That'll be nice, won't it?

TERRY: I don't know. You make me sound like a fool, but I know I'm not. All I know is I want to stay on the stage. I just don't want to be in pictures. An actress in the theatre, that's what I've wanted to be my whole life. It isn't just a career, it's a feeling. The theatre is something that's gone on for hundreds and hundreds of years. It's—I don't know—it's part of civilization.

JEAN: All right, you stay here with your civilization, eating those stews and tapiocas they shove at us, toeing the mark in this female seminary, buying your clothes at Klein's. That's what you like, eh?

TERRY: Yes. I like it!

JEAN: And I suppose you like this insane racket going on all night!
(She throws open window street noises start)

TERRY: *(Yelling above noise)* Yes, I do!

JEAN: And that Cadillac car sign going on and off like a damned lighthouse! *(She turns off light. Again we see the flash of electric sign, off, on, off, on, full up and flashing faster.)* I suppose you've got to have that to be an actress!

TERRY: Yes! Yes! Yes! Yes! Yes!

JEAN: *(Not stopping for her)* Well, not for me. I'm going out where there's sunshine and money and fun and–

TERRY: *(Shouting above her.)* And little ermine swimming pools up to here!

(The street noise, the flashing light, and their angry shouts are still going on as curtain descends.)

JEAN: *(As curtain falls.)* I'm going to make something out of my life. I'm not going to stay in this lousy dump.

CURTAIN

ACT II

SCENE 1

Same as Act 1, Scene 1. Mid-morning, sunlight is streaming in.

FRANK *is rather listlessly pushing a Carpet-sweeper, his attention directed toward an open newspaper lying on a chair. He edges nearer and nearer, his movements with the sweeper become slower and slower, until finally they are barely perceptible.* ANN *comes briskly downstairs with a condescending "Good morning, Frank!" and goes into dining room.*

FRANK'S *response having been an absent-minded mumble.* MATTIE *bustles in from dining room, and her face reflects her irritation as she sees* FRANK'S *idling at this busy hour. Lips compressed, she marches straight to him, snatches sweeper from him and goes off with it.* FRANK *follows meekly after. Somewhere in the hall, unseen, a clock strikes eleven.* BOBBY, *gaily singing, skips downstairs and stops for a look through the mail. She finds a letter that gets her full attention, so that she is absorbed in it as she walks more slowly toward dining room. After dropping her coat and hat on table back of couch R.* JUDITH *enters L. with coat over arm.*

JUDITH: Hello, Bobby!

BOBBY: Oh, say! Here's a letter from Madeleine.

JUDITH: Where is she this week?

BOBBY: Let's see. This week, Portland and Spokane. Next week, Seattle. *(Exits dining room)*

JUDITH: Seattle. That's her home town. (KENDALL *dashes downstairs, struggling into one coat sleeve as she comes.*) Heh, where're you going?

KENDALL: Rehearsal!

JUDITH: What's the rush?

KENDALL: Late! *(Exits up R.)*

JUDITH: *(Calling after her as she dashes for door)* You're too conscientious. *(Door slams)* Never gets you anywhere in this business.

TERRY: *(Coming downstairs)* Well, what does get you anywhere, if I may make so bold?

JUDITH: Clean living, high thinking, and an occasional dinner with the manager.

TERRY: *(Taking a look through mail)* What time is it? Shouldn't you be at rehearsal?

JUDITH: *(Drops coat and hat on armchair L.)* No, there's plenty of time. The nuns aren't called until eleven-thirty today.

TERRY: *(Turning over envelope in her hand)* Mrs. Robert Hendershot—why, that's Louise! Appleton, Wisconsin. It's a letter from Louise.

(Phone rings. TERRY rips open envelope and takes a quick look its pages, which are voluminous.)

JUDITH: *(En route to phone)* Maybe it's a Little Stranger. She's been married a year . . . Hello! . . . She's right here . . . *(Hands phone to TERRY)* The boy friend.

TERRY: Keith? *(Thrusts letter into JUDITH'S hand, who drops down R. to couch and sits)* Read—it's addressed to all of us. *(As JUDITH buries herself in letter. TERRY'S attention goes to phone.)* Keith! Isn't this the middle of the night for you! . . . What about? . . . No, I've got to stay free all afternoon on account of Dad . . . Yes, he's driving all the way from Elvira. Well, you don't have to like it. He will . . . No, I can't, because he's only here a day and a half, and this afternoon he wants to see Radio City and the Medical Center and the Battery.

JUDITH: *(Looking up from letter)* Has he got a bicycle?

TERRY: And don't forget that you've invited us-to dinner . . . No, not at Smitty's . . . Well, Dad and Smitty's just don't go together. And look, darling, don't wear a black shirt and don't be one of the Masses tonight . . . What? . . . Well, you can tell me about it at dinner . . . No, I can't, I've got a radio rehearsal.

JUDITH: *(Still with letter)* Say, this is a classic.

TERRY: Well, if it's as vital as all that you can come up here . . . That's my brave boy *(She hangs up)*

JUDITH: *(Her first opportunity to read from letter)* Get this. "I have gained a little weight, but Bob says I look better, not so scrawny. He says maybe I like my own cooking too much, but then he is always joking."

TERRY: *(To* OLGA, *who enters L. Crossing to c.)* It's a letter from Louise. *(As she sits on couch R.)*

OLGA: What does she say?

BOBBY: *(Appearing in dining room doorway)* Who said a letter from Louise?

TERRY: Yes, it just came.

JUDITH: *(Reading as* ANN *and* SUSAN *come into dining room doorway to bear the news)* "Dear Girlies: I guess you all wonder why I have not written for so long I honestly don't know where the year has gone to. First there was the house to furnish. We've got the darlingest six-room bungalow on Winnebago Street. And then of course everybody was giving parties for me, and after that I had to return the obligation by giving parties for them. We are all even now. I gave the last-one just yesterday— eighteen girls of the young married set, three tables of bridge and one of mah jong, and two people just talked. The luncheon was lovely, if I do say so. Everything pink."

OLGA: You're making it up.

JUDITH: So help me . . . "I am a member of the Ladies' Committee at the Country Club, which gives wonderful Saturday night dances during the summer." *(To the girls)* Japanese lanterns . . . "But do not think that I have lost track of the theatre. We take the Milwaukee Sentinel daily and last week we drove to Milwaukee and saw Walter Hampden in 'Cyrano'."

TERRY: *(Reaching for letter)* Let me see! "So now I've told you all my news and you've got to write me just everything about the

Club. What about you, Terry, have you got a swell part for this season? I thought I'd die when I saw Jean's picture in Photoplay, all dressed up like a real movie star in a little ermine jacket and everything. Jean a movie star! I've been bragging to all my friends. Well, if you girls think about me as much as I do about you, my ears would be about burned off. We have supper here around six o'clock, just as you all do at the Club, and when it's over I always think, well, the girls are all beating it down to the show-shop and making up to go on and just knocking the audience cold. Only I don't say it out loud any more because Bob says, Oh, for God's sake, you and your club! Love to old Orcutt and for goodness' sakes, write, write, WRITE!"

JUDITH: *(Very low)* Wow.

TERRY: Well, I'll never complain again. This makes my eighteen a week on the radio look pretty wonderful.

OLGA: *(As she goes upstairs)* Everything pink.

BOBBY: We've just been livin' in a bed of roses.

ANN: I could have told her when she left it wouldn't work.

(BOBBY, ANN *and* SUSAN *go back to dining room.* TERRY *and* JUDITH *remain.)*

JUDITH: *(Getting into her coat)* Well, I might as well get down to the factory

TERRY: Look, Judith. Think you'll be rehearsing all afternoon?

JUDITH: How do I know! This thing I'm in is a combination of Ringling Brothers and the Passion Play. You never know whether they're going to rehearse us nuns or the elephants.

TERRY: *(Sitting on couch)* It's just that I'd love you to meet my father, if you have time.

JUDITH: Oh, I want to. He sounds like a cutie.

TERRY: I wonder what's on Keith's mind, getting up so early?

JUDITH: Nothing, is my guess.

TERRY: Judith! Maybe he sold the play!

JUDITH: Maybe. *(Takes plunge)* Look, Terry. Where're you heading in with that guy, anyhow?

TERRY: Why, what do you mean?

JUDITH: You know. He's been coming around here for a year, taking all your time, talking about himself, never considering you for a minute. Sold his play! Well, if he has he can thank you for it. It's as much your play as his.

TERRY: That isn't true.

JUDITH: Don't tell me. It was nothing but a stump speech the way he wrote it. You made him put flesh and blood into it.

TERRY: *(Quietly)* You're talking about someone you don't understand.

JUDITH: O. K. Forget I ever brought it up. Well good-bye. *(Starting off)*

TERRY: *(Rather reserved)* Good-bye. *(Takes 2 typewritten pages out of her handbag)*

JUDITH: *(Stops, drops down to back of couch)* Oh, now you're sore at me. I never can learn to keep my trap shut. But I only said it because I think more of you than anybody else in this whole menagerie. Forgiven?

TERRY: Of course, Judy darling.

JUDITH: *(Indicating papers in* TERRY'S *hand)* What's that? Your radio?

TERRY: Mm.

JUDITH: It makes me boil to think of an actress like you reading radio recipes for a living. *(Peers at script)* "Two eggs and fold in the beaten whites." The beaten whites! That's us!

TERRY: *(She rises aid crosses L.)* Anyhow, it's a living for a few weeks. Aunt Miranda's Cooking Class.

JUDITH: Well, you're a hell of an Aunt Miranda, that's all I can say . . . *(goes out door up R.)*

(ANN and BOBBY come out of dining room. ANN is carrying newspaper. BOBBY crosses R. to table, puts on coat.)

ANN: *(Seeing* TERRY*)* Did you read about Jean out in Hollywood?

TERRY: No. Where?

ANN: They've given her a new contract with a big raise and she's going to play the lead in "Two for Tonight."

TERRY: Really! *(Looking over* ANN'S *shoulder)* How marvelous *(Takes paper from* ANN *and goes into dining room.)*

BOBBY: It's all a matter of cheekbones. You've got to have a face like this. *(She pushes her round little face into hollow curves.)*

ANN: *(Gets her coat from piano)* Are you going out job-hunting this morning?

BOBBY: Uh huh.

ANN: Where are you going?

BOBBY: Ah thought Ah'd go round to Equity and see what's up on the bulletin board. Maybe there's something new casting.

ANN: *(Applying lipstick)* I'm going to try a couple of agents offices. *(Becomes unintelligible as she paints the cupid's bow)* Sometimes they know about new things.

BOBBY: What kind of lipstick's that?

ANN: It's a new one. It's called "I'll Never Tell."

BOBBY: Let me see. *(Tries a daub on back of her hand)* Mm. It's too orangey for me. Ah like Hibiscus good and red as if you'd been kicked in the mouth by a mule.

(They gather up their handbags and go. KAYE *comes downstairs like a little wraith. Near the foot of stairs she glances over railing and it is evident that she is relieved to find the room empty. As she is about to go to street door* MRS. ORCUTT *swoops down on her up L. with a promptness which indicates that she has been waiting for her.)*

MRS. ORCUTT: Oh, Kaye! Could I speak to you just a minute, please?

KAYE: I'm just on my way to rehearsal.

MRS. ORCUTT: *(Crossing to dining room L. As she carefully closes din-*

ing room doors) I won't detain you but a second. I just want to—
(The door is closed.As she comes back L. C.) You must know how reluctant I always am to speak to you on this subject. I try to be
as easy as I can with the girls but, after all, I have my bills to pay,
too.

KAYE: But, Mrs. Orcutt, I'm rehearsing. You know that. And just
the minute we open I can start paying off.

MRS. ORCUTT: Yes, I know. But plays are not always successful, and
the amount has grown rather large. So, taking everything into
consideration, I wonder if you'd mind a little suggestion.

KAYE: No. No.

MRS. ORCUTT: Well, it occurred to me that perhaps it might be
wise if you were to find some place a little cheaper. By a lucky
chance, I think I know the ideal place. Of course the girls are a
little older, and it's not strictly a theatrical club—more the
commercial professions. However, I think you'll find it almost
as conveniently situated. Forty-ninth Street, this side of Tenth
Avenue. Perhaps, when you have time, you might drop in and
look at it. (KAYE *only nods a silent assent.)* Now, now, we mustn't
be upset by this. It's just a little talk *(A rather grim pause which
suggest the alternative)*—Now, let's put it out of our minds. Shall
we? And let me see a little smile. *(As there is no response from*
KAYE, MRS. ORCUTT *smiles for both.)* There! Well, we both have
our day's work to do. (MRS. ORCUTT *goes up L.)*

*(PAT singing blithely, comes down stairs. As she passes KAYE U. C,
she chucks her gaily under the chin, says, "H'ya, Baby?" by way of
morning greeting, and executes a brief and intricate little dance
step, all this without pausing on her way to dining room. KAYE
stands, a little wooden figure. Starts to go as TERRY comes in from
dining room.)*

TERRY: What are you doing—going without your breakfast? *(Going
upstairs)*

KAYE: I don't want any breakfast. I'm not hungry.

TERRY: *(On her way upstairs)* Well, you're just an old fool, rehearsing on an empty stomach.

(As KAYE *goes the* TWO MARYS *come into sight on stairs, talking as they descend. They pass* TERRY *as she goes up.)*

BIG MARY: *(In the throes of trying to memorize a part:* LITTLE MARY, *who is cueing her, follows with the part in her hand.)* "Three weeks now since he first came here. What do we know about him—uh anyhow?" Is there an "anyhow"?

LITTLE MARY: Yeh.

BIG MARY: What do we know about him anyhow?"

LITTLE MARY: "I tell you—"

(Doorbell rings)

BIG MARY: "I tell you there is something mysterious going on in this house." Well, that's all, give me the cue.

LITTLE MARY: *(Scans part.)* Uh huh.

BIG MARY: Oh, for heaven's sake! "We must call the police."

LITTLE MARY: Oh, yeh. "We must call the police."

*(*MATTIE *crosses through hallway to answer bell.)*

BIG MARY: Now let's go back and do it right. "I tell you there is something mysterious going on in this house."

LITTLE MARY: *(As they go into dining room)* "We must call the police."

(Outer door is opened and we hear a voice subsequently identified as that of MRS. SHAW, LINDA'S *mother.)*

MRS. SHAW: Good morning.

MATTIE: How-do.

MRS. SHAW: This is the Footlights Club, isn't it?

MATTIE: Yes, ma'am, Won't you come in?

MRS. SHAW: Oh, thank you. *(*MRS. SHAW *comes into sight. She is rather cosy little woman of about 55, plainly dressed, sweet-faced and inclined to be voluble. She speaks rather confidently now to* MATTIE.*)* I'm Mrs. Shaw, Linda's mother. She doesn't know I'm coming. I'm surprising her.

MATTIE: Oh—you Miss Linda's mother! For land's sakes!

MRS. SHAW: She doesn't know I'm here. We live in Buffalo. I just got off the train and came right up. Linda hasn't gone out, I hope?

MATTIE: *(As she goes toward stairs)* No, I haven't seen her around yet.

MRS. SHAW: Well, you just tell her there's somebody here to see her, very important. Only don't tell her it's her mother.

MATTIE: Yes'm. *(She disappears)*

(MRS. SHAW sits on couch and looks about her with bright-eyed interest. SUSAN comes out of dining room, and nods politely.)

MRS. SHAW: Good morning.

SUSAN: Good morning.

MRS. SHAW: Are you a little actress?

SUSAN: Yes, sort of.

MRS. SHAW: I'm Linda's mother. I've come to surprise her.

SUSAN: Oh, what fun!

MRS. SHAW: Which one of the girls are you? Perhaps Linda's written me about you.

SUSAN: I'm Susan Paige.

MRS. SHAW: Are you acting a part on Broadway?

SUSAN: I'm in "Petticoat Lane," but I'm only an understudy.

MRS. SHAW: Understudy?

SUSAN: That means I play the part in case the leading woman gets sick.

MRS. SHAW: Oh! That's nice. And does she get sick often?

SUSAN: Never! *(SUSAN goes upstairs as MATTIE descends.)*

(MATTIE appears slightly flustered.)

MATTIE: I'm awful sorry, I must have made a mistake. I guess Miss Linda must have gone out already.

MRS. SHAW: *(Rising)* Oh, dear! Does anybody know where she went?

MATTIE: *(Edging toward dining room)* Well, I'll see—maybe Mrs. Orcutt knows. *(We have not heard the front door open or close, so silently has* LINDA *entered the house. She is swiftly tiptoeing upstairs as* MATTIE *turns and sees her.)* There she is! Miss Linda! Miss Linda! *(Linda has not heeded the first call, but the second one stops her.)* Your ma's here.

MRS. SHAW: Oh dear, I was going to surprise you.

LINDA: *(Frozen on stairs)* Why—mother!

MRS. SHAW: I guess I have. Well, aren't you going to come down?

(Holds her arms open wide to embrace her)

*(*LINDA *makes a slow and heavy-footed descent, eyeing first her mother, then* MATTIE. *She is wrapped in a camel's hair ulster, a little too large for her.)*

LINDA: *(Coming downstairs)* Mother, how how wonderful. When did—you——

MRS. S.: Why, Linda, child, aren't you glad to see me?

LINDA: Of course I am, mother. *(Kisses mother quickly and backs away)*

MRS. SHAW: *(As she surveys* LINDA'S *strange attire)* Well, of all the funny get-ups!

LINDA: Yes, isn't it silly—I——*(She turns to the gaping* MATTIE.*)* Mattie, I'm sure you have your work to do. Why don't you run along?

MATTIE: *(Reluctant to leave)* Yes—Miss Linda. *(She goes)*

MRS. SHAW: Where did you get that coat? I never saw that coat before.

LINDA: It belongs to—to one of the girls. I had to go down to the drug store.

MRS. SHAW: Why—you've got on evening slippers!

LINDA: I just put the first thing on I could find.

MRS. SHAW: Linda Shaw, if you've run out in your pajamas——
(*Goes to* LINDA *as though to open the coat*)

LINDA: (*Backing away from her mother*) No, I haven't. I——(*She realizes she has made a blunder*) Yes, I have. Yes.

MRS. SHAW: Linda, what are you wearing under that coat? Take off that——(*She jerks it open so that it slides down the girl's arms and drops to the floor, revealing* LINDA *in a black satin evening dress of extreme cut—the narrowest of shoulder-straps, bare shoulders, a deep décolletage, the bodice almost backless.*) Linda!

LINDA: I spent the night with a girl friend.

MRS. SHAW: Oh—Linda!

LINDA: Oh, mother, don't make a scene.

MRS. SHAW: (*With repressed emotion*) Linda, go up and pack your things. You're coming home with me.

LINDA: Oh, no, I'm not.

MRS. SHAW: Linda Shaw!

LINDA: We can't talk here, mother. And there's no use talking, anyhow. I'm never coming home. I'm twenty-two years old, and my life is my own.

MRS. SHAW: Who—who is this man? Are you going to marry him?

LINDA: He is already married.

MRS. SHAW: I'm going to send for your father. He'll know what to do.

LINDA: Mother, if you make a fuss about this I'll have to leave the club. That girl knows already. And if I leave here I'll go live with him, and the whole world will know it. Now take your choice.

(MRS. ORCUTT *enters from dining room, apprehension in her face, steeled for any eventuality. Her quick eye goes from the girl to the mother.*)

MRS. ORCUTT: I'm Mrs. Orcutt, Mrs. Shaw. My maid just told me you were here.

MRS. SHAW: Oh, how do you do, Mrs. Orcutt?

MRS. ORCUTT: I understand you arrived unexpectedly.

MRS. SHAW: Yes, I came down to do a bit of shopping and surprise my little girl here, and we practically came in together. She spent the night with my niece and her husband—86th Street—they had a rather late party and Linda just decided to——I don't see how these young people stand it . . . *(A little laugh)* Doesn't she look silly—this time of day? Linda darling, do run up and change. Why don't you meet me for luncheon at the hotel? Can you do that?

LINDA: Of course, mother dear.

MRS. SHAW: I'm at the Roosevelt, darling. Shall we say one o'clock?

LINDA: *(In quiet triumph)* Yes, mother darling. *(She goes upstairs)*

MRS. SHAW: Oh, well, I must run along. I'm only going to be here a day or two and—well, good-bye.

MRS. ORCUTT: *(Accompanying her to door)* Good-bye. It's been so nice. I'm always happy to meet the parents of our girls. And I hope that whenever you are in the city again you won't fail to drop in on us. Well, good-bye.

(As MRS. ORCUTT *passes back along hallway* OLGA *descends stairs. She is wearing a hat, her coat is over her arm. In one hand she has a few sheets of music, in the other a music portfolio. She tosses her coat over piano. She sits at piano, plays a few bars of music.* BERNICE, *in hat and coat, comes downstairs. She looks in on* OLGA *and listens to music, which is the second part of Rachmaninoff's Prelude in G Minor.)*

BERNICE: Are you going to play that at your concert?

OLGA: *(Playing)* Yes.

BERNICE: When's it going to be?

OLGA: In the spring.

BERNICE: Whereabouts, Town Hall?

OLGA: Yes, yes.

BERNICE: Are you going to play under your own name?

OLGA: *(Stops playing and turns)* Certainly.

BERNICE: Well, you've got an interesting name—Olga Brandt, It sounds like a musician. But Bernice Niemeyer! I think that's what's holding me back in the theatre. *(OLGA continues to play)* Do you know what? I thought maybe I'd take one of those one-word names, the way some actresses do. I thought, instead of Bernice Niemeyer, I'd just call myself—Zara. *(BERNICE goes)*

(OLGA continues with her music. Chopin B Minor Etude, Op. 25, No. 10. Doorbell rings. MATTIE answers. As door opens we hear the voice of DR. RANDALL, TERRY'S father. His first words are lost under cover of OLGA'S music.)

MATTIE: Just go right in and sit down. I'll tell Miss Terry you're here. *(She goes upstairs)*

(DR. RANDALL is a gentle-looking, gray-haired man touching 60. There is about him a vague quality—a wistful charm—that is not of the modern professional world. OLGA, as he enters, is about to launch herself on the finale of the selection she has been playing. It entails terrific chords, discords, and actual physical effort. The length of the keyboard seems scarcely adequate. DR. RANDALL stands arrested by this. Three times the music pauses as if finished, each time DR. RANDALL steps forward to speak, and OLGA starts again. He gives a little nod of approval as OLGA finishes, rises, and gathers up her music and her coat. OLGA acknowledges this with a little inclination of her head, and goes. The front door slams on her going. Immediately the dining room doors open and the TWO MARYS come out, still deep in rehearsal, and start upstairs.)

BIG MARY: "I tell you there is something mysterious going on in this house."

LITTLE MARY: "We must call the police."

BIG MARY: *(With no particular expression)* "Last night I heard moans and shrieks, and this morning a dead man was found on the doorstep, his head completely severed."

LITTLE MARY: "What about the blood in the library?"

(Both exit upstairs. PAT emerges from dining room, intent on mastering a fast and intricate dance routine for which she provides her

own music. She, too, goes toward hall and upstairs. DR. RANDALL
*has barely had time to react to these somewhat bewildering encoun-
ters when a gay high voice form stairs calls, "Dad!" and* TERRY
comes running down. She hurls herself into her father's arms.)

DR. RANDALL: Terry!

TERRY: Dad! Darling! I couldn't be more surprised.

DR. RANDALL: Glad to see me?

TERRY: Glad! I should say so! It's been almost a year.

DR. RANDALL: Too long, my dear. Too long to be separated . . . .
Let me look at you.

TERRY: Bursting with health, Doc.

DR. RANDALL: Mmmmm. *(Pulls down first one eyelid, then other)*
Look kind of peaked to me. Eat enough greens?

TERRY: Greens! I'm a regular Miss Popeye. Now let me look at
you. Say Ah, say Oo, say you love me. *(He laughs as he kisses her)*
Now come on and tell me everything. *(As she takes his coat and
hat)* How's Aunt Lucy? And she is taking good care of you!

DR. RANDALL: *(Goes to couch, sits)* Say, you know Lucy! You'd think
I was ten years old.

TERRY: *(Sitting on couch)* I know. Wear your rubbers, have you got
a clean handkerchief? Didn't she fuss about your driving all this
way?

DR. RANDALL: Carried on like mad.

TERRY: How did you get here so early? You said afternoon. What
happened?

DR. RANDALL: Well, when Stacy invited me to come East with
him, I didn't know what kind of driver he was. Turned out he's
one of those fellows slows down to eighty going through a
town. I dozed off a couple of minutes, once, and missed all of
Pennsylvania.

TERRY: He shouldn't have done it, but it does give me more time
with you.

DR. RANDALL: Now maybe you've got things to do. You weren't expecting me till three or four.

TERRY: I've got nothing but a silly radio rehearsal. You know—I'm the big butter-and-egg girl. I'll be all through by quarter past one. Let's have lunch way up on top of something. Shall we?

DR. RANDALL: (*As he takes envelope from pocket*) That's fine. Give me time to drop in at the Polyclinic a few minutes. 345 West 50th Street. Where's that?

TERRY: It's not five minutes from here. And I'll pick you up at your hotel. Where are you?

DR. RANDALL: New Yorker. Stacy's idea. Full of go-getters.

TERRY: After lunch we'll whirl all over town. We'll see everything. Tonight we're going to the theatre, and Keith's taking us to dinner.

DR. RANDALL: Oh, yes. Your young man. I want to meet the boy.

TERRY: Yes, but Keith's not like anybody you ever met. He's brilliant, and he's written the most marvelous play, and he hates the government and won't wear evening clothes.

DR. RANDALL: Sounds as if he didn't have nickel.

TERRY: Oh, but he will have! This play will put him over. It's thrilling and beautiful! And oh, Dad, I'm going to play the leading part.

DR. RANDALL: Why, Tress, that's wonderful. Your mother would have been very proud.

TERRY: Of course he hasn't sold the play yet. But he will. He's bound to.

DR. RANDALL: Say, I'm going to come back and see you in it, if it takes my last nickel.

TERRY: (*Who has been eyeing him a little anxiously*) Dad.

DR. RANDALL: Yes, Tress?

TERRY: You look as though you'd been working too hard. Have you?

DR. RANDALL: I wish I could say I had. But the fact is my waiting room looks pretty bleak these days.

TERRY: Isn't anybody sick at all? How about old Mrs. Wainwright?

DR. RANDALL: Yes, folks get sick, all right.

TERRY: Well, then!

DR. RANDALL: Well, it seems just being a medical man isn't enough, these days. If you had a cold, we used to just cure the cold. But nowadays, the question is, why did you get the cold? Turns out it's because, subconsciously, you didn't want to live. And why didn't you want to live? Because when you were three years old the cat died, and they buried it in the backyard without telling you, and you were in love with the cat, so, naturally, forty years later, you catch cold.

TERRY: But who tells them all this?

DR. RANDALL: Why—uh—young fellow came to town a few months ago; opened up offices.

TERRY: Oh!

DR. RANDALL: Sun lamps, X-ray machines, office fixed up like a power plant. He's the one's looking after Mrs. Wainwright. She's bedridden with sciatica, arthritis and a heart condition, but fortunately it's all psychic.

TERRY: Dad, do you mean he's taken away your whole practice from you!

DR. RANDALL: Mm—not as bad as that. The factory folks still come to me.

TERRY: But they haven't any money!

DR. RANDALL: They still have babies.

TERRY: Never you mind. I'm going to buy you the biggest, shiniest sun-lamp machine ever invented; and fluoroscopes and microscopes and stethoscopes and telescopes. You'll be able to sit in your office and turn a button and look right through Mrs. Wainwright, six blocks away.

DR. RANDALL: How about that new doctor? Will it go through him?

TERRY: It'll dissolve him.

(KEITH *strides to front of stairs. The black sweater has given way to a black shirt. Otherwise his costume is about the same. No hat, of course*)

KEITH: *(Shouts upstairs)* Terry!

TERRY: Oh——Keith!

KEITH: *(Dropping down C.)* Oh!——The door was open. I came right in.

TERRY: Here's father! He got here this morning.

KEITH: *(Advancing, shakes hands)* Well! This is indeed a pleasure, sir.

DR. RANDALL: Thank you, young man. I'm glad to know you.

KEITH: Terry has told me much about you. I've been looking forward to this meeting for a long time.

DR. RANDALL: Oh, that's very good of you.

KEITH: *(Takes out a crumpled pack of Camels)* May I offer you a cigarette, sir?

DR. RANDALL: Thank you. *(Takes cigarette)*

TERRY: *(Who has been observing all this courtliness with a growing bewilderment)* Keith, what are you up to?

KEITH: You never told me, Theresa, that you and your father had such a strong resemblance. The same fine brow, the deep-set, thoughtful eyes. Allow me, sir! *(Lights DR. RANDALL'S cigarette)*

TERRY: Keith, will you stop it! What is this act, anyhow?

KEITH: *(Blandly)* It's no act. What are you talking about?

DR. RANDALL: *(Pats KEITH on shoulder)* I guess you'll do . . . . Well, children, I've got to be off. You said quarter past one, Terry?

TERRY: *(As she gets his coat and hat)* Yes, father. I'll pick you up at your hotel.

DR. RANDALL: *(To* KEITH*)* Understand we're seeing you later. That right?

KEITH: *(Absent-mindedly crossing L.)* What? Oh. Yes.

TERRY: *(As she accompanies her father into hallway, their arms about each other's shoulders)* I can't tell you how grand it is to have you here, Dad . . . Now, don't cross against the lights, and promise to take taxis. Don't try to find places by yourself.

DR. RANDALL: All right, all right.

TERRY: I'll be at the hotel at one-fifteen.

DR. RANDALL: I'll be waiting.

TERRY: Good-bye, darling.

DR. RANDALL: Good-bye.

*(*TERRY *returns to living room and* KEITH*)*

TERRY: Really, Keith, you can be so maddening. What was all that "Yes, sir," and "How are you, sir?"

KEITH: Can't I be polite?

TERRY: One of the least convincing performances I ever saw.

KEITH: That's right. Hit a fellow when he's down.

TERRY: Keith, what's the matter?

KEITH: I come to you in one of the toughest spots I ever was in my life, and you jump all over me.

TERRY: I'm so sorry. I didn't know. How could I—what's happened? Is it the play?

KEITH: *(Unhappily)* Yes.

TERRY: They all turned it down?

KEITH: *(Reluctantly)* N-no.

TERRY: Keith! Tell me!

KEITH: *(Unwillingly)* I—I could sign a contract this afternoon

TERRY: You don't mean it! Who with?

KEITH: Gilman.

TERRY: *(Almost with awe)* Gilman! Why, he's the best there is!

KEITH: *(Crossing R. to couch)* That's what makes it so tough.

TERRY: *(After him)* Keith, for heaven's sake, you're not being unreasonable about this! A Gilman production—why, it's—Keith, no matter what he wants you to do, you've got to do it. What's he want you to change? The second act?

KEITH: No. He likes the play all right. He's nuts about it.

TERRY: Well, then I don't—understand what——

KEITH: *(Squirming)* I just can't let him have it, that's all.

TERRY: *(Something clicks in her mind)* Keith! It's me. He doesn't want me.

KEITH: Well—you see—Gilman's got Natalie Blake under contract, and she is a big star, and it just happens to be the kind of part she's been looking for——

TERRY: *(Crushed)* Did you tell him you thought I would be good in it?

KEITH: Of course. I gave him a hell of an argument. But he just won't do it unless Blake is in it.

TERRY: *(Turns, moves L.C.)* Well, then, that's—that. I wouldn't do anything to—I bow out, Keith.

KEITH: *(After her)* Gosh, Terry! You mean you really would do that for me!

TERRY: The play is the important thing, Keith. I love every single line of it. You didn't think, after the way we've worked on it for a whole year, that I was going to stand in the way, did you?

KEITH: God, you're wonderful, Terry! You're a great kid! I'm crazy about you! *(He tries to embrace her.)*

TERRY: *(Evading him)* Please, Keith.

KEITH: There isn't one girl in a million would have taken it like that. And I love you for it. Love you, do you hear!

TERRY: Yes, Keith.

KEITH: I knew I could count on you to——

(LINDA *comes down stairs, dressed for the street, carrying a small and costly looking dressing-case. Her manner is that of a determined and scornful girl.*)

LINDA: *(Pauses as she sees* TERRY. *A swift glance down hall. She decides to use* TERRY *as her messenger.)* Terry, Terry, will you do something for me?

TERRY: *(Absorbed in her own thoughts)* What? Oh, hello, Linda.

LINDA: I don't want to see Orcutt. Will you give her a message for me?

TERRY: Yes, of course.

LINDA: Tell her I'm leaving. I'll send for my things this afternoon. Give her this. It's for the whole week. *(Thrusts some bills into* TERRY'S *hand)*

TERRY: Linda, what's the matter! You're moving? Where?

LINDA: You bet I'm moving. Fast. And nobody'll ever know where. *(*LINDA *goes off R.)*

KEITH: What was all that about?

TERRY: What? . . . Oh, I don't know. She's a strange girl.

KEITH: Well, look, I've got to run. Gilman's waiting in the office for me. He's lining up a hell of a cast. And I'm going to meet Natalie Blake this evening. I'm having dinner with her and Gilman.

TERRY: Tonight! Keith, you're having dinner with father and me.

KEITH: Oh, for God's sake, Terry! I get a chance like this with a top manager, and a big start and you expect me to say, "I can't meet you tonight, I've got to have dinner with my girl and her father." That's what you want me to say, I suppose?

TERRY: No, no!

KEITH: I'll do the best I can. You know that. This whole thing is for you as much as for me. You know that, don't you?

TERRY: Yes.

KEITH: Well, then. Now, look, darling——

(KAYE *comes in, and, seeing* TERRY, *halts in doorway. She is a figure of despair.*)

TERRY: Why, Kaye! What are you doing back?

KAYE: They let me out.

TERRY: Oh, Kaye!

KAYE: There was another girl rehearsing when I got there. I'm fired.

TERRY: But they can't do that! How long had you been rehearsing?

KAYE: They still could. This was the seventh day.

TERRY: Darling, don't let it upset you. It happens to all of us. *(A realization of her own recent disappointment comes over her)* To me. It's a part of this crazy business.

KAYE: Terry, I haven't a cent.

TERRY: Who cares! I've still got my radio job. We'll get along.

KAYE: *(Dully)* Don't try to fool me. I know about the radio job. You've only got two more weeks. I can't take any more money from you. I owe you more than a hundred dollars.

TERRY: What of it! Now look. Come on. Have lunch with Dad and me. Come on down to my radio rehearsal.

KAYE: *(Starts for stairs)* No, I couldn't, Terry, I just—couldn't. Don't you bother about me. I'm all right.

KEITH: It's tough.

TERRY: Oh, dear, I hate to leave you like this. Don't be low, darling.

KAYE: *(As she goes upstairs)* I'm all right. Thanks, Terry. *(Exits)*

TERRY: *(To KEITH)* This meant everything to her.

KEITH: The season's just begun. She'll get something else. Now look, darling, you and your dad have a nice dinner some place and leave my ticket at the box-office and I'll be along just as soon as I can. Will you do that, Sweet?

TERRY: Yes.

KEITH: O.K.! That's my girl! You're the swellest kid that ever lived. (*He goes. Door slams*)

(TERRY *stands for a moment, then moves R. to table. Looks upstairs, then at money in hand.* MATTIE *comes into room intent on tidying the ash trays, etc. She makes the rounds with an ash receptacle and dustcloth.*)

TERRY: Mattie, where's Mrs. Orcutt?

MATTIE: Back in her room.

(TERRY *goes in search of* MRS. ORCUTT. *Off up. L.* MATTIE *hums a snatch of lively songs as she works about the room. A piercing scream of terror is heard form above stairs.* SUSAN *hurtles down stairs, her face distorted with terror. Simultaneously,* TERRY *rushes in.*)

TERRY: What is it? What is it?

SUSAN: Up in the hall. She drank something. She's——

TERRY: No! No! (*Rushes upstairs followed by* MATTIE *as* MRS. ORCUTT *and* FRANK *run on from up L.*)

MRS. ORCUTT: What's the matter? What happened? What happened?

(SUSAN *motions upstairs and* MRS. ORCUTT *and* FRANK *run up.*)

TERRY: (*Upstairs*) Kaye! Kaye! Can you hear me?

MATTIE: (*Upstairs*) Oh, Lord, look at her.

TERRY: Kaye, darling! Why did you do it!

MATTIE: Oh, look at her face. (*Simultaneously in hushed tones*)

TERRY: Here, let me hold her! Kaye!

MATTIE: Poor little lamb.

MRS. ORCUTT: Oh, this is terrible!

FRANK: Want me to carry her in her room?

MATTIE: What'd she swallow? What was it?

FRANK: Here's the bottle. Don't say nothing on it.

MRS. ORCUTT: I'll get a doctor.

(During above dialogue SUSAN *has dropped down slowly to piano, where she sinks on bench sobbing.* MRS. ORCUTT *comes downstairs and quickly goes to phone, dialing number, as she does so* TERRY *comes down slowly.)*

TERRY: *(Coming into room)* It's no use, she's——

MRS. ORCUTT: *(Hangs up receiver)* It'll be in all the papers. I never should have let her stay here. I felt it from the start. There was something about her. She was different from the rest of you.

TERRY: Don't say that! It might have been any of one of us.

CURTAIN

ACT II

SCENE 2:

The same 7 o'clock in the evening, about two months later.

JUDITH'S *hat and coat on piano at rise. Again,* SAM *is waiting for a tardy* BOBBY. *Obviously it has been a long wait and his patience is frayed. He peers upstairs, paces the room, crosses to piano and impatiently fingers a few notes of "Old Man River."* BOBBY *floats downstairs, as Southern as ever.*

BOBBY: Hello, there, Honey Bun.

SAM: Hello, Sugar!

BOBBY: Ah didn't keep you waitin', did Ah?

SAM: No. No.

BOBBY: *(Fussing with this necktie)* Just look at your tie! Ah declare, Ah don't see how Ah can keep on lovin' you, the way you get yourself up.

SAM: *(On their way out)* Go on! Everybody knows you're crazy about me.

BOBBY: Ah sure enough am. Ah just can't sleep or eat.

SAM: Honest, Honey?

BOBBY: Mm . . . Where we going to have dinner?

(They go, exit up R. TWO MARYS *enter from dining room, crossing to stairs deep in an argument.)*

LITTLE MARY: Well, what do you want to do all evening? I'm sick of movies and you don't want to sit around here.

BIG MARY: I'll tell you what. Let's go and see Keith Burgess's play.

LITTLE MARY: Keith Burgess' play! We couldn't get into that. The paper says eight weeks in advance and fifty standees last night.

(They start upstairs)

BIG MARY: Then two more won't matter. That's all we want to do—stand up.

LITTLE MARY: Yes, but I don't think we ought to ask.

BIG MARY: Good Lord, you don't want to pay, do you?

LITTLE MARY: Pay? For theatre? You must be out of your mind.

BIG MARY: Well, some people must pay.

(Doorbell. MATTIE enters from dining room. Looks back)

MATTIE: Did you put a new 'lectric bulb up in Miss Kendall's room?

FRANK: *(Enters from dining room)* I will.

MATTIE: Give Miss Terry that telephone message? From Mr. Kingsley.

FRANK: *(Entering)* Land-sakes, I forgot.

MATTIE: Well, you better tell her—he's important. And you can close up the dining room—everybody's been in that's going to eat. *(FRANK closes dining room. At outer door)* Well, I declare!

(The reason for her exclamation becomes apparent as KEITH comes into the room. He is a figure of splendor in full evening regalia—white tie, top hat, white muffler, beautifully tailored top-coat. MATTIE goes toward stairs with her astonished gaze so fixed on this dazzling apparition as to make her ascent a somewhat stumbling one. KEITH, waiting, puts coat on R. bookcase, drops down C., takes out platinum-and-gold cigarette case, symbol of his seduction, taps a cigarette smartly, lights it. JUDITH, the last to finish her dinner, comes out of dining room eating a large banana. As KEITH bursts upon her vision she stops dead, and all progress with the banana is temporarily suspended.)

KEITH: *(Removing his hat)* Hello, Judith.

(JUDITH advances slowly to him, grasps the hand that holds the hat, moves it up so that the hat is held at about shoulder height, backs

up, lifts her skirts a little, and is about to kick when KEITH, *outraged, breaks his position and walks away from her.)*

JUDITH: Well, if you don't want to play. *(Takes final bite of her banana)*

KEITH: Pixie, eh?

(JUDITH *tosses banana skin on the floor between them, beckons him
enticingly.)*

MATTIE: *(Descending stairs)* Miss Terry'll be right down.

JUDITH: *(Shakes head dolefully as she picks up banana skin)* You were
more fun in the other costume.

KEITH: You'd better watch your figure, eating those bananas.
Starches and show business don't go together.

JUDITH: *(Putting on coat which was on piano at rise)* They do in my
show. I got nothing to compete with but elephants.

KEITH: Are there idiots who really go to those childish things—pay
money?

JUDITH: Say, you can't have all the idiots. You're doing pretty good;
give us some of the overflow.

KEITH: I suppose you know we broke the house-record last week.

JUDITH: Oh, sure. I stayed up all Saturday night to get the returns.

KEITH: *(Under his breath)* Wise-cracker.

*(*TERRY'S *voice is heard as she comes running downstairs)*

TERRY: So-o-o sorry, Mr. Burgess! At the last minute I had run in
my stocking and I had to—*(She stops short down C., as she sees*
KEITH'S *magnificent effect. She herself is wearing her everyday
clothes.)*

JUDITH: *(Sensing trouble)* Well, I'll—I'll leave you two young people together. *(She gives the effect of tiptoeing out of room, exits up
R.)*

TERRY: *(Dazzled)* Keith! *(She curtsies to the floor)* Did you remember
to bring the glass slipper?

KEITH: What's the idea, Terry? I told you on the phone we were dressing.

TERRY: I thought you were joking. You said, "We'll dress, of course," and I said, "Of course!" But I didn't dream you were serious.

KEITH: We're going to an opening night! And our seats are third row center!

TERRY: Downstairs?

KEITH: Down——Where do you think?

TERRY: Darling, we've been to openings before, and we always sat in the gallery.

KEITH: Gallery! We're through with the gallery! I've got a table at Twenty One for dinner, and after the theatre we're invited to a party at Gilman's pent-house. You can't go like that!

TERRY: *(As she starts for stairs)* Give me just ten minutes—I'll go up and change. *(She suddenly recollects—stops)* Oh, dear!

KEITH: What's the matter?

TERRY: I loaned my evening dress to Susan.

KEITH: Oh, for God's——*(Turns away in disgust.)*

TERRY: *(Starts again)* It's all right. I'll borrow Judy's pink——*(Stops)* Oh no! Olga's wearing it.

KEITH: *(Crossing L.)* This is the damnedest dump I was ever in! Sordid kind of life! Wearing each other's clothes! I suppose you use each other's toothbrushes, too!

TERRY: *(Quietly)* Would you rather I didn't go, Keith?

KEITH: I didn't say that I——

TERRY: *(Still quietly)* Yes—but would you rather?

KEITH: Now you're playing it for tragedy. What's the matter with you, anyhow?

TERRY: *(Drops down C.)* There's nothing the matter with me, Keith. I just can't see us as third-row first-nighters. We always went to see the play, Keith. That whole crowd—it makes the audience more important than the show.

KEITH: Listen, I don't like those people any better than you do. They don't mean anything to me.

TERRY: Then why do you bother with them?

KEITH: They can't hurt me. I watch them as you'd watch a hill of ants. Insects, that's what they are.

TERRY: Keith, listen, you wrote your last play about people you understood and liked. You lived with them, and you knew them, and they gave you something. You'll starve to death in third row center.

KEITH: I'm going back to them. I'm no fool. They're keeping my room for me just as it was.

TERRY: Keeping it? How do you mean?

KEITH: Oh, I don't want to talk about it now. Come on, let's get out of here.

TERRY: But I've got to know. Do you mean you've moved without even telling me?

KEITH: *(Decides to face the music, crosses to couch R.)* Well, I was going to break it to you later. I knew you'd jump on me. But as long as you've gone this far—I'm going to Hollywood.

TERRY: Hollywood!

KEITH: Yes, to write for pictures.

TERRY: No, no, Keith!

KEITH: Now don't start all over again! If you don't watch yourself you'll turn into one of those nagging——*(He stops as* KENDALL *comes downstairs)*

(She is dressed for the street. Throws a glance into the room, in passing, and notices KEITH'S *unusual attire.)*

KENDALL: *(Impressed, very friendly)* Hel-lo!

KEITH: *(With no cordiality)* H'are you?

KENDALL: *(Senses she has walked into hornets' nest)* Good-bye.

(Beats a hasty retreat via front door up R.)

KEITH: Let's get out of here.

TERRY: Keith, you can't go to Hollywood! I won't let you! You said you'd never go no matter how broke you were, and now that your play's a big hit you're going. Why? Why?

KEITH: Well, they didn't want me before it was a hit.

TERRY: Keith, listen——

KEITH: I know what you're going to say. All that junk about its shriveling up my soul. Listen! I'm going to use Hollywood. It's not going to use me. I'm going to stay one year at two thousand a week. That's one hundred thousand dollars. I'll write their garbage in the daytime, but at night I'll write my own plays.

TERRY: But will you? That's what I'm afraid of. Will you?

KEITH: You bet I will! And in between I'll keep fit with sunshine, and swimming, and tennis, and——

TERRY: Little ermine jackets, up to here.

KEITH: Huh?

TERRY: It doesn't matter.

KEITH: Believe me, they'll never catch me at their Trocaderos or their Brown Derbies.

TERRY: *(Quietly)* When are you going, Keith?

KEITH: I don't know. Next week.

TERRY: Well—good-bye.

KEITH: What!

TERRY: Good-bye, Keith, and good luck. It's been swell. *(She turns, runs swiftly upstairs)*

(KEITH goes to foot of stairs and calls.)

KEITH: Terry! What's the——Terry! . . . Terry! Terry!

(Only silence from above. He claps his hat on his head, and goes. Door slams loudly after him. Immediately on the slam of the door BERNICE tiptoes downstairs with a catlike swiftness and soundless-

ness. Obviously she has been eavesdropping. A quick comprehensive look around the room, then she scurries to window, peers out guardedly, so as not to be seen from the street. Turns back from window just as the TWO MARYS *make swift silent descents. The three at once plunge into an elaborate pantomimic routine revealing their knowledge of the scene which has just taken place between* TERRY *and* KEITH, *and their unbounded interests in its consequences.)*

BIG MARY: *(Whispered)* Is he gone?

BERNICE: Yes. How's Terry?

LITTLE MARY: She's in her room.

BERNICE: Do you think she can hear us?

BIG MARY: She might.

LITTLE MARY: Wasn't it terrible?

BERNICE: I thought I'd die.

LITTLE MARY: Poor Terry.

BIG MARY: I never did like him.

BERNICE: Me neither.

LITTLE MARY: We'd better go back up or she'll be suspicious.

(They start upstairs.)

BIG MARY: Yes, be very quiet.

BERNICE: Shall we ask her if we can do anything?

BIG MARY: No.

(Doorbell rings, they vanish upstairs. FRANK *appears, getting into his housecoat and casting a resentful glance back at the unseen* MATTIE. *As door is opened the voice of* KINGSLEY *is heard: "Does Miss Terry Randall happen to be in?"* FRANK: *"Yessuh, I think so. Will you come right in?"* FRANK *comes into sight. "What's the name, suh?")*

KINGSLEY: Mr. Kingsley.

FRANK: Oh, yeh. You the gentleman telephoned. I clean forgot to tell Miss Terry.

KINGSLEY: Well, as long as she's here . . .

FRANK: Yessuh. (*Pulls himself together and goes upstairs.* KINGSLEY *comes into the room. He stands a moment, then takes out cigarette case and lights cigarette.* FRANK *comes down again.*) I told her you was here.

KINGSLEY: Oh, thank you.

FRANK: And I told her about the phone call, too. (FRANK *goes about his business as* TERRY *comes downstairs.*)

TERRY: (*To him C., shakes hands.*) Why, Mr. Kingsley, how dramatic! You're just in the nick of time.

KINGSLEY: I'm glad of that. What's happened?

TERRY: (*Starts R. to couch*) Oh—sort of an emotional crisis. I dashed upstairs to have a good cry, buried my head in the pillow just the way you're supposed to, and guess what?

KINGSLEY: What?

TERRY: The tears wouldn't come. In fact, I felt sort of relieved and light, as though I'd just got over a fever.

KINGSLEY: How disappointing. Like not being able to sneeze.

TERRY: Perhaps I'll be able to manage it later. Tonight.

KINGSLEY: If a shoulder would be of any—help?

TERRY: No, thanks. I'm afraid I have to work this out alone . . . . (*Sits on couch*) Do take your coat off.

KINGSLEY: (*Takes off coat, drops it in armchair L.*) Thanks. This is rather a strange hour for me to drop in. I did telephone——

TERRY: Oh, Frank doesn't believe in phone messages.

KINGSLEY: (*Crossing to couch*) They do in Hollywood. They just called me up. Can you take a plane for California tomorrow?

TERRY: Me! (*He murmurs an assent*) What for?

KINGSLEY: They didn't say what the part was—sort of character comedy, I believe. Of course the put the picture in production first and then started looking for a cast—the Alice-in-Wonderland method. At any rate, they want a new face in this particular part; they ran off all the screen tests they had on file, and finally came to that one of yours. So there you are. And— oh, yes—they want to know in twenty minutes. Of course it's only four-thirty on the Coast.

TERRY: You're joking.

KINGSLEY: No, all important things are decided in twenty minutes out there. The more trivial ones take years. Shall I phone them you'll be there?

TERRY: Why—I don't know.

KINGSLEY: You don't mean to say you're hesitating?

TERRY: But it's so fantastic! How can I——?

KINGSLEY: *(Sitting next to* TERRY.*)* Dear child, do you mind if I tell you something? *(*TERRY *looks up at him.)* I've been watching you for several seasons. You've been in the theatre for two—three— what is it?

TERRY: Three.

KINGSLEY: Three years. You've appeared in, perhaps, half a dozen plays. I wouldn't call any of them exactly hits—would you?*(*TERRY *merely shakes her head)* And one or two of them closed before the week was over.

TERRY: You've been doing a lot of detective work.

KINGSLEY: No, I didn't need to. I know all about you.

TERRY: You do! That's a little frighten frightening.

KINGSLEY: It's part of my business—watching the good ones. And you are good. You're fire and a variety and a magnetic quality that's felt the minute you walk on a stage.

TERRY: *(As he hesitates)* Oh, don't stop!

KINGSLEY: But off stage you're nothing at all. *(*TERRY *wishes she had left well enough alone.)* When you walk into an office the average manager doesn't see anything there. You might be the little girl who's come to deliver the costumes. They wouldn't see that spark. If Elizabeth Bergner walked in on them unknown—or Helen Hayes—what would they see! Little anemic wisps that look as if they could do with a sandwich and a glass of milk. But put them on a stage, and it's as if you had lighted a thousand incandescent bulbs behind their eyes. That's talent—that's acting—that's you!

TERRY: Now I—am going to cry.

KINGSLEY: But what if they don't see what's hidden in you? Suppose they never see it. You might go tramping around for twenty years, and never get your chance. That's the stage.

TERRY: Twenty years!

KINGSLEY: (*Rises, pulls* TERRY *up.*) But let's say you go to Hollywood. They'll know what to do with you out there. Light you so as to fill those hollows, only take your—(*He is turning her head this way and that to get the best angle.*) right profile. That's the good one. Shade the nose a trifle. (*Opens her mouth and peers in as though she were a race horse.*) Perhaps a celluloid cap over those two teeth. Yes, they'd make you very pretty. (TERRY *steals a quick look in mirror. Her morale is somewhat shaken.*) Then you play in this picture. Fifty million people see you. Fan mail. Next time you get a better part. No tramping up and down Broadway, no worries about money. A seven-year contract, your salary every week whether you work or not. And if you make a really big hit, like Jean, they'll tear up your contract and give you a better one.

TERRY: (*A sudden idea*) Wouldn't they let me do just one or two pictures, instead of this seven-year thing?

KINGSLEY: I'm afraid not. If you make a big hit they don't want another studio to reap the benefit. That's not unreasonable, is it?

TERRY: (*As she crosses to L.*) No, I suppose not. Oh dear! Everything you say is absolutely sound and true, but you see, Mr. Kingsley, the trouble with me is—I'm stagestruck. The theatre beats me and starves me and forsakes me, but I love it. I suppose that's the kind of girl I am—you know—rather live in a garret with her true love than dwell in a palace with old money bags.

KINGSLEY: (*Moving in C.*) But it looks as though your true love had kicked you out of the garret.

TERRY: Oh, dear, if there was just somebody. Mr. Kingsley, won't you help me? Won't you tell me what to do?

KINGSLEY: Me?

TERRY: Please!

KINGSLEY: But I work for the picture company.

TERRY: But if you didn't?

KINGSLEY: *(Quietly)* I'd think you ought to tell them to go to hell.

TERRY: What!

KINGSLEY: *(Indignantly)* Go out there and let them do all those things to you! *(Again he has a finger under her chin, raising her head as he scans her face)* That lovely little face! And for what? So that a few years from now they can throw you out on the ash heap! The theatre may be slow and heart-breaking, but if you build solidly you've got something at the end of seven years, and seventeen years, and twenty-seven! Look at Katherine Cornell, and Lynn Fontanne and Alfred Lunt. The tramped Broadway in their day. They've worked like horses, and trouped the country, and stuck to it. And now they've got something that nothing in the world can take away from them. And what's John Barrymore got? A yacht!

TERRY: You're wonderful!

KINGSLEY: Are you going to Hollywood?

TERRY: No!

KINGSLEY: Will you go to dinner?

TERRY: YES!

KINGSLEY: That's really all I came to ask you.

TERRY: Just a minute, I'll get my hat. *(Runs for stairs as curtain falls.)*

CURTAIN

ACT III

SCENE 1:

Same. A Sunday morning. The following October. The girls are scattered about room in various informal attitudes and various stages of attire. Pajamas, lounging robes, hair-nets, cold cream, wave combs. Four or five Sunday papers, opened and distributed among the girls, are in drifts everywhere, girls are lying on the floor reading bits of this and that, lounging in chairs, coffee cups, bits of toast, a banana or an orange show that Sunday morning breakfast is a late and movable feast. KENDALL *is in riding clothes and bound for a day in the country. All the girls are present except* TERRY. *During the year two new girls have joined the club, and now are sprawled at ease with the others.* OLGA, *at piano, is obliging with the latest popular tune.* MADELEINE *rather absent-mindedly sings a fragment of the song, leaving a word half-finished as her attention is momentarily held by something she reading. A foot is waggled in time to the music.* PAT, *sprawled full-length on top of grand piano, is giving a rather brilliant performance of dancing with her legs in the air.*

LITTLE MARY, *on hands and knees, is making a tour of the re-cumbent figures in search of a certain theatrical news item. In one hand she holds a half-eaten banana.*

LITTLE MARY: *(Crawling from C. to D.L.)* Where's the list of next week's openings? *(She finds that* BIG MARY, *lying on floor L., has the page she wants. She settles down to read over her shoulder.)*

BOBBY: *(Sitting on arch bookcase L.)* Anybody got a roll they don't want?

TONY GILLETE: *(One of the new girls, sitting on R. end of couch)* Here!

BOBBY: Toss!

(The muffin is hurled through the air)

MADELEINE: *(Lying full-length stage R. C. Turning a page of ro-togravure section)* Autumn Millinery Modes. Oh, look at the hats they're going to wear!

(OLGA stops playing)

SUSAN: *(From behind L. end of couch)* Let me see. *(Traverses the distance to MADELEINE by two neat revolutions of her entire body, and brings up just behind the outspread papers, Reads:)* Paris says "Hats'll be worn off the head this winter."

PAT: *(On piano. Suspended in mid-air as her attention is caught by this remark)* Where?

SUSAN: That's what it says. "Hats'll be worn off the head this winter."

BERNICE: *(At the desk R.)* Where're they going to put 'em?

LITTLE MARY: *(OLGA starts playing Für Elise. Busy with American)* Did you know that in Ancient Egypt five thousand years ago the women used to dye their hair just like we do?

JUDITH: *(Seated in armchair L. Furious)* Who's we?

BIG MARY: *(To LITTLE MARY, who is reading over her shoulder)* Take that banana out of my face, will you!

(SUSAN crawls over to ELLEN, lying R. of JUDITH.)

ELLEN FENWICK: *(The other new girl. Perusing the department store ads)* "Two-piece Schiaparelli suits—$5.98. You cannot tell the model from the copy."

JUDITH: The hell you can't.

SUSAN: *(Emerging from newspaper)* Oh, they're postponing that "Lord Byron" play because they can't find a leading man.

LITTLE MARY: What are they looking for?

SUSAN: He's got to be young and handsome.

ELLEN: There are no handsome men on the stage any more.

JUDITH: There's a shortage off stage, too.

PAT: Looks don't count any more. It's good old sex appeal.

(OLGA *stops playing*)

KENDALL: Would you rather go out with a handsome man without sex appeal, or a homely man with it?

BERNICE: I'd rather go out with the handsome one.

JUDITH: Sure, and stay in with the other one.

ANN: (*Who has been seated over R. rises as* JUDITH'S *sally is greeted with a general laugh.*) I think you girls are simply disgusting!! Men, men, men! It's degrading just to listen to you. (*As she moves up to L. of desk*)

JUDITH: Isn't it, though?

BIG MARY: Say, Terry! . . . Where's Terry?

JUDITH: She's still asleep. It's the only chance she gets—Sundays.

BIG MARY: I see that old beau of hers is coming back.

(OLGA *starts Chopin's C Sharp Minor Waltz.*)

TONY: Who's that?

BIG MARY: Keith Burgess. He used to hang around here all the time.

TONY: Really? What's he like?

JUDITH: He's one of those fellows started out on a soapbox and ended up in a swimming pool.

LITTLE MARY: Terry was crazy about him, all right.

BIG MARY: Yeah.

PAT: And if you ask me, I think she still is.

LITTLE MARY: Really! What makes you think so?

PAT: Somebody just mentioned his name the other day and you ought to've seen her face!

JUDITH: She's forgotten he ever lived—that Left-Wing Romeo.

KENDALL: Well, I should think she might, with David Kingsley in the offing. Now, I call him attractive!

PAT: Oh, Kingsley isn't her type. Anyway, he's just interested in her career.

KENDALL: If it's just her career they eat an awful lot of dinners together.

LITTLE MARY: If it's art he's got on his mind why doesn't he get her a job? Not much of a career standing behind a sales-counter.

BOBBY: Yes, Ah think it's perfectly awful the way Terry has to get up at half-past seven every morning. That miserable job of hers.

MADELEINE: It's no worse than what I've got ahead of me.

SUSAN: Well, anyway, you'll be acting.

MADELEINE: *(Rising, crossing to chair R.)* Acting! A Number Three Company of "A Horse on You," playing up and down the West Coast. God! I came to New York to get away from Seattle, and they keep shipping me back there. *(Sits R.)*

BOBBY: You'll be earning some money! Look at Sam and me! We can't make enough to get married. Ah declare Ah'm so bored with livin' in sin.

(OLGA stops playing)

ANN: Well, really!

LITTLE MARY: Oh, shut up!

JUDITH: Speaking of Seattle, Miss Vauclain, would you be good enough to take that load of lumber off my neck! After all, you put it there.

MADELEINE: It isn't my fault if he fell for you.

PAT: Oh, is Lumber in town again?

JUDITH: No; but I've had a warning. *(Drawing letter from her pajama pocket)*

ANN: *(Impatiently, rising, OLGA starts Debussy's First Arabesque.)* Oh, I'm not going to waste my whole Sunday! What time is Jean coming?

MADELEINE: Stick around. What have you got to lose?

ANN: My time's just as valuable as Jean's is.

MADELEINE: Sure. You're in big demand. Sit down.

ANN: Well, if Jean wants to see me I'm upstairs. (OLGA *stops playing.*) This conversation isn't very uplifting. (ANN *goes upstairs.*)

OLGA: She should be teaching school, that girl. (*Starts playing Beethoven Sonata in D Minor*)

TONY: Is Jean Maitland as pretty off the screen as she is on? I've never seen her.

ELLEN: Neither have I.

KENDALL: She's much better looking off. They've made her up like all the rest of them on the screen.

(OLGA *stops playing*)

OLGA: I hope she will soon be here. I must be at the Winter Garden at one o'clock.

LITTLE MARY: On Sunday!

OLGA: (*Bitterly*) On Sunday. (*Goes into a few bars of the newest Winter Garden melody. Something very corny*)

LITTLE MARY: Yeah, we know. Kolijinsky.

(*A voice which we later find is that of* LOUISE MITCHELL HENDERSON *calls out from dining room.*)

LOUISE: Olga!

OLGA: What is it?

LOUISE: What's that you're playing?

OLGA: (*Not very clearly heard above the music*) "Hill-billy Sam."

LOUISE: (*Off*) What?

OLGA: Ah! Come in here if you want to talk.

PAT: Yes, stop stuffing yourself and come in here . . . Heh, Louise!

LOUISE: (*As she comes out of dining room*) I was having some pancakes. (*Crossing to C.*)

PAT: Listen, you've got to cut out those farmhand breakfasts, now that you're back in New York.

LOUISE: *(Settles herself in the group C.)* Imagine getting the Times the day it's printed instead of three days later!

JUDITH: You mean you're not lonesome for good old Appleton?

LOUISE: I haven't been so happy in years. *(She turns her attention to the paper.)*

JUDITH: Everything pink, eh?

BIG MARY: *(OLGA plays E Major Brahms Waltz.)* Oh, say, Irene Fitzroy has been engaged for the society girl part in "River House."

(A series of highly interested responses to this.)

SUSAN: No! . . . Really! . . .

KENDALL: That's wonderful!

LITTLE MARY: She'll be good in it! . . .

LOUISE: Isn't it exciting!

BERNICE: *(As she rises from desk)* I could have played that Fitzroy part. I don't know why I couldn't be a society girl. *(Assumes a supercilious expression to prove her fitness for the part. A chorus of:)*

PAT: Sure! . . . We know . . .

LITTLE MARY: You're always the type.

BERNICE: A real actress can play anything. I may play the French adventuress in "Love and War."

(OLGA stops playing. A little chorus of astonishment: ALL turn to her.)

LITTLE MARY: Really!

BIG MARY: No kidding!

KEN: Do you mean they offered it to you?

BERNICE: Well, not exactly, but I'm writing 'em a letter. *(Back to desk, sits)*

(Another chorus)

PAT: Oh, we see . . .

(OLGA *starts E Flat Major Nocturne of Chopin.*)

KENDALL: Letters! . . .

MADELEINE: You and your letters!

(MATTIE *comes out of dining room with large tray. She is intent on gathering up coffee cups.*)

MATTIE: You-all knows Mrs. Orcutt don't allow you girls to go laying around downstairs in your pajamas.

(LOUISE *rises, give* MATTIE *two cups, then goes up to L. arch.*)

JUDITH: (*Dreamily, as she reads*) Don't give it another thought, Mattie. We'll take 'em right off.

(MADELEINE *rises and up to L. of desk.*)

MATTIE: Besides, look-it this here room! Banana skins and newspapers and toast! I should think with Miss Jean coming you'd be getting all slicked up. Big moving picture star. (*Takes a grapefruit off a small piece of statuary, where it has been draped as a hat. She goes back to dining room with her laden tray.*)

(*For a second there is a lull as the* GIRLS *are absorbed in their papers.*)

MADELEINE: (*To* BERNICE) Are you still writing that letter about yourself?

BERNICE: (*Rises and down a bit*) Look. How many X's are there in sexy?

MADELEINE: Why don't you give up, anyhow?

BIG MARY: Yeh, why don't you take up ballet-dancing, or something?

BERNICE: (*Springs suddenly to her feet, her hands clutching back of chair behind her.* OLGA *stops playing.*) Don't you say that to me. I'm never going to give up. Why, I'm as good as——(*She realizes she is making a spectacle of herself.*) Leave me alone. (*Back to desk, sits*)

KENDALL: (SUSAN *rises and sits R. end of table.*) Ah, they were just kidding. Can't you take a joke?

(OLGA *starts A Flat Major Brahms Waltz.* TERRY *runs down stairs, stopping halfway to toss a word of greeting to the girls below.*)

TERRY: *(A gesture that embraces them all)* Ah! My public!

LOUISE: Hello.

BOBBY: H'ya!

JUDITH: Well, Terry, the Beautiful Shop-Girl.

PAT: Thought you were never going to get up.

TERRY: I wouldn't, if it weren't for Jean's coming . . . . Heh, Mattie! *(A "Yes'm," from* MATTIE *in dining room)* Draw one in the dark! . . . Oh, isn't Sunday heavenly! *(Stretches luxuriantly)* I woke up at half-past seven; said, "Nope, I don't have to," and went right back to sleep. Not all day long do I have to say, "This blouse is a copy of a little import that we are selling for $3.95. I am sure you would look simple terrible in it." *(Sits L. arm of couch)*

JUDITH: I'm going to come down there some day and have you wait on me.

TERRY: If you do I'll have you pinched for shoplifting.

BOBBY: *(Getting off bookcase, drops down C.)* Honest, Terry, Ah don't see how you tolerate that job of yours. Moochin' down there nine o'clock in the mawnin.' Slaving till six, and after.

TERRY: Oh, it isn't so terrible if you keep thinking that next week that part will turn up. I keep on making the rounds.

ELLEN: But when do you have time for it?

TERRY: Lunch hour.

SUSAN: Then when do you eat your lunch?

TERRY: Sundays.

(BOBBY *exits in dining room.*)

PAT: *(Getting off piano, starts for stairs)* Just goes to show how cuckoo the stage is. You can act rings around all of us. Well— *(Stretching a bit as she makes for stairs)* I guess I'll go up and put the face together. I look like and old popover. *(Going up)*

SUSAN: Me, too. Don't say anything good while we're gone. (*As she goes upstairs with* PAT)

JUDITH: What are you going to do today, Terry, after Jean goes?

(BOBBY *comes on and goes to piano L.*)

TERRY: I don't know. Who's doing what? Kendall, you're going social for the day, h'm?

KENDALL: Yes, I'm going out to Piping Rock.

TERRY: Piping Rock—isn't that where your ancestors landed?

KENDALL: Thereabouts.

JUDITH: Mine landed in Little Rock.

BIG MARY: Oh, say, Terry! The paper says Keith Burgess gets back from the Coast today. Did you know that?

(*A little hush. The eyes of the girls are turned toward* TERRY.)

TERRY: Yes, I know. Why do they call California the Coast instead of New York?

LITTLE MARY: I wonder if that sunshine has mellowed him up any.

BOBBY: (*Holding up paper*) Girls, here's Jean stepping out of an airplane!

(OLGA *stops playing.*)

BERNICE: (*Jumping up*) Oh, let's see it. (*To* BOBBY *at piano*)

BOBBY: (*As three or four girls cluster around her including* TERRY) "Blond Hollywood Screen Start Alights at Newark Airport."

LITTLE MARY: That's a darling costume!

BIG MARY: I don't like her hat.

BERNICE: (*Takes paper, crosses R. to window. Reading*) "Lovely Jean Maitland, Popular Screen Actress, Arrives for Rehearsals of Broadway Stage Play."

JUDITH: That belle certainly is shot with luck.

BOBBY: That's what she is! (*As she crosses R. to table*)

JUDITH: First she goes out and knocks 'em cold in pictures, and now she gets starred on Broadway.

BIG MARY: And she isn't even a good actress.

(MATTIE *brings* TERRY'S *coffee from dining room.*)

MATTIE: *(In dining room door)* Here's your coffee, Miss Terry.

TERRY: Thanks, Mattie.

ELLEN: What's she going to do? Quit pictures and stay on the stage?

BIG MARY: No, no. The picture company puts on the play. It's like a personal appearance.

BERNICE: *(Who has drifted over to window)* Girls! She's here!

BIG MARY: *(Darting to window)* Let's see!

(A wild scramble to tidy the room. Newspapers, cigarette butts, etc.)

BOBBY: Look at that car, would you?

LOUISE: Isn't it gorgeous!

LITTLE MARY: There she is! She's getting out!

BERNICE: Oohoo! *(Raps on window)* Jean!

(With a concerted rush they make for front door.)

(NOTE. Lines A to B are read simultaneously as girls rush out in hall to meet JEAN *and as those remaining in room tidy it up.)*

(A) BOBBY: She looks marvelous, doesn't she!

BIG MARY: I wonder if she's changed!

BERNICE: Isn't it exciting!

TONY: Don't forget to introduce me!

ELLEN: Yes. Me, too!

LOUISE: *(Calling upstairs)* Girls! Yoohoo! She's here!

(Meanwhile, on the part of the remaining girls, there is a wild scramble to tidy up room.)

LITTLE MARY: She's got on Red Foxes. *(Cue for* TERRY *to speak)*

TERRY: Here—pick up the papers! Give them to me! *(With a great bundle of newspapers she dashes into dining room and out again.)*

MADELEINE: We should have got all dressed up.

JUDITH: Not me. She's seen me worse than this.

OLGA: She will be dressed up enough.

KENDALL: We're acting like a lot of school girls. We'll be asking for her autograph next.

(The squealing in hallway now mounts to a burst of ecstatic greeting.)

LITTLE MARY: Jean! Jean!

BERNICE: DAR-ling!

LOUISE: WON-derful!

BIG MARY: Look grand!

BOBBY: Jean! Welcome home!

JEAN: *(Still in hallway)* Oh, I'm so excited! How darling of you all to be here!

(SUSAN and PAT run downstairs. From among the group:)

LOUISE: Are you glad to be back?

(B) LITTLE MARY: You haven't changed a bit.

(JEAN comes into view. Her costume is simple and horribly expensive. Her fox furs are fabulous, her orchids are pure white.)

JEAN: *(Embracing girls)* Hello, girls! Madeleine! Olga, how's the music? Kendall!! Hello, Judy. This is worth the whole trip——

(TERRY comes from dining room.)

TERRY: Jean, darling!

JEAN: Terry!

(They embrace.)

MRS. ORCUTT: *(Looming up in the dining room doorway,* FRANK *and* MATTIE *just behind her)* Well, well! My little Jean!

JEAN: Hello, Mrs. Orcutt! Mattie! Frank! *(In turn she throws her arms around all three of them. As she embraces* FRANK *a laugh goes up from the group.)* Well, let me get my breath and have a look at all of you.

BERNICE: It's the same old bunch. *(Grabs* JEAN'S *furs, runs to mirror down K)*

TERRY: No, there are two new ones. Ellen Fenwick and Tony Gillette. Miss Jean Maitland.

TONY: Hello.

PAT: *(The trumpet sound)* Ta-da-a-ah!

JEAN: Hello, girls. I hope you don't think I'm crazy—all excited like this.

ELLEN: Oh, no!

TONY: We think you're darling.

*(*BERNICE, *before mirror, is having a private try-on of* JEAN'S *fox and orchids. Enchanting effect.)*

ANN: Hello, Jean!

JEAN: *(In greeting to* ANN, *who has come rather sedately downstairs)* Ann! I was just going to ask for you.

ANN: My, you look Hollywood!

BERNICE: Do you think it goes with my coloring?

BIG MARY: Let me try it.

JEAN: *(Recalls two men who have accompanied her, and who are standing in hallway. One has a huge camera and tripod.)* Oh, boys, I'm so sorry. Girls, this is Mr. Larry Westcott, our New York publicity man—and a wonder. And this is Billy—uh—I'm afraid I never heard your last name.

BILLY: Just Billy.

LARRY: Just want to snap a few pictures. Do you mind?

MRS. ORCUTT: *(A hand straightening her coiffure)* Not at all.

LARRY: Human interest stuff.

BERNICE: You mean with us!

JEAN: Of course!

BOBBY: Oh, I've got to go and fix up.

(*A chorus of:*)

LOUISE: So do I!

LITTLE MARY: I look a fright.

BERNICE: Me, too!

BIG MARY: We won't be a minute.

(*Up the stairs go* BERNICE, BIG *and* LITTLE MARY, BOBBY *and* LOUISE. MATTIE *is doing a little sprucing up, preparatory to being photographed, and* FRANK *buttons his housecoat.*)

JEAN: Well, Terry!

TERRY: Jean, darling, aren't you thrilled at doing a play? When do your rehearsals start?

JEAN: (*Abstracted*) On Wednesday.

BILLY: (*Speaking to* MRS. ORCUTT *and the two servants. He has his electric apparatus in his hand.*) I've got a pretty strong light here. All right if I plug in?

FRANK: Yes, sah. I'll show you.

(BILLY *and* FRANK *disappear into hallway toward rear of house.*)

LARRY: Pardon me, Miss Maitland. You were going to ask about our taking some shots upstairs. (*Glancing from* JEAN *to* MRS. ORCUTT)

JEAN: Oh, yes. Do you mind, Mrs. Orcutt? They want to take some stills of me up in my old room.

MRS. ORCUTT: Of course not.

LARRY: You know—Humble Beginnings in The Footlights Club. They love it.

MRS. ORCUTT: Why, yes, I'd be delighted.

TERRY: Wait a minute! I've got my Sunday wash hanging up there. You can't photograph that!

LARRY: Great! Just what we want!

TERRY: All right. But I never thought my underwear would make Screenland.

OLGA: So you are a big actress now, eh, Jean? You are going to be starred in a play.

JEAN: Isn't it silly! I didn't really want them to star me in it. I'm scared stiff.

LARRY: She'll be great. Look, Miss Maitland, we haven't got a lot of time. Mr. Kingsley is picking you up here at twelve forty-five and then you're meeting Mr. Gretzl.

TERRY: Who?

JEAN: Mr. Gretzl.

JUDITH: What's a Gretzl?

JEAN: He's the Big Boss—Adolph Gretzl.

LARRY: President of the Company.

MRS. ORCUTT: Of course! Adolph Gretzl.

OLGA: (Dashing to piano. Improvises and sings.)
Of course Adolph Gretzl,
    He looks like a pretzl——

JUDITH: (Picking it up)
So why should we fretzl——

PAT: And fume. Boom-boom. (She times last with a couple of bumps)
(The TWO MARYS come dashing downstairs.)

LITTLE MARY: We're ready!

LARRY: Okay! Everybody here now?

BIG MARY: Oh, no. There's more yet. Girls! Hurry!
(LOUISE'S voice from upstairs: "Coming!")

JEAN: Terry, darling, when am I going to see you? I've got loads to tell you and I want to hear all about you. Let's see—rehearsals start Wednesday. How about lunch tomorrow?

LARRY: Oh, not tomorrow, Miss Maitland. You're lunching with the Press.

JEAN: Oh, dear. Let's see—I'm going to that opening tomorrow night with David Kingsley . . . How about tea?

LARRY: Not tea! You've got the magazine people. And you've got photographs all day Tuesday.

JEAN: *(Turns to* TERRY*)* But I want to see her. How about Wednesday? I'll get away from rehearsal and we'll have lunch. One o'clock?

TERRY: You won't believe it, but my lunch hour's eleven-thirty to twelve-thirty.

JEAN: Eleven-thirty! What do you mean?

(Down come BOBBY *and* LOUISE *refurbished.)*

LOUISE: Are we late?

BOBBY: Ah hope we didn't keep you waitin'.

LARRY: *(Impatiently glancing at his watch)* All right, Miss Maitland.

JEAN: Oh, fine. Now before we start, everybody, I've got a tweentsy-weentsy surprise for you.

BIG MARY: Surprise?

JEAN: Billy, will you bring it in?

(BILLY goes into hall.)

BOBBY: Bring what in?

LOUISE: What?

JEAN: It's for all of you, dear Mrs. Orcutt and the whole dear Footlights Club.

(BILLY enters from hallway carrying what is evidently a large picture, framed and covered with a rich red drapery which conceals the subject.)

BOBBY: Oh, look!

KENDALL: Oh, how exciting!

PAT: What is it?

TONY: Looks like a picture.

LITTLE MARY: What of, I wonder?

JUDITH: Papa Gretzl.

JEAN: All right, girls?

BOBBY: We're ready?

> (LARRY *has placed picture on a chair, upright.* JEAN *steps forward, and with a sweeping gesture throws aside velvet drape. It is a portrait of* JEAN. *All eyelashes, golden hair and scarlet lips. A series of delighted and semi-delighted exclamations.*)

PAT: It's Jean!

ELLEN: Lovely!

TONY: How beautiful!

BOBBY: Darling.

> (JUDITH: *a snap of the fingers*)

MRS. ORCUTT: *(Her dismayed glance sweeping the walls)* It's lovely, Jean, lovely! Now if we can only find a fitting place to hang it.

LARRY: Well, let's see. *(With a look that alights on the Bernhardt portrait and rests there)*

JUDITH: So long, Sarah! (JUDITH *makes a gallant gesture of Hail and Farewell toward the portrait of the Divine Sarah.*)

LARRY: Now, if you'll all just gather around the picture. . . .Okay, Billy!

BILLY: *(Who has been glimpsed now and then busy with his apparatus)* Okay! Ready in a second.

LARRY: Now then, Miss Maitland. Your tight there behind the portrait and you, Mrs.—er——*(Snaps finger at Mrs. Orcutt)* Yes, right here beside Miss Maitland. Now you girls fill in here, making a little circle.

BIG MARY: Sure.

LARRY: And look toward Miss Maitland. That's right—all of you right in here. You, too, girls. That's right, you, too, girlie. We want a nice little informal group. No, you'll all have to crouch down. Everybody down. You, too, sister. (*This is to* MRS. ORCUTT, *who gets down painfully.*) That's fine. And all looking at Miss Maitland.

JEAN: (*Very sweet*) Frank and Mattie have to be in it. Come on, Frank and Mattie!

(*They have been looking a little crestfallen and now take their places at extreme edge, much elated.*)

LARRY: Sure, sure! It wouldn't be a picture without 'em. We want the whole Twilight Club. Now then, have we got everybody? (*Looks over his shoulder just as* BILLY *turns on his special light*)

LITTLE MARY: No, no, where's Bernice?

BIG MARY: Bernice isn't here!

BERNICE: (*Her voice from top of stairs*) I'm ready! Here I am! (BERNICE *has seized this opportunity to register as undiscovered Hollywood star material. She has made her self up to look like a rather smudged copy of Joan Crawford. Her entrance is undulating and regal.*)

PAT: Heh! That's my new dress!

BERNICE: Well, I had to be right, didn't I?

LARRY: Come on, girlie. Right here. (*Pushes her to her knees. Immediately* BERNICE *stares out toward camera.*) No, no! Look at Miss Maitland. Everybody look at Miss Maitland. And remember this will all be in the papers tomorrow.—Ready, Billy?

BILLY: Okay.

LARRY: Hold still now. And everybody look at Miss Maitland! Right! (*Just as* BILLY *squeezes bulb* BERNICE *makes a lightning full-face turn toward camera, all smiles, and back again before they can fairly accuse her of it.*) Now, then for the pictures upstairs ... Miss Maitland!

JEAN: Want to come along, girls?

(Chorus)

BOBBY: Sure.

BERNICE: We'd love to.

(Simultaneously as girls go upstairs.)

TONY: Yes.

(The whole procession streams toward stairs, talking as they go.)

JEAN: I haven't heard a bit of Club news. What are you girls all doing? What's happened? Who's got jobs?

BIG MARY: I have. And Kendall's working. And Judy. And let's see—who else?

SUSAN: I'm understudy in "Roman Candle."

LITTLE MARY: You read about Linda, I suppose. Getting all smashed up?

JEAN: Oh, wasn't it ghastly!

BERNICE: And Kaye's taking poison. I suppose you know about that.

JEAN: Oh, I almost died.

BERNICE: That was awfully exciting. Pictures in the paper, and everything.

FRANK: *(Bringing up the rear with electrical apparatus)* You-all usin' this upstairs too, ain't you?

(TERRY and JUDITH, unable to face a second such scene, remain behind, with only the smiling portrait of JEAN as company. Their eyes meet understandingly. There goes JEAN)

TERRY: *(Blandly)* You're not going to be in the—other pictures?

JUDITH: No, if I'm going to work as an extra I want my five dollars a day.

TERRY: *(Crosses to R. of table)* I do hope I left my room looking sordid enough.

JUDITH: *(L.)* Say, what about the play they've got her doing? Do you suppose it's really something?

TERRY: Oh, it is. David Kingsley told me about it. He says it's a really fine and moving play.

JUDITH: *(A glance at portrait)* Then why does he let her do it?

TERRY: He couldn't help it. They got it into their heads out on the Coast. It's Gretzl's idea. What do they care about the theatre? They think the stage is something to advertise pictures with.

JUDITH: Listen, Jean can't act. If the play's as good as all that, she'll kill it. It doesn't make sense!

TERRY: Now, Judy, haven't you learned not to——

(Of all people, KEITH suddenly appears in archway. Though he has been gone a year, he barges right in as though he had left only yesterday. His clothes represent an ingenious blending of the Hollywood style with his own Leftist tendencies. He still wears the sweater, but it is an imported one, the trousers are beautifully tailored, the shirt probably cost eighteen dollars, no necktie, and course, no hat.)

KEITH: *(His voice heard in hallway. Enter up R. down to C.)* Where's Terry Randall? Oh, there you are!

TERRY: *(Rises)* Why, hello, Keith!

JUDITH: Well, if it isn't the fatted calf!

KEITH: *(Surveying room D. R. to table.)* God, a year hasn't made any difference in this dump! *(He casts an appraising eye over TERRY.)* What's the matter with you? You're thin and you've got no color.

TERRY: *(R. of table)* Well, I haven't been having those hamburgers at Smitty's since you left.

KEITH: That reminds me, I haven't had any breakfast. *(He selects a pear from bowl of fruit on table R. L. end.)* Hope this is ripe . . . Heh! What's her name out there? *(Shouting toward dining room)* Bring me a cup of coffee! *(Finding pear too juicy for him)* God! Give me your handkerchief, Terry.

TERRY: *(Coming around front of couch)* You've got one.

KEITH: That's silk. (*Grabs hers*)

TERRY: Well, Keith, tell us about yourself. Are you back from Hollywood for good?

KEITH: What do you mean? I'm going back there in three days. I've been working on a plan to put the whole studio on a commonwealth basis with the electricians right on a footing with the executives. But they won't have it.

TERRY: Who won't have it, the executives?

KEITH: The electricians! (*Finishing up pear*)

TERRY: Well, anyway you look wonderful. All healthy and sunburned. And I never saw such beautiful trousers.

KEITH: (*Taking a last bite of the pear*) You're looking terrible. (*The core of the pear in hand, he glances about for some place to deposit it. Lightning-fast, the perfect servant, JUDITH is by his side, offering a little ash tray which she gets from piano. He drops the pear-core on it without a word.*)

JUDITH: Thank you. (*Replacing tray on piano, R. end.*)

KEITH: (*Eases to C.—Suddenly he notices JEAN'S portrait.*) What's this chromo doing here?

TERRY: It's a little present from Cinderella.

KEITH: (*Back R. C.*) Those autograph hounds out there waiting for her?

JUDITH: (*Drops D. L. C.*) No, they want another glimpse of you.

KEITH: Did it ever occur to you that I didn't come here to see you?

JUDITH: You mean there's—no hope for me at all? (*Crushed, she goes into dining room, L.*)

TERRY: (*On L. arm of couch*) Well, Keith! Give me an account of yourself. You've been gone a year—I hardly know what's happened to you.

KEITH: (*L.C.*) Why—I wrote you—didn't I?

TERRY: Oh, yes. A postcard from Palm Springs, showing the cactus by moonlight, and a telegram of congratulations for my opening in February, which arrived two days after we closed.

KEITH: I got mixed up.

TERRY: Keith, tell me—what do you mean you're only going to be here three days? Your year's up, isn't it?

KEITH: Yeh, but they wouldn't let me go. I had to sign up for another year.

TERRY: But, Keith, your plays! You are writing another play?

KEITH: Yes. Sure. I haven't written it yet, but I will this year.

TERRY: *(Rises, drops down front of couch)* I see. I saw the picture you wrote—what was the name of it? "Loads of Love."

KEITH: *(Moves D. and R.)* Oh, did you see that? How'd you like it?

TERRY: Very amusing. Of course, Keith, the Masses got a little crowded out.

KEITH: Masses! It played to eighty million people. That's masses, isn't it?

TERRY: *(Sits couch)* Yes. Yes, I guess I didn't get the idea.

KEITH: *(Sits L. of her)* Now listen, Sweet. You know why I'm here, don't you?

TERRY: No, I don't, Keith.

KEITH: Well, look! You can't go stumbling around like this forever. You're not working, are you?

TERRY: Yes.

KEITH: You are? What in?

TERRY: The blouse department of right H. Macy & Co.

KEITH: What! You're kidding.

TERRY: I have to live, Keith.

KEITH: Good God! Listen, darling. You spend years on Broadway and finish up in Macy's. And look at Jean? Two years in Hollywood and she's a star.

TERRY: They speed up everything in Hollywood. In two years you're a star; in four years you're forgotten, an in six you're back in Sweden. *(Moves U.L. to piano)*

KEITH: Not any more. *(Doorbell rings)* That's the kind of reasoning that's kept you where you are! From now on I'm going to take charge of you. You're going to be——*(He breaks off as* MATTIE *crosses through hall from L. to R. Moves D. R.)* There's always somebody coming into this place. It's like Grand Central Station.

KINGSLEY: *(Heard at door)* Good morning, Mattie.

MATTIE: *(At door)* 'Morning, Mr. Kingsley.

KINGSLEY: *(Appearing in archway)* Hello, Terry. *(As he sees* KEITH*)* Well, hello, there!

KEITH: Hello.

TERRY: David! How nice to see you!

KINGSLEY: *(Glancing at portrait)* I see I missed the ceremony.

TERRY: They're still shooting up on Stage Six.

KINGSLEY: No, thanks. I'm the official escort, but there are limits . . . *(As he drops down to* KEITH*)* How are you, Burgess? I heard you were coming back.

KEITH: How are you? *(Shaking hands)*

KINGSLEY: So you've served your year, h'm? Well, you're an exception. You've had the courage to quit when you said you would. Another year out there, and you'd have gone the way they all do. Never written a fine play again.

(A moment of embarrassed silence)

TERRY: *(Rather nervously)* Keith is going back to Hollywood for one more year.

KINGSLEY: Oh, I didn't mean to——

KEITH: It always amuses me to hear a fellow like you, who makes his living out of pictures, turn on Hollywood and attack it. If you feel that way about pictures why do you work in them?

TERRY: *(D. L. C. Hurriedly)* Well, we can't always do what we want to, Keith. After all, you're working in Hollywood, and I'm seeing blouses, and David Kingsley is——

KINGSLEY: *(Moves L.)* No, Terry. He's right. I shouldn't talk that way, and I don't very often. But I'm a little worked up this morning. I re-read Jean's play last night. *(Gesturing toward* JEAN'S *portrait)* And I realized more than ever what a beautiful play it is. That's what's got me a little low. When they come into the theatre—when picture people take a really fine play and put a girl like Jean in it; when they use a play like this for camera fodder, that's more than I can stand. The theatre means too much to me.

KEITH: *(Moves L.)* All right! It's a fine play. And you notice it's Hollywood that's doing it.

TERRY: Oh, Keith, let's not get into an argument.

KEITH: It just shows how much you know about Hollywood. You're five years behind the times. They're crazy about fine things. Dickens and Shakespeare—they've got a whole staff digging them up.

TERRY: All right! Let's talk about something else.

KEITH: If you go to dinner in Hollywood, what's the conversation! Books, and Art, and Politics! They never even mention pictures.

KINGSLEY: I suppose they put that on the dinner invitation. Instead of R. S. V. P. it says: Don't Mention Pictures.

TERRY: *(Coming between them)* Oh, what's got into you two? You're a picture man and you're yelling about the stage, and you're a playwright and you're howling about Hollywood!

KINGSLEY: At least I'm honest about it! I work in pictures, but I don't pretend to like it.

KEITH: *(*TERRY *moves L.)* Who's pretending? I like it and I'm going back to there. And what's more, I'm taking Terry with me.

KINGSLEY: You're what?

TERRY: *(Below chair L. C.)* Keith, don't be absurd!

KEITH: It's time somebody took her in hand, and I'm going to do it. I'm going to marry her.

KINGSLEY: Terry, you can't do that!

TERRY: *(Hopefully)* Why not, David?

KINGSLEY: I've told you why a hundred times. You belong in the theatre.

TERRY: So that's the reason? Yes, you certainly have told me a hundred times. A thousand! I've had it with the soup and the meat and the coffee. Actress, actress, actress!

KINGSLEY: Of course I've told you! Because you are an actress!

TERRY: And I've just realized why. Because you quit the theatre yourself, and you've been salving your own conscience by preaching theatre to me. That made you feel less guilty.

KINGSLEY: Terry, that's not true.

TERRY: Oh, yes, it is! So true! How funny that I never thought of it before!

KEITH: *(Who has vastly enjoyed all this)* Look, I've got to get out of here! *(To* KINGSLEY*)* If you'll let me have just a moment. *(Moves L. to* TERRY*)* When are we going to get married?

TERRY: *(In a deadly tone)* When are we going to get married! We are going to get married, Mr. Burgess, when Hollywood to Dunsinane doth come. That's Shakespeare; you know—the fellow they're digging up out there.

KEITH: *(Stunned)* Huh?

TERRY: It's too late, Keith. When you walked out on me a year ago, you walked out on yourself, too. That other Keith was cocksure and conceited, but he stood for something! What was it?—thunder and lightning and power and truth! Wasn't that what you said? And if you believe in something you've got to be willing to starve for it. Well, I believed in it, Keith. *(She moves to D. R. between them and stands looking from one to the other.)* So I guess that leaves me just a young lady with a career. Or shall we say just a young lady! *(She turns and goes upstairs)*

CURTAIN

ACT III

Scene 2:

Same. It is midnight, and the room is in semi-darkness. There is a pool of light in the hall and on stairway from overhead chandelier and desk lamp. A little later, when the lights go on, we see that Bernhardt has given way to Jean Maitland.

After a moment of stillness there is the sound of the front door opening, and the TWO MARYS *are heard coming home and starting upstairs.*

LITTLE MARY: Well, I didn't like either the play or the cast. And I thought Laura Wilcox was terrible.

BIG MARY: Of course she's terrible. You know how she got the part, don't you?

LITTLE MARY: Sure. Everybody on Broadway knows. The trouble with us is we've been hanging on to our virtue.

BIG MARY: Maybe you have.

(They disappear upstairs. Somewhere in hallway a clock strikes twelve. Then door is heard to open again.)

JUDITH: *(Off R.)* Well, good night. And thank you ever so much. *(Enters R.)*

MILHAUSER: *(Enters)* Thank you. I certainly had one swell evening, all right.

JUDITH: Yes, so did I! What time is it? About two o'clock?

MILHAUSER: No, it's only twelve.

JUDITH: Oh, really? I guess my watch is fast.

MILHAUSER: Look, I'm going to be here all week. What are you doing tomorrow night?

JUDITH: Tomorrow? That's Tuesday—Oh, that's my gymnasium night.

MILHAUSER: Well, about Wednesday?

JUDITH: Wednesday? Oh, I've got friends coming in from Europe, on the Mauritania.

MILHAUSER: The Mauritania? I thought they took that off.

JUDITH: Did I say Mauritania? Ah—Minnetonka.

MILHAUSER: Well, I've got to see you before I go. Of course I'll be back next month.

JUDITH: Next month? Oh, I spend November in the Catskills. My hay fever.

MILHAUSER: Well, I'll call you anyway tomorrow, on a chance. *(Exit R.)*

JUDITH: Swell chance! *(Starts up stairs)*

FRANK: *(Enters up L. Crosses to window R.)* 'Evening, Miss Judith. You in early, ain't you?

JUDITH: It may seem early to you. *(Exit up stairs.)*

(Frank turns out lamp. Crosses L., and doorbell rings. He goes to door.)

FRANK: Who's there?

KINGSLEY: *(Outside)* Hello, Frank.

FRANK: *(A change of tone as he opens the door.)* Why, Mr. Kingsley!

KINGSLEY: *(In hall)* I hope we didn't wake you up, Frank. May we come in?

FRANK: Yessah, yessah. Pardon my shirtsleeves. I thought one of the young ladies forgot her key.

(KINGSLEY and ANOTHER MAN have come into view. The stranger is a short thick-set man who carries himself with great authority in order to make up for his lack of stature. Instinct tells you that this is none other than ADOLPH GRETZL himself.)

KINGSLEY: We wouldn't have bothered you at this hour, but it's terribly important. We want to see Miss Randall.

FRANK: Miss Terry! Why, she goes to sleep early. She got to get up half-past seven.

KINGSLEY: (*Gently turning* FRANK *around and starting him toward stairs.*) It's all right. Wake her up and ask her to come down. (*Drops over L.*)

FRANK: Yessah. You ge'men want to wait in here? (*He turns on light in living room, then goes upstairs*)

GRETZL: (*Looking about with disfavor*) I don't like the whole idea. A fine actress don't live in a place like this.

KINGSLEY: But she is a fine actress, Mr. Gretzel.

GRETZL: (*Drops down C.*) It don't look right to me. Something tells me it's no good.

KINGSLEY: (*L. C.*) Mr. Gretzl, you've had this play in rehearsal for almost two weeks now. And she can't make the grade. You've got to face it—Jean is a motion picture actress. And that's all.

GRETZL: But she is a beautiful girl. When she comes on the stage people will gasp.

KINGSLEY: You saw that rehearsal tonight. And that's the best she'll ever do.

GRETZL: But she's Jean Maitland! People will come to see Jean Maitland.

KINGSLEY: (*Eases L. a bit*) No, they won't. Theatre-goers won't come to see movie stars just because they're movie starts. They've got to act.

FRANK: (*Comes downstairs*) Ah woke Miss Terry up. She's comin' right down. (*Goes down hall off up L.*)

KINGSLEY: Thank you, Frank. . . . (*Points a stern finger toward head of stairs*) Believe me, this girl's an actress.

GRETZL: All right, all right—an actress. Let's see her.

KINGSLEY: (*Crosses R. Puts hat and coat on table*) She's got presence and authority and distinction! And a beautiful mobile face.

She's exactly right for this play.

GRETZL: *(In front of couch)* If she is such a great beauty and such a wonderful actress, where's she been keeping herself?

KINGSLEY: She's been learning her business.

GRETZL: *(Crosses L.)* All right, we'll let her read the part. What else am I here for in the middle of the night? She's got to start to-morrow morning—tonight, even. It's a great big part. Everything depends on it.

KINGSLEY: *(Over R.)* She can do it. She's young and eager and fresh. Wait till you see her. *(TERRY comes downstairs, wearing a loose flowing robe over her long white nightgown. Her hair is loose on her shoulders. Her feet are in low scuffs. She is anything but the dazzling figure described by KINGSLEY. She comes into the room wordlessly, looking at the two men. KINGSLEY, going to meet her C.)* It's sweet of you to come down, Terry. I wasn't sure you would.

TERRY: You knew I would, David.

KINGSLEY: Terry, this is Mr. Gretzl. This is Terry Randall.

TERRY: How do you do, Mr. Gretzl?

(GRETZL mumbles a greeting. "How do you do?")

KINGSLEY: Terry, I suppose I needn't tell you why we're here at this hour. Could you start rehearsing tomorrow morning in this play of Mr. Gretzl's, and open in a week?

GRETZL: Wait a minute, Kingsley. Not so fast, there! Let me look at her. *(He slowly describes a half-circle around her, his eyes intent on her face. As the inspection finishes she turns her head and meets his gaze. But GRETZL'S inquiring look is now directed at KINGSLEY.)* This is the party you just now described to me?

KINGSLEY: *(Crossing GRETZL to TERRY. Pulling a typed "part" out of his pocket.)* Terry, I know what you can do, but Mr. Gretzl doesn't. Will you read a couple of speeches of this—let him hear you?

TERRY: *(A little terrified at the thought)* Now?

KINGSLEY: Would you, Terry?

TERRY: I'll try.

KINGSLEY: *(Giving her the part)* How about this bit here?

TERRY: May I look at it a second, just to——?

KINGSLEY: Of course. *(Turns to GRETZL)* You know, it's rather difficult to jump right into a character.

GRETZL: *(Crossing L. to armchair)* What's difficult! We do it every day in pictures. . . . Come on, young lady. Well——*(He turns a chair around, seats himself ostentatiously, and beckons TERRY to stand directly in front of him and perform.)*

TERRY: *(A deep sigh, takes the plunge. Reads:)* "Look, boys, I haven't' got any right to stand up here and tell you what to do. Only maybe I have got a right, see, because, look——" No, that isn't right. "Because, look——" Do you mind if I start all over?

GRETZL: *(Annoyed)* All right, go ahead. Start over. *(Gets cigar from pocket)*

TERRY: *(To KINGSLEY)* What's she want them to do?

KINGSLEY: Strike. *(Sits L. arm of couch.)*

TERRY: Oh. Uh——*(She is off again, less certain of herself than ever.)* "Look, boys——" *(A bad start again, GRETZL spits out end of cigar he has bitten off, but she quickly recovers herself.)* "Look, boys, I haven't got any right to stand up here and tell you what to do. Only maybe I have got a right, see, because, look, I'm engaged to be married. You all know who it is. He's right here in this hall." *(GRETZL rises abruptly and up to piano for match. TERRY goes on.)* "——in this hall. So if you fellas vote to go on strike, I guess it's no wedding bells for me. Don't kid yourself I don't know what I'm talking about. Because I've been through it before. I've been through it with my old man, and my brothers, so I ought to know." *(GRETZL has picked up a match-box from piano, and now strikes a match with a sharp rasping sound and lights a long cigar.)* "It means hungry, and maybe cold, and scared every minute somebody'll come home with a busted head. But which would you rather do? Die quick fighting, or starve to death slow! That's why I'm telling you—strike! strike! Strike!" *(GRETZL has again seated himself in front of her, and as he throws back his head, the better to survey her, a cloud of cigar-smoke is blown upward toward her face.)* "That's why I'm telling you—strike! Strike! S——" *(She has been choking back a cough, but it now becomes too much for her. She stops and throws part to floor. Tears and anger struggle for master.)* I can't do it! I can't! I won't go on!

KINGSLEY: *(Rising, angered)* You're a fool if you do

GRETZL: *(Rising and buttoning his coat with a gesture of finality. Crosses to couch, gets his hat.)* You must excuse me. I am a plain-speaking man. I don't want to hurt anybody's feelings, but in my opinion this young lady is not anything at all. Not anything.

TERRY: *(To* GRETZL*)* But, Mr. Gretzl, nobody could give a reading under these conditions. It isn't fair. It isn't possible for an actress—you don't understand.

GRETZL: All right. I don't understand. But I understand my business and I know what I see. So I will say good night, and thank you. Come on, Kingsley.

KINGSLEY: I'm sorry, Terry. No one could look a great actress in bathrobe and slippers, and Mr. Gretzl only knows what he sees.

GRETZL: Are you working for or against me, Kingsley?

KINGSLEY: I'm working for you. What are you going to do about your play tomorrow?

GRETZL: I'm going to throw it into the ash-can. All I wanted was Jean Maitland. So she could make a picture of it. All right. She does something else. I can get plenty material.

KINGSLEY: It's incredible that anyone should be so stupid.

GRETZL: *(Rising to his full height)* Mr. Kingsley, you are out. You will hear form our lawyers in the morning. *(Starts up)*

TERRY: Oh, David!

KINGSLEY: *(After* GRETZL. *Both stop C. in hall.)* It's all right, Terry. Gretzl, if you've lost your interest in the play, how about selling it to me?

GRETZL: I see. You're going back into the theatre, eh?

KINGSLEY: I might. Will you sell it to me?

GRETZL: How much?

KINGSLEY: Just what it cost you.

GRETZL: All right. See Becker in the morning. He'll fix it up. Good night.

KINGSLEY: Good night.

GRETZL: *(As he goes)* And I am the stupid one, huh! *(Exits up R.)*

TERRY: David, David, oh my dear, you mustn't do this just for me.

KINGSLEY: *(Drops down L.C. to her.)* No, I'm not one of those boys who puts on a play just so that his girl can act in it. . . By the way, you are my girl, aren't you?

TERRY: *(Brightly)* Oh, yes, sir.

KINGSLEY: I just thought I'd ask. *(Kisses her)* You know I had a couple of pretty nasty weeks, since you drove me out into the cold.

TERRY: Weeks? It seemed like years to me.

(Another embrace. MRS. ORCUTT enters in dressing-gown and slippers.)

MRS. ORCUTT: I'm sorry, Mr. Kingsley, but this is against the rules.

TERRY: Mrs. Orcutt, it's the play!

KINGSLEY: My apologies, Mrs. Orcutt. This may look a little strange. But I came up on business.

MRS. ORCUTT: Frank said there was another gentleman.

TERRY: *(Gaily)* But he's gone! And, oh, Mrs. Orcutt! I'm going to do the play! *(At the end of this announcement, as she says "play", her hand goes to her mouth, like a little girl's, she is surprised to find herself crying in KINGSLEY'S arms.)*

MRS. ORCUTT: Terry, my child!

KINGSLEY: Darling, you're tired. You must get your sleep. *(There is a farewell kiss, with the full approval of MRS. ORCUTT.)* Good night. *(He picks up part where Terry has thrown it. Hands it to her and gets hat and coat from table R.)*

TERRY: Good night.

KINGSLEY: *(Starting for hall)* Eleven in the morning, at the Music Box.

TERRY: *(In a low voice)* I'll be there.

(Kingsley is gone off up R.)

MRS. ORCUTT: Terry, dear, I'm so happy for you. Aren't you thrilled?

TERRY: It was like Victoria. When they came to tell her she was Queen.

MRS. ORCUTT: Dear child! But now you must run along to bed and get some sleep.

TERRY: No, no. I must learn my part. And I must be alone. I want a room by myself tonight. Please Mrs. Orcutt.

MRS. ORCUTT: I'll see what I can do.*(She goes, first switching off main light, exit up L.)*

(Terry stands alone in the semi-darkened room. A light from a street-lamp shines through her window and strikes her face. For a moment she stands perfectly still. Then the realization of her new position comes over her. She seems to take on a height and dignity.)

Now that I am the Queen, I wish in future to have a bed and a room, of my own. *(She stands transfixed as the curtain falls.)*

CURTAIN

FERBER

EDNA FERBER AND HER CIRCLE
by Julie Gilbert

This major biography casts Ferber in a wholly fascinating feminist light, one that could make her a darling of the women's movement." — CHICAGO SUN-TIMES

"…I have, I suppose, lived the life of a stage struck Jewish nun: working very hard, occasionally running around doing good deeds: footloose but the hands tied to the typewriter for hours daily…"

Thus Edna Ferber described her artistic dedication and love of the theatre in a letter to her friend Noël Coward. Everyone knew the Edna Ferber of the books and plays, but her personal life was an enigma. Those who knew her more intimately loved her for her acute wit, but she was also cantankerous, had a temper any grown man would fear, was given to spurts of eccentric generosity, and, above all, was never predictable.

This enduring biography of the popular writer begins with Ferber's last years in New York City, exploring the setting in which she did all of her great writing: the novels *So Big* (Pulitzer Prize winner) *Cimarron, Giant,* and *Show Boat,* and equally celebrated plays: *Dinner at Eight, Stage Door,* and *The Royal Family,* which she wrote with George S. Kaufman. It was also the place where her wit and talent established her as a leading light among a group of such gifted people as George S. Kaufman, Moss Hart, Richard and Dorothy Rodgers, Marc Connelly, Kitty Carlisle, Alexander Woollcott, Russel Crouse, Howard Lindsay and many others. The book then moves back to Edna Ferber's youth, to her beginnings as a newspaperwoman in Appleton, Wisconsin, and finally to her family: her self-effacing father and tyrannical mother.

$15.95 • paper • ISBN 1-55783-332-X

THE COLLECTED WORKS OF HAROLD CLURMAN

Six Decades of Commentary on Theatre, Dance, Music, Film, Arts, Letters and Politics

edited by Marjorie Loggia and Glenn Young

"...RUSH OUT AND BUY *THE COLLECTED WORKS OF HAROLD CLURMAN*...Editors Marjorie Loggia and Glenn Young have assembled a monumental helping of his work...**THIS IS A BOOK TO LIVE WITH;** picking it up at random is like going to the theater with Clurman and then sitting down with him in a good bistro for some exhilarating talk. This is a very big book, but Clurman was a very big figure."

JACK KROLL, *Newsweek*

"**THE BOOK SWEEPS ACROSS THE 20TH CEN-TURY,** offering a panoply of theater in Clurman's time...**IT RESONATES WITH PASSION.**"

MEL GUSSOW, *The New York Times*

CLOTH •ISBN 1-55783-132-7 PAPER • ISBN 1-55783-264-1

WOMEN HEROES
Six Short Plays from the Women's Project
Edited by Julia Miles

The English Channel, the United States
Government, Hitler, cancer—these are a few of the
obstacles which these extraordinary women hurdle on
their way to ticker tape parades, prison cells and
anonymous fates.

COLETTE IN LOVE Lavonne Mueller
PERSONALITY Gina Wendkos & Ellen Ratner
MILLY Susan Kander
EMMA GOLDMAN Jessica Litwak
PARALLAX Denise Hamilton
HOW SHE PLAYED THE GAME Cynthia L. Cooper

paper • ISBN: 1-55783-029-0

MASTERGATE
&
POWER FAILURE
2 Political Satires for the stage
by Larry Gelbart

REVIEWS OF *MASTERGATE*:

"IF GEORGE ORWELL WERE A GAG WRITER, HE COULD HAVE WRITTEN *MASTERGATE*. Larry Gelbart's scathingly funny takeoff on the Iran-Contra hearings [is] a spiky cactus flower in the desert of American political theatre."
— **Jack Kroll,** NEWSWEEK

"Larry Gelbart has written what may be the MOST PENETRATING, AND IS SURELY THE FUNNIEST, exegesis of the Iran-Contra fiasco to date."
— **Frank Rick,** THE NEW YORK TIMES

REVIEWS OF *POWER FAILURE*:

"There is in his broad etching ALL THE ETHICAL OUTRAGE OF AN ARTHUR MILLER KVETCHING. AND, OH, SO MUCH MORE FUN!"
— **Carolyn Clay,** THE BOSTON PHOENIX

Larry Gelbart, the creator of M*A*S*H, is also the author of *SLY FOX, A FUNNY THING HAPPENED ON THE WAY TO THE FORUM* and *CITY OF ANGELS.*

paper • 1-55783-177-7

CHEKHOV:
THE MAJOR PLAYS

English versions by
Jean-Claude van Itallie

The Cherry Orchard

"A CLASSIC RESTORED TO THE HAND, MIND AND BLOOD OF THE CREATOR."

—The New York Times

The Seagull

"SUBLIMELY UNDERSTOOD CHEKHOV ...ABSOLUTELY TRUE TO THE ORIGINAL"

—The New York Post

Three Sisters

"CAPTURES CHEKHOV'S EXUBERANCE, MUSIC AND COMPLEXITY"   *—The Village Voice*

Uncle Vanya

"THE CRISPEST AND MOST POWERFUL VERSION EXTANT."   *—The New Republic*

Paper•ISBN 1-55783-162-9 • $7.95